Asset Assessments and
Community Social Work Practice

Asset Assessments and Community Social Work Practice

MELVIN DELGADO

AND

DENISE HUMM-DELGADO

OXFORD
UNIVERSITY PRESS

OXFORD
UNIVERSITY PRESS

Oxford University Press is a department of the University of Oxford.
It furthers the University's objective of excellence in research, scholarship,
and education by publishing worldwide.

Oxford   New York
Auckland   Cape Town   Dar es Salaam   Hong Kong   Karachi
Kuala Lumpur   Madrid   Melbourne   Mexico City   Nairobi
New Delhi   Shanghai   Taipei   Toronto

With offices in
Argentina   Austria   Brazil   Chile   Czech Republic   France   Greece
Guatemala   Hungary   Italy   Japan   Poland   Portugal   Singapore
South Korea   Switzerland   Thailand   Turkey   Ukraine   Vietnam

Oxford is a registered trademark of Oxford University Press in the UK and certain other
countries.

Published in the United States of America by
Oxford University Press
198 Madison Avenue, New York, NY 10016

© Oxford University Press 2013

Library of Congress Cataloging-in-Publication Data
Delgado, Melvin.
Asset assessments and community social work practice / Melvin Delgado,
Denise Humm-Delgado.
p. cm.
Includes bibliographical references and index.
ISBN 978-0-19-973584-6 (hbk. : alk. paper)   1. Social service.
2. Community organization.   3. Community health services—Planning.
I. Humm-Delgado, Denise.   II. Title.
HV40.D4393 2013
361.3′2—dc23
2012022972

1 3 5 7 9 8 6 4 2
Printed in the United States of America
on acid-free paper

To our beloved daughters, Laura and Barbara

CONTENTS

SECTION 4 Future Rewards and Challenges

The subject of urban based community assets is one that is near and dear to the authors' hearts and has been so for well over 30 years. In many ways, its appeal is that it represents a positive alternative view of how to think about marginalized urban groups and communities that society has effectively "written-off." This alternative view or paradigm is much more than semantics. It represents a drastically different paradigm, or world view, with all of the requisite changes, rewards, and challenges that follow such a perspective.

This book went through a variety of stages in the conceptualization, writing, and editing and is best thought of as a pleasant journey with numerous stops along the way. In similar fashion to some other writing projects, there were periods during which we simply could not stop thinking and writing on the subject; true, there were other periods in which we simply could not stand the thought of writing on the subject. The latter reaction did not have to do with the subject matter not being important or fun to think and write about. It had, however, more to do with the complexity of the subject matter. What started out as a straightforward writing of a book on urban community asset assessments resulted in many detours, stops, and stages, during which we were quite confused! It pains us to acknowledge this, but we have to be honest to ourselves and the reader.

ACKNOWLEDGMENTS

The authors wish to acknowledge the work of Boston University School of Social Work research assistants Lisa Lofaso and Sarah Schufreider.

Definitions, Values, and Principles

"We do not believe in ourselves until someone reveals that deep inside us something is valuable, worth listening to, worthy of our trust, sacred to our touch. Once we believe in ourselves we can risk curiosity, wonder, spontaneous delight or any experience that reveals the human spirit."

(E. E. CUMMINGS)

Section 1 provides a foundation regarding definitions, types of assets, values, roles, and ethnical challenges one can expect to encounter in undertaking a community asset assessment. Chapter 1 provides the requisite road map for the book. Chapter 2 identifies the multiple ways that community assets can be conceptualized and the rewards and challenges associated with a better understanding of these assets. Chapter 3 focuses on the values that underpin asset assessments, and Chapter 4 focuses on the ethical dilemmas regarding the undertaking of this form of research.

Introduction

"The beginning of wisdom is calling things by their right name."
(*A Chinese Proverb*)

INTRODUCTION

All professions evolve and go through stages of development over the course of their history. The field of social work is no exception and has continued to evolve over the past century in a myriad of ways. One form of evolution has been in how practice is conceptualized and carried out from an almost exclusive focus on direct practice, one to one interventions to encompass groupwork and macro social work practice (community organizing, management, research, planning/program development, and policy practice), but not without experiencing tensions and controversies along the way (Specht & Courtney, 1995; Haynes, 1998).

At both the direct practice and macro practice levels, advocacy is now a vital part of social work practice. Currently, the National Association of Social Workers (NASW) *Code of Ethics* (2008) calls for promotion of social justice and social change in all forms of social work. Particular attention is to be given to needs and empowerment of people who are vulnerable, oppressed, and living in poverty.

A parallel evolution also has occurred in regard to guiding intervention paradigms and practice settings. The profession has gone from an almost exclusive reliance on a deficit paradigm to an asset/capital and community focused paradigm, bringing with it exciting opportunities for innovative thinking on how social interventions can fulfill a variety of community social change goals (Hardcastle, Powers, & Winocur, 2011). However, it also has encountered challenges in how to conceive, plan, and carry out these assessments and interventions that lend themselves to evidence-based practice and evaluation. The inherent challenges of researching the effectiveness of community practice will be encountered in asset assessments as well (Ohmer & Korr, 2006).

Community, in many ways, represents a valid and meaningful social concept that has found a prominent place in social work practice (Beckley et al., 2008; Nicotera,

2007). It has been conceptualized as instrumental in a social change process. Yet, it remains a concept that is elusive and filled with both promise and pitfalls from a practice and research perspective, as the reader will see in Chapter 5.

The importance of community as a setting, a vehicle, and a target for social change, however, has only increased in significance as the field has broadened its reach from a narrow to a broad perspective on how best to carry out its historical mission. Community engaged scholarship has found greater acceptance across helping professions, but it has also generated considerable concerns about academic enterprises, and social work faculty have not escaped these challenges (Calleson, Jordan, & Seifer, 2005).

Communities, particularly those that are urban and undervalued, have experienced dramatic changes in composition as the nation has experienced rapid increases in newcomers, particularly those of color. These changes in population have filtered throughout all facets of community life and the formal and informal institutions that comprise the community. These, and other social and economic trends, have necessitated the development of research and scholarship that embrace social work's historical mission of addressing the needs of marginalized population groups, but doing so within a community context with all of its rewards and challenges (Checkoway, 2009; Checkoway & Goodyear, 2004; Defilippis, Fisher, & Shragge, 2006). Nevertheless, the field of community practice within the pantheon of social work interventions can only be expected to increase in importance in the next decade, if we are successful in reaching and engaging new population groups or population groups that are not new but are striving to achieve equality in society.

Communities will need to integrate increasing numbers of people who are aging and disabled. They also will need to change their views and revise their policies and practices as marriage equality for the gay and lesbian community expands. In addition, the burgeoning issues of the unemployed, the under-employed, and the widened differences between the rich and poor need to be addressed. Some examples of the assets that such new or extra marginalized groups bring will be used throughout the book, as will some considerations for their inclusion. Furthermore, the goals of national health insurance, now deemed as Constitutional by the Supreme Court, will be supported by identifying communities' strengths in pursuing health.

The field of community social work practice has enjoyed a significant resurgence this past decade as the numbers of books and scholarly articles on the subject have increased in quantity and quality (Chaskin, Brown, Venkatesh, & Vidal, 2001; Delgado, 1999, in press; Hardcastle, Powers, & Wenocur, 2004; Murphy & Cunningham, 2003; Netting, Kettner, & McMurty, 2004; Weil, 2004a). These books have tackled some of the most difficult conceptual and practice issues on the subject, particularly how practice within a community context can be achieved in a manner that is affirming and inclusive and that respects peoples' autonomy and unique as well as common needs.

Other avenues for scholarship have also emerged to weigh in on the subject matter. The *Journal of Community Practice*, for example, has emerged during the past decade or so and has continued to wield significant influence, as evidenced by its impact in the field. The shaping of what constitutes community social work is far from being fixed in structure and content. As a result, its evolution generally has gone unabated, and the prospects of its continuance are all but assured for the near future. Community social work has shown tremendous progress in reaching out to marginalized groups in urban and rural areas of the country, with social work scholars bringing many of the key concepts underlining community practice into other fields such as health promotion (Delgado, 2009; Delgado & Zhou, 2008), and population groups such as Latinos (Delgado, 2008), for example.

Community practice has also fostered highly imaginative approaches such as involvement of beauticians in providing a wide range of services (Lieberman & Harris, 2007; Linnan et al., 2005; Solomon et al., 2004). The use of community gardens to address food security, beautifying a community, community participation, and the teaching of various educational subjects offers much promise for the field (Allen, Alaimo, Elam, & Perry, 2008; Delgado & Zhou, 2008; Gearin & Kahle, 2006; Hancock, 2001; Wakefield, Yeudall, Taron, Reynolds, & Skinner, 2007). These two practice examples also serve to increase social capital.

Lyon (1999), Netting, Kettner, and McMurty (2004), Popple and Stepney (2008), and other scholars have argued effectively for the importance of community as the context for all forms of social work practice. Weil (2004b, p. 4), in addressing contexts and challenges for twenty-first century communities, identifies five critical community practice issues with direct implications for asset-based assessments and interventions:

1. *Expanding and refining practice approaches* that can build toward social and economic justice;
2. Focusing practice on the *expansion of basic human rights* for women, children, and men;
3. *Building opportunity structures* for disadvantaged populations, and working *to build multicultural strategies and coalitions* for positive social change based on specific situations and common human needs;
4. Focusing community practice activities *on social and economic development, strengthening civil society, and enlarging civic and political participation*;
5. *Finding effective multinational approaches to reducing absolute poverty*

Each of the above five challenges can be accomplished only through the embrace of a social intervention that is predicated on a paradigm that stresses participatory democracy principles and community capital/assets. These interventions can be carried out only upon the successful completion of a community focused asset assessment. Furthermore, this form of assessment is an intervention unto itself, as well as its serving as the basis for interventions based on the findings. Once an assessment is thought of as an intervention, then the process used to gather data goes far beyond this task and also actively seeks to achieve positive social change as one of its many goals. Community asset assessment is conceptualized as falling into what Lather (2006) refers to as an "emancipate" paradigm, which stresses actions such as participatory research, critical ethnography, critical cartography, critical race theory, feminist theories, and gay and lesbian theories. Hardcastle, Powers, and Wenocur (2011) refer to community asset assessment as a process of discovery, and, in this case, one focused on capacities and assets.

The subject of community assets is certainly not new in the social sciences and field of human services, including in social work. Ross (1967), for example, speaks to the importance of identifying a community's resources (internal and external) for mobilization for action. Specht and Courtney (1995), almost 30 years later, addressed the importance of social workers strengthening community resources that bridge organizations and residents.

Neither are community assets a very esoteric subject. A quick Google search will uncover thousands of "hits" on "community assets," "community asset assessment," and "community asset mapping." A community's abilities can manifest itself in a myriad of ways, such as in "resources," "resilience," "strengths," "organizations," "assets," and "capital," to list but six of the most common ways of labeling these abilities. There is no "standard" way of naming community assets.

The increased popularity of assets, however, also brings with it a set of inherent challenges for social work scholars and practitioners. As the reader will see in Chapter 2, this embarrassment of riches, so to speak, brings with it many ways of thinking about, categorizing, and measuring community assets. Consequently, a "cookbook" approach to undertaking a community asset assessment would be ineffective to help community social work practice to move forward.

Our role as community social workers is to assist communities by identifying and working with their assets. This type of "work" is probably best represented through the use of a metaphor of a "journey," with a clear destination in mind, but with numerous anticipated and unanticipated stops along the way. We plan asset assessments with the community rather than for the community. Thus, the process is of great, if not greater, significance than the eventual outcome. This perspective, however, is not restricted to social work and has found a receptive audience in other community and economic development circles (Phillips & Pittman, 2009; Schensul, 2009).

PURPOSE OF AN ASSET ASSESSMENT

Assessments, be they need or asset focused, fulfill the important function of providing community social work practitioners and other professionals with information that will be used to develop community programs and services. These interventions must be based upon a clear understanding of the goals they are seeking to achieve, necessitating the development of an in-depth grounding of these research methods into local circumstances (cultural, social, economic, and psychological). These results shape our understanding of the phenomena being studied and how best to address the needs of communities or enhance their assets (Gandelman, DeSantis, & Rietmeijer, 2006).

Freire addresses another aspect of research and speaks about the potential role that research can play in giving voice to those without a voice (1982, pp. 30–31): "The silenced are not just incidental to the curiosity of the researcher but are the masters of inquiry into the underlying causes of the events in their world. In this context research becomes a means of moving them beyond silence into a quest to proclaim the world." It is our contention that community asset assessments accomplish this noble goal. Traditional (positivistic), nonparticipatory, research approaches have compromised our understanding of community assets, requiring the development of specific methods of inquiry to uncover this knowledge (Stehlik & Buckley, 2008).

Walters and colleagues' (2009, p. 151) expectation of community based participatory research captures the role and potential of community social work practice and community asset assessments, and the interventions that result from them: "Generally accepted CBPR principles recognize the community as a unit of identity and/or analysis; build on the strengths, resiliency, and resources of the community; facilitate co-learning, co-partnering, and community capacity building throughout all phases of the research project, including dissemination; attempt to strike a balance between research and action; emphasize local relevance and ecological and historical contexts that contribute to multiple determinants; generate systems growth through cyclical and iterative processes; and involve long term commitment to process and community."

In the early 1990s, the concept of "popular epidemiology" emerged to help capture a different way of conducting community based participatory research. Brown (1992, p. 269) defines popular epidemiology as an approach undertaken by community residents to "gather scientific data and other information and also direct and marshal the knowledge and resources of experts in order to understand the epidemiology of disease."

Bradshaw (1977, p. 290), in specifically addressing needs assessments, notes the following about social needs: "The concept of social need is inherent in the idea of social services. The history of social services is the story of the recognition of social needs and the organizations of services to meet them." Unfortunately, "social assets" have not enjoyed the same privileged position as needs, and organizations have largely ignored them in the process of identifying community needs. Needs assessments create a one dimensional image of communities that distorts a balanced view, which requires an awareness of community assets (Sharpe, Greaney, Lee, & Royce, 2000).

The role and importance of assessment in development of health and social services are well accepted in the field, and represent the fundamental building blocks for the creation of any form of social intervention. Needs assessments are, without question, the most common form of assessment in these fields (Altschuld & Kumar, 2009; Royse, Staton-Tindall, Badger, & Webster, 2009). They typically, however, result in a rather narrow view of a community that stresses disease risk profiles and lists of various social problem categories (Sharpe, Greaney, Lee, & Royce, 2000).

Nevertheless, unlike needs assessments, asset assessments bring a range of factors and considerations to the creation of an intervention that are guided by participatory democratic principles and processes. Although needs assessments can also be guided by participatory principles, they generally are profession- ally driven and do not stress capacity enhancement in the process. Thomas, Donovan, and Sigo (2010), for example, detail the value of participatory princi- ples to needs and asset assessment of a Native American community in the Pacific Northwest, and illustrate how participatory principles can be implemented.

Asset assessments' emphasis on participatory democracy creates sufficient distance from their needs counterpart through the use of values, language used to communicate, and how research methods get conceptualized and carried out. Katz (2004, p. A1) rightly advocates that community asset assessments make it a priority to start with positives rather than negatives: "Good researchers will focus their questions on community assets, resources, and capacity, rather than barriers. From the beginning, they will formulate a plan to sustain the project's benefits within your community and impart ownership of the project to com- munity members."

Community asset assessments can be viewed as a goal, a strategy, a set of guiding principles, method, and a process. These different perspectives make a consensus definition of an asset difficult to arrive at in both scholarly and practice realms. Consequently, it is best to view asset assessments from an evolutionary point of view in order to appreciate the variety of perspectives, tensions, and potentials for achieving positive social change. In essence, asset assessments are both an instru- ment of discovery and an intervention to achieve community change. Findings, as a result, serve both critical descriptive and prescriptive functions (Smith, 2005, p. 91): "Research, like schooling, once the tool of colonization and oppression, is very gradually coming to be seen as a potential means to reclaim languages, his- tories, and knowledge—to find solutions to the negative impacts of colonization and to give voice to an alternate way of knowing and being."

Generally speaking, asset assessments can address any one or any combination of the following goals (Meridian, 2006, p. 3): "(1) Identify the current strengths, concerns, and conditions of a particular group of people; (2) Assess community capacity to meet the needs of a particular group of people; and/or (3) Identify community assets and challenges related to meeting the needs of a particular group (or groups) of people." Each of these goals can stand alone or in com- bination with the other goals, with local circumstances dictating the primary purpose(s) of an asset assessment. The more goals that are addressed, the more complex, time consuming, and demanding it becomes as well.

Community assets, not surprisingly, must be viewed through a broad lens, as addressed in Chapter 2, in order to better understand and appreciate their community transformative potential (Beckley, Martz, Nadeau, Wall, & Reimer, 2008; Murphy & Cunningham, 2003). However, it is necessary to focus the lens whenever possible to bring about greater clarity. This statement is not contradic- tory. A broad perspective helps ensure that no community asset is systemati- cally left out in any assessment. However, there is a concomitant need to focus in order to better understand the nature and strength of the capital as it relates to an intervention. This focus helps ensure a depth of knowledge that lends itself to a detailed understanding of community geographic boundaries, history, and relative strength of assets.

There is still a need for the gathering of disparate opinions before a consensus is achieved (Beckley et al., 2008). For example, asset assessments must actively seek to tap resident strengths, a geographic definition of what constitutes its boundaries, the amount and location of open space, natural resources, and historical events of significance in the community, for example. This requires community social work practitioners to suspend conventional views of what constitutes an "asset" or "capital."

Bandura (2006, p. 316), however, raises a voice of concern about a focus on the concept of efficacy that bears heeding in an asset assessment: "A group's attainments are the products not only of shared knowledge and skills of the different members, but also of the interactive, coordinate, and synergistic dynamics of their transactions. Therefore, perceived collective efficacy is not simply the sum of the efficacy beliefs of individual members. Rather, it is an emergent group level property." Collective efficacy is exciting from a community social work practice perspective, but it is also hard to capture in capital assessments that focus almost exclusively on individual assets.

It would be unrealistic to expect a community to have a uniform opinion on what constitutes an asset and, if an asset is present, to what extent it wields influence in the life of an individual and community as a whole. There may be, for example, assets that are age specific and cater to youth or older adults. However, these assets may be totally invisible to those outside of the particular groups. The same can be said for gender. Community assets, for example, may be extensive for females but very limited for males. Beauty parlors fulfill a variety of nontraditional roles. However, when compared to barbershops, beauty parlors are far more of an asset for women than their counterparts, which cater to men (Delgado, 1999).

Asset assessments differ dramatically from their needs assessments counterparts along a variety of key dimensions. Asset assessments generally attempt to (1) focus on capacities rather than problems/needs; (2) actively seek community participation and develop collaborative partnerships; (3) seek to tap and enhance community competencies; (4) seek to equalize power between residents and professionals; (5) be proactive rather than reactive to problems; and (6) stress community contributions and ownership of the process and are, thus, empowerment driven.

A quick review of the differences outlined above will convince the reader that asset assessments will never be confused with needs assessments in composition, process, and outcomes. The attempt to equalize power dynamics between undervalued communities and the dominant society means that asset assessments have a strong social engineering component that goes beyond just gathering data, and ultimately seeks to redress some form of injustice, but will do so from a position of community strength.

DEFINITION OF ASSETS

One of the greatest challenges facing any effort to assess a community's assets is determining and arriving at a consensus of what constitutes a community asset. As addressed again in Chapter 2, a widely accepted definition would provide the field with the requisite foundation to make significant contributions. However, the field is far from ready to offer and accept such a definition. This lack of consensus, we believe, is evolutionary and therefore normative in the social sciences. This section will provide the reader with a brief overview of the various perspectives on assets before arriving at a definition that will shape how this book unfolds.

The Asset-Based Community Development Institute's (2001, p. 54) position examining the relationship between individual residents and a community's capabilities sets a wonderful stage for why assets are important: "In each community, within each person, is a capacity to achieve something of worth. How we recognize and encourage such capacity will have a great impact on how we build strong ties and communities. Building on existing capacities for growth and achievement also helps us avoid turning to outside experts for help. Communities have the capacity to develop themselves."

Community assets can be defined in a multitude of ways, not surprisingly, resulting in numerous rewards and challenges for community social work practitioners, particularly for scholars and practitioners wishing to develop a definition with clear boundaries and directions (Haines, 2009; Laverack, 2006b). Chapter 2 certainly attests to this conclusion. Furthermore, assets, once defined, do not fall into a simple binary position, either present or absent. Level of strength brings a richer and more in-depth perspective that is more realistic of conditions in real life (Bridge, 2006). Consequently, any effort to categorize assets must also take into account the level of presence in a community.

The following are but a few other examples of how community assets can be identified and categorized. Carson, Chappell, and Knight (2007) identified and mobilized a community arts program as an intervention in a health promotion project. Community gardens, too, have found saliency as urban focused community assets (Delgado, 1999; Hung, 2004). Rotegard and colleagues (2010) advance the use of a health asset concept (genes, values, beliefs, and life experiences) that results in the development of mastery and self actualization. Morgan and Ziglio (2007), in similar fashion to McKnight and Kretzmann (1996), propose to classify community assets along three dimensions: (1) individualized; (2) community level (family, neighbors, social networks); and (3) organizational and institutional levels. Each of these dimensions can incorporate a wide range of assets.

O'Meara, Chesters, and Han (2004) developed four capacity domains to capture community assets: (1) vision and leadership; (2) structure and partnerships; (3) community engagement; and (4) indigenous resources. Carr and Servon (2009), in turn, identify three potential assets in neighborhoods with strong vernacular culture: (1) consumer markets; (2) ethnic areas and heritage sites; and (3) arts and culture venues and districts. Community art, as a result, can be viewed as a cultural asset. Green and Haines (2012) developed a framework for categorizing community assets that parallels closely the framework that we use in this book. The authors identify seven types of community capital: (1) cultural; (2) environmental; (3) financial; (4) human; (5) physical; (6) political; and (7) social.

There has been an emerging perspective of viewing art, particularly art that is informal, as community assets. Semenza and Krishnasamy (2007) use community art and art installations as community assets (cultural capital). Phillips (2004), too, identifies community art as an asset that can be converted to a community economic resource. Tourism venues such as San Francisco's Mission District community murals represent artistic (cultural) and economic assets. Tours of these murals have been organized to both showcase the community's art talent and serve as a community revenue source. Moreno's (2004) study of El Museo del Barrio (Museum of Spanish Harlem) in New York City does an excellent job of identifying this institution as a community asset and the potential role arts can play in displaying cultural icons and values for the community and outside world. O'Donnell and Karanja (2000) note the historical contribution, both national and international, that the African Americans of Bronzeville on Chicago's South Side made in jazz, blues, and gospel.

Another perspective on art as a community asset is its accessibility to people with disabilities. The obvious way in which art is accessible is with universal design in museums and galleries that incorporates elements such as ramps, elevators with audible signals, and accessible parking, restrooms, lecture rooms, eating areas, and outdoor spaces. A less obvious way is in the access to the individual sculpture, paintings, and other art. This sometimes is done with group or self guided tours that allow touching of artwork or tactile diagrams or facsimiles of artwork within a general art museum. Few museums are fully designed to be accessible to people who are blind or visually impaired, but one notable international example is the Museo Tiflológico in Madrid, Spain (ONCE, 2012). The authors found this museum to be fully accessible and enjoyable for those who are not blind or visually impaired as well.

Assets can be expressive (psychological), instrumental (physical), and informational (knowledge) that get represented through a sociocultural prism. Assets also can be categorized as individual (protective mechanisms/strengths/resiliency), nontraditional, and formal organization based (Deeds et al., 2006; Delgado, 1998a). All communities, regardless of how "disadvantaged," nevertheless, have assets (social, human, economic, cultural, and intangible capital). It is rare that the outside general population reads or hears about these assets in the local media. The fundamental question guiding an asset assessment becomes "what are the assets" rather than "are there assets?"

These two perspectives, in turn, shape how residents and professionals/scholars view community recourses and their potential. These differences in perspectives, however, are not insurmountable, but they certainly are challenging for all those who are involved. The challenges take on greater significance when addressing the needs of those whose primary language is not English and/or are undocumented. Undocumented residents are still part of a community, but their status in this country makes them invisible to those who live outside of their community. When they become visible to those outside of their community, tremendous misunderstandings emerge related to cultural values and traditions.

The field of asset assessment is in desperate need of a nomenclature similar to that advanced by Bradshaw (1977) in the mid-1970s, with all definitions and needs assessments being traced back to one of four definitions of social need. Bradshaw identified four types of needs: (1) felt; (2) expressed; (3) normative; and (4) comparative. The saying *"All roads lead to Rome"* is extremely relevant when discussing needs assessments. All needs assessments are based upon one or a combination of the four definitions of needs conceptualized by Bradshaw. These four definitions, however, can also serve as the basis for conceptualizing and operationalizing asset assessments, with requisite changes.

Felt assets seek to tap community resident perceptions of local assets. In essence, what resources are identified by community residents as benefiting a group or community? These felt assets very often represent perceptions based upon cultural values and norms that are largely invisible to any out group member. Furthermore, felt assets, like their needs counterpart, are the most democratic or empowering of all the definitions because of the emphasis placed on capturing the "voices" of people. Felt assets, for example, can generate data on the type and extent of volunteerism taking place in a community that is not organization or agency related.

Expressed assets capture the actions of residents and can be recorded, such as the number of murals in a community or the amount of fruits and vegetables generated from a community garden. Statistics can also be generated concerning the number of plots being cultivated, the number of individuals or families working the plots, the amount of money generated or saved by producing food from a community garden, and the number of social events taking place. In addition, in the case of gardens that have replaced vacant lots, crime rates can be traced before and after the gardens emerged. Community gardens, in essence, can effectively convert vacant lots into community assets (Kearney, 2009; Tortorello, 2011). When this happens, though, home values often go up, and the chances of communities becoming gentrified also increase.

Normative assets, unlike their counterparts that rely upon standards that are determined by "experts" with educational and institutional legitimacy, need to reflect community standards of what constitutes assets. These normative assets would be shaped by the community and its experiential expertise rather than "experts" with educational legitimacy. Reliance on such qualitative standards helps ensure that a community's voice shapes this definition of assets.

Finally, comparative asset assessments would attempt to "compare" one community with another community and allow local communities to "judge" how well they stand in comparison to comparable communities (local, state, and national). For example, the number of community gardens in a neighborhood can be compared with a similar neighborhood, taking into account demographic composition, population density, and land availability. Data can also be generated on the amount of produce grown, food cost savings, and type of produce grown, and then compared with another neighborhood.

BOOK GOALS

Tebes (2005, p. 213) outlines three major dimensions of community based research that must be addressed in any initiative wishing to move the field of community asset assessments forward in the twenty-first century: "Embedded in community science are implicit theories on the nature of reality (ontology), the justification of knowledge claims (epistemology), and how knowledge is constructed (methodology). These implicit theories influenced the conceptualization and practice of research, and opened up or constrained its possibilities." The goals that are soon to follow in this section attempt to meet Tebes' (2005) three challenges.

There is general acknowledgment that capacity and capacity building concepts need much greater conceptual and measurement clarity (Chaskin, 2001). Lepofsky, Kick, and Williams (2003) make this very argument and note that community capacity building is an undercriticized paradigm. This book, as a result, seeks to further define and refine this paradigm and, in the process, raise and address requisite concerns that must be acknowledged for the field to progress.

It is important to note that this book does focus on urban areas as opposed to a broader arena, and this is purposeful. This is, in part, the result of our experiences in conducting asset assessments in city neighborhoods as opposed to suburban or rural areas of the country. Many of the examples, case illustrations, and studies used in the book are derived from these experiences. Nevertheless, every effort will be made to broaden the content, whenever possible, to include other settings as a means of reaching a broader audience. Fortunately, there are a growing number of examples related to asset assessments in rural parts of the country, and these efforts, too, embrace many of the values and principles integral to this book. However, geographic context does wield considerable influence in how these assessments get conceptualized and implemented.

This book addresses eight goals that can be descriptive or prescriptive in nature, depending upon the subject matter and the needs of the practitioner. These goals are presented as if they were discrete entities unto themselves, but, in reality, there is tremendous overlap between them. Also, these goals are not in any particular order of importance:

1. Provide the reader with the requisite foundation from which to examine the values, goals, philosophy, and principles guiding asset assessments (Chapters 1, 2, 3, and 4).
2. Provide an historical context from which to better understand how asset assessment has gained in importance within community social work practice (Chapter 2).

3. Ground asset assessments within a community capacity enhancement paradigm (Chapter 5).
4. Review a range of methods that can be utilized to carry out an asset assessment within an urban context, including a critique of the advantages and disadvantages of each method, and ways of disseminating findings (Chapters 7 and 8).
5. Identify the rewards and challenges social work practitioners will encounter as they undertake asset assessments (Chapters 4 and Epilogue).
6. Utilize a series of urban case illustrations to assist the reader in operationalizing asset assessments in their respective communities (Chapters 9, 10, and 11).
7. Provide a definition and operationalization of assets/capital assessments that both contextualize this practice as well as provide boundaries that will facilitate implementation of this approach in the field (Chapter 6).
8. Highlight the role and function of community asset mapping as an in-depth illustration of the several forms of assessing community assets (Chapter 7).

AUDIENCE FOR THIS BOOK

There is certainly a clear vision for whom it is that we wrote this book. This book is intended for a social work audience, and more specifically for students taking community organization, planning, program development, advocacy, social action, and management courses. However, we hope its usefulness will go beyond the social work classroom into other fields. Community social workers practice within fields such as criminal justice, community development, education and recreation, and urban planning. Thus, it is hoped that other practitioners will also find this book helpful.

Nevertheless, the authors are under no illusion concerning the difficulty of writing a book that seeks to reach both scholar and practitioner. There are very good reasons why these two worlds have, at times, existed as if they were in parallel universes. However, we believe that community asset assessments provide an excellent bridge between these two contexts because there is a natural link and common social change agenda that are part of any community capacity enhancement paradigm, to which asset assessments subscribe.

BOOK OUTLINE

This book consists of 11 chapters (and an epilogue) and four sections: Section 1: *Definitions, Values, and Principles* (four chapters); Section 2: *Analytical Framework, Methods, and Mapping* (four chapters); Section 3: *Lessons from the*

Field of Practice (three chapters); and Section 4: *Future Rewards and Challenges* (Epilogue). These sections systematically build upon each other as in a story with a beginning, middle, and end. Thus, this book is best read accordingly, although there are readers who may wish to skip chapters and even sections to get to the case illustrations.

CONCLUSIONS

Community asset assessments have had a relatively short history within the social work profession, but that does not negate their importance in helping to define the profession in this new millennium and century. Some practitioners would go so far as to argue, and we certainly count ourselves among them, that the next decade will have a profound influence on the profession as we venture into new and generally unexplored social arenas. Community asset paradigms hold much promise for the profession and the communities we seek to reach.

Community asset assessments also effectively seek to generate and nurture community centered conversations, bringing different perspectives to the assessment process (Gueye, Diouf, Chaana, & Tiomkin, 2005). When communities are well informed about asset assessments, there invariably is a sense of hope and excitement that emerges and must be captured as part of any assessment. Community asset assessments are not without a host of challenges that must be successfully addressed in order for this method to achieve its grand potential. Nevertheless, we sincerely hope that the reader is as excited about this topic as we are. Community social workers, as a result, are in a propitious position to move this field forward in a progressive manner and assist other professions that are slowly finding the value of community centered practice that embraces the principles of social and economic justice!

2

Definitions, History, Elements, and Boundaries

"'Community' in the twenty-first century seems to be everywhere and nowhere. On one hand, the rhetoric of community is omnipresent, as nonprofit organizations, civic organizations, government agencies, and even multinational corporate entities routinely describe their activities to be community-oriented. On the other hand, community in the broader sense of shared interests or solidarities appears to be under unrelenting attack, challenged by sociological forces and intellectual currents that point toward more fragmented social orders."

(SITES, CHASKIN, & PARKS, *2007, P. 519*)

INTRODUCTION

The world and this nation are ever changing. Global economic, social, and demographic forces are causing major dislocations in the United States that have been felt through all strata of this country, and the most recent recession of 2008 is such a case in point. The twenty-first century, as a result, will bring rewards and challenges to community social work practice that will necessitate new forms of conceptualizing and implementing social interventions, particularly in urban areas (Kolzow & Pittman, 2009) with newcomer population groups and other marginalized groups (Delgado, 2011; Falconi & Mazzotti, 2007; Singer, Hardwick, & Brettell, 2008).

Kolzow and Pittman (2009, p. 333) sum up the challenges of globalization quite well for any profession interested in practicing within a community arena: "It is virtually impossible to ignore the reality of the global economy and its impact on a particular community, no matter where it is located. With respect to responding appropriately to globalization, the decisions made are not easy ones, because the issues are complex and much disagreement exists on what is happening and why. The challenge is to research these issues carefully and think about the implications for the local economy." Any effort to assess the global impact on a community must ultimately identify assets, and not just rely upon needs. Otherwise, it provides only a partial, and a very distorted, picture of a community. Immigrants for example, often arrive from extremely difficult circumstances. Yet, they also have extraordinary coping skills in addition to other cultural assets about which social workers need to learn.

Therefore, before community social work practice can advance the field of asset assessment and initiatives seeking to enhance community capacities, it must build upon a foundation that takes into account community history and present day circumstances. Communities with histories of experiencing and welcoming newcomers, for example, will, in all likelihood, be accepting of newcomer groups and have the desire to learn from them. This chapter attempts to orient the reader rather than provide an in-depth treatment of the definition and history of assets (capital) and community capacity driven initiatives.

In the 1990s, asset driven community social work practice was conceptualized as being an integral part of community capacity enhancement, and this conceptualization has continued into the present and guided our research and scholarship (Chaskin, Brown, Venkatesh, & Vidal, 2001; Delgado, 1998, 1999). Other scholars, such as Kretzmann and McKnight (1993), Poole, (1998), and Smith, Littlejohn, and Roy (2003), for example, have been a part of a movement to shift how marginalized communities, particularly those that are urban, are viewed and provide a vehicle through which professions with missions similar to social work can implement asset focused interventions.

The countering of the conventional "deficit" paradigm that stressed needs and problems, to one that first seeks to identify assets or strengths, has fueled the development of highly participatory and empowering interventions incorporating social justice values and principles that are important to the field of social work (Donaldson & Daughtery, 2011; Hardcastle, Powers, & Wenocur, 2011). Thus, community capacity enhancement is reflected in all stages of a community asset intervention, from the posing of the key questions to be answered in the initial assessment to the evaluation of the intervention (Saegert, 2006).

A community capacity enhancement paradigm can be defined as the systematic identification and mobilization of indigenous community resources in the development of a social intervention (Delgado, 1999). Although this definition may appear quite simple, in reality, it hides the complexity and potential for tensions and conflicts that invariably are part of any community effort to achieve change. Community capacity enhancement is a philosophical stance, a set of values, a goal, and a method for supporting people and communities (Delgado, 2001b). In essence, it is an all encompassing perspective that permeates feeling, thinking, and doing. Those who embrace this form of intervention often do so with vigor or passion associated with a mission that is near and dear to them and their identity. Therefore, this is much more than just a "job."

DEFINITION OF ASSETS AND ASSET ASSESSMENTS

Moving the knowledge base forward of community capacity and asset assessment is hampered by multiple definitions of these concepts (Flaspohler, Duffy, Wandersman, Stillman, & Maras, 2008). The concept of "assets" is often called by many different names in the literature and in practice, with "capacity" and "capital" being two of the most prominent usages, and this adds to the challenge of developing a body of knowledge to which all relevant professions can contribute in a systematic manner. Although the concept of "capital" has a legion of followers, as the reader will see later in this chapter, it, too, has its share of critics. Both perspectives will be highlighted in this chapter to allow the reader to make an informed judgment of how best to conceptualize and categorize community assets.

A number of scholars in the past decade and one-half have tackled how best to conceive of community assets. They (1993, p. 25), two of the early pioneers in advancing the concept of community capacity enhancement, for example, refer to assets as individual, association, and institutional "gifts, skills, and capacities." Kretzmann and McKnight (1993) have wielded considerable influence in the early efforts among scholars. However, since their initial work, considerable progress has resulted in examining a multitude of ways to conceptualize community assets, particularly in marginalized urban communities, although not restricted to this geographic location, and drawing upon an extensive theoretical base.

Theokas and Lerner (2006) conceptualize community assets along three domains or settings (family, school, and neighborhood) and four dimensions (human, physical, collective activity, and accessibility) that correspond to a variety of social capital forms. Green and Haines (2011) conceptualize assets or capital as capacities to improve the lives of community residents. They initially (Green & Haines, 2008) conceptualized these assets as falling into five types and later expanded them to consist of seven types (Green & Haines, 2012). Stokols, Grzywacz, McMahan, and Phillips (2003), in conceptualizing community assets for health promotion, divide them into two major conceptual categories: (1) Material Resources (economic, natural, human made environmental, and technical) and (2) Human Resources (social capital, human capital, and moral capital).

Sail and Abu-Samah (2010) conceive of community assets as consisting of knowledge, attitudes, skills, and practice. Oliver (2001, p. xi), however, defines assets from a social intervention and empowerment perspective by stressing the importance of residents accessing and mobilizing these "stocks" for enhancing their well-being and the well-being of their community: "An 'asset' in this paradigm is a special kind of resource that an individual, organization, or entire community can use to reduce or prevent poverty and injustice. An asset is usually a 'stock' that can be drawn upon, built upon, or developed, as well as a resource that can be shared or transferred across generations."

Hardi and Pinter (2007) advance the concept of quality of life as a means of capturing community assets as well as community concerns and problems.

A quality of life perspective represents an emerging way of capturing community capital and needs and, thus, may be very appealing in comprehensive efforts to assess community assets. Community well-being, too, has emerged as another way of capturing a wide array of community assets as well as concerns, and does so in a manner that emphasizes capital concepts (Parker et al., 2006).

The reader, however, is duly warned that there are many different meanings of what constitutes "community well-being" (Cuthill, 2002). Although using this concept offers great promise, it is certainly not a "short cut" for assessing community assets and dealing with a host of thorny conceptual issues (Saunders, 2008).

For example, the concept of community well-being is often determined by the cultural background of a community's residents. Residents who have an upbringing that is based in agriculture will view trees and forests differently from those who come out of urban upbringings. In the case of the former, trees and other forms of greenery play an instrumental role in dictating trees and flowers as essential elements of a state of well-being. Even the United Nations' measure of nations' well-being has evolved over time in its conceptualization of what constitutes positive community development. Each year, it commissions a *Human Development Report* that assesses the quality of life throughout the world. In its 2010 report, it conceptualized quality of life as having a long and healthy life, access to knowledge, and a decent standard of living and then adjusted its findings according to the occurrence of inequality, gender disparities, and serious or multiple deprivations. Significantly, it strived to look not just at each nation's average well-being but also the well-being of its most marginalized members.

Its 2011 Human Development Report retained the focus on marginalized members of society and looked at disparities in power and sexual inequalities. It introduced, too, findings on how environmental sustainability and equity must be considered together because of the very real effects of factors such as clean water, clean air, and sanitation. It concluded that environmental degradation hurts poor and vulnerable groups the most.

Furthermore, the emergence of evidence-based practice has caused additional tensions in the profession. Some social workers have a commitment to evidence-based practice, even in situations that do not lend themselves to this form of practice, such as with new contexts that are difficult to control for or new population groups. Bisman (2004) argues that the social work profession's emphasis on expanding its knowledge base has been accomplished at the expense of the profession's values of human dignity, service to humanity, and social justice. Hoefer (2012, pp. 21–22) says that the term evidence-based practice "is increasingly being used to describe social work practice that has been evaluated as being effective" but that it is "still somewhat controversial" and has not had much impact on advocacy practice. However, he encourages social workers doing advocacy to continue to develop their competencies in this area. Franklin and Hopson (2007), too, emphasize ways to use evidence-based practice in social work and how to overcome barriers to its use.

BRIEF HISTORICAL OVERVIEW

Tracing a social concept's etiology is a precarious journey under the best of circumstances, and some readers may well argue that it is not necessary and a poor use of time and resources. This journey is made even more difficult because the concept of "community assets" may not have been used to capture the significance of indigenous community resources (Van Willigen, 2005). However, it is one that is important, nevertheless, to undertake. Understanding the origins of a social concept or paradigm provides both academics and practitioners with a historical and social contextual appreciation and understanding of the forces that led to the creation of a viewpoint, including asset assessment and community capacity development (Fraser, 2005).

The history of asset based community social work practice is relatively short. A review of the more conventional approach to assessment based upon needs would necessitate a series of volumes to fully do justice to how this concept has emerged and been modified over the years, including how it has influenced fields and professions. Unfortunately, a similar approach to the history of community asset assessments will cover only a relatively short period of time. Nevertheless, the fact that community asset assessments have a relatively short history does not mean that the history it does have is not significant and worth some degree of attention, even if only an overview. Furthermore, there are some antecedents in social work history that bear reflection for the values they embody.

The history of asset assessments, not surprisingly, shares many similarities with the histories of community social work practice and community based participatory research (Delgado, 2006; Fisher, 2004; Weil, 2004a). It has been only in the past decade, though, that asset assessments have found their way into the professional literature and practice across a wide expanse of fields, settings, and population groups. Asset assessments, as is to be expected, have taken on unique sociocultural manifestations depending upon what part of the world is using them (Delgado, 2006).

Health promotion, nationally and internationally, has opened up vast opportunities for using asset assessments and asset focused interventions (Brough, Bond, & Hunt, 2004; Delgado, 2008; Delgado & Zhou, 2008; Freudenberg, 2004; Parker et al., 2006; Raeburn, Akerman, Chuengsatiansup, Mejia, & Oladepo, 2006). Morgan and Ziglio (2007) argue that historically most of the evidence used by policy makers was deficit oriented. However, an assets based approach promotes the use of "salutogenic" resources that stress self esteem, coping, and community participation in creating a health development process.

Community asset assessment is closely integrated with community capacity development or enhancement, and talking about one is not possible without also talking about the other (Hardcastle, Wenocur, & Powers, 2011). This is because asset assessments are part of a process rather than an end in themselves. A number of scholarly efforts at grounding assets, assessment, and their guiding paradigm of community capacity have served to help the field better appreciate the origins of these three concepts as they relate to each other (Haines,

2009). Each of these concepts, however, has many different streams and elements informing their development (Van Willigen, 2005).

The early to mid-1990s are widely accepted as the critical period in which assets, asset assessment, and community capacity emerged to wide acceptance from a scholarly, as well as practice, perspective (Mattessich & Monsky, 1997; Zautra, 2008). More recently, for example, there has been the emergence of the concept of "resilient communities" that may appear to be the same as community capacity (Campannell, 2006; Norris, Stevens, Pfefferbaum, Wyche, & Pfefferbaum, 2008). Mowbray and colleagues (2007) propose a resilient community model that includes community level risk and protective factors. Sturtevant (2006) finds similarity and differences between the concepts of community capacity and community resiliency and argues for greater conceptual refinement, such as differentiating foundation (physical, natural, and economic) from mobilizing (social and human) assets. Landau (2007) draws parallels between resilient families and communities and the significant role resilience plays in change.

The subject of resilient communities has started to gain attention in the professional literature. However, resilient communities generally have been defined as communities that have the ability to successfully recover from some form of natural disaster (Adger, Hughes, Folke, Carpenter, & Rockstrom, 2005). This conceptualization is heavily weighted toward natural disasters and therefore is too limited. We, in turn, prefer a much broader view of community resiliency. Magis (2010), for example, defines resilient communities as those that are able to build and thrive when confronting change, uncertainty, unpredictability, and "surprise."

Resilient communities involve much more than rebuilding infrastructure (Campanella, 2006, p. 142): "It is clear that the modern city is virtually indestructible. At the same time, there is no question that a catastrophe will profoundly alter a city's fortunes and fate; and therein lays the more compelling matter of resilience and recovery. Indeed, it is possible for a city to be reconstructed, even heroically, without fully *recovering*. Put another way, resilience involves much more than rebuilding." Community assets, however, like their protective mechanism counterparts on an individual level, can help communities to weather difficult times, such as during periods of massive unemployment, natural disasters, or crime waves.

Undervalued urban communities can counteract and compensate for a lack of social status within the broader community and society, and the negative attention they receive from media and the government, by effectively generating information that enhances a community's reputation (Craig & Elwood, 1998). Unfortunately, marginalized communities cannot expect to see positive media coverage of local events, volunteerism, and indigenous leaders performing important community functions. Thus, any positive community information will need to be generated internally and shared with the outside world, as respondents such as Barnard J. Stein (2012), Editor of the *Mott Haven Herald* (Bronx, NY), did in response to an article in the *New York Times* (Davidson, 2012) titled *The Bronx is Yearning*, in which deficits in the Bronx were highlighted; the response noted public policies that hurt Bronx residents and the residents' positive work via grassroots organizations. This is an important activity for advocates and social activists. The concept of community assets provides these communities with a language and, through assessment, a process or mechanism that can be used to identify capacities or assets.

VALUE OF A CAPITAL CONCEPT FOR ASSET ASSESSMENTS

All definitions of community assets have limitations that need to be addressed in any effort to assess community assets, and "capital" certainly is not unique in this regard, as the reader will see in the section that follows. Bedola (2004), for example, recommends that any effort to make social capital relevant to urban communities of color must take into account race as an independent factor, account for structural factors, and recognize the role and influence of gatekeepers on the process of developing social capital. Overcamp-Martini (2007, p. 199), in turn, notes that limitations of capital concepts should not prevent us from using them: "Confusion over the boundary-expansiveness of the theory should not be allowed to deflate all of the energy this concept is generating. Abandoning the concept of social capital before it is fully pursued would be unfortunate, rare as it is to obtain the benefits of the attention of the larger non-academic community, while pursuing a potential lead in social sciences."

Relatively speaking, community assets or capital are "data poor" when compared to deficit focused data. Some would argue that the deficit driven assessments and interventions have a long standing history when compared to asset oriented research. Nevertheless, the data poor label does have a way of capturing the state of affairs. Capital as an asset, however, has a rich body of literature that can be drawn upon to bring this concept to community assessments, and generate data for this data poor field, if modifications to needs assessment and other research practice are made (Green & Haines, 2012). Capital concepts, in addition, have great potential for community development or capacity enhancement, but much greater clarity and understanding of successful examples are needed for this potential to be realized (Fukuyama, 2002).

Crowell (2008, p. 1) strongly advocates for the use of community asset mapping as a mechanism that can be comprehensive in conceptualizing a community's various forms of capital, and as a means of minimizing disconnectedness between them: "Asset Mapping utilizes the concepts of physical capital, human capital, and social capital, as a holistic way of evaluation for revitalization and economic development. Challenges exist within most communities and focusing on only one aspect of development and/or revitalization separate from the others is not beneficial in the long run for sustainable planning and more often than not causes a disconnection between residents, organizations, and local/regional institutions."

Mapping's potential value in community asset assessments increases dramatically when the emphasis of an assessment goes beyond tallying numbers and, instead, or additionally, seeks to provide depth (voices and faces) to these numbers. In addition, the concept of capital necessitates that community social workers develop detailed definitions of what assets mean within a local context that takes into account race, ethnicity, age, gender, abilities, sexual orientation, social class, and culture. These perspectives are certainly not new to social work, and we are in a good position to define capital within this context.

Social activism and social advocacy as a form of capital add relevance for addressing urban social problems such as inequality and poverty (Berg, Coman, & Schensul, 2009; Mayer, 2003). Bringing together community groups that share similar concerns is a form of social capital that can integrate a social and economic justice theme (Barron, Field, & Schuller, 2001; Field, 2008). The more "politicized" a concept becomes, the more it lends itself to community social work practice, asset assessments, and social change.

Wakefield and Poland (2005, p. 2819) argue for the integration of a social justice value base in increasing the saliency of a social capital concept for use in oppressed or marginalized communities: "This examination suggests that social capital cannot be conceived in isolation from economic and political structures, since social connections are contingent on, and structured by, access to material resources. This runs counter to many current policy discourses, which focus on the importance of connection and cohesion without addressing fundamental inequities in access to resources...approaches to community development and social capital should emphasize the importance of a conscious concern with social justice. A construction of social capital which explicitly endorses the importance of transformative social engagement, while at the same time recognising the potential negative consequences of social capital development, could help community organizers build communities in ways that truly promote health." If a social justice framework is not at the heart of the approach to community asset assessments, then we cannot do an adequate job of identifying and using them to secure economic, social, cultural, civil, and human rights.

We believe that the reader will be the ultimate judge about the usefulness of how a capital view of community assets lends itself to community asset assessments. An ecological perspective on capital illustrates the value of having all forms of capital interconnected, and necessitates internal (community) and strategic external investment in built capital and human capital (Flint, 2010). We see value in using a capital concept when sufficiently modified to take into account the values and principles espoused in Chapter 3. We would, however, be disingenuous if we did not provide a balanced picture of "capital" as a concept for identifying community assets, as noted in the following section.

CRITIQUE OF A CAPITAL CONCEPT

Capital has found wide usage in governmental, academic, and practice circles, as the reader has seen, because it can be descriptive of a condition but also represents a process that can generate significant returns to a community, city, or nation. Community embedded resources, as a result, can be identified and, wherever possible, enhanced to further community well-being of various types, depending upon the type of capital used. Nevertheless, a capital concept is not without its critics and limitations for community asset assessments.

The concept of capital, particularly social capital, has been criticized from several perspectives, as evidenced by the amount of literature devoted to this subject, and some of the critiques are covered in this section. Taylor, Williams, Dal Grande, and Herriot (2006), for example, argue that the "inter-relations" dichotomy of social capital is poorly understood, resulting in serious asset assessment limitations when applied to undervalued urban based population groups. Most concerns have focused on the use of social capital, and, therefore, the critique that follows will reflect this attention. The following five concerns highlight the most common areas of critiques, although not all forms of critique.

1. Both Facilitates and Hinders Community Groups

A capital concept must be contextualized in order to fully understand whether it is a facilitating or hindering force in communities (Ronning, 2009). Field (2003, p. 74), for example, identifies four serious limitations with the use of social capital when conceptualized in a nonprogressive manner: "access to different types of networks is unequally distributed; social capital in networks can be used to disadvantage others; social capital in groups can benefit members but reproduce inequality and generate unintended consequences for others; social capital can have a leveling-down effort on people's aspirations, providing disincentives for individuals in a group to save and invest." Social capital is about connectedness and relationships, so context takes on significant importance in understanding what these relationships and connections mean (Paranagamage, Austin, Price, & Khandokar, 2010).

Sobel (2002, p. 146) found that people sometimes view outcomes achieved through social capital as being the same as the existence of social capital itself: "A successful group succeeded because it has social capital, but the evidence that the group has social capital is its success." The implication, explicitly or implicitly, is that social capital is a positive thing for this group, but this is not necessarily the case because it may emphasize individual gains without regard to the broader community (Sobel, 2002, p. 146): "The ability to use network relationships to obtain beneficial outcomes need not be good for society or even for the network. In many circumstances, these benefits come at a cost to individuals outside of the group. Society may lose when group members exploit social capital."

Another example of the negative side of social capital is illustrated with this example (Sobel, 2002, p. 146): "An individual may be better off joining a group than staying out and being the target of attacks from the group, but the group may encourage risky or destructive behavior of its members, so that all group members would be better off if the group did not exist." Van Staveren (2003) also recognizes that social capital can have negative effects, such as those found in organized crime. Gangs, too, illustrate this negative side of social capital.

Navarro (2002) critiques Putnam's (2000) book, *Bowling Alone: The Collapse and Revival of American Community*, regarding both historical and current day analyses of social capital that fail to address power and politics. Navarro states that to describe the labor movement as a movement to increase social capital is erroneous since that movement looked to combat capitalism and competition, which are core values in this society. He also criticizes Putnam's interpretation of the Progressive Era as a period in time in which social capital was built, without recognizing the political context of the period or the influence of certain bottom-up movements during that time that provoked change, instead of leaders implementing it from the top down.

Cleaver (2004), in turn, outlines the general idea of social capital, emphasizing that under this theory "victim blaming" is possible. Social capital is sometimes constructed as a way of improving our life without considering the influence of social structures and the negative side of social interactions (Cleaver, 2004, p. 894): "The 'dark side' of social capital, the possibilities of association leading to exclusion of people of particular identities, or of building trust and capacity amongst networks of people with inherently antisocial norms and activities, is well presented in such critiques (Levi, 1996; Portes & Landbolt, 1996) but rather skated over in policy. Additionally, mainstream analyses are often over simplistic on the relationship between socioeconomic and cultural inequalities and relations of power."

Sobel (2002, p. 139) uses a definition of social capital that is based on the work of Pierre Bourdieau (1986): "Social capital describes circumstances in which individuals can use memberships in groups and networks to secure benefits." This definition makes analyzing social capital dependent on the knowledge of the person's social context. A systems or ecological perspective highlights the interconnectedness of a community's various sectors. A change in one sector will ripple out and result in changes in another sector. Increasing the value of housing stock in one part through the introduction of community gardens in vacant lots, for example, increases the value of property, further accentuating differences with the neighboring section of the community (Been & Voicu, 2006). However, a poor economy may result in increased thefts of fruits and vegetables from a community garden (Abel, 2011) and introduce an element of crime otherwise not present.

The increase in foreclosed homes can be viewed from a variety of perspectives. These homes have been found to have gardens that have been abandoned. There was one instance in the San Francisco Bay Area, for example, in which volunteers have gone around to these abandoned homes and collected fruits and vegetables to be donated to feed the hungry. Over a 3 year period it is estimated that 250 tons of fruits have been donated to feed the hungry programs (Severson, 2011).

2. Can Be All Things to All People

A capital concept can be sufficiently flexible to encompass key elements of multiple types of capitals depending upon who is defining, operationalizing, and measuring it (Dika & Singh, 2002). Human and social capitals are considered complementary by some scholars, for example (Schuller, 2002). Manzo and Perkins (2006, p. 342) see the value of a social capital concept in community asset assessments because of its relationship to other forms of capital and its applicability for analysis of different levels: "We would add that: (1) social capital also has important implications not only for economic and political capital but also for physical capital, or the creation and preservation of assets related to place and the built environment (as planners recognize), and (2) it operates on multiple levels, from individual motivations and behavior to formal and informal neighborhood networks all the way up to a culture of democratic communitarianism as a society (i.e., the value we place on community and on working collectively to improve it)."

Throsby (2006, p. 4) illustrates this important consideration in the following statement: "The elements of natural capital comprise renewable and non-renewable resources, the ecosystems that support and maintain the quality of land, air and water, and the vast genetic library referred to as biodiversity. The economic dimensions of all of these phenomena have been extensively analyzed...a heritage building may have some commercial value as a piece of real estate, but its true value to individuals or to the community is likely to have aesthetic, spiritual, symbolic or other elements that may transcend or lie outside of the economic calculus." Raymond and colleagues (2009) propose the mapping of community values for natural capital and ecosystem services in Southern Australia. Thus, one practitioner may define a particular capital as economic whereas another may view it as cultural, and yet another may label it as intangible or natural. All three may be viewing the same phenomenon but calling it by a different form of capital.

Other scholars, such as Knominga and Van Staveren (2007), argue that social capital should not be applied to the economic arena because the assumptions and the outcomes are significantly different. Furthermore, social capital, in particular, has largely ignored the role of race in this society and thereby missed how broader social and economic forces have impinged on marginalized communities of color (Arneil, 2006; Hero, 2007). Such an oversight, as a result, severely limits its usefulness when used in highly multiethnic/multiracial urban communities.

Any concept that is so amenable to being defined differently according to an agenda, or some would argue, whims, of someone, poses particular challenges for asset assessments. There is the argument that social capital, probably more than any other form of capital, is difficult to measure effectively (Van Staveren, 2003). Consequently, the use of capital as a concept to capture multiple dimensions of community assets will necessitate that considerable time, resources, and energy be devoted to defining it in a manner that minimizes differences of opinion of what is being assessed.

Thus, the value and perseverance of a capital concept rest in the hands of practitioners and the communities they seek to reach, as well they should (Ebrahim, 2004). The use of a capital concept as a means of classifying a community's assets offers great potential, but it also brings limitations and considerations.

Certain activities, such as attending church, have value in themselves aside from having social capital value. Persons may not attend church to increase their social capital but, instead, for the intrinsic value of attending church (Van Staveren, 2003). Yet, Aja, Modeste, Lee, Montgomery, and Belliard (2008–2009) strongly advocate for the inclusion of churches in community asset assessments based upon their experiences in Nigeria and the prevention of HIV/AIDS. These institutions fulfill a variety of expressive, instrumental, and informational needs within their congregations (Trader-Leigh, 2008). Not everything of value can be considered capital. Furthermore, what enters into a capital category and what does not is determined by who is conceptualizing this concept (Smith, 2009).

3. Has Cultural Bias

There is a cultural bias that permeates what constitutes capital (Cheong, Edwards, Goulbourne, & Solomos, 2007; Green & Haines, 2012). This bias even crosses different continents (Daly & Silver, 2008, p. 538): "Social exclusion and social capital are the two most prominent terminologies that are providing frameworks for re-visioning the interrelations between economy and society under conditions of social change. They are influential in different locations. Social exclusion is prominent in debates in Europe and Latin America, whereas social capital is the preferred framework concept in the United States and developing countries."

The concepts of well-being and social exclusion are also finding their way into Australia (Saunders, 2008). Navarro (2002) notes that the influence of a social capital concept goes beyond the academic world and forces authors and researchers to use the language of social capital in related works in order to participate in this conversation, but this language is not recognized as being quite biased. Putnam's (2000) book, *Bowling Alone: The Collapse and Revival of American Community,* captured the imagination of academics, government, and the public and is largely responsible for the wide use of the concept of social capital to explain various types of social phenomena.

Sobel (2002) addresses this cultural bias by focusing attention and skepticism on Putnam's views of decreased participation in clubs and other communal activities as being a factor in the decline of social capital and other negative results, which puts blame on generational differences, television, long commutes, and working women. He takes an issue with Putnam's formulas for improving social capital, such as that some goals (for example, better education) can be achieved by raising voter turnouts by a certain percentage, increasing the number of nonprofits in an area by a certain number, etc. He acknowledges Putnam's passion that an increase in civic engagement is good for individuals and the United States, though.

Sobel (2002, p. 144) reviews *Social Capital: A Multifaceted Perspective,* a collection of articles, in which he summarizes Arrow's (1999) argument that "physical capital has three characteristics: extension in time, deliberate sacrifice for future benefit, and alienability. Social capital shares the temporal aspect of physical capital." Sobel (2002) notes that there are aspects of social capital that are not calculable, such as self-sacrifice, being manipulated, or being born into wealth or into an ethnic or racial group. Social capital is nontransferable (whereas physical capital is), but some aspects of it can be given to another person. The example used is that of a store owner whose social capital lies in the good reputation of her store. If she sells it, that reputation is transferred to the new store owner.

A cultural bias takes on greater significance since capital is elastic and can be all encompassing, meaning different things to different people. Feminists have found that it emphasizes formal participation involving organizations and either ignores or minimizes informal relationships (Adams, 2005; Bookman, 2004; Franklin & Thomson, 2005). Gender is supposed to be a nonentity in a capital concept, yet it is addressed implicitly by an emphasis on male types of participation. This bias emphasizes certain types of behavior and deemphasizes other types. There is also a bias toward adults and the almost total exclusion of children and youth (Holland, 2009). Children, for example, facilitate interactions and connectedness between nonrelated adults in community places and settings, yet they are not considered from a capital, social or otherwise, perspective (Weller & Bruegel, 2009).

4. Interactions and Participation Are Not Panaceas

It certainly is tempting to view marginalized communities from a participatory perspective in which getting residents involved is the solution to all of their problems. Increasing the amount of interactions or participation does not necessarily lead to increased community well-being (Bryson & Mowbray, 2005). An emphasis on amount of interactions without equal attention to the nature of interactions provides a superficial view of a community (Arneil, 2006). Cheong and colleagues (2007), for example, advocate for consideration of alternative conceptions of social capital in communities that are experiencing an influx of newcomers. Social capital has generally been conceptualized as locality based. However, newcomers have been found to maintain an extensive social network that transcends nations. This consideration increases the relevance of social capital to very diverse communities.

Van Staveren (2003, p. 415) defines social capital as "a shared commitment to social values as expressed in the quantity and quality of social relationships, which may enable or constrain dynamic efficiency." Van Staveren (2003) conducted a study in Rajasthan, India, to determine if social capital was an effective way of alleviating poverty and found that social capital had a positive influence on household well-being, if it was paired with individual agency. As social capital theory influences policy, a shift occurs that places an emphasis on an individual rather than broader social forces for their situation (Cleaver, 2004, p. 894): "The dangers of assuming that individuals can use network connections and participation in institutions to move out of disadvantaged positions can lead to a situation where individuals are seen as responsible for their own deficit of social capital and marginalization."

Cleaver (2004) adds two new components to this critique. The first aspect demonstrates a need to see how institutions and their functions connect to people's daily lives. Institutions often promote a "right way" of doing things, and Cleaver argues that those in poverty often are unable to navigate these routines and expectations, which are formulated based on dominant world views. Thus, there can be a tendency on the part of those in authority to "blame the victim."

The second asset questions the proposed potential of social capital to implement changes in the lives of poor people (Cleaver, 2004, p. 895): "Mainstream understandings of social capital are based on an inadequate model of human agency and the ability of actors to strategically invest in social capital." Although those in long-term poverty share an equal potential with others for agency and for utilizing social relationships, Cleaver (2004, p. 895) suggests that "these potential capacities are constantly, routinely, and indeed systematically frustrated by the workings of inequitable social and economic structures and the institutions through which social norms and values are channeled."

Cleaver (2004) identifies three factors that negatively impact the utilization of social capital by those in long term poverty: (1) a reliance on "ablebodiedness," which cannot be maintained; (2) a lack of room to maneuver in their social circles due to social stigma and instability; and (3) rarely being heard and so voiceless, or having their opinions not considered important. Ultimately, it is necessary to advocate for a greater understanding of structural disadvantages that plague the poor, and an understanding of how these disadvantages undermine their social relationships and agency.

Navarro's (2002) most scathing critique of Putnam's social capital points out his lack of discussion of power. He sees the decline of unions as the result of a skewed power balance that is in favor of employers. He also makes a connection between Putnam's more recent work and the recommendations of President Bush after September 11, and attributes these ideas to the further weakening of community.

Van Staveren's (2003) critique, like that of Navarro (2002), culminates into one overarching problem with social capital, and that is its omission of considerations of structures that perpetuate inequality. This raises questions of individual agency or access to groups and resources. Van Staveren says it is necessary to (2003, p. 419) "question differences in types of groups (for example between more and less influential groups), entry barriers and mechanisms of exclusion for some groups of people, or hierarchies within groups which influence who contributes and who gets what benefits." Van Staveren (2003, p. 421) also has serious concerns about how gender equality is addressed in a social capital concept and concludes that the social capital argument in policy effectively acts to place "the burden of poverty reduction policies on the poor themselves."

5. It Is All about Economics (Money)

Navarro (2002) is particularly critical of Putnam's conception of social capital, deconstructs his argument for social capital and communitarianism, and takes issue with Putnam's omission of power and politics in his conceptualization of social capital. He attributes this omission of power and politics to the fact that many fields of study in the United States have become highly influenced by the field of economics.

Accumulation of capital becomes an end in itself. Consequently, by extending our networks, it becomes possible to increase our ability to obtain resources, which is Coleman's (1998) understanding of social capital (Navarro, 2002, p. 427): "Participation, organization, and togetherness make individuals stronger, more resourceful, and finally more competitive, by increasing their capital. Thus the purpose of increasing social capital is to increase the overall amount of capital by making more social capitalists."

Cohen and Prusak (2001), like Navarro (2002), argue that using a capital concept brings with it the danger of reducing social phenomena or goods to an economic value, which fits well with capitalistic values. The more you have, the better off you are. Economic capital, for example, is conceptualized as assets. Yet, some cultures can argue that we are "rich" if we have a family that shows love and is united. Obviously, using economic capital in these cultures will effectively find a very "poor" community from an income and material possession viewpoint.

Van Staveren (2003) criticizes the integration of social capital into economic theory, where social capital is seen as producing a return on an investment, so to speak. The critique of this view lies in the fact that social capital is not simply an individual endeavor, but an interpersonal one, with investment by one being dependent on the investment by others. A social capital concept is often compared to other types of capital, and there is a tendency to define it as a form of concrete resource. However, social capital is actually very different from other forms of capital.

Navarro (2002), in turn, questions whether the lack of togetherness cited by Putnam and others in modern American society is actually a result of capitalism and competition and their effects on the American people. In addition, Putnam does not consider the contradiction between his call for more social capitalists and his call for increased "togetherness," showing how powerful capitalism has become.

Finally, community capital frameworks have their share of critics because there are distractions from taking a sustainable approach toward community development through an emphasis of a "piecemeal" approach toward capital (Flint, 2010). However, Flint (2010, p. 55) notes that a capital framework or perspective is important to community development: "The community capitals framework was important to community development here because it demonstrated how to place many different kinds of community concerns on par with each other by suggesting comparisons and integration through the idea of a common currency, not in the idea of money, but rather in the 'value' and investment that different capital assets of a community possess. With this understanding a community can find it much easier to have discussions about issues that cross boundaries of politics, culture, environment, and economy, for example. And eventually community stakeholders, often with very different ideas and views, can begin to acknowledge that improvements in all forms of capital are truly interconnected and require both internal investment as well as strategic investment in built capital and human capital from the outside."

TYPES OF COMMUNITY ASSETS

Hopefully, the reader is sufficiently grounded in the advantages and disadvantages of using a capital concept as a means of capturing community assets, and can see why we are proposing various forms of capital for use in community asset assessments, taking into account the criticisms in the section above. It should come as no surprise to the reader that community assets can be defined in countless ways, and as a result, measured in a variety of ways. The concepts of community and assets are complex and multilayered. However, when combined, their complexity only increases, but so does their potential for bringing about community well-being and social change. Challenge is closely tied to rewards. Consequently, the definition of assets is evolving and increasingly taking into account cultural and social context and, with this, direction on how best to assess community assets.

Efforts that seek to enhance a community's ability to meet the needs of its residents must be undertaken in a manner that is culturally affirming and efficient (Vega, 2009). This takes on significance when viewed from a social ecological perspective. The health and well-being of one family member, for example, has an impact on the health and well-being of the family. Family health and well-being can have an effect on their neighbors and the well-being of the community. There is general agreement that any serious effort to advance a concept of community wellness cannot be accomplished without a corresponding attention to community assets. Yet, health also is dependent on social policies beyond any one community that provide true access to health care for all.

Identifying and classifying community assets represents one of the greatest conceptual challenges facing any effort to conduct a community asset assessment. It can certainly be argued that all communities possess assets regardless of their socioeconomic circumstances. There are core types of assets that can be considered universal and others that are unique to a particular community or group and, therefore, particularistic in nature. Furthermore, not all community assets may be present or present in equal value. Some assets may be weak in influence, whereas others may be particularly strong. Thus, how to conceptualize and organize community assets represents the next major phase in the identification and assessment of community assets. Chaskin and colleagues (2001), for example, conceptualize community assets as falling into three realms: (1) organizations; (2) social networks; and (3) individual leadership. Donoghue and Sturtevant (2007), in turn, apply the concept of community capacity to ecosystems and differentiate foundation assets from mobilizing assets.

Witten, Exeter, and Field (2003) provide an excellent example of mapping urban environments in New Zealand and developed an index of community opportunity structures and resident health and well-being. They identified six asset domains in their research: (1) recreational amenities; (2) health resources; (3) social service resources; (4) cultural services; (5) public transportation; and (6) communication networks. Emery and Flora (2006) advance the use of various types of capital (Community Capitals Framework) to capture a community's capacity, and their conceptualization, with some modifications, will guide how community assets are conceptualized in this book.

The emergence of a capital concept has had a transformative impact on the social sciences and helping professions. Consequently, it should not be surprising that community assets have found a home in this literature. The reader may well argue that there certainly seems to be a degree of overlap between different forms of capital. We certainly agree, as the reader will see in the way the following capitals have been conceptualized. Local circumstances and goals will dictate how each of these forms of capital gets defined and operationalized in an asset assessment. It is important to emphasize that capital is a concept that is generally dealt with as descriptive rather than prescriptive, making the conceptualization of the particular capital very important, although frustrating to academics and practitioners wishing to have greater guidance on how to mobilize them in community interventions.

The step of categorizing assets or the various forms of capital becomes particularly critical because it informs the actions that follow, particularly the mapping of community assets. Nevertheless, this step is not without its share of perils. Numerous scholars and organizations have put forth their suggestions regarding classification.

There are countless ways of accomplishing this step. A search of the literature will unveil seven prominent ways in which to categorize community capital (Emery & Flora, 2006; Green & Haines, 2011): (1) cultural; (2) natural; (3) physical; (4) human; (5) political; (6) financial; and (7) social. The use of a five domains of capital is also popular (Flora, Flora, & Fey, 2004): (1) cultural; (2) human; (3) natural; (4) political; and (5) financial. Different scholars, however, have their own terms and borrow common terms. Johnson (2002), for example, identifies six types of capital: (1) polity; (2) physical; (3) financial; (4), human; (5) social; and (6) cultural.

The goal of developing community initiatives that purposefully seek to combine multiple capitals is certainly not out of the ordinary. Hancock (2001, p. 275), for example, advances the concept of "community capital" as a means of bringing together four forms of capital: "A healthy community is one that has high levels of social, ecological [natural], human and economic 'capital,' the combination of which may be thought of as 'community capital.' The challenge for communities in the 21st century will be to increase all four forms of capital simultaneously." Some scholars combine two or more capitals under one umbrella. Natural and physical capitals, for example, are combined into environmental assets, or financial capital consists of economic and human capital.

Rothman, Teresa, and Erlich (1994), almost 20 years ago, put forth a conceptualization of participation that brings an added dimension to a capital conceptualization, although the concept of capital was not used by them. Rewards
of participation can involve two distinct types: (1) instrumental (concrete) and
(2) expressive (psychological and supportive). Information, we would argue,
is sufficiently important to be taken out of the instrumental category to form
a third type that can be added to instrumental and expressive. Capital assets,
in turn, can provide communities with information, concrete services, and
emotional-supportive services, in any form or combination. All forms of capital,
as a result, can be combined to increase a community's well-being as well as to
mobilize residents and institutions in social change efforts.

Figure 2.1 is presented as one way of categorizing community assets using
capital as a unifying concept. Community assets are divided into seven different capital domains. Each of these domains seeks to capture information that
is unique to its domain. However, although every effort is made to have these
domains remain mutually excusive of each other, in reality, there may be some
degree of overlap between capital domains. Furthermore, as noted earlier, each
of these concepts can be mobilized along instrumental, expressive, and informational dimensions.

1. Social Capital Perspective

It is appropriate to start the discussion of community capital with social capital
(Hustedde, 2009). The concept of social capital has found its way into almost all
social science fields over the past two decades. However, it has found a particularly hospitable home in fields that pay special attention to communities. Extra

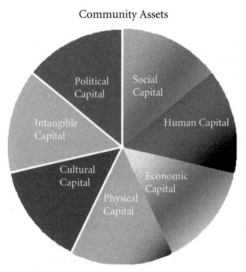

Figure 2.1. Community Capital Assets.

attention will be paid to social capital because of the potential influence this asset can have in any effort to assess a community's assets. That is why this form of capital received extra attention in the critique section of this chapter.

A. DEFINITION

The popularity of a social capital concept does not mean that there is a consensus as to its meaning. Some would go so far as to argue that a vague concept is a popular concept because it can mean anything to everyone (Asian Development Bank, 2001, p. 1): "There is no universally accepted definition of social capital. In the broadest sense, the term encompasses those relationships that help people to get along with each other and act more effectively than they could as isolated individuals. In this view, patterns of social organization, especially trust, mutuality, and reciprocity, are seen as important resources, which can result in benefits to individuals, groups, and society."

It is important to understand the various meanings attached to this type of capital. Although the idea of social capital may be relatively new to the general public, it is a concept that has been well known for quite a long time to sociologists (Portes, 1998). As noted earlier, simply put, social capital is the total potential and actual resources that a person or a group possesses due to social ties, relationships, or networks. Given that definition, it is also as important to recognize that social networks are not a natural given, and that time and energy are needed to build up sustainable and functioning social relationships, whether viewing them from a bonding or bridging perspective.

B. ELEMENTS

One way of conceiving of assets is to look at the categorizing of these resources (tangible and intangible). The use of various types of capital lends itself to developing a better understanding of what assets a community possesses. Usually, when thinking about *capital*, we think in terms of economics and the physical goods that a community possesses. However, it is also important to consider the social and other forms of capital that a community possesses.

Mattessich (2009, p. 49) stresses the importance of social capital in the life of a community: "Social capital or capacity lies at the heart of community development. If citizens cannot plan and work together effectively and inclusively, then substantial proactive community progress will be limited." The presence or lack of social capital can have a significant impact on the functioning of a community and its well-being (Denner, Kirby, Coyle, & Brindis, 2001; Lin, 1999; Portes, 1998; Throsby, 1999).

Estabrook, Sakano, Tubb, Varela, and Williams (2005), for example, studied grocery stores and social capital in a Cincinnati neighborhood and found the stores played important roles in fostering social capital, particularly in situations in which other forms of community assets were either absent or in limited supply. King (2004), in turn, brings up a different dimension and highlights the role of social capital and nonprofit leaders and the pivotal role they play in fostering and using social relationships.

When social capital exists, it can work and combine with other forms of capital, such as economic and cultural capital, to provide access to a greater amount of resources (Portes, 1998). For example, through networking, individuals may gain greater access (information) to subsidized loans and investor tips (Portes, 1998). Investor tips represent a form of instrumental support. They may also receive various forms of encouragement and emotional (expressive) support.

One of the main ways that social capital functions is through the structure and development of community relationships (Portes, 1998). For an individual or group to have social capital, they must be in relationship with others, and it is those others who are the source of the social capital. In social capital, as with economic capital, there is an exchange of goods or resources; however, with social capital, the currency is different. For example, services or favors are one means of currency, or there may be a sense that an obligation needs to be repaid. This phenomenon is known as bounded solidarity and is one explanation for why people do selfless acts. They feel bound and connected to some aspect of society.

In addition, Portes (1998) explains that social capital serves three main functions: (1) It is as a source of social control; (2) it is a form of family support; and (3) it is a source of benefits garnered through extrafamilial social networks. Of the three functions, the third is probably the most commonly used. One example of this is in ethnic enclaves. In enclaves, much of the mobility is network driven, with people connecting to each other with jobs, loans, business tips, etc. Although this is beneficial in some respects, it can also be limiting because it holds people to a small geographic area.

Additionally, it is important to note that, although social capital can connect some, it can function to exclude those who do not fit into the status quo or a community's definition of itself. This point takes on added significance in communities that are experiencing rapid changes in population characteristics, such as newcomers who have different cultural values and speak languages other than English, raising questions concerning how social capital is measured (Veenstra, Luginash, Wakefield, Birch, Eyles, & Elliott, 2005). As noted earlier regarding newcomer communities, the social network can be quite extensive there, stretching thousands of miles in some cases.

Harrison and Falk (1997, p. 41) bring up a different perspective on social capital that stresses the relationship between social capital and informal learning (knowledge that is not school based) as a form of community assets: "In any regional community there may be more potential in terms of people's skills and expertise and in terms of resources and facilities than is generally realised. Social capital is a term used to describe the social organisation and productive synergy underpinning community spirit. Everyday learning activities occur but are not often graced with the term 'learning' as they are not part of an accredited learning policy environment." As the reader will see when the discussion focuses on human capital, informal education is not considered within most typical definitions of human capital. This, unfortunately, systematically fails to take into account a valuable asset in communities that are marginalized by the greater society.

In addition to the above mentioned functions, social capital can also be a protective force, and this aspect makes it very appealing from a community asset assessment perspective. Social capital, not surprisingly, has been referred to as the "capital of the poor" (Gertler, Levine, & Moretti, 2006). This is particularly the case for all lower income groups. This function fits with the idea of the social resources theory, which states that "access to and use of social resources (resources embedded in social networks) can lead to better socioeconomic statuses" (Lin, 1999, p. 35).

C. Illustrations

Many practitioners and social scientists have begun to consider social capital as an asset in social networks (Lin, 1999) as well as being an essential element of social capital (Long & Perkins, 2007). Harpham (2007) argues that community social capital can be effectively captured through quantitative surveys, if a major portion of the instrument focuses on health related questions. Sturtevant (2006) found that collective action can result in the formation of community social capital through the forging of new social networks and mobilizing of local resources for community development.

Lin (1999) explains that, in order to measure social capital, it is necessary to measure the embedded resources, including network resources and contact statuses and at network locations, including the strength of ties and the various bridging ties. To capture embedded resources, there are two different sampling techniques to measure social capital (Lin, 1999). The first technique is a saturation survey, which involves mapping a network. Its advantage is that it gives a complete look at a network location. However, due to the detail that it involves, it should be limited to smaller networks. It is advantageous because it customizes content areas and eco-centered network mapping, but it has a lack of a sampling frame and tends to be biased toward strong ties.

The second, the position generator technique, "samples positions in a given hierarchy representative of resources valued in the collective" (Lin, 1999, p. 39). In this technique, individuals are asked to rank certain things and are asked about their ties, relationships, and familiarity with them. From their responses, it is possible to derive network resource indices. The advantages of this technique are that multiple resources can be mapped, it is content free, and it allows for direct and indirect access. Nevertheless, it lacks specificity of relationships.

The literature on social capital is replete with examples of how to mobilize social capital. The following two examples focus on Latinos and African Americans; however, other examples will be integrated throughout this book. Farquhar, Michael, and Wiggins (2005) report that their project entitled Poder es Salud/ Power for Health, which addressed health disparities in African American and Latino communities using community based participatory research, was successful in enhancing community level social capital.

The Chicano-Latino Youth Leadership Institute (Bloomberg, Ganey, Alba, Quintero, & Alcantara, 2003) also reported success in gaining community capital (social and human) related to increased levels of community service, improved peer relationships, and higher graduation rates than those of white, non-Latino nonparticipants. Bryce (2006) introduces a different conceptualization by stressing the role of nonprofit organizations as social capital because of the role that they play in facilitating connectedness within communities. Jarrett, Sullivan, and Watkins (2004), in turn, report on how youth programs foster development of social capital, including access to and relationship building with adults.

2. Human Capital Perspective

Human capital, like its social capital counterpart, has enjoyed a relatively long history in the social sciences and is often mentioned in any discussion of a community's assets, particularly when discussing economic aspects of communities. Unlike social capital, human capital has had minimal disputes concerning what constitutes this form of capital, as noted earlier in the critique of capital section. This is largely due to the narrowness of this form of capital and its reliance upon quantitative measures.

A. DEFINITION
Beckley and colleagues (2008, p. 63) provide a succinct definition of human capital: "The concept of human capital is rooted in economic theory and refers to the education, job experience, acquired skills, and the health of individuals." This definition favors capital that is acquired, although health is an exception. Most definitions of human capital generally avoid health. It is included in this section because it seeks to tap a dimension of community assets that generally gets overlooked in an asset assessment, yet wields considerable influence on employment.

B. ELEMENTS
A human capital perspective attempts to capture dimensions related to the talents (competencies) and knowledge of community residents (Haines, 2009). Work history and formal educational attainment are often associated with human capital. Another way of viewing human capital is to focus on the skills and knowledge possessed by the labor force. Duration of formal education and levels of qualifications are typical measures used to measure its strength (Schuller, 2002). Green (2010b), however, cautions that any comprehensive effort to capture this type of capital must be prepared to also tap the assets possessed by youth, older adults, and people with disabilities, which are groups usually overlooked in any discussion of human capital.

Attitudes, aspirations, and informal education, unfortunately, are rarely a part of this capital. A narrow definition of human capital effectively disenfranchises numerous talented individuals in marginalized urban communities. Asset assessments of these communities, as a result, must broaden their definition of what constitutes human capital.

As already noted, it is also important to broaden our understanding of human capital from an exclusive focus on adults. Youth, for example, can be just as effective as adults in community development. Therefore, it is imperative that their human capital be considered just like their adult counterparts. The net to capture a community's human capital must not systematically miss groups that can be tapped to help achieve the goal of community well-being. For example, youth are much more adept at using various forms of information technology than many adults, and are in a propitious position to tutor adults on this matter. Last, human capital implicitly places value on residents without disabilities. Residents with disabilities, too, must be included in this concept (see Chapter 4).

Human capital, like its social capital counterpart, is dynamic in nature and particularly sensitive to social, economic, political, and demographic changes in the community. Human capital, like other forms of capital, is incapable of standing still. Haines (2009, p. 41) draws a contrast between human and physical capital that is important to note in any effort to address a community's assets: "In contrast to physical capital, human capital is mobile. People move in and out of communities, and thus, over time, human capital can change. In addition, skills, talents, and knowledge change due to many kinds of cultural, societal, and institutional mechanisms."

Campbell's (2008) study of 20 undocumented Mexican women in a South Carolina community found these women to be both resilient and creative in finding ways of earning an income and so brings a different dimension to human capital. Several of the women opened up informal businesses such as a bakery, day care center, restaurant, and dress shop. These businesses were invisible to those outside of the community but well known, respected, and patronized by those in the community. None of these women had training in running a business or possessed high levels of formal education.

C. Illustrations

A human capital perspective on a community's assets necessitates taking into account the number of residents who are workforce ready but are not gainfully (formally) employed because of lack of access to employment. In addition, it is not unusual to have a research study focused on human capital totally exclude the informal economy of a community. Informal economic activity is prominent in communities consisting of undocumented newcomers, for example (Delgado, 2011).

Delgado (2011) notes that an informal economy represents economic activity that is legal, but unregulated by government. This economic activity relies on cash transactions. However, bartering may also be a form of payment, and one that gets overlooked in estimating the economic impact of this form of exchange. Unfortunately, the broader community often associates any form of informal business as nefarious when it applies to urban communities of color, with drug transactions, gambling, and prostitution being the three most popular stereotypical visions. The informal economy does not refer to these criminal activities. Some examples of informal economic activity include street vendors, car repairs done out in the street or in someone's garage, housekeeping, lawn and yard work, home baking and cooking, and family child care not sanctioned by local government.

Community asset mapping has been used successfully to assess the human capital of people with disabilities in both the United States and other countries, such as Canada (Canadian Association of Business Incubators, undated). The Canadian Office of Literacy and Essential Skills has adopted asset mapping as a tool in building learning networks within and across communities. To bring disability and business development organizations together, asset mapping workshops were sponsored by the Project's five community sites. Each workshop brought together representatives from a diverse group of community based organizations that serve people with disabilities interested in self employment. Workshop participants created an inventory and map of the physical location of services and assets that support persons with disabilities in their community.

Urban communities experiencing the rapid influence of newcomers are another example of how human capital is dynamic. Newcomers of color may possess advanced graduate degrees in their homelands and be professionally credentialed there. However, these credentials may not be formally recognized in this country. Thus, it is possible to find doctors and lawyers who have resettled in this community but who cannot practice medicine or law. They may take jobs that normally would be filled by other people of color with less than a high school diploma, displacing residents who may move to other communities because the job opportunities and possibly racial or ethnic composition of the community is changing. On the surface, it may appear that only demographic changes have transpired, but these changes can be quite profound from a human capital perspective.

3. Economic Capital Perspective

Economic, or sometimes referred to as financial, capital may be the least familiar form of community assets for community social workers but one of the most common ways of conceptualizing a community's assets. Nevertheless, this form of capital represents a critical element in any serious discussion of community well-being with a specific focus on economic development (Green & Haines, 2012).

A. DEFINITION

Economic capital is sometimes defined as consisting of two dimensions: fixed assets and liquid assets (Beckley et al., 2008). This definition is remarkably simple, and that makes it quite popular in some circles. However, this definition is too narrow in other circles, particularly those occupied by community practitioners interested in advancing economic justice agendas. Some scholars and practitioners can argue that economic capital is often a direct benefit of any form of capital that can be enhanced. An increase in formal education or training of residents can translate into qualifying for higher paying jobs. Thus, economic capital can be a primary or secondary goal of any assessment of community centered intervention.

B. Elements

There are many different ways of thinking about economic capital, such as strengthening the local economy through having money circulate and recirculate through the local economy (Rossing, 2000, p. 8): "The benefits produced by those dollars are retained within the community. This makes local people better off and makes economic growth possible. Many elements go into local economic development including local purchasing, local hiring, new business creation, development of human productive capacity, physical resources development, local investing, local credit provision and mobilizing external resources."

Another perspective is the percentage of homes owned by residents as an indicator of community economic assets (Pastor, Morello-Frosch, & Sadd, 2005). A high percentage of resident owned homes results in a stable population base. An emerging viewpoint on economic capital is the availability of land that can be used for food production, tying this form of capital to natural capital (Kristjanson, Radeny, Battenweek, Ogutu, & Natenbaert, 2005). Community access to financial capital is another way of conceptualizing a community asset. The concept of Individual Retirement Accounts (Mckernan & Sherraden, 2008; Schreiner & Sherraden, 2007) addresses the importance of this financial mechanism. The availability of microenterprises, too, adds an important dimension that may be overlooked (Miah, 2003).

Peredo and Chrisman (2004, p. 309) argue for the interrelation between cultural, natural, and social capital in facilitating the creation of community based enterprises: "Theoretical models that separate social, political and environmental factors from the economics dimensions of entrepreneurship cannot account for the failed experiences in business development among very poor populations...We maintain that in this emerging form of entrepreneurship, typically rooted in community culture, natural and social capitals are integral and inseparable from economic considerations, transforming the community into an entrepreneur and an enterprise."

Rossing's (2000) rationale for local (informal) economic capital, in turn, brings a dimension to this form of capital that is considered unconventional, yet is needed to present a holistic or comprehensive view of a community's economic resources and potential. It is important that this form of capital go far beyond conventional views of "economic capital" that stress income and wealth. As a result, community assessment of economic capital can encompass a wide range of possibilities. For example, identifying potential community members who wish to develop their own businesses can be part of an assessment (Emery, Wall, & Macker, 2004; Delgado, 2011).

C. Illustrations

Community asset assessments should attempt to include the economic sector (formal and informal) whenever possible, even though there may be considerable challenges in so doing (Walker, 2006b, p. 27): "A capacity assessment should be undertaken to spark business collaboration and promote the long-term benefits of a diverse economic base. Then when loans or grants become available, investment should be directed to group-defined goals and be available to all. If major revitalization grants become available, microloans and job training should be part of the package."

Providing opportunities for youth to open up savings accounts is a way of stressing the value of savings. The senior author, for example, used stipends that were part of a federal substance abuse prevention grant targeting Latino youth as a way of encouraging participants to save. Youth were paid a stipend for participating in a demonstration project. Half of the stipend was set aside and placed in a bank account for each participant. At the end of the project, as part of the graduation ceremony, each was provided with a certificate for successfully completing the project and a bank account. Efforts such as these, however, may go unnoticed in an assessment of community economic assets.

Delgado (2011) specifically addresses the need for community asset assessments to identify, assess, and map formal and informal businesses within urban Latino communities. Although these businesses can be assessed from a purely economic viewpoint, other forms of capital are needed to fully appreciate the role that they play in the well-being of Latino communities. Local media such as community focused radio and cable programming represent economic capital as well as other forms of capital. Furthermore, these media outlets will play influential roles in helping disseminate findings from the asset assessments, as noted in Chapter 8.

Community economic development cannot be successful without attention being paid to human capital (Lu & Halseth, 2009). Squazzoni (2007) specifically encourages the identification of local community (human capital) assets to be marshaled in support of economic development initiatives. Korsching and Allen (2004) demonstrate how EDGE (Enhancing, Developing, and Growing Entrepreneurs), a community based development program in Nebraska, builds locality based entrepreneurship, and ties together economic and human capital.

The example of merging cultural capital in the form of art districts and tourism illustrates how one form of capital can bring other forms of capital to enhance a community (Breen, 2007; Cohen-Cruz, 2005; Currid, 2007; Delgado, 2011; Grodach, 2010; Shaw, Bagwell, & Karmowska, 2004). Miami's Calle Ocho is an example of various forms of capital (human, cultural, social, economic, intangible, and physical) that have combined to create a community district that attracts tourists, artists, and various types of small businesses, to enhance a community's well-being. This Latino community has undergone significant changes in Latino population from the initial days of Cubans to a point now in which the majority of Latinos are not of Cuban origin. Nevertheless, the various types of capital, including economic, are still present today in the restaurants, grocery stores, and other small businesses.

Aref, Redzuan, and Emby (2009) report on the use of community assets and capacity building in developing a tourism district in Shiraz, Iran. Attracting tourists has enhanced local restaurants and other small businesses. Lange and Fenwick (2008), in turn, report on a very interesting community mapping project in two Canadian provinces focused on small business owners and their moral commitment to their community. The findings highlight how these owners' sense of social responsibility is closely tied to their degree of embeddedness within the community they serve, thereby enhancing their institutions' roles in community well-being.

4. Physical Capital Perspective

The reader may rightly appear puzzled by the inclusion of this form of asset. Social workers and community organizations often are drawn into community asset projects without adequate information about the physical assets of their neighborhoods. Emphasis of community asset assessments invariably focuses on social, human, and, on occasion, cultural capital. Yet, particularly in the case of urban communities, physical surroundings (capital) must be part of any assessment (Skerratt & Hall, 2011). Media very often emphasize the less desirable aspects of housing and physical space within low income urban communities. This negative portrayal must be countered whenever possible.

A. DEFINITION
Haines (2009, p. 41) provides a short but comprehensive definition of physical capital that captures how this concept is used in this book: "Physical capital comprises the roads, buildings, infrastructure and natural resources." This definition does cover considerable territory, so to speak. However, as already noted, physical capital usually is not thought of as a form of capital by human service providers. Yet, it is a very important and distinct form of capital that must be captured in a community asset assessment, particularly when focused on urban communities.

B. ELEMENTS
A "sense of place" as an important component of identity, sometimes prominently, alongside culture, is very much tied to physical space (Oliver-Smith, 2005). Miller and Scofield (2009), for example, report on a Cleveland (Slavic Village) initiative that changed the physical environment of the community, and, in the process, altered internal and external views of the community for the better.

Mallach's (2010) book, *Bringing Buildings Back: From Abandoned Properties to Community Assets*, illustrates the importance of physical structures in shaping positive community definitions of self, and in creating hope for the future, and in the process stresses the shifting of views on abandoned property from one that is deficit driven to its potential for urban transformation. Abandoned properties represent incredible opportunities, or assets, for a marginalized community.

The definition and counting of abandoned property are influenced by local circumstances, making it arduous to compare statistics across communities. For example, views of residential properties (multiple units versus single families or apartment units) may be differentiated from industrial properties (environmentally compromised such as toxic brownfields versus locations not being suitable for private use), and can vary considerably in how they are counted. Vacant lots, too, can vary according to size and specific locations from one community to another.

Hoff, Mahfood, and McGuiness (2010, p. 1), for example, identify brown-fields, sites formerly used for industrial or commercial purposes, from a potential asset perspective: "For brownfield sites where HHRA [Human Health Risk Assessment] indicates that the nature and extent of contamination prohibits agriculture for food consumption because of uptake concerns, returning properties to a more natural state or farming to support an emerging industry like cellulosic ethanol production may be viable alternatives. From an urban planning and policy perspective, converting brownfield sites into urban farms also creates a 'land bank' that provides planners with resources for future redevelopment opportunities. When evaluated both quantitatively and qualitatively, using HHRA to support urban farming as a remediation alternative gives stakeholders a viable and flexible alternative to conventional brownfield redevelopment." Lowrie and colleagues (2011), too, have conceptualized urban brownfields from an asset perspective and how community organizations and residents can come together and develop these fields in the interests of communities.

Glover (2003, p. 190), in turn, notes that marginalized communities often struggle with narratives they dislike and that cast them in negative terms to the outside world: "Tragically, damaging images imposed by outsiders are often powerful contributors to the ongoing development of a negative collective identity...as illustrated by communities affected by urban decline. As urban neighborhoods undergo a dramatic descent due to a variety of economic and social factors, residents face the often overwhelming challenge of resisting the ills, such as crime and urban decay, which accompany such events. Subsequently, as a neighborhood deteriorates, it is not uncommon for it to develop a negative reputation among nearby neighborhoods and within the broader locality in which it is situated. The onset of urban decline, in this sense, introduces a plot twist to the neighborhood's story that changes the very character of the neighborhood and embeds its residents collectively in a tragic narrative. The collective identity of residents is, thus, tied to misfortune, which is only reinforced by outsiders and serves to disempower community members, depleting their optimism to liberate themselves from their ill-fated situations."

Thus, community gardens, as addressed again in greater depth in Chapter 11, represent an effort at revitalization, creating human and social capital and, in the process, improving a community's image outside of the community. Stewart, Liebert, and Larkin (2004) come to a very similar conclusion by also stressing the role of changing a community's landscape as a means of improving identity within, and reputation outside of, the community. Urban landscapes, like their suburban or rural counterparts, consist of much more than trees and sky. City landscapes involve buildings, sidewalks, streets, and parks, for example, that must be tapped in an asset assessment.

Flexibility as to where community gardens can be established represents an important dimension of this form of capital. Community gardens can be established on rooftops, fire escapes, and windowsills (Mazereeuw, 2005). Local community circumstances will dictate the most propitious place for these gardens to thrive. Thus, the locale, size, and focus of the gardens are influenced by the local talent of residents and the type of space that can be used.

The reader may take issue with why some or all of the forms below are included in the physical capital category, and instead, would include them somewhere in the other categories of capital. It was a judgment call on our part that we believed that the items selected for inclusion would best be served by highlighting them here rather than having them get "lost" in the other forms of capital that enjoy much greater attention in the professional literature (Skerratt & Hall, 2011).

Several physical assets stand out in urban communities: (1) Population density; (2) Structure of housing stock and land; (3) Open space; (4) Transportation; (5) Exercise space; (6) Universal design and disability accommodations; (7) Nontoxic environment; and (8) Natural. The reader will notice that some of these assets have been touched upon as part of other capitals in this chapter. As noted earlier in the critique section, what constitutes all of the parts or elements of a capital is very much determined by who is using it and local circumstances.

(1) Population Density

Neighbors are never far removed from each other in urban neighborhoods. High concentrations of residents often have been framed against a standard that is rooted deeply in this nation's agrarian past. Rural living equates with low population density and considerable distances between neighbors. However, urban areas have residents and neighbors living in close physical proximity to each other, leading to greater opportunities to foster social capital. A high density of population can increase social capital, and provide a concentration of human and economic capital, making it an asset that is more abundant in urban communities when compared to rural communities.

Population density, as a result, should not automatically be equated with deficits. In fact, many aging baby boomers have been moving to cities for retirement (Christie, 2006). Furthermore, the international cohousing movement has been growing in the United States and has spread throughout all of its regions, including its cities (Cohousing Association of the United States, 2011). Although cohousing design may not be what we would call dense and may even include significant open space, facilities are shared, and social contacts and a sense of community are encouraged.

(2) Structure of Housing Stock and Land

A creative view of this category seeks to identify the number and size of buildable lots, housing available for purchase or rental, and proximity of housing to key formal and nontraditional institutions in the community (Mallach, 2006, 2010). Urban areas are significantly different from suburban and rural areas for very good reasons. The structure of buildings and the availability of land clearly stand out in how urban communities differ from those found in other geographic sectors of the country.

Who owns the land in a community becomes important information in any effort to identify physical capital. Government, for example, often owns sizable parcels of land in urban marginalized communities (Wills, Chinemana, & Rudolph, 2010). These tracts often go unused or underutilized, making them a prime source of physical capital for use in the community for little or no money.

(3) Open Space

It is always interesting, and some would argue provocative, to think of "highly congested" urban areas as having any form of open space. Yet, even in the most congested communities, open space can be found in the form of sidewalks, streets, and sometimes even green space in the form of parks. These spaces, however, clearly are "different" from what we associate with suburban and rural open space in this country.

Any in-depth conversation with anyone growing up in the crowded streets of New York City neighborhoods will involve countless stories of how streets became playgrounds for children and youth. Sports such as soccer, football, and baseball are all associated with large open and specific spaces of various types. However, rarely are these sports related to a city's streets, where they may actually be played. Rooftops also are often open spaces for families to picnic or simply for sunbathing or flying kites.

We do not mean to make these spaces and places romantic. However, they do exist and are considered assets. Parks, although existing, are rarely close to poor and working class neighborhoods. Public transportation, although available, is still costly for those on fixed budgets. Yet, it does not take a vivid imagination to conceptualize city spaces as places for community activities. Street parties in which city streets are closed off to automobile traffic illustrate how spaces that are not conducive to community gatherings can still become such spaces.

(4) Transportation

Access to public transportation is an aspect of urban life that does not get the attention and credit it deserves. In fact, the only time this topic gets mentioned is during some energy crisis when the price of oil and gasoline makes national news or public transit prices increase. The presence of major intersections or roads adds an additional dimension to this topic because it increases accessibility to a community. The availability of "unlicensed" taxis, for example, is part of a community's intangible capital. These vehicles, however, will not be listed in business directories and may be overlooked in formalized efforts relying on these directories for listings. Nevertheless, this form of transportation is a capital, and, furthermore, it is, in all likelihood, owned by community residents.

(5) Exercise Space

Exercise space is not limited by the extent of open land. Exercise, as anyone who has lived in cities knows, is very much in the eye of the beholder. Streets can be closed for festivities, and sporting activities such as touch football and stickball and handball can be played on sidewalks. Parks, of course, lend themselves to exercise space requiring large open spaces. Unfortunately, what is "ideal" open space for exercise is generally conceptualized by those with very limited experience in living in urban areas.

Exercise space need not necessarily fall under the concept of open space. An urban school may have a small outdoor area that allows younger children to run freely and older children to shoot baskets. An indoor gymnasium makes these activities available during all seasons. For other members of the community, public recreation centers and public pools provide needed exercise for all ages. Although competitive sports may be beneficial for those with suitable skills and abilities, exercise space is a benefit to the least physically able as well as skilled athletes. None of these will require the large open space of a park or a zoo, although they may require creative modifications to make them accessible to people with a range of physical abilities.

Krieger and colleagues (2009) undertook a community asset assessment in Seattle to uncover ways of increasing walking exercise in a public housing development. The findings served as a basis for the development of sponsored walking groups, improved walking routes, provision of information on walking options, and advocating for pedestrian safety. These activities succeeded in increasing walking exercise and reflected the input of the community in their design. Dabson and Gilroy (2009) also utilized a community asset assessment in Portland, Oregon, to increase active living goals that were based upon local assets.

(6) Universal Design and Disability Accommodations
In the United States, 5% of children ages 5 to 17 years have disabilities, 10% of people ages 18 to 64 years have disabilities, and 38% of adults 65 years and older have disabilities (United States Census Bureau, 2010); among the population aged 18 to 64 years, of course, are our returning war veterans. Although the Americans with Disabilities Act requires various accommodations, these have not necessarily been implemented. Where they have been implemented, or universal design principles have been utilized, these are an asset to the population with disabilities as well as others who benefit from more accessibility in the built and social environments. For economic purposes, cities and businesses that are well equipped and have welcoming attitudes that have been recognized and publicized should reap economic benefits as the populations of people with disabilities and elders increases in the twenty-first century. Beyond this, of course, is the fact that opening up environments to people with disabilities and elders is congruent with a social justice framework.

(7) Nontoxic Environment
Lower income communities are the sites of some of the most toxic elements in the United States (Corburn, 2005, 2009). The environmental justice movement has focused strongly on this phenomenon. Whereas a needs assessment may uncover illnesses related to a toxic environment, such as asthma, an assets assessment may uncover action that has been taken to clean up a community's

toxic elements. These local efforts to turn unhealthy sites into healthy and productive sites, such as in the case of urban and community gardening, often go
unnoticed by those outside of the community. Furthermore, governmental entities rarely collect data on the number, size, and location of community gardens.
Consequently, these assets can often go unreported and unrecognized by outside
entities. Furthermore, an urban community with strong environmental laws and
enforcement truly has an asset to offer its residents.

(8) Natural

Natural resources as a form of physical capital, for example, have increasingly
found acceptance because of efforts to identify and tap renewable resources, and
thereby find a niche among researchers and practitioners embracing ecological
processes (Throsby, 1999). Green (2010a) labels these types of capital as "natural
amenities," or nonmarketed qualities of a community that result in increased
community well-being. Nevertheless, this type of natural capital can include but
not be limited to weather, vistas, and unobstructed or limited obstructed views
of rivers, sky, and greenery, for example. There may be natural beauty that can
go unrecognized.

Nowak and colleagues (2010, p. 1) comment on the importance of urban
forests as natural assets: "While the aesthetic values of urban forests might be
eye-catching, the many critical services they provide tend to be overlooked. In
addition to being attractive, urban forests provide a myriad of essential services to the more than 220 million people who live in urban areas in the United
States—including reduced energy use, improved water quality, diverse wildlife
habitat, and increased human health and well-being. Urban forests are an essential component of America's 'green infrastructure' and their benefits extend well
beyond the cities and towns where they are located." The nonprofit community
organization American Forests (2012) also points out absorption of pollutants in
soil, improvement of air quality, cooler microclimates, reduction of energy use,
and increase in property values due to urban forests.

C. ILLUSTRATIONS

The very encompassing qualities of physical capital often result in initiatives
that use this type of capital as a central organizing asset for other assets to be
addressed. Semenza, March, and Bontenpo (2006), for example, highlight how
various forms of physical and cultural capital (public beaches, trellises for hang-
ing gardens, murals, planter boxes, public benches, and information kiosks with
bulletin boards) in public right of way urban spaces of Portland, Oregon, resulted
in social capital and the creation of community well-being.

Kwon's (2002) scholarship on site specific public art and locational identity
illustrates the close relationship between physical capital and cultural capital. Public art, for example, derives its power of community transformation
through its physical location within a community. Public art that is highly
visible and centrally located in a community has a high degree of exposure
and presents opportunities for community dialogue, as compared with public

art that is in some obscure corner of a community where there is just light public traffic.

Minneapolis' Latino community Mercado Central (Cooperative Mercado Central) is another example involving space and economic capital. This section of the community is home to 44 small businesses that were created through a coalition of residents, community organizations, and a faith based organizing group (Asset-Based Community Development Institute, 2009). The development of the Mercardo Central resulted in numerous benefits to the community, city, and state. Three dilapidated buildings were purchased and renovated through an investment of $2.4 million. An estimated 70 new jobs were created, and most of these new hires were from the community. The businesses generated over $2 million in sales and $80,000 in sales taxes during the first year of operation. In August 2009, the Mercado Central celebrated its tenth anniversary. These small businesses reflect local economic needs and are based upon cultural traditions of importance to residents.

5. Cultural Capital Perspective

The reader may question what is meant by cultural capital, and that certainly is a legitimate question. Historically, communities of color were considered to have only negative cultures that were believed to hold them back from progressing in this society. The terms "culturally disadvantaged" and "cultural deprivation" found a receptive audience during the 1960s and 1970s in this country and clearly capture the bias of the middle class and upper class views of what constitutes desirable "culture."

Cultural values such as cooperation and interdependence, as in the example of Latinos, effectively emphasize the importance of getting along and that concerns about the family and group trump individual concerns and competition (Delgado, 2007, 2008). This contrasts with values of competition and individualism that historically have been held in the United States. Furthermore, the knowledge associated with cultural assets was either ignored by institutions and those in authority or actively undermined (Yosso, 2005). Consequently, the question of whose knowledge and culture are worthy emerged.

A. DEFINITION
McLaren (1998, p. 130) provides a definition of cultural capital that emphasizes it as including personal and group qualities and also material objects: "the general cultural background, knowledge, disposition, and skills that are passed on from one generation to another...Cultural capital can exist in the embodied state, as long-lasting dispositions of the mind and body; in the objectified state as cultural artifacts such as pictures, books, diplomas, and other material objects." This definition brings a multidimensional perspective to culture that facilitates this capital being a stand alone capital, as well as allowing aspects to be incorporated into other forms of capital such as social and economic. Local situation and

circumstances will ultimately determine how this capital is conceptualized and operationalized for the purposes of a community asset assessment.

B. ELEMENTS

Cultural capital is both a set of activities undertaken within a certain culture and the attitudes, practices, and beliefs of a certain society (Throsby, 1999). Additionally, it is important to understand that culture can be defined as an expression of the collective aspects of people's behaviors (Throsby, 1999). The inclusion of a spiritual/religious dimension of cultural capital enriches this understanding of this form of capital (Hodge & Limb, 2010; Verter, 2003). Hodge and Limb (2010), for example, address the importance of spirituality in the lives of Native Americans and the role this plays as a community asset and how it can be assessed. Thus, it is not surprising why spirituality/religious beliefs are receiving greater attention in community asset assessments regarding their contributions to community well-being.

Although cultural capital's value is different from economic value, they are connected. This is seen through the existence of both tangible and intangible cultural capital. An example of tangible cultural capital is seen in buildings such as historic places (Throsby, 1999). An example of intangible cultural capital is a country's signature music. Fernandez-Kelly (2008) brings an interesting perspective to this discussion by arguing that cultural capital is transferable between the newcomer generation and its children, helping the second generation move up economically and socially. Both forms provide a culture with a sense of identity and pride, and both are subject to being maintained and rebuilt to keep them vibrant, lively, and usable over time.

Economic value, in turn, has items that can be considered cultural capital. An urban arts festival illustrates the multifaceted dimensions of cultural and economic capital (Quinn, 2005). It provides a community with a venue (space and place) to show off its cultural talent to the outside world (Grodach, 2010). However, these very same festivals also provide a venue for generating economic capital through the sale of art as well as food to patrons. Thus, the services that are connected to items with cultural value serve as the link between economic value and cultural value (Throsby, 1999). In social work, we tend to look at cultural capital as intangible, such as the beliefs and values of an ethnic or racial group; as an asset that can be concrete, such as food and religious and folk medicine practices; and also as representing a worldview that facilitates social navigation in this society.

C. ILLUSTRATIONS

Creativity has historically been conceptualized from an individual perspective to the exclusion of community. Creativity is a community asset that is best appreciated within a cultural context in order to better understand its meaning to a community (Borrup, 2003). The literature has numerous examples of how cultural capital can be an integral part of any community effort to assess capital or enhance capacities. Adams and Goldbard (2005) wrote a book entitled *Creative*

Community: The art of Cultural Development that provides practitioners with countless ways of bringing this form of capital to the practice arena.

Goldbard (2006, p. 22), in a follow up book titled *New Creative Community: The Art of Cultural Development*, argues for the role of cultural based art as a means of capturing and responding to social conditions: "Community cultural development work inevitably responds to current social conditions: the work is grounded in social critique and social imagination. The precise nature of this response always shifts as social circumstances change." Cultural capital, as a result, represents a form of capital that lends itself to being identified, being assessed, and serving as an instrumental component of interventions.

Delgado (2007) addresses cultural capital by examining Latino community assets from a variety of perspectives. The inherent strengths derive from cultural beliefs, values, attitudes, and practices reinforce a cultural pride identity. Fernandez-Kelly (2008) examines the role of cultural capital (assets), how it gets transported from the country of origin for Latinos to this country, and how it helps second generation Latinos. Fernandez-Kelly (2008) conceptualizes cultural capital as consisting of three domains: (1) cognitive correspondence; (2) positive emulation; and (3) active recollection. Richard (2003) provides a detailed description of the use of cultural assets for Latino community building in East Palo Alto, California, and illustrates how cultural assets can attract economic, social, and intangible capital to this effort.

Cultural pride on an individual and collective level serves to help address life's trials and tribulations, and remembrance of nation and ancestry are direct manifestations of cultural capital (Fernandez-Kelly, 2008). Possessing a deep appreciation of cultural traditions and values helps newcomers ground their experience in the United States through the use of this form of capital. One Australian community asset assessment and capacity enhancement project focused on tapping indigenous community cultural assets as a "cultural thread" to draw in participants (Parker et al., 2006). Development of forms of outreach and public information that utilize cultural symbols and meanings serve as cultural assets.

Denner, Kirby, Coyle, and Brindis (2001) present another example specifically focused on one social issue (adolescent birth rates) with one group of people in an exploratory study that examined the roles and interplay of two capitals (cultural and social). They studied the differences between low income Latino communities with either a high or low adolescent birth rate. They interviewed youth and adults in these communities as to why they felt the birth rate was high or low and found that communities with strong social and cultural ties were the ones with the lower birth rate. These communities had a number of nontraditional resources, people living in homogeneous areas, new housing, many community businesses that were run by local business owners, and higher police visibility. Additionally, social capital was visible through shared child care responsibilities and the fact that families had longstanding relationships with one another. Interestingly, longstanding nonprofits, which were mostly staffed by residents of the community, were identified by community members as playing a role in keeping the birth rate low.

In addition to social norms, cultural norms were a protective (asset) factor in the low birth rate communities. Low birth rate areas had higher rates of Latinos, had more residents who were foreign born, were linguistically isolated, and had most people still viewing themselves as being a part of Mexico. As a result of all of these factors, the traditional values were still intact.

Interestingly, no one from the community identified a high adolescent birth rate as a part of the Latino culture. Furthermore, adults in this community viewed a high birth rate as a problem and were more open to options concerning contraception despite religious views. Conversely, in high birth rate communities, there was no general consensus that a high birth rate was a problem (Denner et al., 2001). Overall, the study suggested that high social capital and strong cultural capital were associated with lower teen birth rate.

Cultural capital can capture another dimension, such as spiritual/religious assets or artistic talent within a community. Hodge (2005, p. 314) reports on the emergence of a new form of asset assessments focused on spiritual community assets: "Increasingly, social workers are being called on to conduct spiritual assessments, yet few assessment methods have appeared in academic literature . . . . five complementary assessment approaches that have recently been developed to highlight different facets of clients' spiritual lives. Specifically, one verbal model, spiritual histories, is discussed, along with four diagrammatic approaches: spiritual lifemaps, spiritual genograms, spiritual ecomaps, and spiritual ecograms . . . The aim here is to familiarize readers with a repertoire of spiritual assessment tools so that the most appropriate assessment method in a given client–practitioner setting can be selected." Aja and colleagues (2008–2009), in turn, report on the role of religious institutions and spiritual assets in addressing HIV/AIDS at the community level.

Delgado and Barton (1998) specifically identify Latino community murals as indicators of community cultural pride and talk about how a community asset assessment introduced quantitative measures (number of murals, size, and location in highly traversed sites) and qualitative measures (nature and themes of content) that can be used as indicators. Cultural capital as represented through community public art allows creating together, discovering, and building upon shared meanings and understanding (Better Together, 2001).

The example of Latino youth in Boyle Heights, Los Angeles, illustrates the importance of cultural capital and economic capital (Lopez, 2009, p. D1): "Sandwiched between an underpass and a new police station, this part of Boyle Heights may not seem like anyone's pick for L.A.'s next cultural hot spot—but then again, neither did Spring Street when some rather precocious signage declared a gallery row on the edge of skid row a few years ago . . . But these days if you brave the crowds of families, hipsters and party-seekers every second Thursday of the month in downtown L.A., you'll encounter one of the city's most popular art walks with 45 galleries, a tour bus and, the surest sign of success, illegal street vendors." Latino youth created an art district based upon an asset assessment of this community's public art, and so community cultural capital intersected with community economic capital.

6. Intangible Capital Perspective

Intangible capital, or sometimes called "invisible" capital, is ever present in a community. Yet, like dark matter in the universe, it plays influential roles in daily life. Bronn (2008), for example, advances the proposition that communication within communities and organizations is a form of intangible asset that wields considerable influence and should be identified, assessed, and mobilized.

These forms of assets help shape how communities negotiate daily life and even how communities may define their geographic boundaries. Consequently, the influence they have on how communities think of themselves is quite evident by the presence, or absence, of this form of capital. Not surprisingly, intangible capital is challenging to measure, and no comprehensive community asset assessment would be complete without tapping this form of capital (Svendsen & Sorensen, 2007).

Michiotis, Cronin, and Devletoglou (2010) speak of the importance of revealing hidden issues and assessing intangible assets in both organizations and communities. Yoon (2009), in a rare article focused on invisible capital community assets, found the importance of a community having a sizable portion of its residents being senior citizens helping a community rebound from a major flood because of their experiences with prior floods and how best to recover from these disasters.

Furthermore, this capital does not enjoy the wide acceptance that the other forms of capital covered enjoy. This will prove to be a challenge in any form of community asset assessment, from how to capture it to how best to report its presence. Denton and Robertson (2010) show the importance of a community having a long history of innovation and generosity as forms of capital. This illustrates that intangible capital does provide enough flexibility to help capture community assets that normally would be overlooked or subsumed under other forms of capital and get lost because they lack the prominence of other forms. Intangible assets seek to capture community capital that normally goes unnoticed.

As already noted, intangible community assets are largely invisible. Nevertheless, any effort to arrive at a comprehensive inventory (asset audit) of a community's capital must also involve its intangible assets (Svendsen & Sorensen, 2007). James' (2004, p. 1) observations about intangible assets in the business sector can also be applied to communities: "The contemporary manager has a problem. It is no longer possible to touch or see the things that matter to business performance. A long-term shift from tangibles to intangibles is occurring in many industries. The focus is no longer mainly on cash, inventory, plant and equipment or land, which typically account for one-fifth of a firm's value. Instead, more slippery considerations such as vision, motivation, various types of explicit or implicit knowledge, customer and employee loyalty, and brands are the key determinants of an enterprises' performance." The intangible items covered in this capital either get addressed in this capital or must find a place in the other forms of capital.

A. DEFINITION

The intangible capital asset, by definition, is unorthodox, but needed nonetheless in order to capture a more holistic and realistic portrait of a community's assets. This form of capital seeks to tap assets that are not easily captured or measured but still wield considerable influence in a community's life and well-being. Because there is a certain illusive nature to this capital, unfortunately, this can result in a community asset assessment overlooking its presence and influence in the daily life of a community. Yoon (2009), for example, notes that this type of capital is not typically identified through the use of various existing social indices.

B. ELEMENTS

Intangible assets, by their very nature, are either taken for granted or are very difficult to measure. Dahm (2004), for example, conceptualizes intangible assets in the Latino community by bringing together cultural and spiritual elements such as language, culture, faith life, and spirituality. These elements can also be thought of as being cultural capital. How they get classified, as a result, becomes a local community decision and illustrates the challenges faced in categorizing various forms of assets. Nevertheless, these types of assets cannot be overlooked, particularly if we are assessing the assets of marginalized urban communities.

Ganapalis (2008) stresses the importance of public and civic spaces as venues for generating community capital, and intangible capital taps into this conceptualization. Emery, Fey, and Flora (2006), in turn, conceptualize intangible assets as political influence, pride in heritage, diversity of residents, older adults, and community norms. Haugh (2005) emphasizes that improving a community's image to the outside world is an intangible community asset. Some scholars go so far as to posit that social capital is a form of intangible asset (Kay, 2006; Siegel, 2005). Arizmendi and Ortiz (2004) identify community leadership potential and community moral support for social justice issues as intangible Latino assets. Gardberg and Fombrun (2006), in examining businesses, argue that citizenship programs, too, are a form of intangible asset that can help companies overcome nationalistic barriers in reaching existing and new markets.

Zhou and Kim (2006, p. 1) comment on the interactional and synergistic effects of intangible and tangible capital with community social structures and say that "cultural attributes of a group interact substantially with structural factors, particularly tangible ethnic social structures on which community forces are sustained and social capital is formed." The authors conclude that "culture" is not static and requires structural support to constantly adapt to new situations. Finally, Schuler (2004, p. 2) advances the concept of "civic intelligence" as a means of capturing an emerging form of intangible community capital: "Civic intelligence describes the capacity of society to consciously adapt to its environment and shape a future environment that is healthy, equitable and sustainable. Although individuals contribute to civic intelligence, the concept describes a phenomenon that is *collective* and *distributed*."

We identify four types of intangible capital: (1) historical; (2) temporal; (3) momentum; and (4) hopes and dreams. Certainly, these four do not represent all types. However, we believe that these four capture the spirit of this form of capital, and the reader can examine local circumstances to see which of these assets stand out or can be replaced by others not mentioned here.

(1) Historical

All communities share a history. For some communities, it is extensive and well documented, but for others this history is more recent and minimally documented (Goldbard, 2006, p. 69): "Official histories reliably leave out many of the most resonant truths of marginalized communities—the reminders that sustain pride and hope. When such things pass from living memory, they deplete the stock of images and ideas from which an imagination of the future is constructed." Regardless of the extent and documentation of a community's history, it still must be assessed carefully for its possible contribution as an asset or intangible capital.

Communities with extensive histories of being undervalued by the broader community rarely have a formalized historical document to capture their trials, tribulations, and successes. Probably, the only documentation will be local newspaper articles chronicling the decline of a community or the extensive arrests of its residents. In those instances, oral history must be captured in order to uplift the positives within a community (Hudson & Santora, 2003; Thomas, 2004).

In their analysis of the play "Chavis Ravine," Yasso and Garcia (2007, p. 145) illustrate how oral histories can be transformed into various forms of capital: "Drawing on a critical race theory framework... [the] article weaves together sociology, education, history, and performance studies to challenge deficit interpretations of Pierre Bourdieu's cultural capital theory and to analyze Culture Clash's play 'Chavez Ravine.' The play recounts a decade of Los Angeles history through the perspectives of displaced Mexican American families from three former neighborhoods of Chavez Ravine. Culture Clash's performance recovers and personifies the community cultural wealth cultivated by these families. This multifaceted portfolio of cultural assets and resources includes aspirational, linguistic, social, navigational, familial, and resistant capital. 'Chavez Ravine' affirms the continuity of Chicana/o communities, utilizing culture as a source of strength that facilitates survival and nurtures resistance."

Oral history has a prominent place in the lives of many groups of color and other marginalized groups, and, in some cases, has continued to exist over centuries. Often, there are long time members of the community who were in place as youngsters when important events occurred that were either tragic or celebratory in nature. These individuals represent intangible assets who can help a community recapture its history, and this recaptured history can inform the identity of a community.

(2) Temporal

Timing and momentum are different. "Timing" as an intangible capital that seeks to capture a state of being that is optimal for undertaking community projects. A community festival creates a positive climate for a community to come together and celebrate. However, the creation of this good spirit is also an optimal time for reflection on how to make aspects of community life more appealing. The moment right after a community festival may be a rare moment when this happens in the life of a community. It may be that a sizable number of youth enter school age or adolescence, and the moment is right for developing a project that seeks to maximize their participation in a community initiative. Or it may be a period during which a high number of residents enter retirement age, and an opportunity presents itself for an older adult set of initiatives (Delgado, 2008). This set of circumstances will not happen again for a long period of time. Thus, time becomes an asset.

This capital may be fleeting in nature, but it is still an intangible capital. Time in the life of a community is often a "given" in community practice, and it is so important throughout any stage of an intervention, including its beginning. The reader may dismiss this form of capital because it simply is so unusual and because it requires grasping a changing characteristic of a community. However, timing is always a critical element in community practice, and there is no reason not to consider it in asset assessments.

(3) Momentum

Momentum seeks to capture a moment in time in which key factors and considerations are aligned in such a manner that what normally may appear to be improbable becomes probable. Seyfang (2004) refers to momentum as "social energy." The importance of momentum is certainly well understood and appreciated in community social work practice, and community asset assessments must seek to capture this element if social change is to be maximized as a result of the assessment.

Those of us fortunate enough to have worked in the field for an extended period of time have experienced moments when the "stars are aligned" in a particular way, making a project or community change effort seem magical, or even destined. Yet, it does not occur frequently, and that is why it is special. It may be that a community asset assessment is conducted after a series of fortuitous events have occurred in a community. Optimism, as a result, is very high for the community. Capturing this ephemeral capital is important. An assessment is about a "feel good" moment, making residents even more receptive to hearing good news about their community.

(4) Hopes and Dreams

The concept of hopes and dreams is one that often gets overlooked in any discussion of marginalized communities and their expectations. Furthermore, the concept of a miracle is one that resonates in many communities of color and among residents who are highly religious. Thus, a community that still harbors hopes and dreams is a community with an important intangible asset. Community asset assessments must actively seek to capture this asset.

Hollingshead, Allen-Meares, Shanks, and Grant (2009) have used an innovative question of "miracle" to uncover a community's assets and dreams. They pose the "miracle" question as a way of capturing this information for use in community planning. Hopes and dreams of community residents rarely get captured in any form of formalized survey, needs, or even asset driven assessments. However, these aspirations often tap a form of asset that is arguably very difficult to measure, yet is so critical to the life of a community. As noted earlier in the human capital section, aspirations are generally overlooked when discussing this form of capital. The topic is of sufficient importance that it has its own category here, as well as being part of other capitals such as human capital.

Aspy and colleagues (2004), in their study on youth violence and youth assets, found that youth with community involvement and future aspirations (hope) were almost two times as likely not to carry a gun than their counterparts without these assets. Geoffrey Canada's internationally known work with the Harlem Children's Zone (2012) has shown the power of community involvement and that hope exists even in the most difficult of circumstances. Intangible capital concepts such as the ones presented in this section have a great deal of potential for use in carrying out community asset assessments. However, they are only a means to an end, and not an end unto themselves, and should be combined with other forms of capital (Pinkett, 2003).

The Pew Hispanic Center's (2009) study titled *Between Two Worlds: How Latino Youths Come of Age in America* found that Latino youth are beset by a host of social problems. However, they still maintain optimism about their future in this country. This optimism, as a result, should not and cannot be overlooked in any type of community asset assessment. Yet, a traditional form of needs assessment will surely pick up on a range of social problems and totally miss their hope for the future. A community without hope for a brighter future is a community suffering a deep and collective depression about its state of being.

C. Illustrations

The boundaries between each of these forms of capital discussed above are not fixed and can have a certain degree of overlap. Any evaluation of how these capitals can be tapped for use in a social change initiative will quickly reveal the difficulty of disentangling each from the other, making it arduous to arrive at definitive conclusions. The synergistic effect is real but may be difficult to capture in an evaluation effort. Nevertheless, the fact that they are arduous to measure should not exclude them from an assessment and efforts to measure their influence.

Conducting an oral history project that, for example, involves youth interviewing older adults with long histories of living in a community is an inexpensive and highly important asset assessment undertaking. Histories of marginalized communities rarely get recorded by residents, and histories of urban communities generally are written by elites from outside of the community. Consequently, the voices and experiences of residents, particularly those who were the initial settlers of their respective groups, get lost. Capturing this history and making it available for the entire community, including visual taping of the interviews, are ways of preserving the history of a community before it gets lost, empowering both older residents and youth, and preserving this intangible capital in a manner that can be saved for future generations.

The intangible aspect of momentum, in turn, brings many of the elements associated with "right" timing. However, it enters into discussion when a series of events build upon each other. Summer festivals, sports championships, and graduation events, for example, provide communities with an important sense of having turned the corner during difficult periods. These occurrences, however, are rare, and even rarer when their sequencing is advantageous. For example, a community asset assessment that can start during the beginning of one event can extend to cover multiple events, and thus lead to a culmination at the end of the summer. Each event can build on previous ones and lead up to a final event, such as a community forum at the end of a parade or a community dialogue during the celebration of the opening of a community garden.

Using a festival as a venue to conduct focus groups, community forums, and community dialogues, for example, is an effective way to capture an ideal moment in time for an asset assessment, and tapping the perspectives of participants who would normally not be asked their opinions or insights. Developing a project that involves youth from a graduating class in painting a mural that captures their hopes and dreams for their community is another example of beginning at the right time and right place for an assessment. The graduation is an excellent time to celebrate an important event in the life of those graduates and their families. It is also an important event in the life of the community.

The concept of "capital," although not without its share of critics and limitations, as noted earlier in this chapter, has saliency because of its broad appeal across academic disciplines and professions, including social work. The economist, Throsby, (1999) notes that a "capital" concept continually evolves to encompass broader spheres beyond physical, human, and natural capital since its original introduction. He goes on to argue that there are striking parallels between cultural and natural capital and that cultural capital is a distinct entity unto itself, to show that evolution.

7. Political Capital Perspective

Political capital is the final capital or asset to be discussed in this section. Political capital lends itself to being integrated into the other forms of capital discussed earlier in this chapter. However, it is of sufficient importance and complexity to warrant its own attention, while readily acknowledging its capacity to become a part of other capitals or assets. Various forms of political participation have implications for other forms of capital, such as social capital (Green & Haines, 2012).

As stressed throughout this book, each community must ultimately determine what elements will be included under a particular asset or capital. Political capital gets manifested differently if a community consists primarily of citizens as opposed to the undocumented. The former have expanded options of how to develop and exercise political capital. The latter, however, cannot participate in electoral politics, severely limiting their influence on electoral representation of the community. How best to weigh its significance, and how best to utilize and mobilize it, as a result, should be locally determined.

A. DEFINITION

Political capital is usually defined and operationalized as an ability to exert political influence. The concept of political attitude can also be found in the literature to capture political capital. This perspective, according to Ferguson and Dickens (1999, p. 5), and we concur, brings this concept into the realm of other forms of capital: "An entity's political capital comprises those aspects of its physical, financial, social, and intellectual capital that have potential to affect political outcomes." Community political capital or assets seek to tap a community's level of participation in a democratic process.

Ginieniewicz (2010), however, differentiates between civic and political assets. The former focuses on day to day practices and attitudes that result in a higher quality of life. The latter specifically refers to individuals' capacity to alter individual power relations, particularly in those circumstances in which they are socially, economically, and politically marginalized within their community and the broader society.

Practitioners may wish to think of political capital as a distinct form of capital in its simplest manifestation and can do so by identifying the percentage of the community that votes in elections, for example. If community social workers embrace the transferability of political skills and experiences, though, it then opens the door, so to speak, for including a wide range of activities and settings that can be used to enhance political capital. Therefore, we have elected to broaden this form of asset to go beyond electoral voting to include other forms of manifestations, without negating the importance of electoral voting.

B. ELEMENTS

A concept such as political capital, and particularly with the way it has been defined in this book, lends itself to being operationalized along a variety of elements. Li and Marsh (2008) effectively broaden this form of capital to include various forms of political participation. Efforts to achieve reforms and governance strategies represent political capital and can result in the establishment of a "virtuous circuit" that generates political capital in marginalized urban communities (Burris, Hancock, Lin, & Herzog, 2007). Xenos and Moy (2007), for example, found that the use of the Internet to gather information on electoral politics effectively translates into political and civic engagement. Political capital, in turn, can result in various positive influences on well-being (Ferlander, 2007).

Elements related to political capital must break the conventional views of political capital being only participation in electoral voting. This section, as a result, will focus on four types that stress formal and informal settings and activities: (1) volunteering; (2) electoral voting; (3) decision making in community institutions; and (4) engagement in social and recreational activities.

(1) Volunteering

The emergence and popularity of the concept of "civic engagement," particularly its social dimension, emphasizes the need for and importance of having residents engage in activities that increase the welfare of the entire community (Delgado, 2009). Although civic engagement has generally been conceptualized as volunteering, it can also encompass voting and other political acts such as lobbying. Volunteering, however, has been found to foster political participation in a variety of other spheres or arenas, resulting in numerous benefits to those who volunteer (Baines & Hardill, 2008). Haugh (2007) outlines the influential role volunteers play in community led social venture creation and the importance of identifying and tapping this resource. Local residents have an in-depth understanding of community needs and resources and a vested interest in creating institutions that benefit their community, as in the case of social enterprises.

Participation in community service, too, has also been found to lead to greater electoral participation (Seider, Gillmor, & Rabinowicz, 2011). McFarland and Thomas (2006) found that youth participation in volunteering associations positively influenced adult political participation. Hart, Donnelly, Youniss, and Atkins (2007) found that school required community service was a strong predictor of adult voting and volunteering. Although no studies could be found related to service learning and its relationship to political capital among youth, this area has tremendous potential for increasing political participation among students.

(2) Electoral Voting

Electoral voting is arguably one of the most important ways of seeing political capital manifested in a democratic society. Also, the percentage of the eligible community that exercises this democratic right in local, state, and national elections is an element that is more easily measured than the other elements covered in this section.

However, broadening this political capital element to include other forms is essential. Political representation represents a promising dimension that can help capture an outcome of voting. To what extent does the community have elected officials representing its interests at the local, state, and even national levels? The senior author found that there were many instances in which local Latino business owners eventually went on to being elected to political office (Delgado, 2011). Human and economic capital also translated into political capital in those instances.

The development of political connections represents another perspective on political capital (Li, Meng, & Wang, 2008). There may be instances in urban communities in which these communities do not have the political capital to elect their own residents to political offices but do have ready access to elected officials. This access, as a result, cannot be dismissed in a community asset assessment of political capital.

(3) Decision Making in Community Institutions

Viewing political capital from a community institutional perspective introduces richness to a political concept. Curley (2010) found that neighborhood resources, such as parks, recreational facilities, libraries, grocery stores, social services, place attachment, and feelings of safety, translate into social and political capital. Pitre (2009) examines the political capital generated through parental involvement in school decisions.

Hays and Kogl (2007) go so far as to argue that place based social networks translate into place based political ties through involvement in informal association, translating into electoral voting and other forms of political participation. Electoral voting participation is too narrow a way to better appreciate the wide variety of forms and expressions of political capital or assets (Staehell, 2008).

Alex-Assensoh and Assensoh (2001) bring a different dimension to this element and have found that African American churches proved to be excellent conduits for the development of political skills and as vehicles for political engagement and mass mobilization, an instrumental aspect of political capital. The inclusion of houses of worship as an aspect of political capital broadens this capital. The earlier discussion of economic capital encompassing both formal and informal domains is an example that can also be applied to political capital with formal (electoral voting) and informal manifestations.

(4) Engagement in Group Social and Recreational Activities

Informal community contexts can also serve to create opportunities for the battling of oppression and the fostering of democracy (Evenhouse, 2009). Kim and Bell-Rokeach (2006) stress alternative political skills that occur during participation in activities such as soccer and church movements. Urban agriculture has been found to foster opportunities for developing a wide range of skills, including political capital, that can be transferred into other social spheres (Smit & Bailkey, 2006). Seippel (2006) found that participation in community sporting activities translates into generalized trust and political commitment. However, the influence is much greater when there is concurrent membership in other social organizations.

C. Illustrations

Illustrations of ways of increasing political capital have been included in the descriptions of the elements that can comprise this capital. Voter registration campaigns that are community wide, targeting marginalized urban communities, and specifically addressing groups that have historically disengaged from electoral voting, were evidenced during the 2008 presidential election and have increased in popularity.

Youth, for example, have historically been relegated to no opportunities for voting, or being limited to voting for school presidents, for example. However, recent efforts have targeted youth to engage in electoral voting (Wheeler & Roach, 2005). Pacheco and Plutzer (2008) document the economic and social barriers that youth face in addition to age segregated hardships. Delgado and Staples (2008) advance the concept of participatory democracy as a means of engaging youth in social change efforts that foster the creation of various forms of capital, including political. Political participation, as noted in other sections of this chapter, help shape youth experiences with democracy and can translate to electoral voting and reform efforts.

The knowledge and skill sets acquired in exercising political will and decision making in one arena can also lend them to being applied in other arenas and circumstances (Li & Marsh, 2008). This perspective on this asset allows practitioners to either include political capital as part of other assets or focus specifically on this area in the development of community capacity enhancement interventions. The following illustrations help to capture the flexibility and range of political capital that can be found in communities.

The concept of capital or assets is complex for a variety of very good reasons. Thinking about community assets as consisting of different categories or types facilitates breaking down ways of thinking about the multiple assets a community possesses. It brings flexibility to an assessment process and allows each community to decide how best to categorize its capital or assets. This allows assets to be defined broadly or narrowly, depending upon the goals of the assessment and budgetary and time considerations.

This flexibility, however, also results in tremendous challenges for an assessment. In all likelihood, there will not be a consensus about how to categorize assets. Doing so will be labor intensive and can result in hurt feelings among participants when their way of thinking about these assets is voted down. Furthermore, this fluidity may make it difficult for communities to compare assets over an extended period of time because of differences in how particular capital gets conceptualized. It also makes it difficult to compare assets across communities, making a comprehensive understanding impossible.

This section's review of capital concepts illustrates the long history of various forms, social capital being particularly noteworthy. These are all indications that capital concepts will continue to evolve and expand in scope. There is no reason to believe that this evolution will slow down or come to a complete halt in the early part of this century.

COMMUNITY INVOLVEMENT IN ASSET ASSESSMENTS

Any serious effort to implement a community asset assessment will necessitate that community social workers arrive at what community participation means at a philosophical, or value, level and what it means on a practical level. The community engagement process, as a result, is both a philosophical stance and a strategy for social action (Jones et al., 2009; Taylor, 2007).

Jones and colleagues (2009, pp. S6–8) identify a set of five core values that encourage community engagement in community based participatory research. As addressed in the following chapter, these resonate with the values and principles that should guide community asset assessments. They are "respect for diversity, openness, equality, empowerment (redirected power), and an asset-based approach to the work."

The challenges this process has can be quite tension and stress producing for practitioners (Copeland-Carson, 2008, p. 6): "The road to engagement has many unexpected twists and turns. So, for some funders and practitioners, engagement has an intangible, grasping at air quality to it." The "adventure" is one that should be expected the moment practitioners venture into the largely unchartered waters of community asset assessment.

Jones and colleagues (Jones et al., 2009) go on to differentiate between community "involvement" and "engagement." The former seeks community participation without active partnering. Community engagement signifies community ownership and decision making in all of the major aspects of a research undertaking (Wiles, Charles, Crow, & Heath, 2008). Both practitioners and scholars recognize that the concepts of community ownership, participation, and empowerment are inextricably related (Allen-Meares et al., 2011; Charlier, Glover, & Robertson, 2009; Ritchie, Parry, Gnich, & Platt, 2004; Yoo, Butler, Elias, & Goodman, 2009).

Fisher and Ball (2003) write about "tribal participatory research" with Native Americans and have found that research designs may be more or less acceptable to Native Americans, with those that respect a communal orientation and sharing tending to be more acceptable. They also raise cautions about simplistic adaptations of evidence-based practices from the dominant culture to try to make them more appropriate to Native Americans. They caution (p. 213): "For minority groups who have experienced oppression, an adapted intervention developed by the majority culture may have several unintended negative implications. For example, it may perpetuate the belief that the community lacks the capability to define and resolve its own problems; thus, the community must adopt foreign concepts and values to address these issues." Community asset assessment, too, tries to highlight the assets marginalized, oppressed communities have rather than their needs or deficits.

Although community social workers will argue that there is no effort, large or small or technical or nontechnical, that should not strive for maximum community participation, not everyone engaged in community practice shares this perspective. Khwaja (2004), for example, poses the provocative question of when a community based project should seek community participation. He then concludes that the nature of the project (nontechnical versus technical) should dictate the extent of participation.

Butterfoss (2006, p. 335) notes that efforts to determine the level and extent of community participation have progressed considerably: "Measurement of community participation has progressed from merely asking members whether and how much they participate in various activities to actually specifying how they participated and monitoring that participation." Level of participation, in other words, can and must be captured in any process and outcome evaluations. However, because that approach is time consuming, we must ask how disruptive the asset assessment is in the life of the community. Can residents participate in the research and still pursue their day to day duties, experiencing minimal disruption in their activities? The answers to these questions will go a long way toward helping to maximize resident participation in this type of endeavor and engender good will in the community (Foth, 2006).

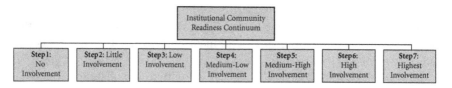

Figure 2.2. Community Involvement in Asset Assessments.

The framework of youth involvement in community research developed by Youth in Focus (2002) lends itself well to conceptualizing community involvement in asset assessments. Figure 2.2 illustrates a continuum that stretches from no community involvement in an asset assessment to one of highest involvement. Each step or stage represents a philosophical stance and brings with it a set of goals with implications for how to conceptualize and implement an asset assessment.

This seven stage continuum helps in determining the measurement of the strength of an asset. This assessment of asset strength, however, is highly subjective, although there certainly is a capacity to use quantitative measures. Operationalizing and measuring community capacity or capital/assets offer the field great rewards (Brown, LaFond, & Macintyre, 2001). These steps are outlined below.

> **Step 1: No Involvement**: No community asset assessment worth doing would eschew any effort at community involvement. It certainly is not in the spirit of how community assessment has been portrayed in this book. Nevertheless, there may be instances in which external sources undertake such a study and avoid community participation in the interest of expediency or cost savings.
>
> **Step 2: Little Involvement**: This step is merely a continuation of the previous step. However, there is recognition that it is important to obtain some degree of community input into the assessment. This means that the process is still dictated by external sources such as funders or experts with educational legitimacy, but there is a willingness to tap community voices as part of the effort.
>
> **Step 3: Low Involvement**: This step represents significant forward movement from an empowerment perspective by having community members participate in various data gathering activities. In essence, they have specific and narrowly defined functions to gather information. However, there is no effort or pretense to involve the community in decision making on key asset assessment questions, preferred methods, and any form of data interpretation. In essence, the community can be considered "hired labor" in this type of undertaking, although labor that does receive some basic training in limited aspects of the research process.
>
> **Step 4: Medium-Low Involvement:** Unlike Step 3, in medium-low community involvement, there is a systematic effort to obtain input from the

community on research questions and culturally grounded methods. Nevertheless, although community participation is expanded beyond "carrying out orders," ultimate sharing or having a community assume major decision making powers is still far off philosophically and practically.

Step 5: Medium-High Involvement: This step acknowledges the importance of the community. However, the importance is narrowed to a community designing and carrying out an assessment. Community input, nevertheless, is not sought out in the interpretation of findings and recommendations that follow. It is almost as if the community is just a secondary member of the research team.

Step 6: High Involvement: This level of community participation involves residents and key stakeholders in all facets of the assessment process, from developing key questions, selecting methodology, carrying out the data gathering, doing data analysis, interpreting findings, and making recommendations. Empowerment and sharing of power are both implicit and explicit in high level involvement.

Step 7: Highest Involvement: The final level builds upon Step 6 and has community residents training each other, and a local institution controlled by the community houses the assessment study and includes it as part of its regular planning process. This does not mean that outside people cannot be a part of this effort. It does mean that this community organization hires and supervises them in the course of carrying out an assessment instead of the "outside expert" doing so.

Lempa, Goodman, Rice, and Becker (2008) developed a scale for measuring community capacity based initiatives. These 10 measures address both resident and leader dimensions: (1) leadership; (2) resources; (3) ability and commitment to organize action; (4) networks; (5) personnel sustainability; (6) sense of community; (7) citizen participation; (8) skills; (9) community power; and (10) critical reflection. None of these measures seems out of place for those who actively work in communities relying on a high degree of community participation.

These measures, in turn, seek to capture community capacity (capital/assets). However, each of these factors is quite complex. A "sense of community," as already noted, is complex and involves membership, influence, integration, and shared emotional connections (Aref, Redzuan, & Emby, 2009). Thus, having a shared understanding of these factors is necessary before the development of any measurement scale.

These factors can be used to help communities better understand and categorize their assets. The items that are eventually used to measure an asset's strengths can include both quantitative as well as qualitative qualities. It is recommended that some form of group decision making process be used to select items and assess their strengths. That responsibility is too immense for it to rest in the hands of one or two individuals, regardless of their expertise and recognition within the community.

As the reader can note, at one end of the continuum there is either an absence of involvement, or it is weak in strength. At the opposite end of the continuum, the involvement is not only present but it is particularly strong. This range of possibilities is a reality in all communities. However, there may be a tendency in marginalized communities not to value their involvement or to minimize their influence and strength. This is a sad commentary on how marginalized communities can be treated as if their community has nothing to offer each other and society.

MEASUREMENT OF ASSET STRENGTHS

Measurement of social phenomena is always fraught with limitations. Defining and measuring any aspect of community are huge challenges. The measurement of community assets and strengths is certainly not an exception and brings an added dimension to this challenge. The identification and categorization of community assets represent but one step, although a critical one, in an asset assessment process. Determining the strength of an asset represents a second step. The fundamental belief is that all communities, regardless of how economically, politically, and socially marginalized in this society, have forms of capital/assets identified earlier in this chapter, necessitating the development of a process of ascertaining their strengths.

Adamson, Baker, and Lewis (2007), for example, advance the importance of assessing a community's capacity and assets regarding health promotion. They state (p. A45): "Community capacity can be measured by the availability of, access to, and trust in facilities such as community centers, parks, schools, grocery stores, farmers' markets, and safe streets, and the presence of committed and engaged leaders in those communities." Clearly, they emphasize community strengths.

Stokols and colleagues (2003) address a variety of considerations concerning community assets and health promotion, one of which is the centrality or peripherality of the asset. Is the asset accessible only to a particular sector or group in the community, such as a house of worship with a small congregation, or is it central and accessible to a wide range of individuals? If it is peripheral, its "value" or "weight" may not be as great as a house of worship that has an extensive congregation and thereby has greater centrality.

Every community must ultimately determine what elements will be included within each particular asset or capital, and how best to weigh these elements relative to each other. Each asset identified earlier in this chapter is multidimensional with the potential for wide deviation concerning what elements must be included. For example, political assets/capital taps a community's level of participation in a democratic process. The percentage of a community that votes in local, state, and national elections can be one element of this form of asset. All communities vote. Some, however, have a higher percentage of eligible voters participating in this form of voting than others. The gathering of this type of data is relatively easy and straightforward, allowing communities to assess how politically connected their various members are in this process.

However, participatory democracy does not limit itself to governmental elections. There are other arenas in which participation and voting transpire. A community, for example, may decide to weigh more heavily voting at annual meetings of various social organizations, PTA, or other arenas that involve voter participation, or to what extent attendance is high at local social agency boards of directors. Adults are not the only ones who vote. Youth, for example, can vote for student government, or to determine some class project. Undocumented residents cannot vote for elected officials because they are not United States citizens. Nevertheless, there can be countless other venues whereby documented status is not a hindrance to voting.

The decision on what elements constitute an asset, and their relative importance from an asset perspective, must ultimately rest in the hands of the community, as does the entire process of assessment. In the case of asset assessment committees, this entity would be the mechanism that is established to make these decisions. It does not mean that communities or committees cannot add or drop elements or change the significance of their weights over time. However, a deliberative process of decision making must be followed to make these determinations.

The development of ordinal scales, for example, is the most common way of assigning weights. Once a determination is made as to what elements constitute an asset, committee members can develop scales or other measures for how best to determine their significance. Each member may assign a particular weight to an element. The committee, as a whole, then adds these weights, divides them by the number of participants, and arrives at a particular weight for the asset.

Needs	Assets
Consumers as Clients	Consumers as Experts
Problem Solving	Appreciative Inquiry
Creates Dependence	Creates Indigenous Leadership
Individual as a Target of Change	Community as a Vehicle of Change
Pessimism	Optimism/Hope/Aspiration
Fragmented Interventions	Collaborative/Partnership/Educational
Educational Expertise	Experiential Expertise
Consumer Disempowered	Community Empowered
Focus on Deficits	Focus on Capacity
Agency Driven	Resident Driven

Figure 2.3. Contrast between Needs and Asset Assessments.

The determination of elements and weights, as a result, is made by local circumstances. This is particularly important because local communities know what is in their best interests and have very localized goals of the assessment.

CONTRAST BETWEEN NEEDS AND ASSET ASSESSMENTS

As noted in Figure 2.3, there is a dramatic contrast between a needs focused assessment and one that is assets focused. This difference in worldview, so to speak, translates into a change in power relationship between provider and community, and an embrace of the importance of process and participation on the part of the ultimate beneficiaries of an assessment, which is the community (Crane & Mooney, 2005; Guion, Golden, & Diehl, 2010).

The schism between skeptics and believers in community asset assessments may be unbridgeable due to the fundamental premises that are used by each camp in determining success (Goodland, Burton, & Croft, 2005). Each of the dimensions outlined in Figure 2.3 brings with it profound implications for language used, role of community social worker, relationships, and community decision making power. In essence, the differences between a need and asset approach are much more than semantics!

CONCLUSIONS

Community social workers are certainly not at a loss for ways to conceptualize, identify, and categorize community assets, since there are numerous ways of viewing them. This chapter has presented a variety of ways of thinking about assets and capital and devoted considerable amount of space to asset concepts and how to identify and categorize them for the purposes of assessing them. This process of identifying and categorizing assets is far from perfect, as noted in the critique section. Nevertheless, we believe our conceptualization offers great promise and is certainly part of the "currency" in any discussion of community asset assessments.

Practitioners in communities with distinct cultural values and practices will find that translating these assets into categories that are easily recognizable by others in the field is difficult to accomplish, or if translated into existing well-accepted categories, can result in artificial categorizations. This risks losing the distinctiveness that a cultural based capital or asset brings to an assessment or initiative. Conceptual dimensions or domains are very much culturally based, whether it is explicitly or implicitly recognized. Consequently, there is no "magical" way of navigating this rough terrain, although this chapter has attempted to minimize the rough waters in this journey. Practitioners and the communities with which they work must arrive at a satisfactory agreement on the key elements covered in this chapter.

3

Values and Principles
Underpinning Asset Assessments

"For community development efforts to be effective, community leaders must know what resources are available to them. In other words, leaders would benefit from having a comprehensive and up-to-date inventory of community assets... The creation of an asset inventory is of great value for a number of reasons. First, it presents community leaders with a broad and inclusive array of resources; this allows leaders to choose community development strategies that are in accordance with their asset base. Secondly, an asset inventory illuminates the gaps, needs, and inefficiencies in the region and helps community leaders to reallocate resources to key challenge areas and avoid unnecessary expenditures. As such, the creation of an inventory of community assets is undoubtedly a worthwhile goal."

(WONG, *2009, p. 1*)

INTRODUCTION

The opening quote by Wong (2009) captures the potential rewards and the richness of data of a well done community asset assessment. Communities, providers, community based organizations, and government can all be considered winners in a successful effort to identify and mobilize community resources or assets (Vega, 2009). Such a win–win approach, however, is predicated on all significant parties sharing the same values, principles, and goals, making it more likely that a consensus on outcomes can be possible. That, unfortunately, is a tall order in most communities, regardless of their socioeconomic circumstances and the best of intensions!

The reader, no doubt, identified a set of core values guiding community asset assessments in the material covered in the previous two chapters. If there is one criticism that can be made about many of the books on capacity development, it is the inattention paid to explicitly laying out the set of values and principles guiding this paradigm. We consider this a fundamental step in any concerted effort to assess a community's assets. Although this process may initially appear to be relatively easy, it is complex, time consuming, and invariably requires reconciliation of significant differences within communities. Communities are not monolithic in composition. In addition, practitioners do practice based upon an explicit or implicit set of values, and these, too, must be articulated prior to the initiation of any collaborative venture with a community.

This chapter, as a result, will make explicit such a set of social work values and principles in the hopes of helping the reader better understand the reasons for undertaking an asset assessment and why, as addressed later in this book, a particular selection of methods for carrying out this form of assessment has been chosen. In fact, research methods per se do not exist in isolation from a foundation of values and principles, regardless of the type of research being undertaken and how "professionally" done and well intentioned (Lietz, Langer, & Furman, 2006; Mertens & Ginsburg, 2008; Shaw, 2005).

The fact that values rarely get addressed and do not get the attention they warrant raises important considerations in any effort to assess a community's assets (Bisman, 2004; Hardcastle, Powers, & Wenocur, 2011; Raymond et al., 2009). Borrup (2005, p. 4) touches upon the practical side of values being explicit rather than implicit: "To say that assets are value-laden is to say that one sees a set of attributes in a person, organization, community or place through a lens that is trained to filter a particular set of political and social values. Someone with a different set of values will see something completely different."

Borrup's (2005) astute observation about how biases dictate what gets constituted as an "asset" is the very reason why asset assessments must actively seek to involve a cross section of a community, as a means of minimizing distortions or oversights of a community's assets. Practitioners and scholars always seem to struggle with navigating this rough terrain. Although much more labor intensive than relying upon a small or, some would argue, elite group, the outcomes will have broader appeal and more far reaching implications as a result. The need to be inclusive far outstrips the demand to be exclusive, even though this makes the task of community asset assessment that much more arduous to complete.

VALUES GUIDING ASSET ASSESSMENTS

The philosophical (values and principles) approach taken toward asset assessments will be felt throughout the entire history of an initiative (Hardcastle, Powers, & Wenocur, 1997, p. 167): "Our philosophy of assessment matters because assessment is a first step in establishing our relationship with a community. The stance taken at the beginning will affect all of the operations that come later... We must believe in the potential of a living system to nourish, to

Figure 3.1. Values Underlying Community Asset Assessments.

grow, and to change." Assessments often do represent the first "formal" attempt to establish a collaborative relationship between organizations and communities. Consequently, how well these efforts are carried out has an impact on how communities view these organizations now, and in the future, as other types of initiatives are launched.

As noted in Figure 3.1, there is a set of seven underlying core value assumptions pertaining to community asset assessments that have much in common with the assumptiohs generally associated with community social work practice (Reed, 2004). We believe that none of the identified values will come as any great surprise to practitioners with a deep understanding and appreciation of communities. Nevertheless, it is essential that these values be highlighted for the reader. These values are addressed separately from each other, but there is no denying the synergistic effect that they enjoy as they interact with each other, to which any practitioner would attest. These values, in turn, are presented without regard to their significance or importance relative to each other.

1. Empowerment

The creation of confidence and the belief that it is possible to alter your environment and circumstances represent essential steps in the empowerment process for individuals and their communities (Gutierrez, Lewis, Nagda,

Wernick, & Stone, 2004; Vega, 2009). Empowerment can apply to all facets of social work practice (Lee, 2001). However, it takes on paramount importance in community capacity enhancement paradigms because the central goal of such interventions is to have communities, particularly those that are marginalized, exercise power and control over their circumstances (Delgado, 2000).

Community empowerment, like community forms of capital, is complex and not one dimensional (Smits & Champagne, 2008; Staples, 2004). Lennie (2005), for example, identifies four forms (social, technological, political, and psychological empowerment). Despite its complexities, it is an important goal in community asset assessments (Kasmel & Andersen, 2011).

It is important to conceptualize empowerment as something individuals and communities do for themselves. Social workers do not empower people or communities as if they were passive recipients of empowerment, and empowerment was something you give to someone. By its very nature, empowerment is the exercise of agency by someone, not by others. Yet, social workers can help to create attitudes, resources, procedures, and policies that are conducive to empowerment rather than putting barriers in the way of empowerment.

Simpson, Wood, and Daws (2003) stress the importance of community empowerment as a key element of any community capacity focused intervention. Empowerment as a value, goal, and intervention must permeate all facets of community asset assessment from the initial formulation of the approach to evaluation (Fetterman & Wandersman, 2004). Pennell, Noponen, and Weil (2005, p. 620) note that, when empowerment is integral to research and program evaluation, it results in "critically examining social conditions or social programs, affirmatively reflecting on their and others' contributions, and responsibly acting to advance individual and collective well-being."

Viewing a community asset assessment as an opportunity to identify community assets of unvalued groups and also to facilitate empowerment in the process only increases the significance of community research. Chow and Crowe (2005), for example, discuss values for identifying issues of saliency to communities of color that also act as vehicles for empowering these communities.

2. Community Participation

The active and meaningful participation of the ultimate beneficiaries of a social intervention represents one of the cornerstones of community social work practice (Checkoway & Gutierrez, 2006). Hardcastle, Powers, and Wenocur's (2011, p. 136) expression of "assessments of, in, and by the community" captures the important role communities can play in assessments. Cargo and Mercer (2008) argue that participatory forms of research effectively bridge the gap between research and practice, particularly when these address social and environmental community themes.

Butterfoss (2006), in a review of the literature on public health and community participation, concludes that how a community is defined, by whom, and who represents the community are critical factors in participatory community based interventions. It would be unrealistic to expect a consensus definition to emerge on what constitutes community. Thus, an effort to determine where the majority of opinions overlap represents a critical step in helping to maximize participation because such an overlap increases self-interest on the part of residents. Yet, there may be more marginalized groups in an already marginalized community. Therefore, special efforts should be made to be inclusive of their opinions, particularly as it is the most oppressed who may need allies for their empowerment.

Communities have people of all ages and all abilities, and some people within an already marginalized community may be further marginalized, based on age or ability. Similar to people who speak languages other than English, people with disabilities of all ages may be missed, if appropriate accommodations are not made. There is a danger both of not obtaining their opinions about assets as well as missing the assets they bring to the community. Although efforts must be made to provide specialized accommodations that are requested by specific individuals, there are some general accommodations that can be made available at the outset of an asset assessment. In fact, making accommodations a regular part of the process may help to encourage people with disabilities to participate. Furthermore, taking a universal design approach would be even better than making accommodations that single out people with disabilities.

Universal design can be defined as the "design of products and environments to be usable by all people, to the greatest extent possible, without the need for adaptation or specialized design" (Center for Universal Design, 1997, p. 1). Therefore, universally designed environments, whether built or social environments, aim to be accessible to all people, whether or not they have disabilities. In addition, they can make environments more accessible for various people in "special" situations, such as persons who are navigating with young children in strollers, have limited or no English language, or are illiterate or have had limited formal education.

The term is used most often regarding architecture, but it need not be limited to that sphere. It can also be applied to materials that convey information. There are several examples that illustrate this, and most are not costly. Written materials should be available in accessible formats for people with visual impairments or blindness and for people with intellectual or learning disabilities. Not all online formats are read correctly by computers that use speech programs, so a person knowledgeable in proper formatting should be consulted about online materials such as websites. In fact, if a community person, whether professional such as a librarian or a layperson such as a student, knows the best way to format information, he or she may be able to be tapped as a resource in the project. Certainly, users with disabilities should be consulted, too.

For open and public meetings, sign language interpreters should be hired. Meetings should be held only in places that are accessible to people who use wheelchairs or walkers or who have limited stamina or mobility, and outreach to offer transportation should be made to elders or others who need assistance to attend a meeting. For people with intellectual or learning disabilities, on the spot reading and processing of materials should not be required to participate, so preparation in advance should be made available to those who would like it. In addition, it should be anticipated that some interviews may take longer than others.

Communities must actively benefit (colearning, reflection, and action) from participation in research projects for the findings to result in meaningful social change (Sutton & Kemp, 2006). Community participation has been framed in a variety of ways, with inclusiveness being arguably the most popular. Asset assessments mandate that residents play decision making roles in order for the assessment to accomplish its primary goals, and that this be accomplished throughout all facets of the undertaking (Titterton & Smart, 2008).

As addressed in Chapters 5, 6, and 7, a number of studies nationally and internationally stress the democratization potential of community asset maps. Fahy and O'Cinneide (2009, p. 167) conclude this very point based on their Galway, Ireland, asset assessment: "As a repository of socially constructed knowledge, community mapping has an important value in the democratization of information both in terms of what is documented and public access to it, in a way that encourages the significant involvement of non-experts in planning and advocacy processes. Findings demonstrated how community mapping is used not just to document and promote the city's social, environmental, economic, and cultural assets but also as a practical tool to encourage public participation in policymaking and to enhance local communities' trust in the municipal authority, thereby influencing sustainability practices through better governance."

Fahy and O'Cinneide's (2009) conclusion about community asset mapping serving as a vehicle for democratizing the planning process highlights the sociopolitical nature of any form of research that seeks to bridge the divide between marginalized communities and all levels of government. Bridging this divide, however, will often result in a "backlash" about making research "political." However, it is our contention, and many others share it, that all forms of research are political, just like all forms of social intervention! An "apolitical" research or intervention is making a conscious decision to avoid upsetting the status quo, and that is certainly political in nature.

3. Leadership Development

Leadership development seems to be a topic that historically has occupied a prominent role in community interventions that seek to enhance the capacities of residents and empower communities. Consequently, this goal should not come as any great surprise to the reader. Ultimate ownership of the results of an asset assessment must rest in the hands of the community, and their leaders are often called upon to validate or "own" those results.

The provision of opportunities for residents to fulfill leadership roles within this endeavor helps foster leadership potential that can play an instrumental role in bringing to fruition the plans for intervention (Emery & Flora, 2006; Riley,

2009). Leadership developed during an asset assessment does not disappear upon completion of the assessment and can play a significant role in helping to carry out programming and a social change agenda that resonates in a community, as well as makes an investment in the future of the community.

Leadership development can be framed under community capacity enhancement, and this facilitates the investment of resources for providing necessary training, consultation, employment, and other forms of support as needed. Furthermore, leadership development should not be focused on the "usual suspects," and this provides an opening for enlisting and supporting women, youth, and older adults, as well as people with disabilities. In essence, the definition of leadership is not the conventional one of one leader and many followers. Leadership qualities should be the guiding force (Delgado & Staples, 2008).

4. Community Investment

Purposeful efforts should enhance a community's capacity to facilitate the acquisition of knowledge about a community's resources but also simultaneously seek to provide resources to further develop local talent. This, incidentally, is accomplished through provision of opportunities for training, consultation, and employment for residents, as noted in the above section on leadership (Delgado, 1999). This form of human capital investment benefits the community in the immediate time period and in future endeavors (Han, Kang, Kim, Ryu, & Kim, 2007).

Providing new mechanisms for communication, such as websites, or assisting local businesses to further update their business plans or obtain financial support from government sources, for example, are other forms of community investment. The time and resources used to facilitate small business development or expansion yield a considerable amount of return that can be classified as social, economic, human, and cultural capital (Delgado, 2011). This is particularly the case in situations in which small businesses represent the "hub" of a community, with investments yielding considerable returns for the business owner as well as the immediate community.

5. Reliance on Local and Self-Knowledge

The popularity of the concepts of "experiential expertise," "local," and "self knowledge" captures the importance of "ordinary" people and their grasp of their operative reality (Gertler, 2003; Goodyear & Checkoway, 2003). Namely, they are the best judges of their conditions, histories, and goals. These concepts shift the power from professionals and academic scholars to communities, and form the basis and foundation upon which asset assessments seek to uncover and document capital for the external community (Quave & Rankin, 2006; Semenza, March, & Bontenpo, 2006).

Rapport, Alegria, Mulvaney-Day, and Boyle (2008, p. 694) advance the concept of "cultural humility," or the practice of self evaluation and examination of assumptions of what the dynamics and context of a mutually beneficial relationship are, which captures the central premises of local and self knowledge: "As professionals entering communities, by maintaining cultural humility, we encourage the community members to teach us their knowledge and practical insights about their efforts to address problems."

6. Social Justice

Social justice plays an influential role in shaping how community social work practitioners think about urban communities, marginalized groups, and major social forces that have an impact on the well-being of communities (Delgado, 2012, in press). Consequently, the presence of social and economic justice as a guiding force in shaping urban community assets is quite natural and expected. An emphasis placed on how socioeconomic forces influence community well-being takes on prominence in assessing a community's assets.

In addition to the National Association of Social Workers' (NASW) *Code of Ethics*, NASW'S (2011b) position statement on social justice supports working to strengthen marginalized communities and notes: "Social work is a practical profession aimed at helping people address their problems and matching them with the resources they need to lead healthy and productive lives. Beneath this practicality lies a strong value system that can be summarized in two words: social justice. Social justice is the view that everyone deserves equal economic, political and social rights and opportunities. Social workers should aim to open the doors of access and opportunity for everyone, particularly those in greatest need." Therefore, key to helping to strengthen urban marginalized communities of color and other communities is the identification of their assets as well as realistic inquiry into the ways in which economic, political, and social forces impinge upon their developing those assets, ignore those assets, or even work to diminish or destroy those assets.

Social justice is not just an abstract concept and calls for policies and actions beyond local communities that support rather than hurt them. A critical contemporary example of how a lack of social justice hurt a community is in the response to Hurricane Katrina in New Orleans, Louisiana. New Orleans is a city with a rich, vibrant history and culture that make it a highly desirable place to live and visit. Yet, when its low income African American neighborhood was hardest hit by the hurricane, the response of all levels of government was inadequate and reflected very little appreciation for what social justice means in action and practice (Cross, 2009; Pyles, 2006). Pyles (2006, p. 80) observes: "These events get to the heart of what social work, social justice and human rights mean to many of us. For millions of people all over the world, bearing witness to citizens who were hungry and thirsty languishing in this great American city and the weak response of federal, state and local agencies was indeed 'news' in the literal sense of the word. Never in recent times did so many people witness the poverty and racism that plague America's urban areas nor had they seen the concomitant lack of dignity that accompanies such oppression. Never had so many become aware of the dysfunction of America's social systems, the fact that they sometimes do more harm than good, are painfully slow or just do nothing at all. However, for those of us who know intimately these social problems and social systems, indeed, none of this was 'news' at all." Despite the unquestionably considerable assets of the African American community in New Orleans, the onslaught of the combination of natural disaster and callous government neglect bore down on those assets in a way that led to gross violations of people's most basic human rights.

Human rights have been recognized internationally in the United Nations *International Declaration of Human Rights* (1948) and are increasingly discussed in contemporary social work literature (Pyles, 2006; Wronka, 2008). The Declaration carefully spells out in Article 2: "Everyone is entitled to all the rights and freedoms set forth in this Declaration, without distinction of any kind, such as race, colour, sex, language, religion, political or other opinion, national or social origin, property, birth or other status." The Declaration does leave unclear who might be included under "other status," and, hopefully, other characteristics will be specified in the future, such as sexual orientation or disability. Still, it does provide a strong moral basis for protection of all people's rights regarding human dignity; nondiscrimination; civil and political rights; economic, social, and cultural rights; and solidarity rights (Wronka, 2008, pp. 16-19). Therefore, it is not difficult to think of its special significance to marginalized urban communities of color whose rights are violated and whose assets so frequently are ignored and underestimated.

Stern (2006) argues that social and economic justice are integral parts of a human rights concept, although they tend not to be equated in Western society. Her call to action to the social work profession (practitioners as well as academics) to make contributions to human rights to support these goals has particular relevance to community social work practice, including advancing research and scholarship using human rights language and concepts. Healy (2008), in turn, traces social work's historical embrace of human rights but notes that we have maintained a "low visibility" in this realm at the international level.

An increasing number of social work scholars and practitioners have started to operationalize social and economic justice from a variety of community social work practice perspectives (Delgado & Staples, 2007; Reed, 2004). The embrace of this perspective, including its prominence in many schools of social work, makes it relatively easy to incorporate this value into community focused interventions such as asset assessments (DeFilippis, Fisher, & Shragge, 2009). Weil's (2004b, p. 8) definition of social justice lends itself quite well to community asset assessments: "social justice implies commitment to fairness in our dealings with each other in the major aspects of our lives...In society, social justice should foster equal human rights, distributive justice, and a structure of opportunity and be grounded in representative and participatory democracy."

Empowerment and inclusion are direct responses from an embrace of social and economic justice (Raeburn, Akerman, Chuengsatiansup, Mejia, & Oladepo, 2006). The importance of practitioners and scholars understanding the influence of external social, economic, and political factors on the status of marginalized communities, and how these residents view their own community, cannot be underestimated (Ganapalis, 2008). Chu, Tsui, and Yan (2009, p. 287), argue that there is a "withering of the moral and political bases of social work practice in the West. The revitalization of the roots of social work is important to the promotion of social justice."

The culmination of a decade or so of neoconservative politics has placed the profession in a precarious position regarding policies that are counter to our mission of social justice nationally and internationally (Ferguson & Lavalette, 2006). Community asset assessments can provide important data that social workers can use to ground their experiences and communities within a context that highlights injustices perpetrated on them because of their ethnic or racial backgrounds. This process also can help to "revitalize" the profession and provide an alternative to the neoconservative focus on the deficits of communities.

7. Cultural Competence

Cultural competence is both a process and a goal of all forms of community social work practice, and asset assessments represent the foundation upon which these interventions are based. Cultural competence takes on great significance because it is within the context of a community's cultural values, principles, and practices that assets are embedded. This grounding is essential in conceptualizing assets, measuring their strengths, and eventually mobilizing them in activities and programming. It must be stressed that cultural competence is a goal for social workers, but because culture is dynamic, and new groups continually arrive in the United States, it is impossible for anyone to become fully competent. Nevertheless, there is an explicit and implicit recognition that there are differences within, and between, ethnic and racial groups that must be taken into account in the development of asset assessments and the actions that follow. Furthermore, the diversity within a community will encompass factors in addition to the crucial factors of race and ethnicity that also require an informed and open understanding.

In addition to the NASW *Code of Ethics*, NASW's position statement on diversity and cultural competence would support taking a strengths based approach toward marginalized communities. It recognizes the need for social workers to educate themselves about and strive to understand people of diverse backgrounds based on factors such as race, ethnicity, language, country of origin, gender, sexual orientation, ability, and age. It states:

Two recent events have made the need for "cultural competence"— understanding the specific cultural, language, social and economic nuances of particular people and families—more important than ever. One is the civil rights movement that began in the 1950s, in which African-Americans, women, gays and lesbians, people with disabilities, and other minority groups alerted the country to their distinct identities and long histories of oppression. The other is the growing number of new immigrants to this country, who bring with them unique cultural, language, religious, and political backgrounds. Histories of internal displacement within their own countries, torture, political oppression, and extreme poverty abound among immigrant communities. Melding these backgrounds with the history, experiences, and expectations of U.S.-born ethnic and diverse populations creates both challenges and opportunities for social workers.

It is fair to say that both helping professionals and society at large have a long way to go to gain cultural competence. Fortunately, social workers represent a group of service providers with a longstanding history of understanding both people's differences and the impact of social injustices on their well-being (NASW, 2011a).

Buttressing this is Article 22 of *The Universal Declaration of Human Rights* of the United Nations (1948) that states that people's economic, cultural and social rights are indispensable for their dignity and free development of their personality. Lum (2003, p. 35), in discussing cultural competence, addresses the importance of social context in better understanding people and circumstances shaping their lives in order for social interventions to be meaningful and effective: "In order to fully understand a person, one must take into account the total context of how the texture of the person is woven together to form a unique being. What pieces or ingredients have been put together to form a mosaic or detailed pattern? What is the total context that transcends the person and the environment and MUST be understood for helping to proceed?" Asset interventions are a form of social intervention and, ideally, lead to social action. Therefore, the interaction of environment and social justice issues, and the cultural background manifested in the beliefs, values, and behaviors of people of color, cannot be viewed as simply a backdrop to an asset assessment.

Part of the effort to understand people and their communities is to understand their strengths, which we too often dismiss. Social workers and others who try to help people to address their problems and obtain services reasonably focus research and other efforts on documenting needs rather than assets. Especially with the inadequate funding of human services and other public benefits, unemployment, and disparities in income and wealth in the United States at the beginning of the twenty-first century, it is necessary to document need to obtain needed services. Yet, a focus on needs should be balanced with a focus on the strengths that allow underserved and marginalized populations to persevere. In addition, when the gaps in services are filled, it should be in a way that builds upon and enriches community assets rather than ignores them.

Community asset assessments explicitly embrace the goal of being based upon the cultural values and norms of the communities being assessed (Delgado, 2007;

Fraser, 2009). Consequently, assessments must be culturally competent in all facets of the research to increase the likelihood that the results are relevant to the ultimate beneficiaries of the social interventions that follow (Bankhead & Erlich, 2004).

Cultural competence in community work necessitates a deep understanding of cultural knowledge and meaning (Torres, Marquez, Carbone, Stacciarini, & Foster, 2008). It is important to emphasize that the definition of cultural assets is determined by the community and not the social worker assisting or facilitating in the assessment. He or she, however, can play an instrumental role in helping the community arrive at, define, and locate these assets, and, as a result, is more of a facilitator or guide in this regard rather than an arbiter of what is an asset and where it is located.

As already addressed in Chapter 2, cultural perspectives on community capital bring a dimension to assets that captures the richness, depth, and importance of cultural values and beliefs. Although capturing these assets in an assessment will prove challenging, a "business as usual" approach to asset assessments essentially undermines the potential of this method for creating social change, and effectively equates this method with its needs assessment counterpart!

The interplay of the above set of core values creates a climate, or environment, that is both exciting and challenging for community social work practitioners. These values are not always shared by society, and, not surprisingly, bring with them inherent tensions and controversies, from an academic and practice viewpoint. Yet, these very same tensions and controversies are essential for moving this field forward nationally and internationally. In addition, this chapter on values sought to provide the reader with an in-depth understanding of how values both guide the asset assessment and influence how it gets operationalized in practice. There certainly are inherent tensions of competing values in any form of social intervention, and that is the case with community asset assessments.

These tensions will be highlighted whenever possible and will provide the reader with direction on how to develop an asset assessment that balances conflicting values and tensions. Parker (2006, p. 482) brings up these tensions when commenting on community mapping in saying that "defining and understanding community mapping projects is problematic, complex, and contingent—but nevertheless important. Community mapping is a growing phenomenon, and evidence suggests that possible outcomes of such projects are possible. Yet closer scrutiny can reveal production processes fraught with tension and marked by unacknowledged privilege."

PRINCIPLES GUIDING ASSET ASSESSMENTS

The values outlined in the previous section can best be conceptualized as the foundation from which we can proceed with an asset assessment. These values, however, are not universally accepted, and there is bound to be tension between those who subscribe to one set of values and those who do not. However, as the reader will see in Chapter 4 in the discussion on ethical considerations, this is to be expected in any implementation of a social paradigm that seeks to accomplish social change, and to do so exercising participatory democratic principles.

Principles represent the essential step in moving from a value base to actual practice (Atkinson & Willis, 2005; Williams, Bray, Shapiro-Mendoza, Reiez, & Peranteau, 2009). Translating theory into practice has been a perennial challenge for any profession seeking to implement social interventions, and social has certainly has not escaped this challenge (Vega, 2009). Practice principles, however, represent the "bridge" between the worlds of academics in their quest to develop theory and the worlds of practitioners in their quest to intervene in the "real world." Consequently, principles are grounded within theory and the practice experience, and thus not only facilitate collaboration between academics, practitioners, and residents, but also serve to inform the uninitiated about the parameters of an intervention (Lasker & Lasker, 2006; Minkler, 2005). In essence, principles are not only descriptive but prescriptive for practitioners.

The following nine principles draw upon a range of scholarly or practice sources that have either specifically embraced asset assessments or community capacity enhancement paradigms (Delgado, 2000); also, these principles are not exclusive to community social work practice and can be found in other forms of social work practice. Nevertheless, these principles have a prominent home in community social work practice. Chapter 5, for example, lays out a set of principles related to research and community steering committees that shares much in common with the following general principles:

(1) A community has the will and ability to help itself in a thoughtful and purposeful manner;

(2) A community knows what is best for itself, and this knowledge is manifested through self and informal sources;

(3) Ownership of how best to assess internal assets rests within, rather than outside, the community;

(4) Partnerships between residents and community social work practitioners are the preferred route for any asset assessment, with assessment being planned with, rather than for, the community;

(5) Reliance and use of community assets in one area will translate into other facets of the community, often creating a synergistic effect;

(6) Asset assessments must be based upon inclusive rather than exclusive community participation parameters and must not reinforce biases between and within groups;

(7) Asset assessments should not be expected to conform to predicted timetables, because each is unique to the community being assessed, although assessments may share a core of similarities between communities;

(8) Assessment findings must be distributed in a manner that reflects culture and community specific preferences for communication; and

(9) An asset assessment must seek to maximize external investment in the community undertaking it.

These principles are conceptually tied with the values outlined earlier in this chapter as a means of facilitating for the reader the close interconnection between values, principles, and actions. Furthermore, these principles bring with them a high level of flexibility in how they are acted upon, allowing local community goals and circumstances to guide their operationalization. Practitioners, however, must be prepared to embrace all of the principles rather than pick and choose among them, in order to achieve the promise inherent in community asset assessments. This is not to say that one or a combination of principles may not be preferred over the others. Yet, the community assets paradigm guiding assessments represents a comprehensive viewpoint, and this should not be ignored by practitioners and scholars.

CONCLUSIONS

Community social work interventions are far from value free. However, it is of paramount importance to be clear and articulate about what values guide us in conceiving and implementing a social intervention such as a community asset assessment. The values and principles outlined in this chapter represent the thinking of two social workers, although there is a rich history backing them.

Some of the values and principles may hold greater appeal to a practitioner than others. Organizations, too, must weigh in and be cognizant of which values and principles are more "valued" than others. However, the values and principles addressed in this chapter have come together to form a particular stance, or picture, of how community asset assessments can be carried out to maximize their benefit to urban marginalized communities or other marginalized communities.

Although it may be tempting for readers to pick and choose the values and principles that are particularly attractive to them, it is strongly advised that these values and principles be viewed as a "total package." An embrace of an asset paradigm such as is proposed in this chapter and throughout this book is not just a "professional stance" but a world view, with all of its attributes. It is very hard to expect communities to be enthusiastic about an asset paradigm if we are not enthusiastic about it, and we do a disservice to marginalized communities if we do not support their empowerment by such a focus on their assets.

4

Rewards, Challenges, and Ethical Dilemmas in Undertaking Community Asset Assessments

"The epistemological approach to participatory research has profound implications for rethinking our ethical commitments, and raises a series of critical questions. What do participatory theory and practice tell us about the nature and location of 'ethics'? What are the ethical dimensions of participatory work? Are there fundamental principles at play in ethical decision-making in participatory projects? And, finally, is there such a thing as an 'ethic of participation'; and if so, what does it look like?"

(CAHILL, SULTANA, & PAIN, *2007, p. 305*)

INTRODUCTION

The quote by Cahill, Sultana, and Pain (2007) above raises a number of profound, and complex, ethical issues for researchers and practitioners who embrace efforts to actively and meaningfully involve communities in the undertaking of community based participatory research (CBPR), such as that proposed in this book. Community asset assessments are a distinctive form of CBPR, with all of its rewards and challenges. This form of research, as the reader will see, has its share of tension areas that are natural points for the ethical dilemmas that are quite familiar to most social work practitioners. These dilemmas are partly tied to the tensions inherent in practicing in communities (Staeheli, 2007) as well as tensions related to being "outsider" researchers (Minkler, 2004).

There is little question that community asset assessments have tremendous potential for helping community social workers carry out initiatives that reinforce key antioppression aspects of our mission and *Code of Ethics*. These rewards, so to speak, are limitless, and so, unfortunately, are the challenges. This chapter highlights some of the most obvious and significant rewards and challenges. Local circumstances wield considerable influence on the rewards and challenges of community asset assessments. Readers, as a result, may well have additional examples of both that have been dictated by what is happening in their respective communities. A total of five key rewards and nine challenges have been identified and addressed because of their significance for this type of assessment.

Any form of community intervention, regardless of whether or not it embraces assets or needs, is bound to elicit both positive and adverse reactions in the community. It is not a question of preventing ethical dilemmas from occurring but of how to minimize the consequences of these dilemmas, and to have a process of decision making to help resolve them when they emerge (Hardcastle, Powers, & Wenocur, 2011; Khanlou & Peters, 2009). Community based asset assessments are no exception (Arundel, Clutterbuck, & Cleverly, 2005). We should not be misled by the label "assessment" because it is a form of intervention and not just a precursor to an intervention. It, therefore, has the distinction of having the challenges associated with being both a research and intervention method (Minkler, 2004).

REWARDS

Much can be written about the multitude rewards that can be derived from an asset assessment at the local, city, state, and national levels (Beckley et al., 2008). The rewards of undertaking an asset assessment can be viewed from the organization initiating the assessment, community social workers and community residents participating in these assessments, and, ultimately, the target of these assessments, the broader community itself.

A well "orchestrated" asset assessment is like a beautiful symphony with all musicians (team players/participants) playing their instruments according to the music score. It is a win–win experience. Foth (2006), however, goes so far as to actively advocate for the field to undertake a vigorous debate about the issues inherent in action research and, as is the case in this book, community asset assessment as a means of moving this field forward in a manner that minimizes ethical dilemmas and uncovers ways of addressing them when they arise. Romanticizing community action research seriously hinders important progress in using this method in marginalized communities.

Elliot's (1999, p. 12) concept of "appreciative inquiry" should find resonance with community social workers embracing social justice and cultural assets in urban communities of color: "What the appreciative approach seeks to achieve is the transformation of a culture from one that sees itself in largely negative terms—and therefore is inclined to become locked in its own negative construction of itself—to one that sees itself as having within it the capacity to enrich the quality of all its stakeholders—and therefore move towards this appreciative construction of itself." Appreciative inquiry is a method that incorporates numerous rewards for all of those who use it in pursuit of social and economic justice, and particularly those of us who practice community capacity enhancement.

Five rewards of undertaking a community asset assessment stand out for the authors of this book: (1) Help marginalized communities enhance their profile; (2) Identify indigenous leadership; (3) Enhance community competencies; (4) Mobilize resources for social change; and (5) Tap the assets of overlooked population groups. We are sure, however, that the reader has found other favorite rewards that may or may not be mentioned here.

1. Help Marginalized Communities Enhance Their Profile

Community asset assessments fulfill a vital "discovery" role in communities that have had their histories modified or destroyed by the dominant society and help reclaim their cultural heritage (cultural assets) and contributions to their own community and the greater society. This process, it must be emphasized, is empowering at an individual and community level. Marginalized communities often get their share of unwelcome publicity, and, as a result, develop identities in the broader society that are devalued.

Appreciative inquiry, as noted earlier, is an asset or strength based approach that is premised on the belief that all communities and organizations have a value or "good" elements. It is a labor intensive process that relies upon dialogue and conversation that stresses depth and acknowledges the difficulty and emotionality of the research process. Consequently, appreciative inquiry lends itself, as its supporters would argue, to a qualitative approach because conventional research methods rely on quantitative approaches that essentially render complex experiences and perspectives into easily discrete categories. A stress on a process of engagement can result in the creation of considerable social capital, such as linking, bridging, or bonding in communities, that can be mobilized to seek numerous goals, with one being an assessment or inventory of a community's assets.

Fenn and Moore (2010) describe a cultural asset mapping process that embraced community identity development and resident engagement as two of the primary goals of the assessment. Community cultural assets, as covered in Chapter 2, play an instrumental role in helping to shape the identities of ethnic and racial groups through an emphasis on what is good about their cultural heritage and why efforts must be undertaken to maintain these cultural assets in the future. An ability to speak more than English, for example, is a cultural asset that can also be thought of as a human capital. Language, as a result, forms a vital part of cultural identity.

2. Identify Indigenous Leadership

All communities, regardless of socioeconomic circumstances, have indigenous leaders. The absence of elected officials and individuals occupying high profile appointed positions makes indigenous leadership of much more importance. In some communities, there are no restrictions as to who can assume this role. Consequently, women as well as men, youth as well as adults and older adults, gay men and lesbians as well as heterosexuals, and newcomers as well as long-time residents, for example, can play leadership roles beyond their respective groups. Asset assessments can help tap these leaders but, just as importantly if not more so, also help identify future leaders.

The discovery of potential leaders results in an important contribution on the part of any "good" community assessment. Investment in these leaders, in turn, enhances a community's capacity. Emery, Fernandez, Gutierrez-Montes, and Flora's (2007) study of training of indigenous leadership and its contribution over a 20 year period to the community illustrates the value of indigenous leadership identification and investment.

Kim-Ju and colleagues (2008) provide an excellent case study of the East Bay Chinese Youth Council and how investments in the past have resulted in the creation of a cadre of youth leaders 15 to 30 years later. Youth involved in community efforts received necessary training and support to carry out their responsibilities. An unanticipated benefit of this attention resulted in these youth assuming community leadership positions upon their transition to adulthood. Thus, investment in community through training and support has added significance when potential leadership is part of a community segment that has minimal or no voice within the community.

Identification of new entrepreneurs is another example of how various types of capital can converge. Delgado (2011), for example, details the importance of Latino small businesses providing youth and other community residents with an opportunity to do internships in these establishments with the hopes of helping them learn about community economic development, so that they can eventually open up their own small business catering to Latinos. An asset assessment can help identify the interests of residents and possibly help establish a network of individuals with similar interests to meet and learn from those with these skill sets and experiences.

3. Enhance Community Competencies

Asset assessments can serve as vehicles for enhancing existing assets at the community level. Weissbourd (2010, p. 1) rightly stresses the importance of neighborhoods and communities being the building blocks of society: "Neighborhoods are important. They are the front lines and core building blocks through which people and other assets get developed and deployed to constitute the national economy, society and polity." Any asset assessment of a community must not only seek to identify assets but must also enhance the competencies of residents who play active roles in any aspect of the assessment.

Enhancing capacities, as a result, can either be an explicit or implicit goal of an assessment. It certainly must be an integral part of any initiative that seeks to address social and economic justice themes. Communities, as a result, not only gain new insights into their assets but also experience human capital gains through active participation in the process. Cameron and Gibson (2005), for example, show the value of community asset assessments in the creation of locally based economic enterprises. Asset assessments can help uncover potential economic markets for goods and services, as well as identify residents with unique experiences and abilities who may wish to develop a business but do not have access to technical assistance to help them to do so.

Using community assets, however, does not mean that a community cannot benefit from external resources and partnerships (D'Alonzo, 2010). Partnerships can and must be an outcome of asset assessments (Lindau et al., 2011). Asset assessments are not intended to have communities exclusively rely on themselves and "pull themselves up by their bootstraps" or reinforce a "blame the victim" approach. Consequently, a politically conservative ideology of having communities help themselves after external forces have placed these communities in precarious situations is not the intent of community asset assessments!

Community assets lend themselves to being enhanced, but we must be very careful in what is labeled an asset, as noted by Mallach (2006, p. 205): "Assets that go unmarketed have only limited value; but marketing not supported by bona fide assets—whether in place or being created—has little meaning." Communities that can identify and enhance their assets are in a better position to attract investments and external support and resources. Neighborhoods and communities, as a result, can engage in active marketing campaigns as a means of increasing patronage of local establishments, for example, but also for altering their images to the internal and external community in the process.

4. Mobilize Resources for Social Change

A community asset assessment is never an end in itself, even though much can be gained instrumentally and expressively for a community in carrying out this form of research. The bottom line, so to speak, is the "so what" that follows an assessment. In essence, how will the assessment enhance a community's capacity? Is the community ready to undertake a change effort or project (Parker, Alcaraz, & Payne, 2011)? It is necessary to keep in mind that assessments are never just about assessing, since communities expect changes to result from these research endeavors (Allison et al., 2011; Hernandez-Cordero, Ortiz, Trinidad, & Link, 2011; Lindau et al., 2011).

This book cites numerous authors who advance the importance of positive community directed social change resulting from an asset assessment. Still, needs assessments per se, too, must have change as an outcome. Assessments for the sake of assessment, whether they are need or asset focused, are of very limited use in any community, but particularly those that are marginalized. Community asset assessments are intended to achieve positive change by helping to mobilize indigenous assets. The combination of internal and external resources increases the likelihood that the outcomes of interventions based upon assets start where the community is, rather than with outside authorities making this determination.

Community members can determine which assets within their communities they want local, state, and federal social policies to support. The community can note how those assets are enhanced and how those assets are hampered. All civil rights movements have worked to raise awareness of the larger society and social policy makers regarding their failure to develop attitudes and social policies that enhance life experiences and life chances that they consider assets to their quality of life. People who lobby for marriage equality for same sex partners point to the legal and social benefits that accrue to heterosexuals who are allowed to marry and the discrimination when these benefits are denied to people who are gay, lesbian, bisexual, transgender, or intersex. People who lobby for community living supports for elders or people with disabilities point to the benefits that accrue from freedom from coercion in institutions. In addition to the obvious social justice reasons for their demands for equal treatment in society, there are very concrete, day to day assets derived from the rights they want ensured by social policies. This demand for asset enhancing social policies comes from the persons themselves who have presented their demands to the larger community. Like these social action groups, communities can advocate for policies to support the strengths and quality of life they have identified as crucial to them.

5. Tap the Assets of Overlooked Population Groups

There is no population group or community that cannot benefit from an asset assessment, as attested to by the range of studies reported in the following literature. Community assets mapping, for example, has been used to address childhood obesity, a pressing problem in urban communities of color across the country. A New York State initiative identified individual and community assets to form a community partnership in support of reducing television viewing and childhood obesity (Baker, Dennison, Boyer, Sellers, Russo, & Sherwood, 2007). Latino immigrants and family planning, too, has been addressed using asset maps (Schwartz, Sable, Dannerbeck, & Campbell, 2007).

There have also been a number of highly innovative and exciting efforts to assess the capital or assets of people with disabilities, adults as well as youth. Crane and Skinner (2002) describe a community asset mapping project in Lexington, Kentucky, that focused on helping youth with disabilities enhance school and postschool options. Balcazar, Keys, and Suarez-Balcazar (2001), too, used a community asset assessment to better understand Latinos with disabilities in their quest to achieve independent lives.

Fox, Suryanata, and Hershack (2005) report on an Asian community mapping project. Wade (2007), in turn, describes an asset focused assessment of women. McClusky and McClusky (2003) show how grandparents are community assets and describe how a community can benefit from identifying them as a community resource. Delgado (1995), too, advocates for grandparents, in this case Latinos, to be conceptualized as community assets, and to have their inputs and talents sought out in assessments and used in the development of social interventions. Delgado (2011) also describes a community asset assessment of Latino small businesses and the role they can play in community social and economic development. An earlier special education interagency coordination demonstration project identified successful methods community agencies used to recruit bilingual/bicultural Spanish-speaking and Portuguese-speaking staff to serve children and youth with disabilities (Humm-Delgado, 1980).

CHALLENGES

Practice would be so much easier if there were no challenges involved in carrying out responsibilities. However, practice would not be as rewarding, either. Much can also be said about the incredible challenges that await community social work practitioners in carrying out such an assessment. The importance of achieving awareness and transparency cannot be overly emphasized (Reason, 2006). Kerta (2003), for example, raises a series of challenges for conducting a community capital or asset assessment, such as a lack of clearly defined process, lack of time, resistant agencies/professionals, or negative attitudes and fear on the part of undervalued community groups. Additionally, when federal, state, and local budgets are inadequate, individuals and organizations often will see an asset assessment as a luxury they cannot afford. These challenges are, no doubt, familiar to those of us with experience in community social work practice.

Identification and assessment of social capital, for example, as noted earlier in Chapter 2, also present a wide range of challenges in community asset assessments. The role and importance of social networks and relationships are not new in the field of social sciences and social work. Some of the most ardent critics of social capital argue that it is really "old wine in a new bottle." Nevertheless, there is no denying how the concept of social capital, even though it is difficult to measure (both by normative and resource oriented approaches), has transformed dialogue and debate about social networks in contemporary society.

Some scholars consider social capital to be the most difficult form of capital to measure, when examined within the constellation of the other forms of capital proposed for use in community asset assessments. The challenges in measuring this concept, however, are offset by its importance in the life of communities, particularly those that are on the social and economic margins of society. Many practitioners and scholars would successfully argue that social capital is the "glue" that binds together all forms of capital in communities.

Minkler (2004), a strong proponent of community based participatory research, raises several ethical challenges that can also be applied to community asset assessments, such as tensions between provider driven and community driven agendas, insider–outsider tensions, real or perceived racism, limitations of various participatory models (lack of consensus on key concepts such as community and assets, for example), owning and sharing outcomes, and use of findings for social change. Khanlou and Peter (2009) advocate for the development of ethi-cal review boards to help ensure that communities are not compromised when they get involved in participatory action research. Compliance with community views does not automatically make research more ethical, yet it helps minimize potential ethical dilemmas (Molyneuz, Wassenaar, Peshu, & Marsh, 2005).

Foth (2006, p. 5) comments on the inherent "minefield" of any form of action research: "Research that situates itself within the nexus of people, place and tech-nology has to cope with the sum of the individual characteristics that each vari-able brings to the study. This nexus is fraught with ethical dilemmas that will only increase in severity and frequency as technology continues to advance at a pace that further disconnects undervalued communities from communities that are privileged." Horowitz, Robinson, and Seifer (2009), in turn, argue for the need for CBPR researchers to balance rigorous research with ethical considerations regard-ing partners and communities. Finally, Marshall and Rossman (2011) advance the need for practitioners and researchers to be able to articulate the ethical challenges of the research being proposed to all stakeholders, including the communities they wish to better understand, before embarking on a research project.

The following are nine of the most obvious challenges: (1) trust; (2) lack of consensus; (3) spatial justice; (4) funding; (5) lack of preparation; (6) limited case examples; (7) labor intensity and time limitations; (8) assets being dynamic; and (9) hidden capital. Each of these challenges can exist by itself. Unfortunately, it is more common to see multiple or all of these present at the same time, making the endeavor that much more challenging.

1. Trust

Rogler, Barreras, and Cooney (1981), over 30 years ago although still relevant today, identified a series of challenges in undertaking research (nondeficit focused) among Puerto Rican families in New York City. Coping with distrust was clearly at the top of the challenges faced by researchers and their teams. The importance of mutual trust and respect very often represents the most critical element in forging a pro-ductive and mutually rewarding partnership between community and providers/scholars (Christopher, Watts, McCormick, & Young, 2008; Johnson et al., 2009).

Marshall and Rotimi (2001), too, stress the importance of community based research engendering both respect and trust as a foundation. Barnidge and colleagues (2010) identify trust as a key element in the establishment of partner-ships. Trust is a multifaceted concept and often involves the organizations spon-soring the assessment, the universities with which they are involved, the research team, and various community groups (Christopher, Watts, McCormick, & Young, 2008). Gaining the trust of emerging population groups that are undocumented and/or stigmatized in society, for example, represents a particular challenge in urban focused community based research that actively seeks the involvement of residents (Martinez, Carter-Pokras, & Brown, 2009).

Asset assessments, too, are predicated upon achieving a high level of trust and respect. There is general agreement that the creation of new social capital is arduous, if not impossible, in communities in which general distrust exists (Rusch, 2010). The distrust between community and academia has been characterized in numerous ways, and this distrust usually has a long history of perceived and actual exploitation on the part of academia of marginalized communities in the name of advancing knowledge and, some residents would argue, careers, too. Thus, the "prestige" that academics enjoy in the broader society may not be shared in urban marginalized communities. In addition, academic institutions sometimes even encroach geographically into low income communities as they buy land and/or buildings for physical space expansion.

In addition, Beckley, Martz, Nadeau, Watt, and Reimer (2008) note that it is not surprising to see a gap between academia and the field regarding how community capacity is viewed, and how these differing perspectives translate into how assessments and interventions are conceptualized and implemented. Waldern (2006), in turn, argues that the tension or struggle between these two worlds is associated with the need for sensitivity on the part of academics to social inequality and the need to maintain scientific rigor. Nicotera (2007) raises the point of how the differing perspectives between researchers and practitioners need to be resolved when viewing neighborhoods and that, until these differences are eliminated, tension will continue to persist and is to be expected.

Although this gap or barrier can be substantially minimized when lead researchers share ethnic and racial backgrounds similar to the communities from which they are attempting to assess assets, it does not guarantee that mistrust or ethical dilemmas are not present (Wiles et al., 2008). Kanuha (2000) differentiates between "being native" versus "going native" in undertaking social work research as a community insider. An embrace of an emic perspective (subjective, informed, and influential viewpoint) facilitates the process of community asset assessment versus an etic perspective (more objective, distant, logical, and removed) that detaches the social worker from the community. This does not mean that social workers of the same ethnic and racial backgrounds as the communities in which assessments are being undertaken do not encounter significant pressures from the community and the community agency sponsoring the study.

Participatory research such as community asset assessment conceptualized in this book will often result in the creation or highlighting of current or past tensions between different participating parties such as community members, service providers, and academics (Cashman et al., 2008; Imm, Kehres, Wandersman, & Chinman, 2006; Scarinci, Johnson, Hardy, Marrion, & Partridge, 2009). Tensions also may be present between different age groups. Youth do represent a vast untapped community resource that is simply waiting to be discovered and cultivated in service to communities (Kelly, 2009). Adult ability to address their distrust represents one of the key barriers to active civic involvement. Tensions between different ethnic and racial groups also may be present. A Latino community, for example, may consist of numerous different Latino origin groups.

On the surface, this community appears to be similar. However, different Latino origin groups may have a long history.

Having clear parameters pertaining to the research does help to establish trust between researchers and communities because it minimizes differences in expectations between participating parties. However, there is also a considerable amount of ambiguity, making flexibility and transparency necessary to the process (Chutuape, Willard, Kapogiannis, & Ellen, 2009; Marshall & Rotimi, 2001).

The rewards of establishing a beginning of trust between sectors that have historically not enjoyed it can have profound implications for future endeavors that can be mutually beneficial (Reisch, 2012). Academics, for example, can still pursue knowledge and have careers enhanced, without the exploitation of the community, if the academic agenda coincides with that of the community. Having social and economic justice principles at the forefront helps increase the likelihood that these two agendas are not mutually exclusive.

2. Lack of Consensus

Arriving at a consensus of what constitutes a community asset or capital and capacity enhancement is a critical step in any concerted effort to bring these concepts to life in a community initiative. However, as noted earlier, different definitions of community "capital" and "capacity" are quite common in the field (Chaskin, 2001; Lempa, Goodman, Rice, & Becker, 2008; Maclellan-Wright et al., 2007). Furthermore, there are different definitions of what constitutes a community. These differences of definition are normative and should be expected to appear throughout the assessment process.

Is consensus a goal or an impossible dream in community centered practice? This question wields considerable influence in the determination of what constitutes a community asset and what the best ways are to measure its presence. The quest to achieve consensus is certainly central to community asset assessments and the capacity enhancement projects that follow. It would be simplistic to believe that communities do share a set of values (Shirlow & Murtagh, 2004). Value conflicts at the community level pose serious ethical challenges for planners and others interested in community initiatives (Watson, 2006).

The decisions concerning which values are to be embraced and which ones are to be ignored for the "greater good" can be found in almost any form of community practice, and will emerge in community asset assessments. Nevertheless, the goal of achieving consensus has been criticized along a variety of dimensions and, at times, quite unfairly (Innes, 2004, p. 15): "Many critiques of consensus building have been uninformed about the nature of this practice or the theory on which it was built, though there is extensive literature on both. It is grounded in the theory and practice of interest-based negotiation and mediation. It is not grounded in Habermas' concept of communicative rationality, though theorists have found useful illumination in his ideas. Claims are often made about pathologies of consensus building based on cases where the conditions for authentic dialogue recognized by both practitioners and theoreticians were not met. Documentation of cases shows that when these conditions are met, many desirable outcomes occur."

Innes (2004, p. 15) goes on to examine "the various critiques, including the claims that external power differentials are deterministic, that lowest common denominator solutions are the outcomes, that valuable tensions are lost in the process, and that agreements are fleeting at best." Although arriving at a consensus is highly desirable, it cannot be expected to be achieved without its compromises (Innes, 2007, p.5): "Consensus building is time consuming and requires skill and training. It is only appropriate in situations of uncertainty and controversy where all stakeholders have incentives to come to the table and mutual reciprocity in their interests."

Arriving at a consensus between nonprofit directors and community residents, for example, is considered an even greater challenge (Kissane & Gingerich, 2004) when directors refuse or are unable to believe in residents possessing capital (Nicholas, 2004). This bias makes it impossible for the varied goals associated with community asset assessments and capacity enhancement to be achieved. In fact, this inability or refusal is more in line with conventional needs assessments than asset assessments and probably represents one of the greatest challenges to effectively carrying out an asset assessment. This bias may be deeply ingrained and may be the result of racism, classism, and other oppressive beliefs and forces that effectively render urban communities isolated from external resources.

Community participation, when legally required, or funding is contingent upon it, may not be carried out wholeheartedly (Innes & Booher, 2004). Also, stakeholders are not all of equal importance or influence in communities, and this certainly is the case in community asset assessments. Bowen (2005), for example, in a rare article specifically focused on "low level" stakeholder collaboration as a means of facilitating successful community initiatives, differentiates between various levels of stakeholder influence, showing the complexity of this process. Community asset assessments must be sensitive to this nuance for the purposes of program development (Ozanne & Anderson, 2010).

3. Spatial Justice

Spatial justice refers to the inequitable distribution of resources, services, and access as a fundamental human right, and utilizes geography as a way of determining how certain communities are signaled out by society to be deprived (Soja, 2010). The concept of spatial justice can be viewed either as a hindrance or a facilitating force for community asset assessments. It is included in the challenges category because it has the potential to overwhelm a community and those wishing to highlight its assets. The emergence of a spatial justice perspective has provided the field of social work and other professions interested in the subject of social justice with a concept that facilitates the understanding of how ecological circumstances shape the lives of groups and communities in this country (Soja, 2010).

Spatial justice has taken geography as a point of reference and helped frame a wide range of social conditions to illustrate how a community unit of analysis helps focus on a wide range of deficit oriented statistics. Categorical funding of research and services invariably results in communities being viewed from many different vantage points. However, this brings about an inability to view the entire community as a whole. A disproportionate amount of social problems concentrated in a relatively small geographic area shapes community images of itself and those images outside the community, which can result in a defeatist attitude about change, assets, and future hopes (Fainstein, 2010).

Ahn-Redding's (2007) book *The Million Dollar Inmate: The Financial and Social Burden of Non-Violent Offenders* captures this point quite well. Communities that are undervalued by society have a disproportionate number of residents who are incarcerated. Each inmate is estimated to cost taxpayers approximately $29,000 a year to imprison. There are city blocks that have an excessive number of residents in prison, and the annual cost to taxpayers is over $1 million a year.

As noted in Chapter 2, negative identity shapes internal and external perceptions to the point at which a community may not think of itself as possessing assets. Consequently, asset assessments must actively incorporate goals of changing community negative attitudes about itself by highlighting the "good" that exists within its boundaries. However, any social workers with extensive histories of working in marginalized communities will quickly attest to the pervasive and destructive forces operating to undermine a community's quest for a positive identity.

A spatial justice perspective effectively serves to bring together statistics and sources of information that shape community attitudes. A spatial justice approach also facilitates the development of a more in-depth understanding of how social problems get manifested within small geographic areas within a community, and why this is so. There invariably are sections of urban communities that face an increased onus due to an excessive concentration of problems.

4. Funding

The subject of funding is integral to any effort to assess a community's assets, just as it is when discussing a typical needs assessment. Lack of adequate funding to "properly" undertake a community asset assessment is nothing new, and this is particularly the case when discussing insufficiently resourced communities and the organizations serving them. Allen-Meares and colleagues (2011) advance the concept of embedded funders (foundations that have made long term commitments to communities) and the importance of fostering use of evaluation approaches that are conceptualized less in theoretical ways and more in action creating ways.

Unfortunately, any effort at innovation involving marginalized or undervalued communities will face increased scrutiny from funding authorities. Consequently, if an organization is waiting for an opportunity to obtain the necessary funds to carry out an "ideal" asset assessment, it may never be in the position to actually implement it. This point should not come as any great surprise to practitioners who have worked in undervalued communities.

However, lack of funding also can serve to facilitate creative ways of bringing together parties who normally would not join forces and can result in innovative ways of assessing assets with minimal or no actual funding specific to this undertaking (Haugh, 2007). Furthermore, minimal reliance on external funding effectively frees communities to seek answers to critical questions that would normally be unacceptable politically, and thereby "unfundable." This can result in the mobilization of resources for social change.

Although community asset assessments, of course, can be undertaken with generous funding, the question of whether a community can undertake an asset assessment with no funding can be answered with a resounding yes! It may not provide the "optimal" results. However, such efforts require not just creativity but also extensive contributions of time and materials from the community. In fact, such efforts often prove to be much more fruitful than those undertaken with government funds. Community grocery stores and restaurants, for example, can contribute food and meals. Key community institutions such as houses of worship can donate space and supplies. The community asset assessment undertaken with minimal or no money takes on a version of a quilt, with many different pieces of cloth coming together to create a work of woven art!

5. Lack of Preparation

The necessity of all participating parties being adequately prepared to undertake a community asset assessment also should not come as any great surprise to community social workers. However, it has only been in the past 5 to 10 years that community asset assessment has started to find its way into common practice and the professional literature. Consequently, case examples and educational programs preparing community social workers and other community practitioners for this form of research are still in their infancy, particularly when compared to their needs assessment counterparts.

This lack of preparation effectively means that practitioners are forced to learn a research method "on the job" that would be challenging even for those who have formally learned it in the classroom. Consequently, "on the job training" applies to community residents, too. In many ways, this lack of preparation serves to level the playing field for all those involved in a community asset assessment. That can be very empowering but also quite distressing.

6. Limited Case Examples

Local circumstances wield incredible power over how community asset assessments should be planned and implemented, and this is a strength as well as a weakness in this type of research method. The professional literature, and this book is certainly no exception, provides case illustrations and case studies (with greater depth of detail) to highlight the value and tensions associated with this type of endeavor. However, rest assured, the reader will be in a community that may not look exactly like the communities being described in these examples, or the configuration of assets may be unlike anything the reader has come across in the literature.

Community asset assessments, unlike clinical social work where numerous case studies can be found in the professional literature, do not enjoy the same range of information that clinical case studies enjoy. Consequently, any effort to draw from the examples in the literature to help a local community effort may encounter a lack of similar or relevant case examples. This requires local communities to problem solve complex situations, making the task of community asset assessment that much more arduous and time consuming to accomplish. One of the recommended methods for use in community asset assessment, as addressed in Chapter 6, is the development of case studies capturing the process of conducting an assessment, as a means of encouraging other organizations and communities to engage in community asset assessments.

7. Labor Intensity and Time Limitations

Community asset assessments are very labor intensive undertakings. In fact, any endeavor that actively seeks to engage communities and include residents in all facets of the study would be labor intensive. If these efforts are conceptualized as community capacity enhancement, then the time, money, and effort can be justified to funders. However, viewing community asset assessments as simply research would do a serious injustice to this field of practice for social work, or any other profession wishing to address social and economic justice issues in this nation's urban areas.

We cannot think of any facet or phase of a community asset assessment that is "simple," "quick," "easy," or amenable to a "shortcut." Thinking of these assessments in this manner will quickly result in disappointment and failure. True, there are actions and approaches that can minimize the labor intensity of the effort. However, a desire for a "quick and dirty" community asset assessment would be detrimental to the community being assessed, and to those doing the assessment. A highly focused asset assessment is recommended in situations in which time and resources are limited. Comprehensive assessments are the most complex, labor intensive, and costly undertakings.

8. Assets Being Dynamic

Community capital or assets are not a fixed entity and, as a result, are highly influenced by external forces and internal events in a community (Beckley et al., 2008, p. 63): "Community capacity does not simply happen. Rather it is developed and formed, or diminished and lost through response to changing conditions. Observable community capacity becomes manifest when there is a reason to act or to react. These reasons, or catalysts for action, may be positive or negative and we therefore describe them as opportunities and threats."

Consequently, one of the greatest challenges facing a community asset assessment is the difficulty in maintaining up to date results so that the findings may remain relevant. Some urban communities, for example, have histories of attracting newcomers. The influx of newcomers has a profound impact on all aspects of a community, including its manifestations of capital or assets. One store owned by Colombians, for example, may be purchased by Mexicans, as the latter increase their representation in the community. The store will remain a community asset. However, it will increase in significance for the Mexican community, although it will lose its significance for Colombians. Additionally, a community grocery store that has enjoyed a positive reputation under one owner may have a new owner who has replaced quality products with inferior products, and so the store will no long enjoy a positive reputation and position in the community. On the surface, it still will be an establishment owned by a community resident, so it may give the appearance of being a community asset. However, in reality, it will not be an asset.

9. Hidden Capital

Asset assessments are, by their very nature, only as good as their ability to uncover community capital or assets. For some assets, it is relatively easy to capture and ascertain their influence within a community. Favorite community grocery stores or houses of worship that are respected by membership and non-membership alike, or individuals whom it seems everyone either knows personally or knows about because of their generosity or good deeds, are relatively easy to identify and assess.

Moore and Roux (2005) studied the associations of neighborhood characteristics with the location and type of food stores in urban communities and found that low income communities of color had four times as many small grocery stores as the wealthiest neighborhoods but half as many large supermarkets. Also, liquor stores were far more present in low income communities when compared to wealthier neighborhoods. Their study, however, focused only on formal businesses and made no effort to identify informal establishments. It can be reasonably concluded that informal food establishments would have made the differences even greater regarding both food and liquor businesses. The authors offer an important conclusion regarding this disparity that has implications for access to nutritious food (Moore & Roux, 2005, p. 331): "The infrastructure of the local food environment is yet-another feature of the built environment that varies substantially across neighborhoods and may contribute to disparities and social inequalities in health. Accurate description of area differences in the local food environment is an important step."

Short, Guthman, and Raskin (2007), however, report on a community asset study of food establishments in a low income San Francisco community and found that many of these small businesses promoted food security (a variety of low cost and nutritious foods). Nevertheless, limitations related to access (geographic unevenness), overall affordability, and a focus on co-ethnics (no differences between racial and ethnic backgrounds) limited their potential to provide sufficient access to a broader community clientele.

There are, however, community assets that are hidden from public purview and, therefore, are much harder to capture in an assessment (Bergsgaard & Sutherland, 2003). Some assets are either invisible or have very low profiles, so to speak (Riley, 2009). For example, diversity can be considered a community asset (Clark et al., 2003). Urban community assets encompass places, spaces, activities, and events that may not be easily visible to the outside community, creating challenges for defining and measuring urban community assets (Montgomery, 2005; Ozanne & Anderson, 2010). Residents learn about other cultural traditions, festivities, and values, thereby enriching their own lives and giving them a more global appreciation. Castka, Bamber, and Sharp (2004), in turn, use the concept of intangible capital to assess organizational teamwork performance.

Gardner and Mathias (2009) emphasize that people with disabilities, too, have social capital that can benefit a community and have much to offer if they are provided with an opportunity to do. Before this can occur, however, systematic efforts to assess their assets must be undertaken. Asset based community development and organizational development efforts can incorporate people with disabilities. Forman (2004) also touches upon a rather large hidden population group in youth. He critiques the community policing movement and highlights how these efforts systematically excluded youth as assets in these policing efforts, instead, relying solely on adults.

CRITIQUE

The field of community asset assessment has suffered from a lack of critical thinking and serious critique, as noted in the introductory chapter. Gaarder, Monai, and Sollis (2003) offer a rare critique of asset assessments and mapping of community capacity. The authors focus their attention on several critical areas: (1) communities are not monolithic in composition, and there are bound to be different definitions of what constitutes an asset; (2) cultural belief systems may put professionals and communities at odds over how best to approach a local problem; (3) a quest for feasibility of an asset assessment may result in simplification of complex social phenomena, effectively disempowering the community; and (4) even though the focus of asset assessments is on assets, communities may inadvertently revert to needs, limiting the potential of asset assessments and mapping.

Wiseman (2006) acknowledges the role and importance of efforts to tap community assets. However, he criticizes efforts that put the onus of achieving significant social change on communities themselves, instead of these assessments advancing the need for initiatives to address redistributive taxation, income security, and labor markets that result in "sustainable reductions in poverty and social exclusion." Thus, community asset assessments, in effect, are seen as a social engineering tool with minimum potential to achieve significant social change.

Efforts to get communities to take more action, and, therefore, responsibility to address internal needs, have sometimes been framed as conservative in ideology, particularly when external resources are not marshalled in these endeavors (Delgado, 2000). A similar type of criticism has been made toward community self help efforts (Berner & Phillips, 2005; Williams & Windebank, 2000). A philosophical focus on "pulling oneself up by one's bootstraps" has a long history in this country, making indigenous efforts to help communities without external resources quite popular in conservative thinking circles. From a social work ethics standpoint, however, the identification of assets that can encourage social action would be critical.

ETHICAL DILEMMAS

The National Association of Social Workers *Code of Ethics* (2008) is not a prescription for exactly how to act in any particular practice decision. Yet, it provides guidance that is critical to doing community asset assessments. For example, the preamble states: "Social workers seek to enhance the capacity of people to address their own needs. Social workers also seek to promote the responsiveness of organizations, communities, and other social institutions to individuals' needs and social problems." These are goals of community asset assessments. The code's ethical principles also stress the importance of human relationships in saying: "Social workers seek to strengthen relationships among people in a purposeful effort to promote, restore, maintain, and enhance the wellbeing of individuals, families, social groups, organizations, and communities." Community asset assessments focus strongly on the value of relationships within communities that provide strength to their members. The code's focus in its ethical standards on cultural competence and diversity must permeate the process, and confidentiality, conflict of interest, and informed consent ethical standards must be addressed as seriously as in any research endeavor.

The subject of ethical dilemmas and decision making has historically found a home in the clinical realms of social work practice. However, practice in the community is certainly not exempt from ethical dilemmas (Watson, 2006), as noted earlier in this chapter and other parts of this book. Furthermore, it is impossible to discuss any form of research, community focused or otherwise, without also raising ethical dilemmas (Save the Children, 2000, p. 8): "Every piece of research is context specific, and ethical considerations must bear this in mind .... Ethical decisions occur at all levels of research ... Any researcher who does not give due considerations to ethics is potentially damaging the people researched and those carrying out the research."

There is an increasing call for research on social work's ethical decision process in community focused practice (Banks, 2008; Doel et al., 2010). Clark (2006, p. 75) raises the importance of social work's "moral character," and this concept has profound implications for community social work practitioners involved in asset assessments and ethical conduct: "The social work role, as in other human service professions such as teaching and nursing, sometimes requires more than the competent delivery of standardized service: it also involves modelling ways of life and counselling over morally problematic issues. Value neutrality over many pressing contemporary social issues is thus neither feasible nor desirable for human service professionals. The requirements of the role include demonstrating a virtuous character. This has long been implicitly accepted in practice, if not always clearly acknowledged."

The National Association of Social Workers *Code of Ethics* (2008), however, explicitly states that all aspects of the code apply to practice in communities and all methods of practice. In addition, integrity is specifically noted as a social work value, with the corresponding ethical principle being to behave in a trustworthy manner.

Healy (2007) addresses the increased globalization (values of diversity and human rights) and multiculturalism, and advocates for universalistic and cultural relativism to be integrated into social work ethical decision making. Grey (2005) raises paradoxical forces that further challenge ethical decision making processes. These forces can be found in an extenuated form within urban marginalized communities. Delgado (2006) addresses the ethical challenges involved when youth are engaged in research. The ethical dilemmas that follow will not surprise the reader based upon the content covered in the previous section.

Buchanan, Miller, and Wallerstein (2007, p. 153) note that CBPR lies at the nexus of two major underlying ethical concerns that involve respect for community autonomy and the fair allocation of limited public resources: "Growing use of CBPR raises two new ethical issues that deserve greater public attention: first, the problem of securing informed consent and demonstrating respect for community autonomy when the locus of research shifts from the individual to community level; and second, fair distribution of scarce public resources when practical constraints make the most rigorous research designs for assessing the effects of community interventions virtually impossible."

Delgado (2006) identifies seven key areas for ethical dilemmas involving youth led research that have applicability to community asset assessments: (1) participation and protection (no harm from participating); (2) conflicting agendas; (3) informed consent; (4) agreement on purpose of research; (5) confidentiality and trust; (6) clarity in process (no misunderstandings); and (7) payment (maximum exchange of funds for the community). These seven areas of potential ethical dilemmas touch upon the range of potential areas of tension that can be expected to emerge as part of a participatory community asset assessment.

Hardina (2004), in a rare article specifically focused on ethical dilemmas for community organizing practice, raises many of these concerns when examining this form of practice. Discussion of ethical dilemmas regarding community asset assessments, and community capacity development, though, has largely gone unaddressed in the literature, although these are certainly present in any community change effort (Verity, 2007).

Ungar, Manuel, Mealey, Thomas, and Campbell (2004) address the need for detailed guidelines to help community social workers navigate the challenges of engaging informal community helpers in practice. "Lay helpers," for example, can be found in most communities, and these individuals fulfill important service provision functions that often go unrecognized by formal service providers. In Latino communities, these individuals may take the form of folk healers practicing out of their homes, away from public scrutiny. Residents know how to access them, but formal service providers do not even know they exist, let alone how to access them (Delgado, 2006).

Ethical dilemmas related to confidentiality are not uncommon in community asset mapping (Aronson et al., 2007b). Community asset assessments, like their needs assessment counterparts, have the potential to invade the privacy of residents and can expose participants to risks within and outside of the community (Wang & Redwood-Jones, 2001). These risks have included youth asset assessors getting into altercations with gang members as they "invade" a gang's territory, exposure to experiences that can bring back painful memories, or witnessing sad or frightful situations that can compromise youth's psychological state of being (Delgado, 2001).

Concerns about personal safety can compromise the integrity of the research by excluding sections of a community with high crime rates. Community social workers, too, are not above having safety concerns. Suarez-Balcazar and Kinney's (2006, p. 306) comments on realities and myths of community safety, although specifically addressed to community psychologists, have equal applicability to social workers: "When working in a community that is facing economic and social hardships, it is challenging for researchers to recognize the negative events that pose safety concerns while also acknowledging the positive responses to marginalization coming from the community. Unfortunately, the negative often overshadows the positive, and researchers are more likely to distance themselves by avoiding contact, limiting community visits, or by working through intermediaries or third persons, such as hiring others."

Having community "backing" or "trust" will go a long way toward helping to ensure that those involved in community assessments, staff as well as volunteers, are supported and cared for by the community. Such support, however, does not guarantee safety. It does, nevertheless, increase the likelihood that participants will not be harmed, or, in the case of communities with high percentages of undocumented residents, not be feared to be authorities interested in deporting them.

Although ethical challenges are inherent in community asset assessments, like other forms of CBPR, Minkler (2004, p. 654) sums up quite well why these challenges should not prevent these types of research partnerships from moving forward in service to a community: "CBPR frequently involves thorny ethical challenges for outside researchers and their community partners. Yet despite such challenges and obstacles, CBPR provides an approach to research that shows increasing promise as we attempt to address many of today's most intractable health and social problems. By involving and building on the strengths of multiple stakeholders in the research process CBPR offers the opportunity to achieve ... 'partnership synergy,' tackling difficult issues more effectively than any one partner could do alone."

Community assets may be uncovered that exist in the informal sector, such as businesses being run from homes, child care being provided without local government sanctions, or car repairs being conducted on the street as a business. Some of these informal businesses are run by individuals who are undocumented and wish to remain "underground." Making this information public can cause these individuals, and the community, hardships, if authorities close down these businesses and deport those who are undocumented. Atkinson and Willis (2005, p. 7) touch on this very point in regard to community capacity building (CCB): "CCB projects that fail may also damage the social networks and community relationships that previously existed so making it all the more important that the process as a whole is taken seriously."

Community social networks are not always harmonious, and these relationships must be taken into account when conducting a community asset assessment. The senior author conducted a community asset assessment in a New England Latino community, and significant differences emerged as to what constituted an asset in the community. Folk healers were considered an asset by a large portion of the community. However, certain religious fundamentalist groups considered folk healers to be an extension of the devil and could not label them as assets. The same tension occurred when community botanical shops (cultural variations of pharmacies) were identified and labeled as assets by one group and not considered assets by another group. Communities are not monolithic in structure and composition, and neither are assets.

CONCLUSIONS

Community asset/capital assessments are complex and require numerous decisions to be made throughout the process. These assessments bring significant rewards for communities undertaking this form of research. However, there are inherent challenges and ethical dilemmas that will be encountered during implementation, as addressed in this chapter. This necessitates a critical review of the process.

All forms of research can be considered "political" in nature, and community asset assessments are certainly no exception. Entering a community means having to interact with various groups who may not share the same world view, histories, and goals. Furthermore, it necessitates establishing and maintaining relationships founded upon mutual trust and respect. Nevertheless, a successful asset assessment is able to negotiate these points in a manner that builds community solidarity in the process.

The greater the awareness of potential "fault lines" prior to undertaking an asset assessment, the greater the likelihood of achieving a meaningful outcome, with minimal disruption to the life of a community. However, much will remain to be discovered or uncovered along the way, and no amount of "preparation" can provide community social workers with all of the answers. In essence, community asset assessments always mean entering into a journey that will bring great rewards but will also bring expected and unexpected turbulence. That is what makes this journey so exciting and meaningful.

Analytical Framework, Methods, and Mapping

"Some communities may be particularly well endowed with effective individuals working on behalf of the community, whereas others may have productive organizations and social groups. However, each illustrates the existence or building of community capacity only as far as it is connected to a collective agenda or to the realization of collective well-being at the community level. When this happens, the different levels of agency can be seen as the vehicles through which community capacity operates."

(CHASKIN ET AL., *2001, p. 21)*

Section 2 brings community assets to life by specifically addressing the "how to" of carrying them out in an urban community context. Chapter 5 discusses the importance of determining how a community gets defined and how to conceptualize all of the stages associated with an assessment. Chapter 6, in turn, talks about the varied methods that can be used. Chapter 7 focuses on how to conduct a community map. Finally, Chapter 8 addresses the dissemination of findings.

5

Analytical Framework for Undertaking Assessments

"In all manner of community-based work there has been much chatter the past few years about identifying and mobilizing assets—human, organizational and community strengths, resources and capacities. A growing number of practitioners and funders in community development and social-change work are adopting this strategy, and its terms have increasingly become part of the lexicon."

(BORRUP, *2005, p. 1*)

INTRODUCTION

Unlike its needs assessment counterpart, asset assessments strive to create a wide range of opportunities for community involvement, and this often represents the "signature piece" that distinguishes this form of assessment from its needs counterpart. Needs assessments can actively involve community members in the conceptualization and implementation of an assessment. However, the decision to do so rests in the hands of those carrying out the assessment, and there are no philosophical principles requiring them to involve community members. Recent attention and funding devoted to carrying out community asset assessments have done much to increase the popularity of these forms of assessments in the field, in urban as well as in rural areas (Marre & Weber, 2010).

Green (2008, p. 50) argues for the conceptualization of community development practice as a form of social movement because of the emphasis placed on social action: "Approaching community development from an action-oriented direction requires that we borrow from, synthesize and augment existing theoretical perspectives within the realm of social movements, including those focused on political-economic constraints and opportunities, resource mobilization and organization, and framing of grievances and collective action. This approach will help to inform researchers, community development practitioners and poli-cymakers to better understand the enterprise of intentional social change at the local level. Additionally, it holds promise for those scholars engaged in applied research with change initiatives who want to pursue a more critical assessment of community development work."

The evolution of a community capacity paradigm upon which asset assess-ments are based has continued into the present day, offering encouragement to the field and those who practice and undertake research based on this para-digm (Chino & DeBruyn, 2006; Delgado & Zhou, 2008; DeRienzo, 2008; Salem, Hooberman, & Ramirez, 2005). Green (2010a), for example, provides case stud-ies reflecting a variety of settings in which asset assessment and asset build-ing form an instrumental role in shaping community development strategies. These examples illustrate for practitioners and academics the flexibility of a capacity enhancement paradigm to tap a variety of community assets and inte-grate them into an intervention.

Asset assessment's acceptance has been broad from a discipline point of view, with social work, health, planning, and education standing out. However, pub-lic health and the health promotion fields, probably more than any other field, have embraced this paradigm (Delgado, 2009; Delgado & Zhou, 2008; Maclellan-Wright et al., 2007; Nam & Engelhardt, 2007). The acceptance of a socioeco-logical perspective in various human service related fields has facilitated the use of community assets in addressing health disparities, for example (Delgado, in press).

REDISCOVERY OF COMMUNITY

As noted in the opening quote in Chapter 2, Sites, Chaskin, and Parks (2007) argue that "community" in the twenty-first century enjoys a ubiquitous status and can be found everywhere and nowhere at the same time. They say that com-munity has been lost, discovered, and rediscovered with "disturbing regular-ity." The discovery, or rediscovery, of community makes community assets both easier and harder to conduct (Kim & Kaplan, 2004).

"Community" plays such a central role in community asset assessments and often represents the "glue" that binds together a wide range of methods that share in common only a community focus. An emphasis on community effec-tively shifts attention from individual and single causative factors in both theory and practice, placing emphasis on community and social forces (Kegler, Rigler, & Honeycutt, 2011; Kim-Ju, Mark, Cohen, & Garcia-Santiago, 2008). Such an emphasis lends itself to an embrace of social justice values and principles in shap-ing how assessments are conceptualized, and the programming resulting from the findings, when focused on marginalized communities (Hardcastle, Powers, & Wenocur, 2011).

Not surprisingly, the definition of community used shapes how commu-nity assets and capacity enhancement are conceptualized (Norton, McLeroy,

Burdine, Felix, & Dorsey, 2002, p. 196): "How we think about community will affect how we think about the concept of community capacity, including the resources that may exist within communities to address common problems." The concept of "community," however, arguably represents the most challenging aspect of community practice, and this concern is evident both in the United States and some other countries. Martinez, Carter-Pokras, and Brown (2009), regarding Latinos in the United States, go so far as to argue that the first principle of any community based participatory research is to arrive at a locally defined definition of "community." This may seem rudimentary; however, it is far more complex than most practitioners may think.

Different population groups may define community differently because of their unique experiences within this ecological context (Kelger, Rigler, & Honneycutt, 2011). Youth, for example, live in communities but are essentially disenfranchised from decision making roles within major institutions in their community (Evans, 2007). Groups that are marginalized not just geographically but also on other characteristics such as disability or sexual orientation may have community reference points that transcend a geographic community and relate to cultural and political solidarity.

The definition of community, not surprisingly, is closely tied to the definition of community participation to which we subscribe. Community participation, like its popular counterpart of civic engagement, can have many different meanings depending on an individual's philosophical standpoint (Bradbart & Braid, 2009). Community social workers, as a result, must be very careful about the uncritical popularity of a community concept.

A number of scholars have raised concerns about the "rediscovery" of community and its implications for community practice. Mowbray (2005), for example, cautions against acceptance of this paradigm without requisite critique when governments expound the virtues of community and support efforts to build community capacity. Maginn (2007) and King and Cruickshank (2011) talk about how community participation has become the buzzword in the United Kingdom's urban regeneration efforts and that there are challenges in determining what this actually means from a policy and practice perspective. Labonte's (2004, p. 115) observations about the evolution of the concept of community over the past generation in Australia have a ring of familiarity and truth to them in this country: "Thirty years ago … governments rediscovered community. From processes (community participation, community development) to attributes (community competence, community capacity) to services (community health, community education), it seemed that all we had to do was to drop the adjective of *gemeinschaft* (community) in front of the noun of our particular preoccupation and the impersonal structures of *gesellschaft* (mass society) disappeared. Of course, we quickly learned it was more complex than that."

Atkinson and Willis (2005, p. 4) sum up quite well some of the most stinging criticisms of community capacity efforts such as asset assessments in New Zealand: "We need to remember that the idea of CCB (Community Capacity Building) is not uncomplicated or without its critics. Some people argue that

CCB can be seen as a 'band-aid' solution for focusing attention on local community problems rather than much wider structural issues such as poverty and unemployment. Others argue that relying on volunteers and voluntary labour has helped make it easier to withdraw funding for health and social services... These criticisms all have some validity—where CCB is useful however, is in allowing communities, often with low political influence, to set their own agenda." The setting of their own agenda, however, can result in tensions and conflicts between the community and the organization sponsoring the asset assessment.

Brennan (2007) counters the argument about volunteers by highlighting the potential role volunteers can play in community asset assessments, and stresses their role in post-assessment in creating a vision and community political will for carrying out recommendations made as a result of the assessment. Voluntarism is not an activity that is restricted to middle and upper-middle class communities and can be found in low income and low wealth communities, too. However, it may not appear in a conventional manner, and it may not involve doing so with organizations and/or formally.

Casswell (2001, p. 23) echoes a line of argument similar to Atkinson and Willis (2005) and notes that an emphasis on community as a place for intervention has had its share of critics in New Zealand: "Community initiatives have been a convenient panacea with a reputation for exercising a stabilizing effect in society, concentrating attention on local-level planning and control... At its worst, the notion [is] that community participation and empowerment can be used to argue for greater reliance on voluntary organizations in order to allow withdrawal of needed health and social services." Concerns about using the presence of community assets as an excuse to withdraw or avoid allocating public funds must be carefully watched. Undervalued communities do not have excessive resources to give back to government, and it would be a cruel policy decision to argue that these communities can take care of themselves.

The expansion of the concept "community" brings with it its share of advantages and disadvantages for practice (Lynn, 2006, p. 110): "The ambiguity of community allows it to be a place for a vast range of imposed and 'organic' social reproduction functions, and an accessible site for meaningful collective action, but it also has the potential for disempowerment. The breadth of the concept of 'community' allows for it to be critiqued as ephemeral or as romantic fiction, but also used and exploited by government." The complexities associated with communities tend to be ignored and underappreciated (Fremeaux, 2005; Kegler, Rigler, & Honeycutt, 2010, 2011).

Lynn (2006) is not alone in being suspicious about the allure of community in the twenty-first century. Gaynor (2010), although specifically commenting on Ireland, notes: "At a time of rising stress for communities, families, and individuals coupled with a growing disillusionment with government, the concept of 'active citizenship' has arrived as a salve to many of the social ills of our time. Emphasizing citizens' own responsibilities, and espousing values of solidarity, community, and neighbourliness, active citizenship embodies all that is good, rendering it somewhat immune from criticism. While agreeing that community values of solidarity and neighbourliness are indeed critical, this paper takes issue with what it argues is a significant re-visioning of the three core concepts embodied within active citizenship—citizenship, social capital, and community development—and argues that active citizenship, as it is currently promoted by state and select civil society organizations alike, substitutes self-help for redistribution and self-reliance for state accountability, in the process depoliticizing the principles and practice of community development and denying community actors a voice in their own development."

Shaw (2008, p. 24), too, raises a cautionary flag regarding the discovery of community and its sociopolitical significance: "In fact, sometimes it seems that policy development needs to reinvent the wheel of community every decade or so. The question, therefore, is what this ideological recycling of community tells us: first, about the meaning of the term itself; second, about the contemporary significance within the wider politics of the state." Foth (2006) refers to community as a "convenient container" for researchers and external sources to describe a defined group of individuals. These individuals, in turn, may not consider themselves to be a part of this definition of community.

It is fitting to end this section on the rediscovery of community with one scholar's assessment of community over the past 100 years (Morse, 2011, p. 8): "Thinking back on the ideas that have really made a difference and stood the test of time, I settle on three: creation and expansion of community development corporations (and their intermediaries), the practice of asset-based community development, and vehicles to provide affordable capital. These three ideas encompass the essential elements of any change strategy: a structure for change, a vision for change, and a strategy for change."

COMMUNITY CAPACITY AND SOCIAL CHANGE

The popularity of community capacity enhancement has made this paradigm appealing for a variety of disciplines (Norton, McLeroy, Burdine, Felix, & Dorsey, 2002, p. 196): "Interest in community capacity touches many disciplines, including organizational development, community development, sociology and social work, criminal justice, political science, and public health." Chinman and colleagues (2005) highlight the importance of a community science research agenda focused on better understanding community capacity for enhancing the potential of prevention projects. A broad reach, so to speak, brings with it a set of inherent challenges for all those professions seeking to incorporate this paradigm in their work with communities as well as a great potential for conceptualizing and carrying out projects that can be ambitious and possible only when different disciplines collaborate (Mathie & Cunningham, 2003a,b).

A number of prominent scholars have written about community capacity efforts in various parts of the country. Chaskin and colleagues (2001, p. 1) reviewed community capacity initiatives and arrive at the not surprising conclusion that an initiative "consists of actions to strengthen the capacity of communities to identify priorities and opportunities and to foster and sustain positive neighbor-hood change. The focus on building capacity as a goal of community building efforts is both explicit and pervasive in the rhetoric, missions, and (to a greater or lesser extent) activities of these initiatives." Diers (2004) provides a detailed description of how the identification, assessment, and mobilization of Seattle's community assets were used to develop participatory democratic processes in the city's neighborhoods. Lindau and colleagues (2011) describe the importance of collaboration and the identification and mobilization of Chicago's South Side assets to inform health policies, research, and programs. Casswell (2001, p. 31) notes the relationship between community initiatives such as those that are capacity enhancing and policy: "Community initiatives depend upon a support-ive policy environment to make a difference in people's lives. Local-level action in isolation is unlikely to ameliorate the effects of a policy environment hostile to its goals. Community initiatives inform the need for central policy change if lines of communication between the community voice and policy advisers are open."

Positive social change represents the "bottom line" in any community capac-ity enhancement effort and, as a result, must be systematically built into every facet of the effort (O'Donnell & Karanja, 2000). Jackson and colleagues (2003, p. 347) bring an added dimension to this goal based on their study of community capacity in Toronto, Canada: "Our approach moves away from the traditional focus on improving the skills and knowledge base of the community members, which often carries the implicit assumption that such capabilities do not already exist. Instead, our approach was to assume that the 'problem' of community capacity is not located so much in the community members as in the facilitating and constraining conditions."

FRAMEWORK

Any serious discussion of theory will undoubtedly uncover tension between those of us who wish to "do" and those of us who wish to "think" before doing. However, there is a clear and powerful relationship between theory, values, and practice (Chinman et al., 2005; Smith, Littlejohns, & Thompson, 2001). We believe that community asset assessments require the application of theory to practice.

Garbarino and Haslam (2005, p. 447) discuss this form of tension: "If it's action you want, North Americans are number one. The slogan 'Just do it!' should probably be our national motto. But if what is needed is to think more deeply about the issue, it's necessary to lean on a much more European tradition, where theory and deep analysis have a longer history and greater kind of social credence. There was a German psychologist (Kurt Lewin) who worked in the United States and tried to bring the European approach to America. Lewin once wrote that 'there is nothing so practical as a good theory,' which, to an American ear, often sounds like a contradiction in terms. We tend to think theoretical is over *here* and practical over *there*. Lewin understood that to do good practice you have to understand things deeply. This is evident in many sound programs."

We may think that Garbarino and Haslam (2005) overstate this disconnect between theory and practice. Yet, Trevillion (2008) goes so far as to argue that there is a disconnect between social work practice, research, and theory, and that "intellectual fragmentation" is largely responsible for this situation, which needs to be reversed for the profession to progress in this century. However, regardless of how this argument is framed, there is no denying the tension that exists between theory and practice, between the "ivory tower" and the "real world." Thomas (2007), for example, holds little hope for planners to be able to achieve significant social changes and believes that having any disconnect between theory and practice certainly does not hold promise for the field.

Nevertheless, there is no denying the potential importance of theory in helping to guide community initiatives such as community asset assessments. Jaccard and Jacoby (2010, p. 3) offer a very liberating suggestion concerning who has the "right" to create theories: "Most students are intimidated by the prospect of constructing their own theories about a phenomenon. Theory construction is viewed as a mysterious process that somehow 'happens' and is beyond the scope and training of a young scientist trying to find his or her way in the field." Shaw (2005), in turn, argues that practitioners should assume a greater role in theory construction through what is called "street market" research.

A proliferation of theoretical paradigms pertaining to community initiatives, including those that are capacity focused, can be viewed in some circles as counterproductive to moving the field forward (Lather, 2006). However, others, including the authors of this book, see this proliferation as positive and an indicator of vibrancy, opening the door to various interpretations and input, including the voices of community residents.

A framework, like principles, is an attempt to bridge this divide in a manner that facilitates these worlds coming together. The framework that follows is offered in the hopes that practitioners and academics can come together and do so with communities. Lyons and Reimer (2006) put forth a six part framework for comparing and contrasting community capacity frameworks that offers the field a useful analytical tool for helping community practitioners find the most appropriate model: (1) Is capacity considered a condition or a process? (2) What are the desired outcomes? (3) How is measurement of capacity to be undertaken? (4) Is the capacity within (endogamous) or external (exogenous) to the community? (5) On what are the primary levels of analysis focused? (6) Are capacity outcomes inherently positive? The answers to these six key questions will help facilitate a better understanding of the goals, processes, and outcomes of community capacity enhancement.

The framework for community asset assessments in this book draws from five critical stages for community capacity enhancement. Each stage has analytical (theoretical) and interactional (sociopolitical) dimensions and multiple steps: (1) identifying and categorizing assets; (2) mapping; (3) building and solidifying support; (4) developing an intervention; and (5) evaluating (Delgado, 1999). This book emphasizes the first three stages as they can be applied to community asset assessment.

Social interventions resulting from an asset assessment can easily necessitate an entire book developed to outline them. Interventions can be as focused or as comprehensive as the asset assessment, not different from needs assessments. However, asset inspired interventions systematically go about including identified assets as key elements, stressing important democratic participatory principles that aim to empower communities in the process. Evaluation of social interventions, too, must follow community participatory principles and assess the extent and success of community assets. Efforts to evaluate the success of interventions, as a result, can utilize many of the methods and techniques used to conduct asset assessments, such as focus groups, ethnography, or photovoice, as well as quantitative tools. There has also been a recent emphasis toward the development of community capacity measurement scales (Lempa, Goodman, & Becker, 2008; Maclellan-Wright et al., 2007; Smith et al., 2008). Particular emphasis will be placed on contextualizing all three stages within an urban context because these stages have been developed with urban communities as a focal point. Rural areas, it should be noted, also have to contend with similar factors, though.

Green, Gregory, and Mason (2009, p. 413) stress the importance of understanding context and its influence in social work practice targeting diverse population groups: "Understanding the context of practice is an essential component of social work practice as is providing service that respects diversity. These twin concepts are necessary to include in planning and delivering services across all levels of practice. However, while we might understand how the context impacts on service users (and such an understanding is a vital part of assessment processes), the context has greater and more far reaching impacts. For example, in rural practice research, there is evidence that the context strongly influences the choice of practice methods, the behavior of the professional as an individual and as a community member, and the management of complex ethical situations...[and] how changes in context impact on professional decision making and choices about intervention."

The context may have such influences when we consider it as it relates to people with disabilities. The United Nations recommends the use of the *International Classification of Functioning, Disability and Health* (World Health Organization, 2009) as a biopsychosocial approach to assessing disability from the individual level to the national level. Social workers have recommended its use by the profession as well (Barrow, 2006; Saleeby, 2011). Of special significance to social workers is that it promotes the concept of environmental factors as restricting participation by individuals in their communities and society. One of the major innovations in the *International Classification of Functioning, Disability and Health* is the presence of an environmental factor classification that makes it possible for the identification of environmental barriers and facilitators for both capacity and performance of actions and tasks in daily living. With this classification scheme, which can be used either on an individual basis or for population wide data collection, it may be possible to create instruments that assess environments in terms of their level of facilitation or barrier creation for different kinds and levels of disability. With this information in hand, it will then be more practical to develop and implement guidelines for universal design and other environmental regulations that extend the functioning levels of persons with disabilities across the range of life activities (World Health Organization, 2002, p. 8).

This approach can lead to social action based on a community wide asset assessment. For example, if one part of a community has accessible subway stations, but another does not, development of that asset throughout the community may be promoted through social action.

COMMUNITY CAPACITY ENHANCEMENT AND ASSETS

The concept of community capacity enhancement is the overarching perspective that guides asset assessments as conceptualized in this book. Beckley and colleagues (2008, p. 61) raise important questions as to what is meant by "capacity," with the responses to this question very closely tied to who is asking the question: "Community capacity can be grounded by asking this basic question: The capacity to do what? Such a question can be answered in a multitude of ways, and in part it depends upon who is asking the question. For instance, policy makers and external community analysts often operate from a macro level, where outcomes are described in broad overarching terms... By contrast, community residents may take a more micro approach and describe capacity in terms of shorter-term goals... Obviously, there is overlap... The point is that capacity outcomes may be legitimately defined somewhat narrowly, or quite broadly." Obviously, these questions bring an "academic" and "real life" perspective to any deliberation on community asset assessments and community capacity enhancement.

Jackson and colleagues (2003, pp. 340–341) further note: "Our review of the literature suggests that the search for conceptual clarity about what constitutes community capacity is an ongoing struggle, and illustrates the complexities and highly interrelated nature of the terms. The paucity of literature on models of community capacity and practical indicators is noteworthy." Clarity, and the specificity that follows, as a result, is an important goal or element of community capacity enhancement practice, including asset assessments.

Mayer (1994, p. 3), over 17 years ago, offered a simple, but significant, definition of community capacity that captures the potential and dynamic nature of this paradigm that is still very relevant today: "Community capacity is the combined influence of a community's commitment, resources, and skills which can be deployed to build on community strengths and address community problems." Labonte and Laverack (2001, p. 114), in turn, define community capacity as the "increase in a community group's abilities to define, assess, analyze and act on health (or any other) concerns to their members." The challenge, however, rests on how to conceptualize "community commitment," "resources," and "skills." We can also easily add "community" to this list.

There certainly are no shortages of opinions (scholarly and practical) on bringing these factors or dimensions to life (Jackson et al., 2003). Lempa, Goodman, Rice, and Becker (2008) characterize the literature on community capacity as generally addressing three interdependent dimensions or domains: (1) social protection of communities; (2) multilevels; and (3) improvement of health and social conditions. However, these authors go on to note that the approaches toward these ends are quite varied and in desperate need of greater specification, with great variability between capacity enhancement approaches in the literature. Nevertheless, the importance of identifying and supporting indigenous leadership generally has been identified as one of the critical elements of successful capacity development initiatives.

Chaskin and colleagues (2001) identify four characteristics that set the foundation for community capacity enhancement initiatives: (1) the community having an identity as a community; (2) a commitment on the part of residents to the betterment of the community; (3) the competence to solve community problems and issues; and (4) access to requisite resources. Each of these elements, in turn, must be conceptualized as existing on a continuum from less to more, in similar fashion to the concept of capital. An "either–or" proposition is not very practical or realistic.

Verity (2007), in an extensive and very well conceptualized review of the literature on community capacity building, concluded that, although there are differences in conceptual logic and emphasis between different versions of capacity enhancement, there is a "common bridge" between these approaches through their emphasis on community, institutions, linkages, transfer of resources, and the necessary knowledge, skills, and abilities to accomplish the goals of capacity building. Reimer (2006), based upon a study in rural Canada but also applicable to other urban centers, identifies four contextual elements that can limit or enhance community capacity by emphasizing the global economy influence, stability of the local economy, proximity to urban centers, and local institutional capacities.

Domains, or dimensions, have emerged as another way of categorizing community capacity or asset focused initiatives. Two efforts stand out in this area. Busch and Mutch (1998) conceptualize assets as falling into four domains, with each domain consisting of various levels of community capacity: (1) network partnerships; (2) knowledge transfer; (3) problem solving; and (4) infrastructure. Gibbon, Labonte, and Laverack (2002) identify nine domains, many of which parallel the forms of capital covered in Chapter 2, seeking to operationalize community capacity from assessment and action perspectives for the purposes of evaluating these forms of initiatives: (1) participation; (2) leadership; (3) organizational structures; (4) problem assessment; (5) resource mobilization; (6) "Asking why," or critical reflection; (7) link with others; (8) role of outside agents; and (9) program management. Another perspective on community capacity is advanced by Flaspohler, Duffy, Wandersman, Stillman, and Maras (2008). These authors developed a taxonomy that categorizes capacity along two dimensions: (1) level (individual, organizational, and community levels) and (2) type (general capacity and innovation specific capacity).

Finally, the Search Institute of Minneapolis, Minnesota, has developed an extensive following among youth serving organizations and professions based on its work with youth and community related assets. Also, books by Clary and Rhodes (2006), Lerner and Benson (2002), Moore and Lippman (2005), Nakkula, Foster, Mannes, and Lewis (2010), and VanderVen (2008) provide countless ways of identifying and utilizing youth and community assets in service to youth. The youth asset constructs (40 types that fall into external and internal assets) developed by the Search Institute have been found to offer great promise for future asset assessment surveys (Oman et al., 2002). Nakkula and colleagues (2010), for example, have shown the importance of conceptualizing assets broadly and bringing together multigenerations to create a stronger and more youth friendly community.

In essence, community capacity must never be viewed in a linear fashion; a cyclical or developmental perspective makes it easier to capture a community's state of well-being (Beckley et al., 2008). This consideration takes on even greater significance in situations in which the intervention that follows the assessment takes an excessive amount of time to implement and does not capitalize on the momentum created by the assessment. Assessments, be they asset focused or needs focused, create excitement and expectations of change that should not be wasted, particularly when addressing marginalized communities with great needs, assets, and hopes for a better future. Asset assessments have the potential of creating momentum and the corresponding high expectations that follow. If these expectations are dashed, it can be counterproductive to implementing a project. Furthermore, it can make the community cynical about future efforts to assess capacities (Beckley et al., 2008).

THE INITIAL GUIDING QUESTION

Morgan and Ziglio (2007, p. 20) note that the initial question posed in a community asset assessment reverberates throughout the entire process: "Learning how to ask what communities have to offer begins a process of building and developing local capacities out into the open, where they can work together to everyone's benefits." Developing a statement or questions that are locally determined and capture the meaning of what "community assets" or "capacity" mean often represents the initial step in an asset identification process. In fact, it is also necessary to get input as to how "community" is defined. A local definition of "community" may share universal elements with common definitions of community but will also bring unique elements (Smith-Morris, 2007). The days of assuming that everyone shares the same definition of "community" are long over, and that necessitates that local definitions be employed when doing community asset studies.

The use of visioning, or "future search," is one common method that helps an assessment steering committee start the process of creating a unifying statement. This approach can ask participants what they want their community to look like in the future. Nakkula and colleagues (2010), for example, describe how the development of a "listening" project assisted Orlando youth in developing priorities for a philanthropy initiative.

The Alameda County (California) Public Health Department (2007, p. 23) makes several suggestions about how to start such a process: (1) focus on a better future; (2) encourage hopes and dreams; (3) appeal to common values; (4) state positive results; (5) emphasize strengths and assets; (6) use words, pictures, or images; and (7) communicate enthusiasm and encourage excitement. Lachapelle, Emery, and Hays (2010) found that doing trainings through workshops set the stage for and facilitated the visioning experience and also resulted in the development of trust and working relationships as a result of participation.

Haines (2009, p. 44) identifies three important elements of this type of exercise: "The first component is inviting a broad spectrum of the community so that many opinions and perspectives are represented. The second component is preparing a process that is meaningful, effective, and efficient...This third component, which is closely related to the second one, involves choosing public participation techniques to accomplish a vision or multiple visions for a community." The elements identified by Haines (2009) are sufficiently flexible to take into account local circumstances that are sociocultural in nature.

For example, people with disabilities are sometimes the focus of needs assessments in communities. Research questions aim to find out what services are unavailable or are not optimal. From an assets perspective, the research questions would aim to determine what services are provided by people with disabilities to the community and what other assets they bring to the community. Although there is discrimination in the workforce, and so their employment may be less than the population of people without disabilities, they may, in fact, be employed. They may also be participating in the informal economy, in part because of exclusion from the formal economy. They may be involved with community service on advisory boards or in a variety of volunteer roles. Anderson (2009), for example, discusses contributions as leaders, volunteers, and staff that people with disabilities can bring to parks and recreational facilities; therefore, their participation in these should not be overlooked as assets in communities. Furthermore, organizations and individuals who promote such inclusion should be considered as community assets.

Community asset assessments are sufficiently flexible to take into account universal circumstances in all communities since all communities have subgroups that experience discrimination in the larger society, and possibly the local community, based on characteristics such as age, disability, sexual orientation, or immigrant status. Therefore, the asset assessment should consider seriously what will bring in a truly "broad spectrum of the community." For example, what organizations are likely to represent older adults; people with disabilities; lesbian, gay, bisexual, transgender, or intersex individuals; or new immigrants? What locations are physically accessible to elders and people with disabilities? How will outreach materials be welcoming in terms of their content? What methods of communication will be accessible to the broadest range of people in their languages and by their individual communication methods? Of course, these are areas that should be informed by people who may be affected.

STAGES PERSPECTIVE

A stage or developmental perspective on community asset assessment attempts to merge theory and practice in a manner that breaks down the process in a manageable way to increase its usefulness for practice. Breaking down a very lengthy process into clear steps, or stages, works both to prevent participants from becoming "overwhelmed" by the endeavor, and helps organize priorities and marshall resources. In addition, it introduces a time element for each stage that facilitates discussion of how ambitious the goals for each step are. Each stage should also be guided by relevant theory.

Domahidy's (2003, p. 75) comments on the power of theory serves as a guiding force on how theory can be presented in a manner that encourages praxis: "Theory is powerful because it organizes what professionals pay attention to and how they pay attention. It shapes beliefs that in turn shape action. Presented as orienting frames, however, theories are available to the user as consciously chosen alternative ways to approach understanding settings and developing strategies to address issues. This approach encourages praxis as disciplined reflection engaging theory to enrich practice." The practicality of a developmental perspective allows practitioners to see how theory is put into practice according to the goals of individual stages. This is descriptive rather than prescriptive in nature, allowing practitioners to modify theory according to local goals and circumstances.

A stages, or developmental, view of asset assessments puts into perspective the process in a manner that facilitates understanding and appreciating all of the major steps and decisions that must be made in order to fulfill the promise of this participatory research endeavor. Furthermore, a developmental perspective increases the likelihood that key decisions get made in an orderly manner with the present time in focus, without losing sight of the long term implications. Such a perspective also facilitates the creation of curricula to undertake training of participants and other key stakeholders in the process.

ROLE AND FUNCTION OF KEY PARTICIPANTS

An endeavor such as a community asset assessment requires multiple roles to be filled from within and outside of the community. For the purposes of discussion and illustration, only two roles (facilitator and steering community) will be addressed. Asset assessment necessitates countless activities and roles for it to be carried out in a manner that reflects a team effort. Just some of the roles and activities include securing space and supplies; being a media contact facilitator or organizational point person in answering inquires from the community, organizations, and government officials; and ensuring that assessment forms are available in multiple languages. Therefore, it is probably wise to conceptualize a community asset assessment as an iceberg, with only the tip that shows above the water being the assessment process and everything that goes into supporting these efforts being underwater.

Eisinger and Senturia (2001), however, based on a range of Seattle community development projects with active community participation, stress the importance of clearly defined decision making roles and procedures. Community asset assessments are certainly no exception.

Facilitator Role

Unfortunately, the scholarly literature on community asset assessment has paid minimal attention to the roles of facilitator or cofacilitator in carrying out this undertaking. For example, the facilitator's role in undertaking a community asset map is of critical importance in the entire process (Chambers, 2006, p. 2): "The medium and means of mapping, whether ground, paper or GIS and the style and mode of facilitation, influence who takes part, the nature of outcomes and power relationships. Much depends on the behavior and attitudes of facilitators who control the process."

Community participation in community asset assessments must be carefully examined to ensure that it generates a sense of a fair process and that every effort is made to maximize the capital participants bring to this endeavor. This necessitates careful assessment of participant abilities and expectations and that every effort be made to weigh these factors in the assignment of roles in the assessment process. It would be unfair and unwise not to take into account the wishes and abilities of participants. It is also important to be inclusive and open to a diversity of possible participants by choice of meeting times and places that are convenient and accessible.

It is important to emphasize that the training requirements for community participants are not to make them "researchers," or even "junior researchers," but to provide them with the necessary foundation (knowledge and skills) to be contributing members of the assessment team (Cashman et al., 2008). They, it needs to be reemphasized, bring knowledge and skills about their community (informal and self knowledge) that outside researchers do not possess and are not expected to have. Rather, like any team, not every member brings the same competencies. There is a distinction between academics and community residents that is real. However, the strengths that each brings to the project complement each other's, and this has a synergistic effect on a community asset assessment.

It is strongly advised that the facilitator role be filled by a community resident with wide appeal and respect as a means of increasing the ownership of the process and to help ensure that the community feels comfortable in participating in the assessment. More commonly, there are cofacilitators in these types of initiatives, though with the cofacilitator being a professionally educated provider, and hopefully of the same ethnic/racial background as the community undertaking the assessment. It is not unusual, however, to find that community resident facilitators are also providers of human services in the community.

Steering Committee

Any community wishing to undertake an asset assessment should first start by establishing a steering committee, or task force, that will play an active decision making role throughout the assessment process (Johnson et al., 2009). The composition of this committee must take into account local circumstances and actively include community stakeholders. It is possible to conceptualize a steering committee as a coalition of interested organizations and community stakeholders who are residents.

Newman and colleagues (2011, p. 3) provide advice on composing a community advisory board (CAB) or committee, in this instance related to community based participatory research, but also applicable to community asset assessments: "To select appropriate board members, specific inclusion criteria should be established that reflect the goals of the research and the intended functions and purpose of the CAB. Brainstorming to identify potential members and determine the best recruitment and selection strategies is an iterative process requiring input from all members of the research team. The process requires consideration of types of expertise and resources needed and who can bring that expertise to the partnership. The intended outcomes of the study facilitate determining what type of person (e.g., service provider, consumer, community leader) or agency is represented on the CAB. Identification of people or agencies with specific expertise in the topic of interest is necessary to create a knowledgeable CAB and to help position the research project favorably in the community. New partnerships are often encouraged to start small and to involve a few community-based organizations that are highly regarded by community members."

The definition of a community stakeholder, for the purposes of a community asset assessment, goes beyond the conventional definition of someone with a decision making position within the community, which generally refers to an elected official or a formal provider of services. A stakeholder is defined as a resident who takes ownership in creating or sustaining a community's well-being (Chaskin et al., 2001). Defining a community stakeholder beyond conventional views of people who hold positions of power and authority allows committee membership to be more inclusive rather than exclusive.

Emery and Flora (2006, p. 31), too, stress the importance of community asset assessments being inclusive rather than exclusive in membership: "A leadership training program alone would have limited impact on human and social capital. A leadership development program designed to include youth and people from various locations within the community using local expertise impacts cultural capital as people socially reconstructed the structure of leadership. Young persons became leaders, local people, experts, and community leaders, collaborators as new relationships were developed outside the previous vision of possible relationships."

Another perspective on membership is to make every effort to enlist participants who bring four key types of legitimacy or perspective to an assessment
(Rein, 1977): (1) expertise (experiential and educational); (2) institutional (formal and informal); (3) ethical (key community members with a high degree of
respect within the community being assessed); and (4) consumer (community
representation that takes into account its composition regarding ethnicity/race
and key undervalued groups such as those who have a disability, are undocumented immigrants, or who are lesbian, gay, bisexual, transgender, or intersex.

Few individuals can be expected to bring all four types of legitimacy. However,
all four types must be present on a steering committee to help ensure that the
results are accepted within and outside of the community. It is best to conceptualize this steering committee as an orchestra with careful attention to making
sure that all of the necessary instruments are well represented. Asset assessment
steering committees are composed based on strategic considerations rather than
relying upon only those who step forward on their own to volunteer.

Steering committees can, however, have subcommittees that can be more
accommodating of additional volunteers with varying interests, capabilities, and
time considerations, allowing for tasks to be performed as decided by the composition of the group. Nevertheless, the steering committee itself becomes the
most visible symbol of a community assessment project for the internal as well as
the external community. Consequently, the time and effort devoted to enlisting
participation are time and effort well invested.

The actual size of a community asset assessment steering committee is
dependent upon the complexity of the assessment being planned. A complex
project will necessitate that each legitimacy category has four or five members.
A more focused, or simple, assessment may be undertaken with a single four-
to six member committee. Training and orientation will be needed for both
focused as well as comprehensive initiatives. However, comprehensive assessments require that more effort be devoted to "team building" and more time be
set aside for meetings.

Finally, the creation of a steering committee would benefit from the establishment of a set of principles similar to those established by the Morehouse School of
Medicine Research Center that helped guide community research in low income,
predominantly African American communities (Blumenthal, 2006). The following
10 principles are presented only as a guide to help communities develop their own
set of principles. Some of the following Morehouse principles share much in common with the principles presented in Chapter 3 (Blumenthal, 2006, pp. 3–5):

1. Policies and programs should be based on mutual respect and justice for
   all people, free from any form of discrimination or bias.
2. All people have a right to political, economic, cultural, and environmental self-determination.
3. The community has the right to participate as an equal partner at every
   level of decision making, including needs assessment, planning, implementation, enforcement, and evaluation.

4. Principles of individual and community informed consent should be strictly enforced.

5. The community repudiates the targeting of people of color and lower socioeconomic status for the purpose of testing reproductive and medical procedures and vaccinations.

6. Present and future generations should be provided an education that emphasizes social and environmental issues, based on our experience and an appreciation of our diverse cultural perspectives.

7. Research processes and outcomes should benefit the community. Community members should be hired and trained whenever possible and appropriate, and the research should help build and enhance community assets.

8. Community members should be part of the analysis and interpretation of data and should have input into how the results are distributed. This does not imply censorship of data or of publication, but rather the opportunity to make clear the community's views about the interpretation prior to final publication.

9. Productive partnerships between researchers and community members should be encouraged to last beyond the life of the project. This will make it more likely that research findings will be incorporated into ongoing community programs and therefore provide the greatest benefit to the community from research.

10. Community members should be empowered to initiate their own research projects that address needs they identify themselves.

A number of scholars recommend the establishment of some form of committee to play an active role in carrying out research. Bluementhal (2006), based upon the Morehouse experience, presents a compelling case for the establishment of a community coalition board, or what we call a steering committee, that can establish a set of parameters of values particular to a community and, thus, facilitate community based research. Brown (2006) also proposes the use of a citizen panel or advisory committee to help in addressing complex community issues and initiatives. Hohenemser and Marshall (2002), in turn, advocate the use of a youth advisory committee as a means of capturing youth voices in research and programmatic undertakings that are youth focused. Finally, Garrettson and colleagues (2010) describe the important role a community advisory committee played in designing and implementing a qualitative focused methodology to uncover community assets. The findings were incorporated into a medical school's curriculum and informed research endeavors.

An asset steering committee, which is the term we prefer because members have decision making powers rather than being purely advisory, can fulfill the necessary functions to carry out an asset assessment. It certainly is fitting to end this chapter with the Morehouse guiding principles. A community asset assessment steering committee will certainly benefit from the development of operating principles to help it navigate difficult decisions associated with community based participatory research. Community social workers will also benefit by having clear expectations of what constitutes research or asset assessment from all participating parties.

CONCLUSIONS

Asset assessments are both an instrument for uncovering indigenous resources within marginalized communities and a vehicle for bringing about social change by helping communities better identify and mobilize their indigenous resources and enhance their capacities in the process. Assessments must actively seek to uncover cultural resources, and this is particularly important when they are undertaken in culturally diverse urban communities because of their high concentrations of people of color.

Paradigms, models, and frameworks seek to simplify phenomena in order to make them more accessible to practitioners and scholars (Beckley et al., 2008). Unfortunately, rarely is the community mentioned as an audience for paradigms, models, or frameworks. Nevertheless, we should not underestimate a community's ability to grasp complex phenomena, if communicated in a manner that makes this information accessible, and there is genuine interest in its responses.

As this chapter illustrates, putting together an asset assessment team and conducting such a study involve numerous decisions and compromises along the way and will engender tensions between differing parties within and outside of the community. Nevertheless, this does not mean that a systematic plan cannot be developed to minimize detours during the journey. Also, local circumstances have a tremendous amount of influence on how assets are conceptualized.

6

Community Asset
Assessment Methods

"Assessment is an integral part of the planning process, as it allows an organization to prepare for implementation. It can also be useful after implementation of the intervention has begun to revisit areas that need modification, reassess agency capacity, and reexamine overall goodness of fit between the target community and agency…"

(GANDELMAN ET AL., *2006, p. 35*)

INTRODUCTION

The above quote by Gandelman and colleagues (2006) stresses the role of assessment throughout the planning and implementation process. This chapter provides the reader with several of the most common methods and, we believe, most useful methods available for undertaking asset assessments as well as emerging methods that offer great potential for use in marginalized urban communities. The field of community asset assessments is expanding rapidly and, in the process, is introducing new or modified versions of commonly used methods. The more common methods, incidentally, are also generally prevalent in needs assessments and will not be new to the well initiated community social worker.

Community social work practitioners and scholars know that, in all likelihood, the gathering of data on community assets, particularly in marginalized communities, will necessitate reliance on generating primary data rather than reliance on existing data sources (Goodman et al., 1998; Grantmakers in Health, 2006). Most data sources (government and nongovernment) are deficit oriented. Generating data offers distinct advantages over using existing data because it allows communities to develop questions that are pertinent to their circumstances, rather than to get answers to questions that are of interest to government and other sources external to the community that may not share the same interests or concerns. However, generating new data is expensive and labor intensive.

There are several methods, technologies, and data sources that lend themselves to asset assessments (Delgado, 2011). As noted, many of these methods have been used for needs assessments but, with the necessary modifications, can also be used in community asset assessments. These include community forums, community gathering event dialogues, focus groups, key informant interviews, ethnographic observations, surveys (open ended), journals, the Delphi Technique, photovoice, expert panel, oral history, CommunityLine, and use of geospacial analysis technology; these generally tend to be qualitative methods because they provide community residents with opportunities to have their voices heard and to actively participate primarily in the gathering of information related to their lives and surroundings, but not all are.

Geospatial analysis technology is part of cartography and mapping, which will be discussed in its own chapter (Chapter 7). The technology, however, will be discussed here because social workers may not be familiar with it because it is relatively new. We think that cartography or mapping of various types has sufficient potential for bringing in the perspectives of a community in such a productive and unique way that its rationales and benefits deserve special attention in their own chapter that goes beyond the description of geospatial analysis technology here.

The goals of an asset assessment project will shape research approaches and methods, rather than the other way around. Qualitative and quantitative methods will be addressed in detail in the hopes of helping the reader implement them in practice. The methods outlined in this chapter can be used in a variety of combinations to take into account goals, time periods, costs, and the history of asset assessments within a community. Each of the methods, in turn, will be critiqued for its advantages and disadvantages in community asset assessment, since no method is "perfect," with local circumstances wielding great influence over the selection of the most appropriate methods.

METHODS, TECHNOLOGIES, AND DATA SOURCES FOR COMMUNITY ASSET ASSESSMENTS

Communities, particularly those that are highly diverse, are nonlinear and, as a result, are unpredictable or "dynamic." Schensul's (2009, p. 243) observations, although based on the prevention field, are easily applicable to community asset assessment in that "evidence based practices in prevention science which may have been tried and shown to be effective in one location under one set of historical and contextual conditions cannot be assumed to be effective in another."

Contextualization is a cornerstone of social work practice and community social work practice, and assessment is certainly no exception. Success in one community with a particular approach toward an asset assessment may not be translated to another without significant modifications, even when the communities' sociodemographic factors share many similarities. The reader is advised that, in reviewing the following methods, local circumstances must ultimately dictate the selection of the most applicable methods, regardless of the prefer-ences of the staff involved in an asset assessment project.

Delgado (2000, p. 42) notes that "no one method or approach to community asset assessments can do justice to the richness and complexity of communi-ties. Consequently, it is essential to conceptualize the assessment process as a multi-method with a clear, if not exclusive, tendency to use methods that rely on interactive and personal contacts, and are shaped by local social, political, and economic circumstances." The greater the reliance on multiple methods, the higher the likelihood of reaching all sectors of a community in a manner that is culturally competent.

Atkinson and Willis' (2005, p. 12) recommendations, although referring to evaluation of community capacity building projects, are also equally applica-ble to asset assessments: "Face to face interaction with project participants is a particularly useful method for gaining an in-depth understanding of commu-nity relationships and dynamics—these issues are much less likely to be appar-ent through survey methods or through simply observing community groups or activities. In other words, for whoever is doing evaluation it is important to spend time in the community and become involved." The attractiveness and value of personal contact will not surprise the reader since this form of interaction has a long tradition in social work.

Although community asset assessments can be conducted through the use of both qualitative and quantitative methods, they generally favor the use of qualitative methods for several major reasons (Onwuegbuzie & Leech, 2006). Qualitative research lends itself to capturing the perspectives or insights of peo-ple or groups that have historically been marginalized or undervalued in this society. Its also involves active participation by community members and organ-izations that leads to ownership of the findings and actions that result.

Iwasaki, Bartlett, MacKay, Mactavish, and Ristock (2006) studied the personal narratives and life stories of "nondominant voices" of Aboriginal persons liv-ing with diabetes, with disabilities, and who are gay and lesbian. This facilitated the development of an interpretative map that highlighted stressors but, just as importantly, coping mechanisms (assets), and thereby underscored the need for this form of qualitative data being an important part of any community study. Heath and colleagues (2009) see much value in using visual methods as a means of facilitating youth producing images to engage youth in research. The authors contend that research too often favors methods such as one to one interviewing, which are more adult friendly.

Long histories of being marginalized by outsiders have resulted in a distorted picture of particular communities in this society. Communities such as Chicago's South Side, New York City's South Bronx and Harlem, Boston's Roxbury, and Los Angeles' South Central and East Los Angeles, for example, all elicit images of downtrodden and "crime infested" communities. In essence, these communities are viewed as devoid of assets.

The voices of residents in these "types" of communities are rarely sought out by researchers and scholars to paint a balanced picture of their lives. Yet, residents are the best experts on their own lives and circumstances (Corburn, 2005, 2009). This form of knowledge is referred to by a variety of terms depending upon the field of practice (self-knowledge, local knowledge, community knowledge, and informal knowledge). Tapping this knowledge is best done through qualitative methods (Eaton, 2010).

Israel and colleagues (2006) stress the value of utilizing a multimethod (qualitative and quantitative) and multidisciplinary community based participatory research as a means of ensuring research instruments and methodology that are inclusive rather than exclusive and are more reflective of the community that subsequent interventions seek to reach. Montoya and Kent (2011) stress the importance of expertise being mutually constructed and the role that qualitative research can play in achieving this goal.

Qualitative methods may set the stage for quantitative methods. Qualitative data take on greater significance in cases in which there is limited information on communities participating in the research process. This is particularly the case in communities of color and, more specifically, groups that are newcomers to this country or are highly marginalized, with relatively little known about them. This information, in turn, helps to shape the questions that can be asked in a quantitative study.

A social justice stance, as noted in Chapter 3, reinforces for social work the importance of qualitative methods playing critical roles in community asset assessments (Mertens & Ginsburg, 2008, p. 484): "Given the commitment expressed by the social work community towards the furtherance of social justice as reflected not only in their ethical codes, but also in their historical legacy and current statements of purpose, the question of how research can contribute to the enhancement of human rights and social change is particularly relevant for the ethical conduct of qualitative social work research. Based on literature from ethics and social work research ... the intersection of advocacy and research is examined from a transformative stance, revealing that strict adherence to the codes and/or regulations as defined by governments, professional associations, and ethics boards are fraught with tensions with regard to such issues as informed consent, confidentiality, and beneficence. In order to investigate topics that are controversial (e.g., pedophilia, drug use) and involve participants who may be stigmatized, the researcher's role may need to be reframed as a member of a team, with differential responsibilities assumed by each team member...[Further, there are] potential ethical alternatives in which the researcher can partner with communities for collection, analysis, and interpretation of data."

Concepts such as experiential expertise, self knowledge, local knowledge, indigenous knowledge, contextual intelligence, community knowledge, and informal knowledge, as already noted, are frequently used in the literature to capture community views (Corburn, 2005, 2009). Community asset assessments, like other forms of community based participatory approaches, seek to uncover knowledge of relevance to undervalued groups in society, and to do so in a manner that is as nonintrusive as possible and that respects the cultural values and beliefs of the community being assessed.

This information is highly contextualized, necessitating active local involvement in making this knowledge known to those outside of the community (Corburn, 2005). Torre and Fine (2007, p. 408), as cited in Cahill, Sultan, and Pain (2007), address the potential of research to achieve this critical goal when they say: "The understanding that people—especially those who have experienced historic oppression—hold deep knowledge about their lives and experiences, should help shape the questions, frame the interpretations [of research]." Thus, the important role of helping to shape the nature and wording of questions is one that is best done by the ultimate beneficiaries of the research, since they have in-depth knowledge of their lives and circumstances.

There is a pressing need to narrow the existing knowledge gap between and among academics, professional providers, and community (El Ansari, 2005; El Ansari, Phillips, & Zwi, 2002). The tension between "scientific rigor" and "community participation" in knowledge creation historically has been identified as being incompatible (Allison & Rootman, 1996). Qualitative methods that value and seek to capture community voices can narrow, and even eliminate, this gap.

Quantitative methods often rely upon expressed data, namely, data derived from agency or government sources. These data, as a result, reflect the dominant society's bias toward deficits or pathology related information. Luke (2005, p. 185), however, argues for a different point of view on biases when examining quantitative methods used in gathering information that captures community context: "[A] survey of empirical articles published in the *American Journal of Community Psychology* shows that community scientists utilize a narrow range of statistical tools that are not well suited to assess contextual data. Multilevel modeling, geographic information systems (GIS), social network analysis, and cluster analysis are recommended as useful tools to address contextual questions in community science." Ennis and West (2010), for example, see social network analysis as a valuable tool in determining the success of asset informed community development.

Rotary International (2008) developed a brief, but informative, document outlining a variety of methods for conducting community asset assessments, many of which are covered in this section (such as surveys, asset inventory, community mapping, daily activities schedule, seasonal calendar, community café, focus groups, and panel discussion). In addition, Rotary International (2008) has provided a detailed description of how to conduct these methods and the materials, time, and other considerations needed to facilitate an assessment, which the reader may find useful.

Selection of methods for conducting an asset assessment must take into consideration the following nine factors: (1) histories of community undertaking an asset assessment; (2) familiarity of assessment team members with qualitative and quantitative research methods; (3) time that can be devoted to the endeavor; (4) season (winter, spring, summer, fall); (5) funding; (6) time period between the issuing of findings and the initiation of an intervention; (7) level of trust within the community being assessed; (8) capabilities of the sponsoring organization; and (9) practitioner preference and competence with particular research methods. Each of these factors can wield considerable influence on the outcome of an assessment. Considering more than one, however, has a substantial impact on the process of assessment by tapping multiple perspectives.

COMMUNITY ASSET ASSESSMENT METHODS

Community Forums

Community forums are sometimes referred to as "listening sessions" and often represent the democratic ideal in which everyone has a voice and a right to exercise this privilege. Witkin and Altschuld (1995, p. 161) define community forums by comparing this method to a New England town meeting "in which a community is called together to discuss a pressing issue…The community forum (also sometimes called a public hearing or community speak up) is used to gather stakeholder concerns or perceptions of need areas, opinions about quality or delivery of services, information on causes of present need, and [to facilitate] exploration of community values." Although this definition relates mostly to needs, it can easily be used to focus on community assets.

Community forums cover many different types of gatherings that take into account various goals (Parker et al., 2006). Typically, a community forum brings together a large portion of the community to present findings and get reactions and suggestions for interventions based upon how the community interprets the findings. Although these are called "community forums," they may also go under different names depending upon local circumstances and traditions. Delgado (1998b, p. 330) comments on the usefulness of this method: "Community forums can also serve to assist researchers in the beginning stages of quantitative research designs. This method can assist researchers in refining concepts, narrowing open ended questions into closed ended response categories, and identifying potential barriers to implementing large scale field-based surveys." These types of surveys can be used to gather data on a broader scale to augment data gathered using qualitative methods.

There is no set format for a community forum. However, it typically consists of four stages or steps:

1. Introduction of the panelists gathering information, including the forum facilitator, which typically takes about 10 to fifteen minutes;
2. Sharing of the forum's agenda with the audience, which takes approximately 5 to 10 minutes;
3. Testimonies, which are the bulk of the time used, with 60 to 75 minutes usually being allotted to this step; and
4. Sharing of the themes uncovered during the forum with the audience and prioritizing the next steps, which takes approximately 15 to 20 minutes.

These time periods, of course, are estimates and will depend upon how concise and detailed the testimonies are and the number of testimonies made. Time also may vary if participants are asked to respond to visual material, such as a map, for example.

Like all methods, there are limitations inherent in community forums, and it is important to note several of the more prominent types:

1. Respondents must have a cultural background that has exposed them to this type of participation. The experiences of the senior author in conducting community forums in Latino communities has shown that Latinos coming from totalitarian regimes (dictatorships) generally eschew participation. Group gatherings in these countries have resulted in revolutions and repressive responses on the part of government.
2. It takes a very self confident community resident to get up before a large group and share his or her thoughts and experiences with community assets.
3. Community forums tend to attract those who are very articulate, organized, and have a personal stake in the outcomes of the forums, thus skewing the tenor and outcome of the forums.
4. Forum facilitators must have excellent group skills because of the nature and potential of disruptions.
5. The unit of analysis is the group, and if the group is highly diverse, it is impossible to draw any generalized conclusions from the testimonies.

These limitations, or considerations, are not to be taken lightly because of the potentially large number of participants who may be involved in a community forum. These large numbers, however, can make the information gathering in these forums exciting and generate good "word of mouth" about the effort. However, these same large numbers can also magnify the consequences of a poorly planned forum.

Sarkissian and colleagues (2009) note that community forums may be perceived as uninviting because of their formality. Youth may find the waiting to go to a microphone off putting and adult centered. They advocate for the use of speakouts, which are less formal than a forum, allow for flexibility of movement between booths and tables focused on specific aspects of community, and have much in common with aspects of community café gatherings (Chapter 8) for dissemination of findings.

However, community forums, like other large public gatherings, do not lend themselves to the participation of residents who are undocumented because of fear of deportation. In addition, communities with large numbers of undocumented residents with origins in countries with dictatorships may have negative associations with large crowd gatherings. These gatherings can elicit images of popular uprisings and harsh consequences from governmental authorities.

Nevertheless, community forums bring tremendous benefits. For example, they lend themselves to television coverage by local stations or cable programs.

The presence of the media not only lends credibility to an event but can also serve as a way of disseminating the results beyond those in attendance. A videotape can serve as a future reference point, too, on the findings and recommendations and can be used in training future leaders on how to conduct a forum. These benefits come at no financial cost to the organization sponsoring the forum, too.

Community Gathering Event Dialogues

Born's (2008) book entitled *Community Conversations* provides a detailed description and practical techniques for fostering community dialogues or discussions that help uncover assets, dreams, and connectedness. Community conversations (Born, 2008, p. 4) provide opportunities for information on assets to surface in a natural or unforced manner: "When a community begins to think and work comprehensively, it naturally attempts to use all of its assets. Assets can take different forms and can come from surprising places .... But most often it is not the organizations but the people who lead them, that represent the true, untapped assets."

These community dialogues have all of the elements typically found in a community forum. However, unlike community forums, these events have as a primary purpose a set of goals other than information gathering. Festivals, health fairs, and sporting competitions, for example, have entertainment and delivery of health and social services as primary goals but also present opportunities for engagement in conversations with participants.

Community events are often viewed as ideal times and places for engaging in dialogues and reaching undervalued groups in a manner that is nonstigmatizing and at a time when they are most receptive to outreach efforts. These gatherings often occur with advance notice, are well publicized, and, in some cases, can attract a wide range of social service providers engaged in health education and prevention. Consequently, efforts to identify community assets can be facilitated at a low cost.

However, it is important that these events capture a wide sector of the community or, if a group specific event, that findings not be generalized to the entire community. A women's health fair would provide important asset questions that are gender specific and cannot be generalized to men, for example. Youth sporting events invariably attract large numbers of youth with similar interests or whose attendance is a form of support for friends or relatives who are competing. If an event lacks physical accessibility and effective communication, that information obtained cannot be generalized to people with disabilities of any age.

Focus Groups

The popularity of focus groups as a qualitative tool is undeniable, as evidenced by its extensive use in assessments of various kinds and the availability of detailed books to help practitioners to use this method (Goebert & Rosenthal, 2001; Krueger & Casey, 2009; Liamputtong, 2011; Stewart, Shamdasani, & Rook, 2006). It is arguably the most popular of all qualitative methods. Unfortunately, it is also one of the most misunderstood and abused qualitative methods (Barbour, 2005; Langer, 2005). Consequently, practitioners using this qualitative method for uncovering community capital must do so with the greatest of caution and profound sense of the misinformation that can be found.

Green (2009, p. 157) is a proponent of using focus groups as a means of identifying community assets but notes that this method is not without limitations: "Focus groups have the advantage of being inexpensive and can be conducted more quickly than surveys. They can also provide more in-depth information on why people feel the way they do on various issues. On the other hand, focus groups do not give most residents an opportunity to participate in the process, and the findings may not be very representative of the larger population." Although Green's assessment of focus groups is largely accurate, it is not necessarily a "cheap" way of tapping community assets because the unit of analysis is the particular group, and so every effort must be made to get participants who share key characteristics, such as gender and socioeconomic class. This means putting extra attention and resources into recruitment.

Clark and colleagues (2003), for example, found focus groups to be a highly effective method to identify community assets in highly diverse communities. Aronson and colleagues (2007b), too, found that focus groups were an excellent vehicle for uncovering aspects of communities that normally would go unnoticed. Nevertheless, it is important to keep in mind that the unit of analysis is the group. The moment the group consists of participants with multiple demographic variables such as age, ethnicity, and length of residence in the community, generalizations are impossible to make. Doing so can certainly lead to misrepresentations.

Focus group efforts are similar to an iceberg. The portion of the iceberg that shows is represented by the actual group, and much effort goes into composing the group to help ensure that it represents a particular segment of the community. In essence, it has limited appeal for generalizations across communities. This aspect of focus groups is not as attractive as the actual conducting of the group session. Nevertheless, it represents one of the most critical elements to consider regarding this method.

The ideal number of participants is open to interpretation and is very much dependent upon the facilitator's skills. However, a number of eight stands out as ideal. The length of the meeting should be around 90 minutes, long enough to allow lengthy discussions but not too long that participants can get anxious. How many questions should be asked of participants? The answer is probably five or six, to allow in-depth probing of responses. This limited number is important because community asset related questions are often very new to group members and will necessitate very serious thinking about the responses. It is usual to have community residents asked problem related or deficit related questions. Thus, it is easier for them to think about community needs and problems rather than community assets. This challenge may also require asset related questions to be posed in a variety of ways.

Key Informant Interviews

McKnight's (cited in Minkler, 1999, p. 14) conclusion, "Institutions learn from studies, communities learn from stories," brings to mind the saying of the Irish folk singer Frank Harte (quoted in Moloney, 2005): "Those in power write the history, while those who suffer write the songs." Valuable "data" are in the eyes of the beholder, and communities definitely have their perspective on what constitutes data or useful information, which often does not get the attention it deserves. Stories, art, and examples of good deeds done in the community need to be shared and validated by the broader community. Obtaining these perspectives necessitates the use of a qualitative method that allows, and even encourages, probing and in-depth dialogue.

Not all qualitative methods lend themselves to this level of engagement and discovery, though. Focus groups and community forums, for example, are qualitative methods. However, neither is conducive to a high level of in-depth probing because of the number of participants and limited time available. Key informant interviews, on the other hand, do lend themselves to capturing these stories, artists' work, and events. This method also lends itself very well to involving residents who are undocumented since they can answer the questions in a nonpublic venue.

Key informant interviews provide community asset assessments with a method that is sufficiently flexible to be used in a wide range of community settings, such as homes, parks, and other places in which residents feel comfortable, and facilitate probing into previously uncharted areas (Aronson et al., 2007b). This method, when conducted well, flows like a very good conversation between two individuals, and its flexibility allows for a range in time devoted to answering questions. For the quintessential example of interviewing, see any of the works of Studs Turkel, such as "Division Street: America" (1993) and "Hard Times: An Oral History of the Great Depression" (2000).

The Access Project (1999, p. 2) provides a clear rationale for the use of key informants: "The key informant interview has a very specific purpose. It involves identifying different members of your community who are especially knowledgeable about a topic (who we call 'key informants') ... The interviews are usually conducted face to face ... The length of the interviews can vary, and will depend on the number of questions you decide to ask." Question construction and sequencing necessitate serious thought and consideration as to how best to build upon answers, particularly when they are community asset related. Mertzel and colleagues (2008) provide a detailed description of the use of key informants in Harlem, New York City, and the richness of data that they uncovered regarding community resources and community identity that served as a basis for a tobacco control initiative.

One of the concerns about using key informants is that a single, general, or only implicit criterion such as "community resident" may be used for their selection. Consequently, it is recommended that the community asset assessment steering committee establish clear criteria as to who qualifies to be a key informant. Useful criteria include length of residence in the community and position in the community, such as resident, formal provider, or residents who are also employed in the community. Furthermore, interviewers should have a clear understanding of the type of information being gathered on assets from each type of key informant.

These criteria serve to focus time and energy as well as seek to minimize different perspectives on what constitutes a community asset due to differing qualifications and backgrounds of key informants. Outreach workers, for example, bring a different perspective on community assets when compared to agency directors, who may have an overall appreciation but cannot provide important details. Readers interested in a greater depth of description should consult the Access Project (1999), which, over a decade ago, published what is probably the most detailed guide for undertaking key informant interviews in community asset assessments. This guide outlines for the practitioner how to structure, conduct, and interpret findings from this method.

Ethnographic Observations

Ethnography is certainly not foreign to social workers. It is probably best defined as a qualitative research method with a central goal of providing a detailed, contextualized, and nuanced description of everyday life (Hoey, 2008). Ethnographic research as a method is well established in the social sciences and in the helping professions, and particularly in social work practice that is community centered. This method has great appeal to those researchers and practitioners with a keen interest in assessing communities. Ethnographic immersion facilitates the creation of a more comprehensive picture of a community's capital, and, as a result, it is recommended as part of a broader methodological approach toward developing greater awareness of a community's informal structure and values (Aronson et al., 2007b; Foth & Adkinsor, 2005). Not surprisingly, development of an in-depth understanding of an urban neighborhood's assets often requires that careful ethnographic observations be undertaken to contextualize findings from other methods. Furthermore, ethnographic research requires a sufficient amount of time to be set aside to ensure that it gets carried out in a respectful and informed manner, in order to fulfill its potential (Jeffrey & Troman, 2003).

Ethnographic research has evolved over time to incorporate a diverse set of ways of gathering data that are qualitative based (Handwerker, 2006; Seymour, 2007). Kusenbach (2003, p. 455) advocates for the use of the "go-along" interview conducted in informal outdoor places as a complementary method to traditional ethnographic approaches using participant observations and interviewing: "I argue that by exposing the complex and subtle meanings of place in everyday experience and practices, the go-along method brings greater phenomenologi-cal sensibility to ethnography." Ethnographic research facilitates the capture of information that may be overlooked in more conventional approaches and does so with an attempt to minimize disruption in daily activities of the community.

There certainly are a number of perspectives related to structuring and focus-ing the ethnographic method. Hall, Lashua, and Coffey (2008), for example, bring a dimension to ethnographic research that complements that of Kusenbach (2003) by emphasizing the role of sound in everyday life, and how it influences community interactions and the use of urban spaces. Urban sounds are definitely different from rural sounds. The "loud" sounds of urban life are not necessarily viewed as negative, by the way, but bring a perspective to an assessment that may emphasize auditory representations.

Ross and colleagues (2009), in turn, advocate for the productiveness of "guided walks" and "car journeys" as two methods that help ground a researcher into a community. These two, by the way, are not mutually exclusive of each other, with each providing a unique vantage point. Scott (2007) describes the use of walking tours of an Atlanta community, and involvement of key community institutions such as houses of worship, in an effort to identify community assets for creating and reinforcing bonding and bridging social capital. Kinloch (2007) illustrates this method through the use of mapping, photography, and video interviews by Harlem, New York City, youth.

Taking public transportation such as buses, too, adds a different dimension that often gets overlooked. Passenger interactions among themselves and also involving bus drivers, for example, help provide insights into social capital that exist only in transit situations. The emergence of visual or virtual networked field sites has started to find a place in ethnographic research incorporating physi-cal, virtual, and imagined spaces, bringing an added dimension to conventional thinking about this form of community research (Burrell, 2009).

There is no population group that cannot benefit from an ethnographic study of its assets. Eloff and De Wet (2007), for example, report on the value of an eth-nographic study focused on discovering community assets for enhancing pre-school learning. This ethnographic research utilized a variety of methods, such as observations, field notes, interviews, photographs, and artifacts. Findings identified cultural, human, intangible, social, and economic capital that could be mobilized in a preschool initiative. McElroy, Davis, Hunt, Dadul, Stanba, and Larson (2011) studied persons with disabilities in Ladakh, India, using inter-views and participant observation techniques to identify the strengths and needs of this population group and its family and community leaders.

Surveys (Open Ended)

Surveys are certainly very popular in identifying and documenting community assets (Green, 2009). They provide insight into how a broader sector of a com-munity thinks about a particular topic such as assets. The fundamental decision of whether the survey will consist of open ended, closed ended, or a combination of questions will be a deciding factor in the cost and time demands for use of this method. The reader will see strong parallels between need and asset focused surveys, and many of the limitations found in the former can also be found in the latter. However, those experienced with conducting asset assessments surely will attest to how difficult it is to get community residents to think about community assets when they are used to thinking about their communities from a deficit perspective.

It is generally recommended that asset surveys rely upon open ended questions and that it is necessary to be creative in how to ask questions about community assets. The same question may have to be asked several different ways in order to capture this information. Thus, we have found that asset surveys generally take three times as much time to conduct as the typical needs focused survey because they necessitate that respondents think about their communities in a dramatically different way.

There are limitations related to surveys that get accentuated only when the information they are trying to uncover is arduous to retrieve. Surveys based upon representative samples are expensive. Interviewers need to be screened and trained carefully and supported, and this process takes on even greater significance when the interviewers are new to this method and/or are indigenous to the community being assessed.

Surveys generally consist of information on multiple categories, with each consisting of numerous questions. The advantage of a survey method, whether need or asset focused, is also its limitation. Surveys lend themselves to the gathering of a broad perspective. However, the depth of information is compromised for breadth. Finally, though, the training and support provided in these instances can be quite empowering and capacity enhancing, and when the study is completed, the interviewers stay in the community and enhance the human capital of the community.

Journals

An asset based assessment not only necessitates the use of a different language that is not pathology driven, it also necessitates the quest for new methods that effectively free up asset team members to tap cultural assets and other considerations generally overlooked by those external to the community (Aronson et al., 2007b). The use of journals is one such culturally bound method, either written or audio recorded. Journals can be called by various names and sometimes have been referred to as events or activity logs (Butterfoss, 2006).

One suggestion for helping to capture the nuances, such as practice and ethical dilemmas associated with asset assessments, is to encourage the use of journals by the steering committee and team members, to help capture the joys, trials, and tribulations associated with conducting this form of community centered research. This mechanism, however, must be sensitive to participating parties who have challenges in writing or recording observations, feelings, and impressions. Journal entries can be done throughout the day or at specific times. There is greater and greater use of electronic journals, particularly among youth, so practical concerns may dictate when these can be done.

In situations in which literacy or disabilities are factors, use of audio recordings has proven successful. When these tapes are transcribed, there are considerable costs involved in this method. However, it may involve only a limited number of individuals within the community, and having audio recording methods helps ensure that no segment of the community is excluded from this process and conveys to the broader community the importance of tapping all sources, regardless of challenges. In addition, speech recognition computer software creates print directly from voice, making transcription unnecessary.

Delphi Technique

Surprisingly, the use of the Delphi Technique as a method to address a community's assets has not been reported in the literature. The Delphi Technique was developed in the 1970s as a research method for developing priorities for "improving the urban social environment" (Molnar & Kammerud, 1977). It has been conceptualized primarily as a communication device to elicit the opinions of "experts" on particular urban problems. It typically consists of several steps or stages that entail establishing a panel and brainstorming, sorting, and ranking of community problem related statements.

Although specifically used to identify the most pressing social problems, it can serve in similar fashion to the more deficit oriented conventional use of this method by stressing assets because of flexibility in how it can be conceptualized. It is a method, however, that will not provide an in-depth look at a community's assets. The Delphi Technique, nevertheless, has the potential to provide broad information on a community and also to allow a more in-depth study of particular geographic areas and a specific asset focus. The financial costs of this method are generally minor, facilitating the use of the Delphi Technique in situations in which funding is very limited.

It is necessary to create a panel of approximately 10 participants representing different significant sectors of a community such as religious, service provider, fire, and safety. These representatives ideally should capture forms of legitimacy (expertise, institutional, ethical, and consumer) as a means of helping to ensure representation. Each panel member, in turn, can recommend 10 potential respondents to a key question that needs to be answered.

Each respondent is enlisted to respond to a question such as "What is the greatest strength of our community?" This information can be conveyed via paper or electronically. Each respondent's answers are then categorized by the panel and sent back to the respondents for rank ordering according to importance. These responses are then sent back to the panel, tabulated, and ranked (each category keeps all of the responses as a means of capturing the sentiments of the responses). A typical set of responses will then be ranked in order from one to 20.

Another step has these 20 categories rank ordered and sent back to respondents to further rank order them according to which asset is most amenable to being enhanced. Responses are tabulated and ranked. At the end of the process, two lists will be made available: (1) the most important assets ranked from one to 20 and (2) 20 assets that respondents wish to have enhanced, in a descending order of amenability to enhancement.

Because the Delphi Technique is usually used to rank order needs or problems, typically one list has the top 20 needs or problems confronting a community. The second list addresses ease (amenability) of addressing these needs or problems. Some of these items may be of great concern to a community, but there is a sense that they are arduous or impossible to address. This information helps guide the use of other methods to further define and narrow a focus of an intervention. Therefore, the Delphi Technique helps focus an asset assessment but should not be considered the only method used in such a study.

Photovoice

What is photovoice? The emergence of photovoice as a method that lends itself to community asset assessments has ushered in a high degree of excitement through the use of digital cameras, making the process less expensive than the use of conventional cameras requiring film to be processed. It is a tool that has been shown to be quite effective in use across a variety of groups and in addressing a variety of issues. This tool lends itself quite well to developing greater awareness of community problems but can also be used to uncover community assets.

Like other participatory research approaches addressed in this chapter, photovoice seeks to accomplish social change goals at the community level, but it does this through use of photograph and corresponding narrative to bring the pictures and stories of community assets to life (Foster-Fishman, Nowell, Deacon, Nievar, & McNann, 2005). Molloy (2007) envisions photovoice as a "tool" for social workers to raise awareness about social justice issues and empower undervalued groups in the process.

The following description illustrates a common approach toward using photovoice, with a focus on maternal and child health (Wang & Pies, 2004, p. 95): "Residents were provided with disposable cameras and were encouraged to take photographs reflecting their views on family, maternal, and child health assets and concerns in their community, and then participated in group discussions about their photographs. Community events were held to enable participants to educate MCH staff and community leaders...The photovoice project provided MCH staff with information to supplement existing quantitative perinatal data and contributed to an understanding of key MCH issues that participating community residents would like to see addressed."

The goals of photovoice are generally threefold (Wang & Redwood-Jones, 2001, p. 560): "(1) to enable people to record and reflect their community's strengths and concerns; (2) to promote critical dialogue and knowledge about personal and community issues through large and small group discussions of photographs; and (3) to reach policy-makers." These goals make photovoice an attractive method for use in community asset assessments by addressing the relevance of concerns some communities may have about participating in asset or deficit driven research projects (Carlson, Engebretson, & Chamberlain, 2006). The popularity of photovoice, in large part, can be attributed to its potential for use across population groups, goals, budgets, and settings as a vehicle for identifying community assets and increasing community dialogue (Brazg et al., 2010; Castleden, Gacuin, & First Nation, 2008; Downey, Ireson, & Scutcfield, 2009).

Marginalized communities obviously benefit from having their stories told to increase positive attention and resources to their communities. However, participants also benefit from photovoice by engendering a sense of control over their lives and an increased awareness of the importance of relationships and their potential to be agents of social change (Foster-Fishman et al., 2005). Participation, in essence, is intended to be a transformative experience and represents a critical element in any form of participatory democratic based intervention (Delgado & Staples, 2008).

Photovoice lends itself to use by a variety of groups, regardless of literacy skills. In addition, it has been a method that seems to be able to engage residents across the lifespan, as well as people with varying degrees of abilities. Photovoice has been found to be a particularly viable method for assessing the assets of people with disabilities (Jurokowski & Paul-Ward, 2007; Jurokowski, Rivera, & Hammel, 2009).

Wang (2006), one of the nation's leading proponents of photovoice, has undertaken numerous studies involving this method and opened the door to other researchers reaching out to marginalized groups in this society. Photovoice has also been used with homeless people, for example, and Wang, Cash, and Powers (2000) report on their effort involving homeless women and men in shelters who photographed their daily existence, documenting strengths and struggles. Participants, in turn, shared their perspectives in group discussions using photographs that best represented their lives. Youth, too, have been found to benefit from using photovoice method research in developing a critical consciousness of their strengths and challenges, and developing a better understanding of their communities (Wang, 2006).

Photovoice has also been effectively used to create community "photo mapping" as a means of integrating health and place research with young people (Dennis, Gaulocher, Carpiano, & Brown, 2008). For example, development of a greater awareness of how place of residence and health are associated has resulted in actions to alter their environment to create healthier options for youth and other residents.

Carlson, Engebretson, and Chamberlain (2006) report on the success of photovoice in an African American community in helping participants identify things in their community of which they are proud and things they wish to change. McIntyre (2003) used photovoice as a means of capturing how women create place and identity within the contexts of everyday life. Internationally, one photovoice project in South Africa sought to promote food security among the poor with HIV/AIDS (Swaans, Broerse, Meincke, Mudhara, & Bunders, 2009). Kelly and colleagues (2006), in turn, used photovoice as a tool for promoting physical activity in communities.

The field of health promotion, in particular, has found this method of engaging community, identifying assets, and translating these findings into health promotion strategies beneficial. Barridge and colleagues (2010) describe the use of "photo-elicitation," or photovoice, as a means of increasing community dialogue on community assets, and incorporating these resources into health initiatives.

Wang and Pies (2004) undertook a photovoice research project on maternal and child health that sought to accomplish three goals: (1) enhance community health assessments and program planning; (2) encourage community use of photovoice to record and communicate health assets and concerns; and (3) educate and introduce this research method for use in grassroots driven initiatives. Catalini and Minkler (2010) conclude, based upon a review of the literature on photovoice, that this method invariably (60%) is closely associated with social change efforts following a photovoice activity, facilitating the empowerment of participants. Hergenrather, Rhodes, Cowan, Bardhoshi, and Pula (2009), too, undertook an extensive review of the literature on photovoice as a research methodology and conclude that, despite limitations, this method holds much promise for facilitating community participation in assessment and bringing about community change and empowerment.

Photovoice does present challenges along a variety of dimensions, though. Mitchell, DeLange, Moletsane, Stuart, and Buthelezi (2005), for example, identify challenges related to technical aspects, documentation and interpretation of findings, ethics, and translating findings into action. The popularity of photovoice and of digital cameras, however, has made the process less expensive than the use of conventional cameras requiring film to be processed, making photovoice a research method more appealing for community asset assessment. This new "tool" in the hands of community residents has provided a vehicle through which a community can be better understood internally and externally (Delgado, 2006).

Expert Panel

The expert panel method generally has been underutilized or unused, even though it provides tremendous flexibility for asset assessments. An expert panel is a group of members specifically selected because of their experiences, expertise, or positions within a community, providing a unique perspective on analysis of data or information. The use of an expert panel provides an opportunity for specific input by a group on a particular form of asset. It can, for example, consist of religious/spiritual stakeholders giving their input into religious capital or small business owners into economic capital assessment. Expert panels also supplement a steering committee and provide flexibility when a particular type of expertise is missing from a committee. These panels are very different from the one established for a Delphi Technique. The Delphi panel gets selected both because of its unique views on a community and also because of the corresponding social network that it can tap.

The size of an expert panel can range from several members to 10 to 15 members, depending upon the importance given to a particular asset. If an intervention that results from an asset assessment will involve the religious/spiritual organizations and stakeholders, for example, it allows a steering committee to engage these individuals early in the process to make an intervention easier to market and implement. The size of this panel must also be taken into consideration if training and extensive support will be needed to facilitate the process. Consequently, local goals and circumstances will dictate the ideal number of members.

Nevertheless, there must be a consensus definition of who constitutes an "expert" for this method to wield influence in asset assessments. Expertise can be defined along educational and experiential dimensions. Although this distinction can appear rather straightforward, who is considered an expert is not simple and is very much dependent upon who is deciding.

Expert panels can meet on a regularly scheduled basis and be asked to respond to very specific questions or findings. This method, however, must not be confused with the role of a community asset steering committee because its "charge" is quite specific and time limited. This method complements the other methods presented in this section and chapter and should not be used on its own.

Oral Histories

Oral history research on community assets can be as broad and exploratory or narrow and focused as the goals of the assessment. Janesick (2007, p. 111), for example, found 70 different definitions of oral history in a review of the literature, many of which overlapped with each other, and defines oral history in the following manner: "It is regularly defined in this era as some variation of a person who has had first hand knowledge of any number of experiences." Although this definition may initially appear simple, oral history projects are far from simple, as evidenced by the number of definitions in the literature.

Methods can vary, for example, according to the use and type of recording device employed (tape recorders, video, paper and pencil, etc.), depth and frequency of interviews (one lengthy interview or a series of interviews over an extended period of time), use of observations, and documents. The focus of oral history projects can also differ. Some may focus on local residents, others may focus on providers or elites, and still others may focus on a combination of these. Language used takes on importance in cases in which English is not the primary language spoken. This necessitates having interviewers who are fluent in the interviewee's language. Also, knowledge of culture takes on prominence because the symbols used in conveying stories and experiences necessitate translating this information in a culturally meaningful manner.

Asset assessment projects utilizing oral histories as the primary mechanism for discovering or, as the case may be, rediscovering community assets have enjoyed considerable popularity in communities that have been marginalized. They include, for example, groups new to this country, those with long histories of oppression such as African Americans, and those that had these histories erased such as Native Americans.

Thomas (2004), in writing about neighborhood planning, discusses the potential for using oral history as a way of obtaining historical insights from community residents. She sees it as a particularly good method to include people who are marginalized and whose voices have not been heard. Thomas (2004, p. 56) states: "The need to tap resident knowledge is particularly important in distressed central-city neighborhoods precisely because they need whatever resources may be available. Resident initiative, wisdom, and participation are important resources." Community asset assessments relying on oral histories are not an "inexpensive" way of tapping community assets, though. Oral history projects are labor intensive and require considerable training, supervision, and support of interviewers and careful recording and analysis of data.

CommunityLine

There have been innovative approaches toward tapping community asset related information, with CommunityLine being one such example. This is the establishment of an Internet site or an around the clock, toll free, telephone number that residents can call to share their views of community assets (Thompson, 2009). This method is particularly appealing for those residents who wish to remain anonymous or whose written and reading skills severely limit their participation in more conventional data gathering methods. Hours and days can be adjusted, and a period of time can be established during which the line will be operational, taking into account budget and other forms of resources. Extensive advertising throughout the community is required for this method to be viable, though.

Specific lines can be promoted for residents who do not have English as their primary language. YouthLine, for example, can target youth, and it can be staffed by them, too, as a method for specifically reaching out to this age group that generally gets overlooked even in more comprehensive asset assessments. Alexander and Cagle (2009), for example, describe the use of an Internet site for lesbian, gay, bisexual, and transgender youth to use to record their concerns, and such a model could also be used to record assets.

A gathering of data in CommunityLine, although with limitations, is relatively easy to implement and staff. Yet, data obtained through this method are not generalizable and will necessitate transcription, which will be expensive, time consuming, and may require bilingual transcribers. This approach is recommended as a supplement to other methods but not as a primary way of tapping community assets.

Geospatial Analysis Technologies

Needs assessments have often relied very heavily upon quantitative data gathered through existing agency and governmental data gathering methods. These data, unfortunately, have been heavily deficit oriented through their focus on problems and needs. Geospacial analysis technologies have the potential to make important contributions to community asset assessments through the gathering and analysis of both quantitative and qualitative data.

The role and potential of computers, software, and telecommunication equipment, such as mobile phones, necessitate that special attention be paid to their use in community asset assessments and mapping. Geographic Information Systems (GIS) is a geographic analysis technology that encompasses a system of hardware and software used for storage, retrieval, mapping, and analysis of geographic data (United States Geological Survey, 2007).

GIS can present and analyze spatial data in formats such as graphs and charts as well as on maps. It has gained in prominence in the new millennium. Also, in the past decade or so, technology has become more readily accessible to community residents without formal training in cartography or geography, and various computer software programs such as MapInfo, ArcGIS, and EpiMap typify this increased accessibility (Aronson et al., 2007a). Therefore, extra attention will be paid in this section to GIS.

It is important to note that GIS is a method that requires specialized computer knowledge, software, and hardware to implement it as well as staff to operate and maintain it. Computers must be available that are adequate to the requirements of the software, and special printers must be capable of printing large maps, if those are desired beyond the smaller sizes that standard printers can print. Although data can be obtained from existing government sources, for example, to input onto maps, often researchers gather data in the community using specialized handheld devices. Therefore, because of the expertise and funding needed to carry out GIS projects, it is often likely that this type of work would best be done in collaboration with an organization such as a university that already has the system in place, or a grant to fund it may have to be obtained.

Some free Internet training modules are available, but the novice also would have to learn about GIS in its entirety in order to understand how to apply the information from the training effectively. In addition, some free software is available, but technical expertise or consultation would be needed to integrate free or "open-source" resources, such as Google Maps, with other parts of a GIS system, such as software for analysis. Like other technologies, though, the expertise needed and costs may decrease over time, and some progress has already been made, which will be discussed below.

A major way in which GIS has become more accessible to communities is the development of applications that can run on smart phones that have greater computer capabilities than earlier mobile phones. Therefore, instead of carrying specialized handheld devices made only for GIS data gathering, regular smart phones can have applications downloaded that work with the Global Positioning

System (GPS) that generally now is built into mobile phones. This makes it easier to include community people in an asset needs assessment data gathering process. Oversight of the large number of people who are able to gather data increases, but the inclusionary aspect of the process is improved as well.

The City of Boston, Massachusetts, provides an example of the use of smart phones to gather data by surveys conducted on foot (L. H. Delgado, 2012). Although more sophisticated handheld devices were used previously, it was found that the smart phones were more efficient. The survey obtains citywide data on foreclosed and distressed properties as part of the Department of Neighborhood Development's ongoing work to help address these issues. Using GIS, the survey data are combined with various other data sources, mapped, analyzed, and interpreted regarding trends and geographic areas that need the City's attention. This method identifies assets and improvements, in addition to deficits and areas needing further attention (L. H. Delgado, 2012).

Another example of the use of smart phones in GIS data gathering is the Beacon of Hope Resource Center's project in New Orleans, Louisiana (ArcNews Online, 2010). In addition, this is an example of a collaboration of a community organization with both a university and a municipality. The Beacon of Hope Resource Center was developed in 2006 in response to Hurricanes Katrina and Rita, and a major part of its work has been to assess neighborhood conditions throughout New Orleans. Although it began with paper surveys done in the field, which it arduously entered into its later GIS system, it progressed to surveying with smart phones (Beacon of Hope Resource Center, 2011). This was an effort that began with the community, which then collaborated with a university, and which finally engaged a municipality, resulting in a three way collaboration. Residents have remained engaged throughout the process and found the spatial data presented on maps of the community and its neighborhoods to be very helpful in conveying information about New Orleans and its recovery (ArcNews, 2010).

A review of the literature on GIS and undervalued communities will uncover a variety of terms that make GIS empowering and inclusive of marginalized groups. Terms such as "public participation GIS" (PPGIS) and "Participatory GIS" (PGIS) are often thought of as postmodern adaptations of conventional GIS applications. GIS has emerged to fulfill a variety of functions, including being used to record community assets. Elwood (2006) sees GIS research methods as offering urban marginalized communities the potential to create their own narratives or stories that reflect their priorities and understanding of community assets and problems. Hyland and Owens (2005) stress the value of computer generated neighborhood asset maps as a means of obtaining and presenting information in a highly visual form that increases its accessibility to residents.

GIS, in a fashion similar to the other methods covered in the chapter, has the potential for positive change or for further oppressing communities. How it is conceptualized, and the values and goals guiding its use, will dictate the approach. GIS is a research tool that can be empowering and liberating, if used by residents to seek social justice and social change. However, its true measure of potential and effectiveness will be when it goes beyond conventional reliance on location of organizational, religious, and educational settings and seeks to uncover hidden talents and gifts not widely recognized within the community.

Turner and Pinkett (2000) advance the notion that tremendous synergy and the capability to empower communities to improve their environment can be found at the intersection between community building and community technology. Glantz and McMahan (2007) also echo the importance of mapping and edited a special issue of *Practicing Anthropology* devoted exclusively to illustrating the benefits of a merger of anthropology and GIS community maps to increase the understanding of the dynamics of health and well-being, and community participation.

GIS serves to provide a more in-depth understanding of resident perceptions of local issues and priorities and can help put multiple variables into a spatial view, which would not be possible through plain statistics. GIS also lends itself to identifying resident perceptions of community assets. It has the potential to improve delivery of social services, too. For example, GIS maps of social service providers can help social workers identify and make referrals to resources for their clients (Hillier, 2007).

Dunn (2007) presents a variety of ways of democratizing GIS to capture and utilize indigenous and local knowledge and increase community control and ownership of geographic information. Dennis (2006) reports on a youth community asset assessment project that utilized a range of qualitative methods (photography, narratives, and drawings), which were then incorporated into GIS. Ghirardelli, Quinn, and Forester (2010) describe the use of GIS and local food store data focused on the availability of fresh produce within low income communities in California to identify resources within food deserts.

Schlossberg (undated) reports on a GIS initiative in Grand Rapids, Michigan, that was spearheaded by United Way. A GIS analysis of assets and needs supplemented an ethnographic and traditional needs assessment. Schlossberg (undated, p. 15) comments on the attractiveness of GIS: "GIS has demonstrated...that it can be an effective methodology for converging the dual goals of bottom up and top down decision making. Data presented with the aid of GIS is more easily understood by the communities served as well as organizational administrators, funders and public officials."

Introduction of GIS as a community participatory mapping tool, as to be expected, will necessitate addressing challenges concerning preconceived perceptions of a "steep learning curve," competing ideology of how to use this tool, and difficulty in interpreting results (Kothari et al., 2008). The challenge is to give community residents more access to GIS and mapping.

Grassroots Mapping is a project that began at the Massachusetts Institute of Technology to do participatory research and democratize mapping by local communities (Warren, 2012). Its work relies heavily on low technology and low cost materials. For example, in Lima, Peru, Grassroots Mapping worked with children and adults to launch their own "community satellites" of helium balloons and kites, obtaining data to enter into maps. It also did aerial mapping using balloons in Louisiana, Mississippi, Alabama, and Florida after the Deepwater Horizon oil spill on the Gulf Coast. The Public Laboratory for Open Technology and Science, which grew out of the Grassroots Mapping project and of which the Grassroots Mapping project now is a part, makes available both free directions for communities to use their own materials and an extremely low cost kit for communities to do their own balloon mapping projects. Currently, many sites throughout the United States and abroad are doing mapping using the Grassroots balloon or kite mapping methods (Grassroots Mapping, 2010; The Public Laboratory for Open Technology and Science, 2012).

Grassroots has benefited from so called Web 2.0 developments that resulted in flexibility in using data (Diehl, Grabill, Hart-Davidson, & Iyer, 2008). Web 2.0 generally refers to the interactive use of the Internet that was developed after the initial Internet was created. Diehl and colleagues (2008), like Talen (2000), recognize that GIS is often for the elite and tends to exclude a large majority of the population. Therefore, Grassroots strives to make maps accessible to the general community in order to harness a "collective intelligence." Most importantly, Grassroots is a mechanism for creating asset maps that allow community members, as well as the general public, to view the community in a new, positive light (Diehl et al., 2008). To achieve this, the programmers made it easy to add and edit information on the maps, facilitating participants' abilities to access their previous and current maps along with other community members' maps. The goal was not only to help users get a feel for mapmaking, but also to give them a better sense of their community as a whole.

GIS, as already noted, has the potential to help to empower communities and get them involved in the creation of a better community. In particular, GIS can be very useful in helping to show disparity in a community. Because the process of getting communities involved is a relatively new concept, though, the reliance of GIS on computers and technology can make it not easily accessible to the general public (Talen, 2000). However, what Talen (2000) calls bottom-up GIS (BUGIS) is trying to combat this trend and involve the general public, specifically community members, in mapping efforts.

Talen (2000) describes two significant efforts at BUGIS in Dallas, Texas, that were conducted at visioning events. The first step was to select an appropriate venue for the mapping. When necessary, groups were broken down into smaller groups according to communities. The second step was to prepare all relevant GIS data for the participants. It was important to keep all the data straightforward and to address all geographic areas of relevance that could be covered. Third, there were GIS facilitators whose role was to work with participants and act as translators in order to make the maps and accurately display the individuals' preferences. This technical support was important in clarifying the process and helping participants with questions.

Participants then constructed their BUGIS, relying on three things: description, evaluation, and prescription (Talen, 2000). First, the participants described their personal patterns within the community and then made greater, broader descriptions. In terms of evaluation, they expressed their opinions as to the value and significance of certain aspects of their communities. Finally, for prescription, they expressed their desires and hopes for the future of their communities. All of these were mapped on a BUGIS map. Interestingly, although individuals were mapping almost the same geographic areas, the maps looked very different. Different individuals, not surprisingly, identified different points of interest as important. A result of the individual maps was the opportunity to increase the knowledge of community issues (Talen, 2000; Talen & Shah, 2009).

GIS has been explored as an aid for people who are blind or have visual impairments. For example, in the 1990s, tactile maps with raised features and Braille were developed using GIS at Pasadena City College, California (Clark & Clark, 1994). A more recent college campus example of a project to develop a tactile map with raised lines and symbols and Braille for students who are blind was done by a Kansas University graduate student who is blind, working in collaboration with the university's Geography Department and Cartographic Services Office. Her insight directly brought in the specific needs and perspectives of a student who had to navigate the campus (Maines, 2006). Although there are challenges for making such maps so that they are effective and truly practical, the concept is promising for wider use. Development of tactile maps could be integrated into an asset assessment, too.

Goldman and colleagues (2008) at the Center for Embedded Networked Sensing at the University of California, Los Angeles, present a compelling case for the use of what they call "participatory sensing" as a resident driven research approach and method. Participatory sensing seeks to increase community participation in the assessment design, implementation, analysis of data, and development of action plans. It utilizes a variety of data collection devices, such as mobile telephones, as a way to enable community residents to take geotagged images of various assets in their community; geotagging attaches location specific information to the images. These images can then be automatically uploaded and displayed on interactive maps. This approach can be used by special population groups to focus on particular assets or interests.

A number of scholars, however, have raised questions about participatory GIS and technology. Perkins (2007, p. 127) raises a voice of concern specific to participatory GIS: "Participatory GIS in theory belies a more democratic spatial governance...but the majority of this work emphasizes the incorporation of local voices into maps produced and controlled by specialists, and articulating *their* agenda, rather than subverting mapping, or changing what is mapped." Perkins (2007), as a result, touches on issues about how existing power structures seek to elicit community voices without themselves being the target of change. There is untapped potential in GIS for mapping community assets. However, efforts to further include community residents in the use of GIS necessitate that a conscious effort be made to do so and that there be a willingness to modify this tool to encourage community participation and ownership.

Anchan and Katz (2003, p. 123), in turn, pose a provocative question pertaining to technology and marginalized groups: "Can we expect that providing access to information technology will change the status of a marginalized population? In the end, it is not whether the marginalized have access to information technology. Rather, the critical issues are whether they want to use it and, if so, how they would use it. Possibly, the use of information technology or the surrounding debate on the digital divide remains an issue that does not relate to their immediate basic needs." Sieber's (2006, p. 491) assessment of GIS points out the potential of this method for creating positive as well as detrimental consequences for communities: "It is an odd concept to attribute to a piece of software the potential to enhance or limit public participation in policymaking, empower or marginalize community members to improve their lives, counter or enable agendas of the powerful, and advance or diminish democratic principles."

It is possible to combine maps to create one that integrates information from all participants. However, Talen (2000) warns that synthesizing data in that way can compromise individual viewpoints. Also, Talen warns that planners must be willing to give control over to the community members instead of professionals, whom they have relied on for years.

CONCLUSIONS

Practitioners have a variety of tools and options that can be used to carry out community asset assessments. We believe that the more tools that can be used for a particular job, the higher the likelihood the results will capture the community's assets. Realistically, though, the selection of methods must be based upon time, funds available, expertise, political will on the part of the community, and the questions one seeks to answer. Community asset assessment does not have to involve computer software, though, and can still be done with manually inputted information, as will be discussed in Chapter 7. In addition, there can be a combination involving computers and manual methods. This flexibility allows local circumstances to dictate how a community asset map can be accomplished.

The abundance of methods also does not mean that practitioners do not have favorite ones that resonate with their skills. However, it is important to warn community social workers that local circumstances must dictate the methods to be used in an assessment and not the practitioners' preferences. This means that as a team is being put together, special attention should be paid to enlisting participants with complementary strengths. Steering committees and research teams must always be composed after deliberative planning and engagement in a thoughtful decision making process. In addition, as noted earlier in Chapter 5, research teams should be inclusive of all significant sectors of a community by race, gender, sexual orientation, age, abilities, and length of residence, to list but a few considerations.

7

Community Mapping Strategies

"We are all mapmakers. Any community can make maps. Community mapping rests on such a claim and assumption. Maps are inspiring. Maps provide a unique language for humans to communicate with one another. Maps can record great losses and discoveries, the changes of physical and political landscapes, great beauty and destruction. Maps reflect our relationship to ourselves, to one another and to the environment. They reflect the geography of our lives and communities."

(LYDON, *2003, p. 132*)

INTRODUCTION

Community asset assessments, as conceptualized in this book, are a form of what is referred to as community based participatory research (Butterfoss, 2006), and community asset maps are one way of engaging communities in this process. This chapter provides the reader with goals and approaches for developing maps based on community assets. Community asset maps can be thought of as visual and geographic representations of assets on a very concrete manner. They literally place identified assets on a physical map of a community in various ways, from manually placing colored pins on a map to using computer programs to place assets on a computer generated map. However, community asset maps can also be thought of from a conceptual viewpoint as an account of information that has lacked a corresponding visual representation or a listing of assets along with their location. This visual representation facilitates communication across various segments within and outside of a community and facilitates the illustration of spatial links and complex concepts.

Asset maps probably are best thought of as visual aids that facilitate the display and analysis of community generated data in a manner that increases a community's understanding of and insights into its resources and abilities (Goldman & Schmaltz, 2005). One of the most appealing aspects of Geographic Information Systems (GIS), for example, is its power to crystallize information in a manner that lends itself to collective visualization for the purposes of developing an intervention (Hillier, 2007). However, it needs to be demystified and made more community user friendly (Rattray, 2006; Talen, 2000), as noted in Chapter 6.

Seeking creative expression beyond the written word opens up previously overlooked avenues for gathering information on community assets, particularly in communities with strong oral history traditions. In those, maps can capture and save information about assets as they have begun, grown, or changed over time, such as religious institutions or parks. A number of institutions that typically would not be considered to be interested in community assets have started to engage in asset assessments utilizing multiple methods that include both mapping and oral histories. Chicago's Field Museum is such an example. This study covered the period from 2001 to 2003 and focused on a variety of communities in and around Chicago and assessed art, gardens, small businesses, and local histories as told by long time residents. The assessment used GIS, oral histories, interviews, participant observation, focus groups, photography, and video to identify and analyze what forces and factors were the most significant in the lives of community residents.

Green (2009), in addressing which methods to use in a community asset map, notes: "The purpose of the project should guide the decisions about which method to use and what specific information should be collected. The goals may range from promoting local economic development or community health to supporting youth programs. The community and/or organizations need to clearly state the purpose of the project." Not surprisingly, goals should dictate which methods are used rather than methods dictating goals.

Community asset maps provide an opportunity for communities to engage in visioning exercises about their communities (Laverack, 2006a; Smith, Littlejohns, Hawe, & Sutherland, 2008). Mapping, as a result, provides a community with a new perspective or optic from which to consider social interventions (Beckley, Martz, Nadeau, Wall, & Reimer, 2008). Maps, in essence, provide visually striking information on hidden or difficult to reach population groups and can reveal previously unknown patterns, even to community insiders (Gesler, Hayes, Arcury, Skelly, Nash, & Soward, 2004). This potential to illuminate known and unknown knowledge, we believe, enhances the value of asset maps and expands the audience for this information in the process, such as government and social service agencies. Social workers and other helping professionals are not the only professions discovering the value of community asset maps. The early part of the twenty-first century has witnessed an increasing number of professions venturing out into the community and displaying a willingness to engage in community asset mapping. Mapping for marketing, by the way, is used by big businesses and advertising, and small community businesses may be able to reach the local community by accessing an asset map as well.

Williment (2009, p. 7) describes a four year project initiated to make libraries more socially inclusive through a community led planning model that stressed community assets and specifically focused on the use and value of an asset map: "An asset map is an excellent instrument that can help library staff identify and conceptualize the potential connections the library could develop within a specific community, while also recognizing current community capacity and gaps." Medical students are also starting to be exposed to the values of community asset assessments in developing a better understanding of how environmental context influences health (Garrettson, Walline, Heisler, & Townsend, 2010; O'Toole, Kathuria, Mishra, & Schukart, 2005). Pineda (2006), in turn, outlines the identification of faith based assets.

School counselors have found that community asset mapping is an effective way of identifying community resources that can be tapped in service to students (Griffin, 2010). Community pediatrics has found value in mapping community assets, too (Pan, Littlefield, Valladolid, Tapping, & West, 2005). The correctional field also has started to use asset mapping, but in a dramatically different way, by locating prisons on GIS and Global Positioning System (GPS) maps to improve their operational management and strategic planning capabilities (Karuppannan, 2005), but obviously, this form of asset mapping is not how it is conceptualized in this book. In addition, community asset mapping has also found an international audience, as evidenced by its use in countries such as Australia (Laverack, 2006a, 2006b; Parker et al., 2006), Canada (Smith et al., 2008), China (Robinson & Perkins, 2009), England (Knox, 2009; Mittelmark et al., 2006), Japan (Mittelmark et al., 2006), Korea (Liou, 2004; Nam & Engelhardt, 2007), and New Zealand (Raeburn, Akerman, Chuengsatiansup, Mejia, & Oladepo, 2007).

WHAT IS MAPPING AND ASSET MAPPING?

Blanchet-Cohen, Ragan, and Amsden (2003) capture well the common perceptions of what constitutes a "map," as well as the potential for reaching new audiences: "Most people envision 'maps' as sophisticated drawings designed by specialists that locate resources, territories, and peoples in a geographic context. Maps have tended in recent times to represent the values of dominant power structures, being used by nation-states and companies to delineate boundaries and ownership. Traditionally, though, maps have had a broader meaning. Indigenous peoples have used maps to illustrate stories, songs and dreams related to places... People have used branches and leaves to draw maps in the sand, on animal hides and on wood ....Maps are talismans that provide form to social reality; they model the world... They take on many forms, portraying the physical, social, spiritual and cognitive realms of a given place and people."

Social work has been using mapping for over a century manually (Hillier, 2007). GIS represents a natural evolutionary step for the profession, though social workers were the pioneers of the social survey movement, which influenced settlement house workers, business people, academics, and others to start studying communities. Some leading social workers of that time included Florence Kelley,

Paul Kellogg, and Charles Booth (who influenced W. E. B. DuBois in his surveys with the African American community of Philadelphia) (Hillier, 2007). At the base of these social surveys and mapping efforts was the idea of ecological systems theory that people and their environments interact. Although social workers generally have been reluctant to use GIS to integrate and analyze spatial data, some argue that it could be useful in testing ecological theories.

Veiller, writing in the 1900–1901 journal *Charities Review*, described how mapping was done in the Tenement House Exhibit of 1899 by advocates for the poor in New York City. The project located tenements and their physical characteristics, such as lack of windows and baths, on maps. Within these tenements, specific individuals who had applied for charity as well as those with illnesses such as tuberculosis, typhoid, and diphtheria were located and documented on maps, and these maps were displayed in an overlay fashion. Although this was a needs assessment of sorts rather than an asset assessment, it was used to advocate for improvements in tenements and low income neighborhoods. Furthermore, issues were located in the environment, not the individuals. For example, lack of bathing facilities, rather than people's personal habits or character, was noted as the cause of lack of cleanliness.

O'Looney (1998, p. 201) identifies four essential goals of community mapping that stress the importance of this form of information gathering and sharing: "Community mapping is defined as follows: (1) efforts to understand the world as a landscape of many different aspects and values; (2) identify areas that appear to make a degree of unity; (3) explain why things are the way they are; and (4) identify opportunities for positive social actions and policy development." The journey of community mapping is one best thought of as a discovery process whereby the actual "discovery" is as important as the actual journey taken, and therein rests the attractiveness and challenges involved in mapping a community's assets or capital.

Maps have evolved over the years and have taken on a variety of functions that transcend the usual narrow dimensions currently associated with this form of information dissemination. Conventional maps have a cultural and social historical context that reflects the biases and worldviews of the map makers. Yet, the form a community asset map can take is limited only by our creativity. Crampton (2009) applies the concept of "performativity" (cultural, social, and political activity) to maps as a means of transforming maps from "objects" to process activities that benefit undervalued groups and communities. Beaulieu (2002) proposes a four stage process for mapping community assets that illustrates the importance of process: (1) identifying assets; (2) relationship building; (3) mobilization for action; and (4) community meeting to envision a common future vision. Consequently, this flexibility allows local circumstances (such as budgets, priorities, and timeframe) to determine the nature and the level of details in a map.

Perkins' (2007) lists of methods and materials touch upon the potential for how maps can be created. They can be sewn, woven, knitted, painted, drawn, filmed, or animated. They can include ceramics, photographs, or posters, and the more conventional paper fold up type with which we are familiar. Culture plays an influential role in dictating the most accessible form of map. The methods and materials provided by Perkins (2007), Crampton (2009), and Blanchet-Cohen, Ragan, and Amsden (2003) highlight the diversity of ways of conceiving a community map.

Maps historically have been developed by the elites in society, and therefore were designed to serve their social, economic, and political needs rather than the needs of communities or specific groups that are marginalized or undervalued. Harley (1988, 1989), well over two decades ago, called attention to the close relationship between maps and power, and how maps reflect political and social agendas. The ability to shape maps based upon assumptions and privilege further accentuates the need for undervalued communities to effectively shape the values and priorities that they bring to social change efforts.

Unlike other forms of maps, community maps open the arena for "amateurs" (Parker, 2006). Historically, maps have been the purview of professionals, and they decided what information was important to gather. Cartography was undertaken by those who had the training, interest, and time. Needless to say, those of low income and low wealth did not fall into this professional class. Mapping favored those who had educational expertise (legitimacy). Asset mapping, however, is quite democratizing because it favors experiential expertise as the primary source of legitimacy. This means that low income and low wealth communities can undertake mapping.

Since the mid-1990s, cartography has been demystified, largely as a result of GIS becoming more accessible to nontrained GIS professionals, ushering in an era of so called "do-it-yourself" cartography (Rattray, 2006). Nevertheless, there are still concerns related to costs, limited technical expertise, and worries about obsolescence that must be addressed (Rattray, 2006). Once cartography is demystified, however, community collective action based on the opinions and decisions of the community can result (Silver, Weitzman, & Bretcher, 2002).

Counter-mapping, otherwise known as "critical cartography," represents the use of community mapping as a vehicle for mapping against dominant power structures to further progressive goals (Hodgson & Schroeder, 2002). Critical cartography's history has been traced back to the late 1980s (Crampton & Krygier, 2006). A social change agenda, or what critics would label as maps with a "political agenda," are a natural extension or outcome of a better understanding of the role of oppressive forces on an undervalued community's well-being.

An important element of critical cartography is its emphasis on participation on the part of the disempowered (Chambers, 2006; Pain, 2004). Herlihy and Knapp (2003), in turn, stress using participatory mapping as a way to generate spatial information of relevance and, in the process, also making it user friendly to the community. Perkins (2007, p. 127), too, points out that community mapping is within the grasp of all people: "Individuals in modern society have, until recently, only rarely mapped; they used maps created by cartographers. Yet all human beings *can* map: people have natural mapping abilities... And, in response to technological and social change in the last twenty-five years, cartography has increasingly been democratized... with an emergence of critical approaches to mapping."

How a community views itself plays a critical role in the implementation of community asset maps. Community asset maps effectively change community perceptions of themselves, and perceptions are critical in changing attitudes and instilling hope for these communities. In fact, social change is not possible in many marginalized communities without a significant change in how these communities view themselves.

An asset paradigm such as community capacity enhancement is premised on the fundamental belief that all neighborhoods or communities, regardless of their geographic location, composition, or economic standing, have assets to offer their own and the broader, external, community. Low income and low wealth urban neighborhoods, as a result, need to recognize, discover, and mobilize their assets (Green, 2009; McKnight & Kretzmann, 1996). A failure to do so effectively limits their potential to take stock of their internal resources, and, thus, they must rely upon the largesse of society to aid them in meeting their needs.

Although community asset maps specifically target assets, the process may also uncover other types of information (Field Museum, 2004). Parker (2006, p. 480), in the spirit of empowerment, notes that community asset maps must be allowed to uncover power differentials within and outside of the community: "The themes of inclusion, transparency, and empowerment offer insight into both particularities and commonalities of community maps, as well as the relationship between community maps and power. These issues form the root of empirical and theoretical tensions in the study of community mapping." A community map will shed light on many different aspects of communities, and not just assets, which will play a role in the development of interventions and social change efforts.

It reminds us of the initial step a group may take in contemplating the virtues of going on an "exciting" weekend outing together. Invariably, each member of the group has a slightly different vision of what constitutes an "exciting" trip. The journey of discovery starts out with great joy and anticipation and quickly emerges as a decision making process that necessitates compromises, tensions, and hard work. The decision on destination is dependent upon the amount of time, money, and willingness of a group to plan and gather the necessary information to make the requisite purchases of transportation tickets, getting the times and dates of the attractions, etc. Consequently, planning a trip can share much in common with community asset mapping. There are certainly rewards to be enjoyed as well as trials and tribulations. It can bring groups together in a decision making process and ultimate ownership of the experience. However, it can also accentuate fault lines and power differentials, just as in a community.

Community maps can consist of many different types. However, mapping related to needs and problems are the most prevalent, such as location of "hot spots," for example, which identify areas in the communities that attract crimes (Ahn-Redding, 2007; Eck, Chainey, Cameron, Leitner, & Wilson, 2005). Maps can take a positive perspective on some of the same information that was obtained with a negative map. Vacant lots are excellent examples. Vacant lots can be attractive areas for crimes to occur. However, they can also be a place in which a community garden can be planted or a playground developed (Delgado, 2000; Tortorello, 2011).

According to McKnight and Kretzmann (1996), the most accessible assets are those that are both in the community and are controlled by the community. Examples of these include residents with particular talents, citizen associations, religious organizations, and locally owned businesses. Of all of these assets, individuals are the greatest asset, although the most challenging to assess. To identify the skills and talents a resident brings to the community, an inventory and assessment of capacities must be undertaken (McKnight & Kretzmann, 1996). Also, community members must play integral roles in successfully mapping their own communities (Parker, 2006; Glöcker, Mkaga, & Ndezi, 2004).

Although asset mapping is useful, it is only one form of community mapping. Witten, Exeter, and Field (2003), for example, look at community mapping as a way of explaining health disparities in certain areas of New Zealand. In their study, they used an alternative approach to understanding health disparities by directly examining "the health-demoting and health-promoting characteristics of areas of residence" (p. 161). They found that the way people felt about their neighborhoods, including the amount of satisfaction that people felt about them, and the social relationships that developed out of them, were linked to the accessibility of opportunity structures in their communities. They also found that local community sports clubs served as major socializing centers as well as informal places for obtaining health information. It is clear that having resources that are geographically accessible is extremely important to health, especially for those with limited mobility and few outside resources.

Witten, Exeter, and Field (2003) developed a community mapping plan using the development of the Community Resources Index that examines where people live and the distance to a range of mostly formal community resources. Their study measured the health and well-being of certain populations (Maori, Samoan, and Pakeha) in different areas around Auckland, New Zealand. As a result of the community map, it became apparent that local governments were not aware of the impact that limited access to services was having on people's health. It is possible that, with further mapping (and this could be applied to a number of other areas), policy makers could have better evidence as to why and how they should be distributing money and other forms of resources.

Another example of community mapping used to help an impoverished community is seen in Dar es Salaam, Tanzania's (formerly known as Mzizima) largest city and capital, with its water and sanitation. At the end of 2001, WaterAid, an organization in Dar es Salaam, along with a few other community organizations, collaborated to take action to change the troubling state of the water and sanitation systems (Glöckner et al., 2004). In their mapping effort, they mapped five States (settlements), with each mapping lasting between one week and one month, that involved a series of planning and implementation stages.

First, they gathered the stakeholders and introduced them to a community mapping exercise and planning process. Then, they held a one day planning seminar for leaders of the participating organizations. Next, representatives from each stakeholder group were invited to participate in a four day facilitator training session. Finally, 25 people from each settlement were identified to work in a community mapping team (Glöckner et al., 2004). Adding local people was important, as with any mapping effort, because it allowed the community to feel empowered and created community mobilization.

During the course of the mapping process, each house and family in the settlement (community) was interviewed, and basic information such as household information, savings, and health status was taken on "enumeration" forms. Following the collection of data, teams drafted maps and, when done, did a transect walk involving local residents (a systematic walk along a predefined path) through the settlement to clarify and double check their maps. Upon completion, they did a one day presentation to stakeholders and also disseminated the information via flyers, leaflets, and reports (Glöckner et al., 2004). The maps were used in a discussion of public policy and to help substantiate conditions to be addressed by local government.

According to Glöckner and colleagues (2004), one of the most significant outcomes of the community mapping exercise was that settlements became more aware of their situation and felt more empowered to challenge it. Specifically, one settlement was able to organize a weekly refuse collection, and other settlements with private connections to water had money put into their accounts for future projects. Also, very importantly, community issues defined by residents were now a part of the government planning process. However, there were some difficulties, such as getting the attention and feedback of important decision makers and issues with dissemination (Glöckner et al., 2004). Overall, the two case studies mentioned above, although internationally based, are good representations of what community mapping can do.

Nevertheless, it should be noted that there are limiting factors to inclusiveness, such as intentional exclusion (such as women's perspectives), limited resources, and lack of critical thinking before mapping (Parker, 2006). Also, Parker (2006) makes a good argument for community authorship or ownership. She says that authors from the communities add credibility to the map because there is an assumption that they have prior knowledge of the community. Therefore, it is helpful to be open about who creates the maps and to cite the people by printing their names on the back of the map, or even on an affiliated website.

Finally, Parker (2006) and other scholars argue that community mapping is good because it can challenge things that were left out or "silent" in other more mainstream maps. Overall, community mapping can be of great benefit; however, it is important to keep in mind power relationships and to remember who the authors are and their motives behind creating it. Having clarity about the central goals will help ensure that the community understands how others' goals interface with their own goals and help explain when bumps are encountered along the road of doing a community map.

MAPPING GOALS

Community symbols of success can be social, spiritual, physical, economic, cultural, natural or green space, and political through access to elected officials

(Emery & Flora, 2006). An annual community festival or parade, for example, can involve multiple symbols of success and self worth. Assessing a community's assets, however, does not entail having to cover all of the assets or capitals addressed in Chapter 2. As already noted, community asset assessments can be limited in scope, or as in-depth and expensive as the goals of the community undertaking this research. This flexibility or elasticity makes this form of research highly desirable.

A number of scholars have put forth community mapping goals. Corburn (2005) argues that maps seek to address at least three key sociopolitical goals in relation to knowledge: (1) aggregation and selection of what is considered to be important data; (2) identity formation vehicles through the use of information that serves to give "life" to key representations; and (3) boundary makers that effectively include and exclude information. Cornebise (1998) poses four essential questions, or goals, developed almost 15 years ago, that should guide any form of community mapping initiative: (1) Why undertake a mapping of community assets? (2) What assets do you want to identify and map? (3) How do you want to map these assets? (4) How will the community's capacity and well-being be enhanced through this mapping? Each of these questions, in turn, consists of potentially numerous subquestions. Nevertheless, these four questions capture important information for community mapping, as well as the trials and tribulations that must be addressed to achieve success.

We have identified five major mapping goals for community asset mapping: (1) Provide data in a visual manner that facilitates wide participation; (2) Help the community engage in a participatory process; (3) Provide direction for the development of an intervention based upon a consensus of the group; (4) Serve as a sociopolitical tool to help gain external support for initiatives; and (5) Help a community gain wider awareness and recognition of its assets. It is not necessary to have all five goals present in an undertaking or to have all five goals share the same degree of importance. However, when all five goals are present and equally meaningful, community asset mapping takes on greater significance in the life of the community.

Community asset maps must ultimately have the visual display of assets as a overarching goal, with the primary purpose of having the information understood by a broad sector of a community. Having the internal community understand the data represents the "bottom line." In addition, the external community must also be able to understand the symbols used in a map, since maps often seek to serve the needs of multiple audiences within and outside of a community and will be the basis for achieving some form of social change.

POTENTIAL OF COMMUNITY ASSET MAPPING

Hu (2002) notes that community mapping can serve as a qualitative and quantitative research tool to create knowledge and insights about a community, and as an action tool for engendering social change efforts through collective understanding of community priorities. Aronson, Wallis, O'Campo, and Schafer (2007a), like other scholars, conceptualize community asset mapping as a powerful tool for engaging residents in a research undertaking, and for further introducing residents to neighborhood social ecology.

Gaarder, Munar, and Sollis (2003, p. 12) draw a close parallel between identifying community assets and setting the stage for strategy development that effectively builds upon local participation: "Community asset mapping is capacity-based, internally focused and relationship driven. By emphasizing the importance of mobilizing and strengthening the asset base of local communities, the community asset mapping approach explicitly recognizes that local actors are likely to be a significant source of solutions to local problems... Asset mapping requires the evaluation and aggregation of assets in order to reach consensus on the scope and influence of each asset type on community life.... The agreements reached are the basis for the formulation of development strategies that relate to, and which seek to enhance, identified capacities."

Community asset maps, when predicated upon community participation, can be quite powerful because they allow communities to determine what kinds of information they want and need based upon their own priorities, and not those of academics or governmental officials. Engaging a community in a mapping activity increases acceptance of the final results, too, increasing the likelihood that interventions resulting from the analysis will be implemented (Bryant, Forthofer, Brown, Landis, & McDermott, 2000). We would argue that community asset assessments are not conceptually and politically possible without active and meaningful participation on the part of the community throughout all facets of the assessment (Hardcastle, Powers, & Wenocur, 2011).

Although there is a tendency to romanticize communities, including their residents, not every resident is a productive and meaningful part of a community. A community asset assessment, as a result, must identify not only residents who are widely regarded, but also those who, for a variety of reasons, have not been active and contributing members of their community but have the potential to contribute. Chaskin and colleagues (2001, p. 13) comment regarding helpful neighbors: "Those who participate in this way are generally a minority of the residents and often have somewhat higher socioeconomic status than most people in the neighborhood." Our experiences do not bear this conclusion out, and we have found that there is a wide range of residents who help each other. Differences, however, may exist as to the visibility, frequency, duration, and type of assistance provided (information, expressive, instrumental), with some forms of assistance being more visible than others, requiring a more nuanced approach in asset assessments.

Capturing these nuances in the neighbor helping neighbor process, as a result, should be one of the goals of a community asset assessment. Focusing on the more visible helpers and systematically identifying them are important. However, going deeper into a community's caring or helping systems represents what we believe to be a more significant contribution for an asset assessment (Delgado, 1999). This information lends itself to quantitative as well as qualitative dimensions. Each informs the other and serves to provide a more comprehensive portrait of a community.

The role of access to information in enhancing community capacity has not received the attention it warrants, and an asset assessment, and specifically mapping, represents one form of effort to provide access to information. Hyland and Owens (2005, p. 105) stress the importance of information in the life of a community: "A growing body of literature has revealed the disparity resulting from poor access to information. In a very real sense, information has become as essential to the creation and maintenance of wealth as the control of capital, land, and natural resources... One could argue that the inaccessibility of information to community-based groups further alienates neighborhood stakeholders."

Parker (2006, p. 481) goes so far as to argue that community map making must be within the reach of both those who are formally and informally educated, effectively democratizing this form of assessment: "community mapping [should] not [be] the sole purview of 'scholars.'" Lydon (2003), too, rightly observes that community mapping is not mapping for or of a community; it is mapping by the community of its vision, which can eventually lead to action. The emphasis must always be on participatory principles more than an actual map.

Community maps ultimately must seek to achieve high levels of inclusion, transparency (lucidity of the goals, context, and legitimacy of the map makers), and empowerment (Parker, 2006; Tulloch, 2007). It is possible to have both participation and a map that is inclusive; it is not possible to have an inclusive map without participation. This point may seem straightforward. However, it is relatively easy to lose sight of the process and emphasize the final product, the map.

The field is increasingly addressing the importance of differentiating between different levels of community participation to draw implications for practice, as already noted in Chapter 2. Wong, Zimmerman, and Parker (2010), for example, offer one focused on youth. Delgado and Staples (2008) also offer their version of different levels of participation regarding youth activism. Snow's (2008, p. 1) observations of community asset mapping as a participatory process reinforce the need to think beyond research methods when discussing this form of assessment: "Asset mapping is not a system or a method, but a way of thinking and acting that reminds us of the assets all around us and the success we have when we work these assets together to get things done as part of a larger community."

Noy (2008), too, proposes to use maps as a participatory means of advancing public sociology's contributions to nonacademic communities or as a way of giving back to a community. Maps, when placed in the hands of community residents, provide a concrete tool to visualize and conceptualize their communities in ways that rarely have been available to them. In addition, maps can be as sophisticated or as "simple" as the community wants them to be (Mittelmark et al., 2006).

Lydon (2003, p. 1) also extols the virtues of community mapping and raises important reasons as to why community social workers have found this tool attractive: "Community mapping is both the recovery and discovery of the connectedness and common ground that all communities share. The emerging cartographic practice is a vital part of a worldwide movement for participatory learning, community empowerment and sustainable planning. Maps visually represent worldviews and knowledge and therefore have unique spatial power. Community mapping assumes that ordinary people and communities can make maps to express their stories about their lives and home places. Viewing community mapping as a learning and planning process, facilitating such story telling and community maps represent the stories." Some common ways that can be used to engage residents to tell about an asset include asking them to create a picture of it, tell a story about it, or do an exercise about it, such as choosing just 15 words to describe it.

Community asset maps, it must be emphasized, go far beyond the role of conventional maps by necessitating that assets be linked or weaved together for a picture or vision to emerge that will eventually lead to interventions by actively integrating how communities view their assets. Beaulieu (2002, p. 12) states that "to be truly effective, asset mapping must take the essential step of linking these various talents and resources together. In isolation, these aspects are likely to realize, at best, only modest advancements in the well-being of local people and their communities. Integration of these assets, however, provides the foundation for genuine improvements in the welfare of those people and their localities." Clearly, these types of maps are not conventional and lend themselves to community wide groups and subcommittees determining what assets are important to enhance daily living experiences.

CAUTION IN USING COMMUNITY ASSET MAPS

The value of community asset maps is well established in select practice and scholarly circles that particularly embrace social and economic justice and participatory democracy. Nevertheless, there are very good reasons why community asset maps have not enjoyed a wider acceptance in both practice and scholarly realms. Kerka (2003), for example, identifies four factors that may act as barriers to community asset mapping: (1) lack of process; (2) lack of time; (3) resistant agencies/professionals; and (4) negative attitudes or fears on the part of residents. Each of these factors is significant. However, they rarely appear by themselves, and a community asset mapping assessment generally can be counted on to involve several, if not all of them.

When maps seek to incorporate cultural assets, as in the case of newcomers who do not have English as their first language, there are additional social and political challenges if community social workers do not share the same background and language skills as the community (Delgado, 2007). Recent national efforts to deport undocumented residents have made this community particularly distrustful of authorities. Also, invariably, there is tension between academics and communities they seek to research (Carroll & Rosson, 2007; Christopher, Watts, McCormick, & Young, 2008; Moser, 2008).

Parker (2006, p. 482) acknowledges the challenges but still sees the rewards being greater than the challenges in that "the defining and understanding community-mapping projects is problematic, complex, and contingent—but nevertheless important. Community mapping is a growing phenomenon, and evidence suggests that positive outcomes of such projects are possible. Yet closer scrutiny can reveal production processes fraught with tension and marked by unacknowledged privilege." This assessment of community asset mapping is very insightful and identifies the inherent political and social realities associated with any kind of venture into the community that has the express goal of bringing about social change.

It is relatively easy to romanticize the role of community asset maps because they often symbolize everything that is "good" about community social work practice. DeFilippis, Fisher, and Shragge's (2006, p. 673) comments about "community" are also applicable about community asset assessments and are worth noting: "As the realm of community has grown increasingly important in the contemporary political economy, the theoretical debates surrounding community have also grown in importance and volume. Too often this literature has been either celebratory or dismissive; either romanticizing the concept and thereby elevating it to primary rank as the focal point of societal initiatives, or objecting to its regulated limits and contradictions and thereby dismissing its importance and political utility. There are important contributions being made by those who dismiss community and those who celebrate it." Community asset maps are an excellent vehicle for channeling the values outlined in Chapter 3. However, they are not the "perfect tool" or "magical tool" that we, and many other advocates, wish them to be.

Craig and Elwood (1998, p. 13) raise a yellow flag of caution about power and representation in community mapping: "We close with a word of caution. Information is power and it is tempting to misuse power, especially for groups that are advocating for a specific outcome. Community groups are able to use maps and geographic information to support their position, but sometimes those positions could be quite parochial or elitist. Grassroots does not always mean, 'in the best interest of society' or 'representing the interests of all members of the community' ... Nevertheless, community groups are playing a key role in balancing interests in American society. Maps and geographic information are helping to support this role, for better or worse." They raise the issue of status and power differentials even within the community.

FREQUENCY OF COMMUNITY ASSET MAPPING

How often does a community need to do an asset assessment and a corresponding map? There is no simple answer, except to say that it depends upon the community. Assets, like needs, are dynamic and can be expected to change in strength, appear, or disappear. This does reinforce the importance of action occurring as quickly as possible to capitalize on the immediacy of the findings. It is important to remember that considerable time and resources were invested in the assessment, and communities do not have the luxury to sit and congratulate themselves for too long a period.

One popular approach is to initially undertake a comprehensive assessment, then focus on a capital specific assessment every year thereafter. Targeted efforts can be limited in scope (e.g., geographic) and rely upon methods that have been used in the community in past efforts, as a means of maintaining consistency and saving on time and funds for training on new methods. As noted in Chapter 6, community forums, focus groups, ethnographic observations, and key informant methods lend themselves to capital specific assessments and are not as expensive as some of the other methods.

This approach may seem dubious, but it is not beyond the reach of most communities. It is important to remember that community asset assessments can be targeted or as broad and comprehensive as the community warrants. The former are less expensive and labor intensive, particularly if there is a cadre of residents with prior experience in conducting asset assessments. The time, money, and effort expended in the initial effort turn into an investment in the subsequent undertakings. Our experiences with youth illustrate this point (Delgado, 2006). Youth who are involved in asset assessments generally stay in the community as they transition into adulthood, thereby maintaining this asset assessment capacity and experience in the community.

TYPES OF MAPS

Contrary to conventional wisdom, there are numerous types of community asset maps, just as there are numerous types of capital. Some are more conventional and use modified standard geographic maps of a community. However, others are quite innovative in design and execution. For example, one very innovative mapping project transpired in the South Bronx, New York City, and had a map of the neighborhood taped onto a closed off street that was the end of a local parade route, which helped to ensure a steady flow of resident traffic. Those residents passing by were asked to list both community problem and asset locations on the map. The information was converted into artistic symbols of varying colors. This example illustrates the integration of art with community participation in a manner that does not have to be labor intensive and expensive and injects a degree of "fun" into the experience (Cohen-Cruz, 2007). This form of mapping can complement other forms of mapping to develop a more comprehensive perspective on a community's assets, bringing in different visual representations.

For the purposes of illustrations, though, only four types of asset maps will be presented: (1) community cultural; (2) community ecological; (3) community economic; and (4) community public. However, community assets, as already noted, can be conceptualized in a multitude of ways. In essence, asset maps are limited only by our imagination.

1. Community Cultural Maps

Cultural mapping taps cultural capital and represents a rather exciting perspective on asset mapping. Michigan State University (2000, p. 3) notes: "Cultural mapping consists of examining long-term customs, behaviors, and activities that have meaning to individuals and to the community. Information for cultural mapping is gathered in face-to-face interviews. Communities can use cultural mapping as a tool for self-awareness to promote understanding of the diversity within a community and to protect and conserve traditions, customs, and resources."

This form of mapping brings forth the potential to reach out to newcomer populations, for example, in a manner that helps these communities take stock of their cultural assets, and concomitantly share these gifts or treasures with the outside community. It can also generate new types of information or data that can result in new scholarship and ways of better serving the community. A focus on assets rather than needs serves an important public relations function, too, that is often needed to counteract negative publicity that generally is associated with "illegal aliens" and how much they are "costing" this country.

Cultural mapping, as noted in the discussion of cultural capital in Chapter 2, can involve efforts to identify informal art as a direct manifestation of community cultural values, history, and symbols (Delgado, 2011). The bias of what constitutes "art" is one that historically has been a source of contention in communities of color across the nation. Community artistic expressions (e.g., sculpture, banners, store signs, or murals) are culturally influenced and are often found throughout urban neighborhoods. Murals painted by residents, for example, generally go unnoticed by those outside of the community. However, these are significant public art projects that are hard to miss within the community because of their size, content, messages, and location in prominent places. In addition, they tap local artistic talent and beautify the community, besides conveying important sociocultural messages (Delgado, 2000; Delgado & Barton, 1988).

Stern and Seifert (2007) tie together the role of informal, or cultural, art and community revitalization with the economic and social benefits that result from this form of art expression. Informal art is rarely viewed as an asset by those outside of the community. However, within communities with minimal access to careers in the field of art or without art museums that are community operated, informal art provides an opportunity to bring these creative impulses and abilities to the public.

2. Community Ecological Maps

Maps that seek to identify community based organizational relationships, or a form of social capital, are another way of focusing a community asset assessment. These types of maps seek to "clarify the place of an organization in the community spectrum" (Best Practice Briefs, 1998–1999, p. 4). Community eco-logical asset mapping is often incorporated into broader community asset maps. Although community ecological maps tend to focus on formal, or traditional, community organizations, they can also incorporate or focus on nontradi-tional organizations (Delgado, 1998) or even combine both formal and informal organizations.

One of the major advantages of community ecological maps is that they facil-itate focusing an asset assessment to answer specific questions about this form of capital. Broadening the category of organization to encompass both formal and informal, however, does complicate the process, but the picture it presents is a more realistic assessment of a community's institutions. There is little dis-pute that local community based organizations wield considerable influence in the day-to-day business of residents. Thus, it becomes essential to view these establishments with very careful attention, and a community asset map can capture the expressive and instrumental roles these institutions play in com-munity life.

3. Community Economic Maps

Economic capital maps are within the grasp of many professions, although this type of map seems to be preferred among economists. As noted in Chapter 2, economic capital can be defined narrowly or broadly, depending upon the values and perspectives of those undertaking an assessment. The advantages of defin-ing it in a broader manner that includes the informal economy are considerable in helping to capture the influence of otherwise invisible economic power within the community (Delgado, 2011).

An asset assessment focused on the informal economy would seek to iden-tify businesses related to child care, meals, and repair services out of residents' homes. Focusing on community owned formal small businesses of a particular type, such as grocery stores, bakeries, and restaurants, allows for an assessment of the food sector and the economic role these institutions play. Broadening the asset to go beyond economic capital can generate data on the roles these insti-tutions play in fostering healthy diets, for example, and thus encompass other forms of capital. Boundaries between different forms of capital are rarely rigid, allowing for local circumstances to dictate the number and types of capital, that can be classified in a variety of ways, depending upon the perspective taken.

The presence and importance of informal businesses in marginalized urban communities are forms of economic capital that generally get overlooked in com-munity asset assessments (Delgado, 2011). Informal businesses are those types of enterprises that legally exist in the broader society. Consequently, it is important to reemphasize that they do not encompass drug dealing and selling of stolen property, for example.

Informal businesses are often owned and operated by local residents, and the nature of local circumstances necessitates that they stay invisible to outside authorities. However, their invisibility does not diminish their influence and importance in the lives of residents. Thus, a community economic capital map that focuses on formal economic institutions can present just a "partial" view. It is only when the assessment ventures out to identify informal businesses that a more comprehensive picture can be captured. Such an effort, however, will prove costly and time consuming, but the results are that much more fruitful and indicative of a community's true economic capital.

4. Community Public Maps

Community public capital assessment first appeared formally in a 1997 report entitled *Back to Basics: Creating New Possibilities for Flint*, which was produced by the Mott Foundation. A multimethod approach was used involving key informant interviews and focus groups. A listing and location of Flint, Michigan, assets were provided in the report, along with recommendations for how to tap public capital. Although this report did not provide any graphic representation maps to present its findings, the potential for use of a visual map does exist, increasing the value of these forms of maps in reaching an expanded audience.

Community public capital maps draw upon a variety of capitals, most notably social capital. Such maps can gather and show four types of community focused information (Best Practice Briefs, 1998–1999, p. 3): "(1) social gatherings that enable people to learn about what is happening in the community; (2) organized spaces for interactions where people can learn about, discuss, and act on community challenges; (3) catalytic organizations that spur discussion on community challenges and marshal a community's resource to move ahead; and (4) safe havens for decision-makers to meet for unofficial candid discussions."

Mapping public capital, however, needs to go beyond "officially" recognized spaces and places and take into account informal or nontraditional settings in which residents feel comfortable meeting and sharing thoughts and insights. The senior author, for example, found a local Latino owned restaurant in Corpus Christi, Texas, that was a community gathering place where an intersection of almost all major segments of the Corpus Christi Latino community and elected officials would gather and exchange information. This setting, as a result, would encapsulate all of the forms of capital covered in Chapter 2, if community asset assessors took the time and effort to better understand the role of this institution in the life of the community.

MAPPINGS STAGES

Community asset assessments are probably best planned and implemented in phases or stages because of the complexity, thought, finances, and sociopolitical considerations involved in undertakings that are innovative, community based, and stress participation and ownership by the ultimate beneficiaries of the undertaking, namely the community itself. In addition, because most community asset assessments involve high levels of volunteerism and extensive preparation to be successful, the process will often take longer than originally anticipated.

Community asset mapping generally has been conceptualized as consisting of one major activity with various facets related to it. We, however, have found it useful to think about this community asset mapping as consisting of four major stages: (1) Pre-Mapping Stage; (2) Preparation Stage; (3) Asset Identification Stage; and (4) Post-Mapping Stage. Each stage, in turn, has a specific set of goals guiding its development and can be further divided into multiple activities. Consequently, the following section has been organized keeping this in mind in the hopes of helping practitioners better assess the forces that are in place to facilitate the assessment as well as the forces that are detrimental to carrying out the project.

PRE-MAPPING STAGE

A pre-mapping stage effectively serves to set the requisite foundation for a community mapping project. This stage, like any foundation, consists of various complementary activities and tasks. These relate to four activities: (1) Sponsoring Organization Selection; (2) Steering Committee Selection; (3) Asset Team Selection; and (4) Publicity. The time, money, thought, and effort devoted to making sure the "right" people are part of this undertaking are well spent.

1. Sponsoring Organization Selection

Community asset assessments are predicated or founded upon active citizen involvement (Bishop, Vicary, Browne, & Guard, 2009). However, the degree of participation on the part of residents may be influenced by their perceptions of social organizations and government (Marinetto, 2003). Interestingly, the professional literature has not paid close attention to the importance of selecting the "lead" organization in a community asset assessment.

The lead organization must be well respected and so have institutional legitimacy within the community, with a requisite history of initiating efforts of high value and meaningfulness to residents. It does not mean, however, that other organizations cannot play an active role in this endeavor. Collaboration, after all, is a key theme in community asset assessments, just as it should be in community based participatory research (Minkler, 2005). Nevertheless, the lead organization will be the public "face" of the assessment, which will eventually lead to an intervention that seeks to enhance community assets and address community needs and concerns.

Ideally, this organization is also in the position to possibly assume a lead role in carrying out recommendations based upon asset findings. In addition, this lead organization must be able to provide or broker the necessary resources such as staff, space, and funding, for the assessment to be carried out in the most efficient manner. Consequently, the lead organization is an important resource in helping to attract other resources and political support for this undertaking.

2. Steering Committee Selection

The composition of a group that will guide an asset assessment may seem like a perfunctory step, but it is not. The composition of the steering committee will influence all facets of a community asset assessment, and the time and thought that goes into its selection and preparation are time and effort that will pay back multifold as the assessment progresses. In essence, there should be no shortcuts taken with a steering committee because its members represent the "glue" and the "vision" that keep a project together.

Community efforts invariably consist of a wide cast of actors such as religious leaders, business owners, residents, teachers, students, and social service staff, to list but a few types. All of these individuals bring with them unique perspectives on a community's assets based upon their histories in the community, personal experiences, sources of legitimacy, languages, vantage points, and sets of values (Chaskin et al., 2001). Therefore, considerable thought and outreach should be undertaken to make this committee inclusive of all the major sectors of a community. As a result, community asset assessments become an opportunity to build social capital, even when this form of capital may not be a primary goal of an asset assessment. Relationships built in this experience can carry over into other projects and spheres well after an assessment is completed. The social capital resulting from the initial experience can pay significant dividends in future endeavors.

The ideal number of steering committee members is certainly open to various perspectives. Unfortunately, the professional literature has not advanced the "ideal" number of members. We believe that it should be around 12 and that this number allows the steering committee to be large enough to incorporate various major constituencies and stakeholders but not too large that it becomes unwieldy in conducting business. Subcommittees, though, can facilitate bringing on board additional members with specific competencies or legitimacies, with the subcommittees disbanded upon completion of their tasks.

In addition, this committee size allows for setting up meeting dates in a less challenging manner than would be possible with a very large steering committee. Making the committee smaller, though, would open up the possibility of it being labeled "elitist," which is probably the most damaging accusation that can be leveled at a community asset steering committee.

3. Asset Team Selection

The composition of the team that will be actively involved in carrying out major parts of the assessment is just as important as the composition of the steering committee. Steering committees are often the primary source for recommending team members, so a highly inclusive and diverse steering committee increases the likelihood that team members, too, will represent significant sectors of the community.

Careful attention must be paid to ensure that all major community constituencies and stakeholders are given an opportunity and are encouraged to play an active role in this undertaking. Particular attention, however, must be paid to age, race, gender, sexual orientation, abilities, and, as in the case of numerous urban communities across the country, legal status. Bringing together this representation may result in "tensions," such as in the case of representatives from religious fundamentalist groups as they relate to lesbian, gay, bisexual, transgender, and intersex (LGBTI) communities. However, inclusiveness must be an integral goal of community asset assessments.

A clear understanding of the goals, activities, and tasks involved in carrying out an assessment will aid in the selection of the team. An assessment focused on a particular sector of a community with a history of attracting newcomer groups, for example, will necessitate finding team members who share this group's background and the use of very specific outreach methods that take into account their legal status. The methods that will be used to conduct the assessment, in turn, will also be another consideration. A highly qualitative approach will necessitate having team members with "people skills" and language competencies other than English, for example.

The legal status of the residents will make the assessment process more labor intensive because of the high level of suspicion that team members will encounter, even if they share the same ethnic background as the residents. The team should also be supported in reaching community members whose communication style or method is not typical based on factors besides country of origin. For example, some community members may have communication differences because of various disabilities, but their input should still be valued. Examples might be skill development for communicating with people who have expressive language difficulties or who use sign language.

The size of this team is very much dictated by the comprehensiveness of the effort, the timeframe, and the amount of funding to support the assessment. A comprehensive effort will necessitate having the capability to reach all subgroups in the community and, ideally, having member representatives of those groups on the team. A highly focused assessment, in turn, will not require a large team. However, this does not mean that the level of training and field support for a small team is any less complicated than for a large team.

The question of whether resident team participants should be paid for their effort seems to be one that invariably emerges. Our position is that the decision be made to pay them. Compensation, however, can be done in a variety of ways. Payment through gift certificates as a token of gratitude is one effective way of recognizing effort and talents. This takes on greater prominence if the certificates are donated by local businesses. Consequently, local circumstances must dictate the most appropriate manner to help compensate participants for their efforts.

Compensation certainly will increase resident participation in the research effort. Youth from economically marginalized backgrounds, for example, may not be able to volunteer to be part of an assessment. However, if they are paid, it increases the likelihood of their participation because participation may be in lieu of an after school job (Tice, 2009). This exchange of funding, however, may compromise their ability to be honest in their feedback (Delgado, 2006).

4. Publicity

The innovative nature of asset assessments makes this form of research less accessible to the average community resident, who is more likely to be used to needs assessments that seek to uncover needs, problems, and concerns. Thus, the more prepared the community is for this undertaking through widespread publicity, the easier it will be to undertake the process and continue to keep the community excited and ahead of developments. There are few urban marginalized communities that would not welcome the creation of positive news about them, and the publicity stage represents the first step in what will eventually become a publicity campaign that will end with the dissemination of positive results.

The initiation of a community asset assessment benefits from a well orchestrated media campaign that informs the community of the effort. Local media outlets such as cable programs and radio programs are excellent venues for disseminating details and information concerning the nature of the study. Community asset assessments are major community events and are deserving of appropriate media coverage. The same media sources can also play important roles in disseminating findings, once the study has been completed. These sources take on added significance in cases in which the community is highly diverse in cultural backgrounds and may not have English as its primary language. Ethnic and racial media outlets, as a result, take on prominence in these circumstances.

Involvement of local houses of worship and key community institutions such as schools, ethnic specific social agencies, eating establishments, and community social centers also provides other avenues for getting information out to different sectors of the community. The second author found libraries to be very helpful in disseminating information in local communities because of librarians' commitment to being of service to all sectors of the community. In essence, researchers should consider a variety of sources to publicize the research

PREPARATION STAGE

Any research undertaking requires time and resources to be set aside for preparing the community and the research team for the undertaking. This preparation or foundation, however, takes on added importance in the case of a community asset assessment that stresses participatory democratic principles because the "community" will play a significant role in all facets of the project. In the case of low income and low wealth urban communities of color, participants will generally have a low formal level of education and no formal training in the area of research, necessitating time and effort being devoted to grounding the research team.

Four phases stand out in importance during this phase, and they are all of equal importance: (1) Orientation; (2) Training; (3) Formalizing Collaboration Agreements; and (4) Trial Run. Each phase, in turn, brings with it a unique set of rewards, challenges, and tasks.

1. Orientation

The orientation phase attempts to address questions and concerns participants may have about such an endeavor since, in all likelihood, few, if any, will have been formally involved in a research project. Just as importantly, the philosophy (values, principles, and goals) of an asset assessment must be shared and discussed. The orientation phase usually takes about two hours, long enough not to rush a dialogue, but not too long for individual participants who may not actually want to be a part of the project.

In addition, final decisions about participation should not be done on the spot. It is advisable that participants be given 48 hours in which to make a decision. This time period gives them an opportunity to talk with significant members of their families or trusted members of the community. This decision making period can result in fewer turnovers of team members once the project commences. Ambivalence concerning participation should be minimized or eliminated once a project gets implemented.

2. Training

The training phase represents an opportunity for organizations and funders to invest in participants with the immediate benefits of an assessment but also the future benefits of enhancing community capacity after the completion of an assessment (Johnson et al., 2009). The level and intensity of the training are influenced by the goals of the asset assessment, whether it is comprehensive or focused on particular assets, and the number of methods used.

Comprehensive asset assessments necessitate an expenditure of considerable time and resources whereas focused assessments require less intense training. Nevertheless, both efforts must conceptualize the training and support needs of the asset team taking place at various junctures, with the initial phase being the most labor intensive. Training and support, however, can also take place throughout the remaining stages of the assessment. Furthermore, it is necessary that mechanisms such as peer debriefing take place on a regularly scheduled basis (Lietz, Langer, & Furman, 2006).

Hands on, experiential training is favored over more didactic and theoretical training. The former often involves team building exercises, role plays, videos, and videotaping. These training methods help to ensure that the voices of those participating in community asset assessments, in similar fashion to other forms of qualitative research, are heard, and heard correctly. Residents with low formal educational levels may have a hard time reading and writing, making their contributions that much more difficult to obtain. Listening to long lectures, too, may prove difficult because residents are required to sit still and in one place for an extended period of time. Experiential training, however, provides different ways of learning and participation and, when done well, makes time go by very fast. This does not mean, however, that didactic lectures cannot be integrated throughout the training. However, these lectures are meant to supplement experiential training rather than the other way around.

3. Formalizing Collaboration Agreements

Preliminary enlistment of formal and informal collaborating organizations can be started during the early period when assessment is being considered. This phase should formalize these preliminary decisions and result in commitments with clear expectations concerning roles, time commitments, and expectations, though.

An asset based initiative must seek to develop collaborative interdisciplinary, organizational, and resident partnerships as part of the effort (Baker, Dennison, Boyer, Seller, Russo, & Sherwood, 2007; Minkler, 2005). Eloff and Ebersohn (2001), based on a South African study, conclude that an interdisciplinary collaborative approach toward asset assessments enhances the likelihood of more effectively assessing community early intervention efforts.

Teufel-Shone, Siyuja, Watahomigie, and Irwin (2006) conclude that communities, practitioners, and scholars can collaborate to produce a culturally relevant and formative community assessment. Levy, Baldyga, and Jurkowski (2003, p. 314) provide a set of recommendations for the development of university–community partnerships that have direct relevance for community asset assessments and involvement of multiple organizations in this type of endeavor: "Although an often desired goal, true partnership between community members and university researchers can be difficult to achieve. The development of selection criteria can be useful for objectively choosing a community organization as a partner agency. The implementation of formal partnership principles is proposed as a strategy for building a successful partnership. Partnership principles are a powerful mechanism to assure ethical relations between collaborators. As a strategy for process evaluation, they can help organize data on the extent to which intent has translated into action. They provide a structure for project stability that can outlast individual commitments and a mechanism to keep project commitment on course and maintain active engagement."

Collaboration across formal and informal sectors is often one of the recommended routes that community asset mapping can take to help ensure that outcomes of such efforts result in positive social change (Robinson & Meikle-Yaw, 2007): "Working together is the first step toward building community. When diverse groups of citizens completed signature project tasks, their actions redefined the local community and improved associational networks. Civic participation provided opportunities for learning, skill building, creating new leaders, and nurturing a culture of participatory development. The substance for building community capacity, social capital, and civic participation will be augmented when diverse people participate and interact in a wholesome and winsome manner with each other in various roles to accomplish the goals they had set for their community. By working as peers to accomplish a goal or task, people learn new things about each other and themselves and discover that they can do things together that they didn't previously recognize."

The development of community partnerships across all significant sectors of a community will necessitate community social workers having a skill set not usually found in social work curricula (Wertheimer, Beck, Brooks, & Wolk, 2004). Interestingly, the importance of collaboration is often mentioned in grant proposals and talked about in passing in social work education. For example, it has been a stated goal of federal government funders to facilitate bringing together educational and human service agencies to carry out special education mandates. However, collaboration is probably one of the most challenging forms of practice for community social workers and other professions interested in this form of work (Lasker & Lasker, 2006; Sirianni, 2007). This is especially true when government funding sources operate in a way that encourages competition and separate "turfs," such as between education and human services, as the second author learned in an interagency collaboration demonstration project (Humm-Delgado, 1980).

Asset focused assessments also increase the likelihood of multidisciplinary collaboration in service to communities (Lasker & Lasker, 2006; Morgan & Ziglio, 2007). Suarez-Balcazar and colleagues (2006) report on the success of their food collaborative project in bringing various sectors of the Chicago African American and academic communities together to establish a connection between an African American farmer and the community, a community grocery store, and a salad bar in a local school. An embrace of an asset framework facilitated the development of this project and minimized the level of distrust between disciplines and between academics and residents.

Deficit oriented assessments often rely upon highly developed diagnostic categories that are very profession driven, for example, in the mental health and special education fields. This historical reliance, including a very specific professional language, makes collaboration across professions difficult to undertake. An asset focused assessment, however, necessitates the use of a relatively "new" language and concepts that do not share the historical baggage of their deficit oriented counterparts. Every profession, so to speak, is starting anew in this area, and as a result, may be more likely to collaborate because history is not weighing it down. New language and nomenclature open up this arena for dialogue, and possibly collaboration, which was either arduous to achieve in the past or simply not possible.

4. Trial Run

It is highly recommended that a trial run be undertaken to help ground team members in all facets of the methodology and to help them better understand their roles. This trial run essentially serves to accomplish three goals of equal importance: (1) better preparing team members for what the experiences of conducting an asset assessment will be like; (2) helping to resolve potential roadblocks or unanticipated challenges; and (3) preparing participants and the community for why and how a community asset assessment will unfold in a particular manner that takes into account local circumstances.

Trial runs, like their more conventional pretests for researchers, are quite common in community asset and needs assessments. A trial run does not completely eliminate all potential problem areas. However, it may provide surprises, such as community members with particular abilities to interview religious members or folk healers in the community. Conversely, some committee team members may have an aversion to interviewing certain key sectors of the community because of prior negative experiences or strong religious beliefs about folk healers and religion, for example. Youth may wish to avoid certain sections of a city because of concerns about gang violence, as another example.

ASSET IDENTIFICATION STAGE

This stage represents the culmination of a difficult and, no doubt, lengthy process for all those who were involved in this undertaking. This stage, as a result, brings added pressure to all those involved in the assessment. Nevertheless, there is much joy and reward in this phase because it represents the actual visualization of information that prior to this point existed in bits and pieces and was not previously visualized by a community. This stage may be the first time a community actually has taken a picture of itself by accentuating its assets.

This stage is considerably labor intensive for very good reasons—so much is expected to happen during this period. Many of the methods covered in Chapter 6 lend themselves to use during this stage. Oral histories, key informants, photovoice, ethnographic observations, and journals, for example, can play instrumental roles in engaging residents in sharing their perspectives on community assets that can then be translated onto community maps. How these methods are combined and used will be dictated by the goal of how broad or specific a map is needed.

There are various factors that must be considered during this stage of asset identification. For the purposes of discussion, three of the most important will be addressed for the development of maps done through manual means because these are the types of maps that are within the scope of all communities, including those without access to geospatial technologies (1) asset related information; (2) symbols; and (3) mapping.

1. Asset Related Information

This stage necessitates gathering of information that is asset specific and provides information that can be useful in the mapping and in the development of social change interventions. The identification of the type and location of an asset will play an important role in the actual mapping of a community. It is also important, however, to provide detailed descriptions of the characteristics and why this is an asset. The more information that can be provided, the easier it will be to have all those involved with the assessment agree on the type of asset and its value to the community.

In the case of assets that are people related, detailed information must be obtained on people's willingness to be interviewed and their willingness to be part of a post-assessment intervention. This latter step can also serve as an opportunity to identify any particular challenges that may be encountered in using this asset in a planned intervention that will follow an assessment.

2. Symbols

This stage can only be accomplished after decisions are made as to how assets are going to be labeled for the purposes of mapping. The decision of symbols is determined either by the Steering Committee or a subcommittee. Symbols related to houses of worship will have one symbol. Food establishments, in turn, will use another symbol. In situations in which the asset assessment is being conducted "low-tech," pins of different colors can be used for specific assets. These pins are then placed on a map of the community and situated where the asset is geographically located.

3. Mapping

Finally, we may wonder why it takes so long to get to what many practitioners call the "fun" part of community asset assessment. When the necessary foundation has been laid in the early parts of the endeavor, the mapping part not only represents hard work but also brings with it the joy and exaltations associated with important discoveries. It represents a positive view of communities that rarely are thought of as having positives.

The process of assigning or pinning assets on a map can be a powerful and transformative experience for the group. The most powerful examples are when teams take turns putting the pins on a map and share their impressions and experiences with the whole group. Each team takes its turn. At the end of the exercise, the entire group shares reactions and impressions. This group process becomes particularly important because, ultimately, the entire team must own the results of the assessment, rather than some subsection of the asset map. The same process can be accomplished with computer graphics. However, this process does not have the power of a group in a room participating in the filling out of a community map, with the possible exception of youth who have relevant computer skills.

The process of actually mapping a community's assets can be celebratory in nature, particularly when it becomes a group project that emphasizes maximum community participation. Situations in which team members gather in a room and use an oversized map that facilitates all members specifically noting assets on a map create a sense of excitement. These situations facilitate group dialogue and present a moment, which in some communities is really rare, for sharing of insights, experiences, and mutual discoveries that no image on a computer screen can possibly match. Furthermore, this form of mapping lends itself to involvement of all age groups from children to older adults. It is not unusual, too, to have food and music as part of the process.

POST-MAPPING STAGE

The post-mapping stage consists of multiple major tasks that set the foundation for a social change initiative. This stage provides an opportunity for the discussion of local history, conditions, and trends, too, which are often qualitative and culturally nuanced in nature. This task is a necessary dimension in order to contextualize assets and goals (Delgado, 2011). Development of community context driven or "meaningful" data is a goal for community initiatives, particularly those that are capacity enhancement focused in undervalued urban communities (Zautra, Hall, & Murray, 2008). These data, in turn, can be used to measure the success of interventions during the evaluation of the asset assessment. The process of arriving at asset indicators will also provide team members with an opportunity to engage in an in-depth discussion of how they identify community assets and why they consider them to be important in the social fabric of the community. In addition, they can also arrive at discussions as to how these assets can be mobilized in a concerted effort to enhance the quality of life in the community.

The time demands of this phase are contingent on the level of complexity of the asset assessment. Was the assessment highly focused on one aspect of community assets, or was there an effort to arrive at a comprehensive listing of assets? If comprehensive, then this stage can take a considerable amount of time and might be measured in weeks. How much time this phase requires varies, of course, and the time and effort devoted to the initial phases of the assessment preparing participants will influence this, too. The post-mapping consists of four phases: (1) data analysis and interpretation of findings; (2) dissemination of findings; (3) evaluation of the experience; and (4) development of interventions.

1. Data Analysis and Interpretation of Findings

The data analysis tasks are often the most rewarding ones because of all the hard work that went into gathering the information. Therefore, this phase should involve as many participants as possible and can be divided into various teams. There may, for example, be members particularly interested in spiritual/religious assets. Other teams may be interested in economic capital and may elect to better understand the formal and informal economy of a community (Delgado, 2011). The breaking down into teams does facilitate analysis of findings because it makes it easier to schedule meetings. However, it is important to have all of the teams report back to the entire group that consists of all the teams.

Bringing the teams together provides groups with an opportunity to share each group's findings, analysis, and interpretations, but, just as importantly, it also provides the groups with an opportunity to learn about other facets of their community. For many, this can be a very rare opportunity, and it is also essential for the interpretation of the findings. Furthermore, this can be quite empowering because no segment of the group is left out, and, eventually, the entire group must own the findings and come up with an action agenda. In essence, there are no mysteries as to why a particular action is being promoted. New perspectives or interpretations can also require additional community members, such as with a community forum or expert panel. Nevertheless, the more methods employed, the more challenging and demanding the analysis and interpretation of findings will be (Levy and colleagues, 2004).

2. Dissemination of Findings

As noted in Chapter 8, decisions related to how and where to disseminate findings provide an opportunity to achieve the greatest impact from the mapping and the conclusions derived from analysis. This task must be carefully planned and implemented to achieve the greatest gain because dissemination of findings and corresponding recommendations will set the stage for the interventions the community prioritizes.

3. Evaluation of the Experience

Evaluating how participation was experienced must not be overlooked. To capture the process, evaluation must occur at multiple levels, including individual as well as group and team experiences. This information will play a valuable role in any future community asset assessment and mapping project. Community asset assessments will have multiple sources of information about reactions to the experience that can be tapped, such as journals, observations, and debriefings that occurred throughout the project. However, it will also be necessary to have a more formalized evaluation that systematically gathers information from individuals, groups, and the team.

4. Development of Interventions

Although the process of conducting an asset assessment and map is important, the "so what?" that follows this process takes on importance when the process has been completed. The design of interventions, location of potential funding sources, and development of collaborative agreements with community based institutions must flow from the findings of the assessment and maps. A well designed assessment will provide insights into possible interventions. Community mapping can even be used to determine where to concentrate services and staff to do the greatest good (Maman et al., 2009).

Community asset mapping provides community social workers and the communities they serve with a vehicle for better understanding the capital or assets of their communities. Inner city merchants, for example, have been tapped to offer suggestions for how to improve economic development in marginalized communities, and this information has been used to map various types of community assets (Loukaiton-Sideris, 2000). Also, Zust and Moline (2003) sought the services of two Latino community leaders in helping to interpret findings from their study of Latino culture and community assets. The post-mapping stage is the assigned time when recommendations for interventions take center stage.

CONCLUSIONS

As the reader has, no doubt, realized, there are few limits to community asset mapping because this method can be used with any population group, when the necessary modifications are undertaken to be sensitive to unique sociocultural characteristics, and they can accommodate a wide range of budgets and time constraints. Maps lend themselves to visually conveying the location of various forms of capital, particularly those that are physical and cultural, such as community gardens, murals, houses of worship, grocery stores, hometown clubs, and other settings (Aronson et al., 2007a). Maps can be used to help communities and providers better appreciate and understand the unique characteristics and nuances of the communities they serve.

As noted earlier, asset assessments, like needs assessments, are intellectual and analytical, as well as political and interactional, exercises in bringing about community change, and they should not be taken lightly. Asset assessments and mapping are excellent mechanisms for generating questions and enthusiasm in a community, and this translates into raised expectations for change. Failure to deliver on the change, however, can have negative consequences for future efforts to undertake an assessment, similar to their needs assessment counterparts.

8

Reporting Findings

"In constant dynamic flux, communities rebuild and redefine themselves without the benefit of social science consultation. Despite community-level agency, however, larger processes of social change—migration, innova-tion, renovation, gentrification, renewal, rebuilding—are not always transparent to individuals or to communities...Communities not privi-leged with information on how global or national economic and social policies may be affecting informationally marginalized communities may seek all the tools necessary to express agency but may have no access to them..."

(SCHENSUL, 2005, pp. 191–192)

INTRODUCTION

This chapter presents various innovative ways of disseminating results to a com-munity beyond the conventional issuing of a report on findings and recommen-dations, but using creative approaches to dissemination does not preclude the issuing of a report. There is certainly a place for official reports, and most funders prefer this method. However, reports invariably are written for a particular audi-ence in mind, and rarely is this audience the community that will ultimately benefit from the findings. Consequently, a multifaceted approach toward dis-semination of findings will go a long way toward increasing community partici-pation and achieving change.

The culmination of all the work that has gone into a community asset assess-ment is often represented in a document with information pertaining to meth-odology, findings, recommendations, and limitations. However, the reporting of findings from an asset assessment is sufficiently important to warrant its own chapter.

Clear presentation of research findings from community based research is a perennial issue in health and social science research, particularly when this research involves marginalized populations (Larson, Schlundt, Patel, Goldzweig,

& Hargreaves, 2009; Linday et al., 2011). Durlak and DuPre's (2008) review of the literature on community changes resulting from community research findings identifies multiple ecological factors influencing this process. Ecological factors such as demographic characteristics, population density, primary language spoken in the home, acculturation levels, and histories of dealing with oppressive forces, for example, help shape the change process, and the extent to which, and nature of, outreach and educational campaigns that are conceptualized.

Guerra and Knox (2008) present an excellent case example of the role of culture in influencing how findings from a community study on Latino immigrant youth can get disseminated in the community to maximize their impact. Culture, in this instance, reflects being Latino and young as well as the organization carrying out the initiative. Young people have a culture, and that is often overlooked or subsumed under ethnic or racial culture, but it is sufficiently influential to warrant its own attention. Use of slang as an integral part of their communication necessitates that asset assessments be able to translate to an older audience. In addition, dissemination in the community in which they feel comfortable and accepted will invariably be different from that of their adult counterparts.

A community asset assessment fulfills many different worthwhile functions, including helping to locate the "best" way of getting information and findings disseminated into the community. An asset assessment will reveal the primary media outlets to which the community turns for information. It can also determine how different population groups get information pertinent to them, as opposed to the broader community. Although a general strategy and the corresponding tactics of doing this do not exist prior to an asset assessment, the process will undoubtedly uncover new or nuanced ways of getting the word out. Chung and colleagues (2006), for example, describe a highly innovative approach to disseminating findings and information related to depression and African American communities. This effort involved the use of poetry, film, photography, and a theatre premiere as ways of grounding communication within a cultural context that stresses visual and artistic forms of disseminating information of particular relevance to this community.

Findings from a community asset assessment need to find their way back into the community in a manner that facilitates and encourages discussion and engagement of residents. However, just as importantly, residents need to inform the intervention that follows. Vaugh, Rojas-Guyler, and Howell (2008) provide such a case example of how a photovoice project involving a Latina girls' photography exhibition set the stage for health interventions. Yonas and colleagues (2009) show how the use of creative arts, such as writing, drawing, and painting, with youth sets a foundation for interventions targeting this age group.

The first step, however, needs to be creatively planned to help ensure that all the significant groups are reached. Finding ways of disseminating findings takes on added significance in situations in which the communities that are undervalued have limited access to conventional sources for information, such as local newspapers and media programs in their primary language, or, because of their undocumented status in this country, they cannot easily engage in public discourse. Also, language, in this instance, goes beyond the spoken language and also requires the use of symbols that are culturally grounded and take into account the level of acculturation. This is not to say that findings cannot also be disseminated through other mainstream sources.

There are numerous ways that communities can report the results of an asset assessment. We will highlight seven that are particularly promising in urban communities: (1) community cafés and other small places; (2) community forums; (3) community events and institutions, including meetings at natural gatherings such as houses of worship, festivals, and fairs; (4) local media, such as at newspapers, cable shows, and radio programming; (5) video or photography premieres; (6) websites; and (7) development of case studies. Each of these ways represents varying degrees of expertise, labor intensity, and costs, but each can be tailored to the specific needs of the community, allowing for great variability.

It is important to emphasize that local circumstances will be the primary guiding force in determining which of these seven, or other methods not addressed in this chapter, are to be prioritized. However, the one clear principle we recommend is that results cannot be disseminated using only one method. The more methods employed, the greater the likelihood that all segments of a community will get the information, which will then set the requisite foundation for an intervention. In addition, in all methods of disseminating information, issues for people with disabilities should be addressed, such as using physically accessible locations and accessible formats in websites.

SOURCES FOR DISSEMINATION

1. Community Cafés and Other Small Places

Small gatherings of residents are highly attractive for sharing of information. Bonham and colleagues (2009) found community small group dialogues or discussions to be particularly viable and attractive in urban communities of color. These gatherings, unlike focus groups, which are highly structured and targeted to a particular demographic group and are primarily intended for obtaining information, provide a great deal of flexibility in how they get designed. The information shared in these dialogues can reach a broader audience.

There are generally several places within a community in which residents and visitors gather for coffee or meals. Little Havana in Miami is well known for its coffee stands, called *cafterias*, where residents congregate to get coffee and play dominoes nearby, for example. These types of settings are considered geographically accessible and "psychologically" safe because they are affirming and accepting and, therefore, lend themselves to an exchange of information. Although the physical size of these establishments does not lend itself to large gatherings, the intimate nature of the settings does lend itself to informal conversations.

Community café gatherings in local restaurants are also intimate gatherings that lend themselves to dialogue in small groups. These settings, unlike a community forum, which usually consists of a large gathering of residents, generally consist of tables with each one representing a community's assets (social, human, cultural, economic, physical, political, and intangible) that have been discovered through earlier research processes. Residents can pick tables that interest them, then spend 20 to 30 minutes at a table sharing their perspectives or answering unresolved questions raised in the assessment. At the end of this time period, they can move on to another table and discuss other assets, or they can simply stop. Food and refreshments are generally available throughout the event, lending a casual feeling to the dialogues.

Laundromats are also excellent sources for reaching residents. These establishments generally require those washing their clothes to stay and monitor this activity. Also, these establishments lend themselves in time, space, and psychologically to discussions of community events and concerns. The senior author has used these settings very effectively to disseminate information to the community, and has even paid the expenses of washing and drying participants' clothes while they participated in an event or activity (Delgado, 1999).

2. Community Forums

Community forums represent one of the most attractive ways of obtaining information from a large gathering of community residents. Delgado (1998b), in an assets and needs study of Latino elders in a New England community, used participants in a community forum, in addition to focus groups, to assist in providing interpretations of research findings that were unexpected or difficult to answer. Community forums are not only a method for gathering data on assets but also a potential venue for disseminating key findings and obtaining reactions from an audience.

These gatherings usually attract a large number of community residents and key stakeholders and are a means of generating political support for an initiative. In addition, they lend themselves to media coverage, further highlighting their political significance in communities, particularly when local media such as ethnic newspapers and public access cable shows are encouraged to cover the event. In advance of the event, a fact sheet should be provided to the media that includes contact information for follow up.

Community forums, however, may not be the best venue in communities that have high levels of distrust of authorities such as immigration authorities (Delgado, 2006; Heritage & Dooris, 2009). In addition, much planning must transpire prior to holding a community forum. Considerations include finding a place that is politically neutral, accessible to people with disabilities, and accessible by public transportation. There also must be a plan for child care for participants who must bring their children, comfortable seating arrangements, facilities for food, and the assignment of language interpreters, to name a few other considerations.

3. Community Events and Institutions (Natural Gatherings)

Communities invariably have numerous venues for disseminating asset assessment results. The frequency and nature of community wide events that bring together residents in festivities and celebrations of various kinds are also a form of social and cultural capital (Brough, Bond, & Hunt, 2004). These events are generally an annual affair and are planned well in advance of the date on which they are scheduled to occur. Community events also have individuals or committees charged with planning and implementing them, lending themselves to easy contact by community asset steering committees.

As noted in Chapter 6, oral histories represent a viable, although expensive and labor intensive, method of uncovering lost histories in marginalized communities. Community cultural events and gatherings at houses of worship lend themselves very well to the sharing of the uncovered assets through photographs of respondents, transcripts, and audio/video presentations highlighting key findings (Matarasso, 2007). Oral histories have also been the basis for plays, making findings readily accessible to audiences that may have limited reading language proficiencies (Goldbard, 2006). Sign language interpreters make the event more inclusive of community members, too.

Cultural events can occur several times over the course of a year in many ethnic and racial communities, presenting ample opportunities for the sharing of oral history outcomes (Grodach, 2010). These events are nonstigmatizing and are excellent places and spaces for presenting uplifting information about members of the community who normally would not be thought of as assets. Community historians, who tend to be elders who may have been some of the early settlers in the community, rarely get an opportunity to share their perceptions of how communities have been transformed over an extended period of time. Having knowledge of a community's history represents a foundation upon which to better understand the present and build toward the future.

4. Local Media (Ethnic Newspapers, Cable Shows, Radio Programming, Etc.)

Dissemination of key findings is facilitated through the use of visual images and personal stories, as in the case of the homeless in Toronto, Canada (Halifax, Meeks, & Kander, 2008, p. 129): "When working on social justice issues, it is easy to become overwhelmed by the problems faced. To maintain morale, it helps to be creative, have fun, and see results. In the spring of 2006, we were able to bring together a group of people to document, first hand, the daily experience of being homeless in the City of Toronto. Using photography and story telling, we were able to give voice to a population not often heard. Our powerful images reached out to the public through events and publications. This resulted not only in great coverage and discussion of the important issues we were addressing, but also in a successful and rewarding group project that benefited group members in many ways."

Local media outlets invariably are seeking information that is relevant to the community, often have a following, and are relatively easy to access. These sources, as a result, provide a good avenue for disseminating information. The fact that this information is positive makes it that much more appealing for local coverage, because broader mainstream media are usually interested only in tragedies and negative stories about urban marginalized communities. In addition, broader mainstream media limit access by community residents and tend to rely on information from elected and appointed leaders, major organizations, and national news services.

5. Video or Photography Premieres

Photographic exhibitions, as noted in Chapter 7, are an attractive way of disseminating asset findings in a visual manner. These exhibitions are sufficiently flexible to take into account different amounts of space. Partial exhibitions, for example, can transpire once a major exhibition has taken place. These more limited exhibitions can be shown in key community locations and even can assume a traveling exhibition schedule throughout the community.

The use of community asset videos is starting to get greater attention as this medium becomes less expensive, and the term "video" in this chapter is used to refer to any technology or format that produces what used to be able to be captured only on a videotape. Parker and colleagues (2006) report on the use of video and the development of a manual to capture assets and develop capacity enhancement interventions in Australia. Chavez and colleagues (2004) report on the use of video making as a means of conducting community based participatory research, on how this method facilitates participation from all segments of a community, and on how it can be shown at community events.

The senior author of this book used video as a means of capturing community assets in Holyoke, Massachusetts. This project involved Latino youth ages 14–16 years and was a result of their suggestion of using a video of their community's assets as one effective way of making their findings more accessible to the Latino community. A "premiere" was held in a community center for the event, which was hosted primarily by youth project participants. Copies of the video were provided to all of the families of project participants to share with their family and friends. Later, there were instances of the video being shown in churches and other community settings. Copies were also provided to local libraries for possible retrieval by the general community and other interested people. More recently, the video sharing website YouTube has been available, and youth frequently share there, so this might have been another dissemination site, had it been in existence.

The development of a video can be very labor intensive and expensive because of the equipment that is needed to record, edit, and produce a final product. Therefore, the development of a collaboration partnership with local colleges and university media departments may facilitate the use of video. Still, video undertaking provides many roles for youth that capitalize on their talents and goals. Videos also lend themselves to using captions as a means of reaching a broader audience, with Spanish language audio and English captions, for example. They also may be useful to people who are deaf or hard of hearing, if captioned, and to people who are blind or have visual impairments, if there is a version with video description. In essence, the outcome of community participation is greatly enhanced through the production of a video that is carefully developed.

6. Websites

The influence of the Internet cannot be ignored in the dissemination of asset findings. This method has been referred to as "virtual ethnography" (Heath et al., 2009). Wong (2009, p. 10) advocates for the creation of a website for the results of an asset assessment to be posted and, thus, made available to all who wish to know about the community's assets: "The ultimate goal in creating an inventory of community assets is for this inventory to be online on a website for the members of the community to access. This way, community members can easily use this resource to make more well-informed decisions. As such, after gathering the information about assets, a website needs to be built and all the information needs to be entered on this site...The inventory also needs to be kept up-to-date. The team must decide how frequently they want to update the inventory."

Wong's (2009) recommendation for online access holds much merit. Access to these data is important, and technology provides a range of options for recording and disseminating oral histories. Bonmayor (2008, p. 188), for example, advocates for the use of "digital storytelling," which is a form of hybrid, multimedia narrative that lends itself to critical and creative theorizing, and states: "As an assets-based social pedagogy, digital storytelling constructs a safe and empowering space for cross-cultural collaboration and learning...using as primary evidence the story script, visual images from the digital story, and excerpts from a recorded interview with the author. It concludes that the process of digital story making and theorizing empowers and transforms students intellectually, creatively and culturally." Heath and colleagues (2009) also highlight how project websites lend themselves to special population groups such as youth.

There may be information that is gathered about certain community assets, however, that does not lend itself to wide public scrutiny. Informal businesses, for example, would not want authorities to know of their existence and whereabouts. Informal appliance repairs may be provided in a community home without the requisite licenses and scrutiny by local authorities. These types of businesses are invisible to those outside of the community and, as a result, are rarely, if ever, covered by local media in stories that are positive about a community. Unfortunately, stories related to businesses that are "off the grid" tend to emphasize criminal business activity rather than positive business activity.

Websites that provide information one way to the reader (not interactive) are not necessarily designed to be accessible to people who have visual impairments, even if they have access to an assistive technology such as one that reads text using a synthesized voice. Therefore, it usually is effective to consult not only experts when doing website design but also readers who are blind and visually impaired themselves. Then, the website has to be tested, too, using the assistive technology that the reader actually would use, to make sure it truly is accessible as it is designed.

Jaeger and Xie (2009), in discussing online accessibility issues for people with disabilities and older adults, further point out that accessibility issues have been addressed even less well with interactive online communities in which users communicate with each other. They make the important point that, in addition to the social benefits of online communities, people with cognitive disabilities of all ages can communicate at their own pace, if the online interactive communication is designed to allow for that (e.g., by not requiring immediate, "real time" responses and allowing sufficient time to complete online forms). Therefore, the design of online communities, too, requires forethought, the input of people with disabilities and older adults, and testing for effectiveness and inclusiveness.

7. Development of Case Studies

The reader may question the inclusion of case studies to end "innovative" approaches toward disseminating community asset findings. Case studies have a long and distinguished history in social work practice for very good reasons. Case studies provide both practitioners and scholars with an in-depth description of community asset assessments and, thus, fulfill important roles in advancing this field. However, there are biases against case studies in scholarly circles.

Flyvbjerg (2006, p. 219) identifies five common misunderstandings about case study research: "(a) theoretical knowledge is more valuable than practical knowledge; (b) one cannot generalize from a single case, therefore, the single-case study cannot contribute to scientific development; (c) the case study is most useful for generating hypotheses, whereas other methods are more suitable for hypotheses testing and theory building; (d) the case study contains a bias toward verification; and (e) it is often difficult to summarize specific case studies." Flyvbjerg's (2006) assessment of the value of case studies is not restricted to scholarly circles and academics. Still case studies can also be developed, along with corresponding maps, for community consumption. These can be shortened versions that, with the proper layouts, can be read by a wide sector of the community. These cases also lend themselves to be translated into various language and Braille, increasing their reach to communicate the results of an asset assessment. In addition, they can be written for various levels of literacy, further enhancing their value in communicating community asset findings.

CONCLUSIONS

Social scientists have advocated for greater creative means of conveying community focused information that can result in community change efforts (Foth, 2004; Sutton & Kemp, 2006). Using unconventional ways of disseminating findings necessitates that those guiding a community asset assessment are well attuned to how the community best gets information. A further challenge will be in how the process and outcome get captured so that the immediate community, as well as the external community, has faith in the endeavor. Efforts must be made to determine and document the most cost efficient ways for the findings to get disseminated to aid other communities in their efforts to broaden the landscape of information dissemination.

Uncovering new ways of disseminating the results of innovative research such as community asset assessments provides community social work with a creative outlet for sharing the voices of the community. We would say that uncovering new ways of disseminating information is just as important as developing new methods for capturing these voices. The material covered in this chapter represents but a few examples of how asset findings can find their way back to the community. The reader will, no doubt, be able to expand on the various approaches used in this chapter and cite other potential ways that focus on other key community institutions that touch the lives of many urban residents in specific ways.

Lessons from the Field of Practice

"Assets, often of untold value, lie within the citizens of our communities, within the groups we form, within our larger organizations, within our land and other physical resources, within our local economy and within organizations and projects that connect us. By recognizing these assets, we reconfirm our own capabilities. Also, we can discover possibilities for mobilizing to meet our interests and needs and fulfill our community aspirations."

(ROSSING, *2000, p. 1*)

This section of the book will include chapters on how community asset assessments can be modified to address different populations, themes, rewards, and challenges. Chapter 9 examines a particular age group, youth. Chapter 10 focuses on one group of color, Latinos. Finally, Chapter 11 examines community gardens. Each of these chapters includes unique information, but there are cross-cutting themes that emerge that highlight universal challenges and rewards with this form of research. Therefore, this chapter and the two chapters that follow will be organized into three topics: (1) *Rewards*; (2) *Challenges*; and (3) *Case illustrations*. These are not mutually exclusive of each other. However, each section will focus on particular aspects of community practice that are relevant to doing community asset assessment. In addition, each will focus only on the most salient points, due to space limitations.

9

Asset Assessments
and Youth

"Children and youth see their surroundings in a different way than adults do. By working with children and youth to identify spaces and places which are important to them, it is possible to gain a whole new sense of community and cultural values."

(COMMON GROUND, *2004, p. 1*)

INTRODUCTION

Why should youth be involved in community asset assessments? Youth perspectives on their community must be sought, and they must also play an instrumental role in conducting community asset assessments. Although youth can help map all aspects of community capital, they are particularly adept at assessing youth related assets and bring a unique set of talents and expectations to this form of research (Delgado, 2002, 2006, 2009; Miller, 2008). Youth live in and are part of community daily life and must, as residents, have a place in community asset assessments (Heath, Brooks, Cleaver, & Ireland, 2009; Yonas et al., 2009). Youth represent a vital asset segment of communities, but their perspectives rarely get tapped, and even more rarely are they asked to play a significant role in obtaining the viewpoint of their peers (Sherman, 2004). Youth are assets in all communities and nations (Aspy, Oman, Vesely, McLeroy, Rodine, & Marshall, 2004; Holland, 2009; Shah, 2011), and any nation that neglects its youth is a nation with a very limited future (Sherman, 2004). Also, it could be argued that no society or community should disempower its youth (Delgado & Staples, 2007; Evans, Ulasevich, & Blahut, 2004; Weiss, 2003). In fact, marginalized communities never have the "luxury" of writing off a significant segment of their residents.

Brennan, Barnett, and Lesmeister (2007, p. 13) summarize the state of affairs for involving youth in community development and the importance of doing so for the ultimate success of these projects: "A need exists for program and policymakers to better understand the factors that influence youth involvement in the community development process. Historically, youth input in local decision making, problem solving, and community action strategies has received only limited attention. However, recent trends suggest that youth are playing an increasingly important role in the development of their communities. As non-profits, volunteer groups, and nongovernmental organizations take on greater responsibilities in providing for local well-being, the active contribution of youth is vital to the long-term success of development efforts." There certainly is no better place to start involving youth than in the beginning when an asset assessment is being proposed.

Amsden and VanWynsberghe (2005) advocate for the use of community asset mapping as a research tool that is particularly appealing to youth. It represents a creative way of engaging youth but must be accompanied by novel approaches to formulating results and outcomes for it to achieve its potential with this age group. A number of scholars have utilized innovative ways of involving youth in asset assessments. Yonas and colleagues (2009) describe the Visual Voices project and how the use of creative arts facilitated youth identifying community strengths for addressing safety concerns. They utilized arts based writing, painting, and drawing activities to engage youth.

Photovoice is another creative method for conducting asset assessments that can be used in mapping. As already defined, it is the use of photographic equipment, usually digital, to capture a visual image and to use this image as a vehicle for generating information and discussion. These images also lend themselves to exhibitions that attract large crowds and convey to the broader community important themes and messages. Photovoice represents an appealing method for use by youth.

Strack, Magill, and McDonagh (2004) provide an excellent example of photovoice that can be used by youth in after school projects. Photovoice was used to assist youth to develop their personal and social identities and increase their social competency. Brazg and colleagues (2010) used this method in the Our Community in Focus project to identify community strengths for addressing adolescent substance use and abuse. Dennis and colleagues (2008), too, describe a youth participatory photo mapping project in Madison, Wisconsin, that utilized digital tools, narrative interviewing, and participatory protocols that resulted in maps that provided direction for youth community based interventions.

Finally, it is important to note that, although this chapter focuses on youth aged latency and older, younger children, too, can engage and benefit from asset mapping (Blanchet-Cohen, Ragan, & Amsden, 2003): "Just as young children have an innate tendency to speak, sing, draw, and count, they also tend to make maps...Children as young as four years of age can depict their community, using blocks, cardboard paper, or sand; environmental planners have successfully used maps of different media to elicit children's ideas and interests. In many regards, maps are an ideal medium for children to spatially express the relationships between organisms and their environment...The children's maps provide valuable information for discussing safety issues, planning for play areas or assessing a child's geographical range. Mapmaking also presents the advantage of not requiring language or literacy skills, making the process appropriate for children of different ages and cognitive capacities. The nature and quality of maps change as children mature; generally, by age 11, children create fairly abstract maps depicting an increasingly wide geographical range that includes special places far from home."

Practitioners may well have a hard time accepting Blanchet-Cohen, Ragan, and Amsden's (2003) argument that children can have a role in mapping their community or that they can, in fact, be community assets. Wilson and colleagues (2006), for example, in an article examining high school students working with fifth grade community research team members, describe the potential of youth teams to undertake community asset and risk maps.

REWARDS

Any youth asset assessment must start with youth themselves determining the initial guiding question to an assessment (Hohenemser & Marshall, 2002). The active and purposeful involvement, including leadership and decision making roles, for youth in community asset assessments is an idea that is no longer foreign in some national and international circles (Delgado, 2006; Delgado & Staples, 2007; Zeldin, 2004). Jones (2009) found the important roles that youth leaders play in the voluntary organizations in which they participate and how it can carry into other spheres. Allison and colleagues (2011), too, found youth assets invaluable in informing and shaping a youth violence prevention project. Deeds and colleagues (2006) also report on 15 community participatory studies on asset and needs assessments involving adolescents.

The rewards of actively involving youth in community asset assessments will result in outcomes with profound implications for the present and future of their communities and for society as a whole (Hernandez-Cordero et al., 2011; Larson, Walker, & Pearce, 2005). There certainly are serious challenges, as addressed later in this chapter. Yet, the advantages unquestionably outweigh the disadvantages of youth participation (Aspy et al., 2010). Four particular advantages stand out because of their importance: (1) Youth develop unique knowledge of their own community; (2) Youth assets are tapped; (3) Youth become social change agents; and (4) Youth can receive short-range and long-range benefits.

1. Youth Develop Unique Knowledge of Their Own Community

Youth views of their community are very much shaped by the position they occupy in their community (Shah, 2011). Consequently, their perspectives will have unique vantage points. Evans (2007) argues that youth live in communities, yet their experiences, positive and negative, are generally overlooked by researchers. Furthermore, youth have their own culture that wields just as much influence on them as the conventional views of culture related to race and ethnicity. Youth culture brings music, language, and behaviors that characterize their world view. This perspective on life and community will vary considerably from their parents and other adults in their community. Youth, in addition to understanding their culture, also bring an understanding of the groups they represent within their respective communities, and this knowledge must be tapped. Asset assessments, for example, lend themselves to a focus on youth subgroups, such as female adolescents (Chen, Weiss, & Nicholson, 2010).

Gearin and Kahle (2006) studied adolescent and adult perceptions of the role of green space in Los Angeles and found significant differences between youth and adult views. Adolescents saw green spaces as places for socializing and relaxing, whereas adults viewed them as places for activities. Laughlin's (2008) study of how youth define public space in Toronto provides an insightful perspective on how space and place become conceptualized and utilized based on a subgroup.

Youth views of what constitutes a "good life" and a "good person" are another perspective from which to contextualize a community's assets. Bronk (2008, p. 713), in a study of early adolescents involving this very question, found these concepts to be viable in a community study: "Analysis of their responses revealed that sixth and ninth graders see care and support from friends and family as requisite components of the good life. Having material comforts, being happy, and achieving personal goals were also important, as were staying out of trouble and helping others. Treating others well was necessary for one to be considered a good person. Good people, according to these youths, also acted in genuine or authentic ways."

Andersen (2011) reports on a community based asset assessment focused on young people to determine what it is about their community that attracts them to stay. This study was in response to concerns about a decade long trend of this community losing population. Duke, Borowsky, and Pettingell (2011) show the importance of adults tapping youth views of their neighborhood to improve their engagement in activities. Heinze, Jozefowicz, and Toro (2010), in turn, report on the use of a youth asset assessment to develop more appropriate programming for homeless and at risk youth.

The 4-H organization, the youth development program of the 109 land-grant universities and the federal Cooperative Extension System, is the largest youth development program in the United States, with more than six million youth in urban, suburban, and rural communities as members (4-H, 2012). Although 4-H Clubs generally have been identified with suburban and especially rural locations, the 4-H organization also has programs in several cities. For example, New York City has the Community Improvement Through Youth (CITY) Project, through Cornell University, a land-grant university. In this model program, youth "identify local problems/issues by using various types of community mapping (e.g., GIS/GPS, photography, and videography) and then create lasting, sustainable changes in their communities" and have documented strengths as well as areas for improvement (NYS Community Improvement Through Youth [CITY] Project, 2012).

Youth possess self knowledge and local "contextualized intelligence" knowledge that often get overlooked by adults. Youth are able to ground their concerns and experiences in a manner that escapes most adult comprehension of their lives. In essence, youth are the best experts on their lives and the neighborhoods in which they live. We as adults are not the sole possessors of "knowledge." This informal expertise is best conceptualized as a form of a community quilt, requiring many different pieces of fabric of various shapes, texture, and colors. Youth, as a result, have their contribution to make to this knowledge quilt, and their contribution is no less valuable than that of their adult counterparts. This ability to contribute, however, does not mean that they cannot benefit from adult support via training opportunities (Ross, 2011).

2. Youth Assets Are Tapped

Viewing youth as community assets has started to garner attention from scholars and research institutes. The Search Institute, for example, based in Minneapolis, Minnesota, has undertaken extensive research in the area of assets and has developed a classification system of youth focused assets that has found wide usage across the United States (Clary & Rhodes, 2006; Lerner & Benson, 2002; Moore & Lippman, 2005; Nakkula, Foster, Mannes, & Lewis, 2010; VanderVen, 2008). The Search Institute, as already noted, identified 40 developmental assets related to positive experiences, relationships, opportunities, and personal qualities that youth need to grow up healthy, caring, and responsible.

Schafer-McDaniel (2004) conceptualizes social capital among youth as consisting of three dimensions: (1) social networks/interactions and sociability; (2) trust and reciprocity; and (3) sense of belonging/place attachment. The professional literature has not paid much attention to youth as assets, though. Consequently, it has only been in the past decade that this subject matter has slowly but prominently appeared in professional journals and books.

Youth social navigational skills can be viewed from an assets perspective. Youth who live in areas with high rates of crime, and are able to socially navigate their ways through these neighborhoods and cope with the stressors of life in these areas, possess incredible assets associated with vigilance and problem solving. This must be captured and shared with their communities (Teitelman et al., 2010).

Youth knowledge of information technology, particularly in undervalued communities in which access to this resource is severely limited, stands out and opens up avenues for important contributions to asset assessments and their community (London et al., 2009). Kasumagic's (2008) vivid description of how youth used technology in Bosnia and Herzeogovina to help postwar healing and recovery attests to their contributions and to why they were instrumental assets in those communities. Santo, Ferguson, and Trippel (2010) found that youth utilization of technology (maps, photography, and blogs) helped them to map their community in general. Youth involvement in the asset assessment supported the planning process and the development of family friendly urban areas and fostered civic

engagement. Rodine and colleagues (2006), in turn, found that youth involvement in the community, as evidenced through volunteering opportunities, also
serves as a protective factor. Thus, both the community and the youth benefit.

3. Youth Become Social Change Agents

Youth and social action are a natural combination (Berg, Coman, & Schensul,
2009; Delgado & Staples, 2008; Gordon, 2010; Wilson, Dasho, Martin, Wallerstein,
Wang, & Minkler, 2007). Their knowledge of their communities and social networks is invaluable in the creation of social change efforts at the community
level. Necheles, Hawes-Dawson, and colleagues (2007, p. 2219) tie together youth
technological abilities and advocacy: "Results were derived from photograph
sorting activities, analysis of photograph narratives, and development of advocacy projects. Youth frequently discussed a variety of topics reflected in their
pictures that included unhealthy food choices, inducers of stress, friends, emo-
tions, environment, health, and positive aspects of family. The advocacy projects
used social marketing strategies, focusing on unhealthy dietary practices and
inducers of stress."

Morsillo and Prilleltensky (2007) advance the argument that social interventions that stress meaningful engagement of youth decision makers in social
change efforts benefit them psychologically and politically and call this psychopolitical validity. Youth develop confidence and competencies in understanding political change at the community level. Community asset assessments that
have youth in central decision making roles do bring benefits to participants
that are social, political, economic, and psychological. In addition, these forms
of assessments serve to nurture current and future leaders in the community
being assessed.

Cammarota (2011, p.828) discusses the concept of social justice and youth
development and its merits for youth empowerment in saying that the social
justice youth development (SJYD) model is "conceptualized to facilitate and
enhance urban youth awareness of their personal potential, community responsibility, and broader humanity. The SJYD requires the healing of youth identities
by involving them in social justice activities that counter oppressive conditions
preventing healthy self-identification... While urban youth engage in social justice activities and become committed agents of change, positive educational and
development experiences will emerge."

4. Youth Can Receive Short-Range and Long-Range Benefits

Youth led community asset assessments result in a wide variety of gains for
youth and their community that can be appreciated only when viewed within a
broad time range. Camino's (2005, p. 3) conclusions based upon two community
asset assessments demonstrate that the benefits of youth led asset assessments

are multifaceted, with short-range and long-range implications: "Asset mapping enabled the youth to increase their own civic understanding of the communities' historical, cultural, social, political, economic, and geographic resources. Armed with such knowledge, youth were able to speak with authority in public forums and meetings. The youth also shared their maps and results with other community groups. This contributed to the success of the teams in changing community adult attitudes from viewing youth as current or potential problems to seeing youth as responsible, knowledgeable, and contributing individuals. Finally, asset mapping formed a basis from which the youth were able to lead community involvement. Youth led various community groups in asset mapping as [a] way to include diverse perspectives, and to facilitate community members' first-hand learning of assets and resources."

Community capacity enhancement results from investment in youth and youth involvement in helping to shape the future of their community. Youth participants will remain in the community at the conclusion of the assessment and can, and should, be expected to influence the interventions that are recommended. Valaitas and O'Mara (2005) cite an example of youth investment by highlighting the role and importance of school based computer supported community development. Youth were placed in a position to help other youth and adults, benefiting participants as well as their community. Youth participation in this project was facilitated through increasing their ownership of the project and receiving due recognition from other youth and adults, thereby enhancing their image in the community. The skill sets developed as a result of participation could be transferred to other aspects of their lives, then, and in the future.

CHALLENGES

Categorizing urban youth as a population consisting of nothing but needs and problems is counter to the goals and principles that underpin community asset assessments. A deficit stance would certainly undermine the credibility of any effort to involve or have youth led community asset assessments. Harper and Carver (1999), over a decade ago, and many scholars since, identified a series of challenges of involving youth as collaborators in community research. However, the benefits of including youth far outweigh the challenges. Nevertheless, there certainly are challenges. This section will address four specific challenges: (1) invisibility of research on youth as assets; (2) adult-youth working relationships in shaping asset assessments; (3) youth as not bias free; and (4) youth aging out.

1. Invisibility of Research on Youth as Assets

As already noted, youth can be considered community assets or capital in numerous ways, particularly if we as adults are prepared to seriously broaden our horizon as to who is capable of possessing assets (Davidson, Schwartz, & Noam, 2008). Youth bring energy, innovation, commitment, and a genuine concern for their environment, but their insights into what makes quality youth programming are often overlooked (Yohalem & Wilson-Ahlstrom, 2010).

The professional literature on youth of color as assets has been sadly lacking. Rodriguez and Morrobel (2004), for example, in a review of the literature of six youth development journals and two Latino specific journals, found that Latino youth were rarely the focus of research and scholarship on the use of youth development concepts, with what little attention was paid being heavily deficit oriented. Consequently, a shift in paradigms is needed to highlight their strengths and assets. Filbert and Flynn's (2010) research on youth assets in Canada's First Nation youth in in-home foster care found that those with higher levels of assets were also more resilient, making the identification and tapping of assets important in any program seeking to reach and help this population group.

Valaitis (2005, p. 3) sees the use of the Internet and computers as vehicles for youth empowerment and youth as community assets because of their competencies with technology: "Youth are among the disenfranchised groups. Adults typically view youth as the cause of community deterioration rather than as a community asset. Youth often feel they have little voice in their communities. Youth participation in their communities can positively influence programs so that they are more responsive to youth's needs and can help support youth's sense of self-determination from a community and individual perspective, thereby promoting their health. Increasing youth community participation, however, has been problematic. Since computers are an important aspect of youth culture, they may offer solutions to increasing and supporting community participation." The invisibility of youth as assets and potential leaders and members of community asset projects is a major challenge that must be addressed for communities and community practice to advance.

2. Adult–Youth Working Relationships in Shaping Asset Assessments

The potential benefits of adult–youth relationships is often matched by, or exceeded by, the challenges in developing them based upon mutual trust and respect (Delgado & Staples, 2008; Gordon, 2010). Unfortunately, both sides invariably hold very little trust and respect for the other. This does not mean, however, that this gap cannot be narrowed or eliminated. This will require extraordinary efforts on the part of adults who are willing to be tested by youth.

Adults control resources and power in the human service field, and society in general. Youth would have difficulties, as a result, in undertaking an extensive community asset assessment without the explicit or implicit consent of adults, and without the resources that they control. The information gathered during this process, however, will generally have implications for an entire community, regardless of the ages of its members.

A key consideration in the successful outcome of a youth assessment effort is to what extent adults trust and respect youth and their abilities to shape the environments in which they live. This goal takes on particular significance in the case of newcomer youth, for example, who must negotiate new found freedoms in this society, despite very traditional views of youth in many cultures in which youth simply do not have power (Delgado, Jones, & Rohani, 2005).

3. Youth as Not Bias Free

Community social work scholars and practitioners with extensive experience in working with youth can certainly be tempted to cast this group as consisting of nothing but strengths. This would be a serious mistake. Youth, like their adult counterparts, have unmet needs and are also biased, bringing all of the foibles that adults possess to any discussion of what constitutes an asset and how best to mobilize it in service to the community (Delgado, 2006).

Youth are human beings and can bring biases related to gender, sexual orientation, class, race, age, and disabilities, to name but several of the most obvious ones. Thus, this necessitates that every effort be made to help youth better understand these beliefs and feelings. Adults, however, bring the added limitation of embracing adultist beliefs. Adultism refers to the belief that adults are superior to youth in all regards and that only adults know what is best for youth (Checkoway, 1996; Delgado & Staples, 2008). Therefore, although youth may be ageist regarding older adults in the community, adults may devalue the young.

4. Youth Aging Out

Youth focused and led community asset assessments are largely an untapped recourse with tremendous potential for transforming communities. Youth bring energy, hope, and talent to this field, just as they have to youth led community organizing and intergenerational interventions (Delgado & Staples, 2008). However, they will age and, in the process, leave this age group, making the aging out process a looming challenge for any organization and community wishing to sponsor and support such efforts (Sherwood & Dresner, 2004). Therefore, poor planning can easily result in organizations losing youth who age and transition into adulthood, along with the leadership that is so essential for community centered efforts for social change. Providing opportunities for these "new" adults to continue working with youth is one way to maintain and benefit from this in leadership in community asset assessments.

Efforts to involve youth at relatively young ages will help to ensure that they will remain with an organization for a long enough period of time to acquire the requisite skills and experiences needed for their adult roles. It is important to remember that youth do not suddenly develop strengths at some magical cutoff point. Thus, matching youth with responsibilities and activities will emerge as an important challenge for the field.

CASE ILLUSTRATIONS

Oftentimes, youth are overlooked when it comes to planning and implementing community change (Weller & Bruegel, 2009). Despite making up a large proportion of the overall community, they are a highly underrepresented part of the population when it comes to having power or say in major decisions in their communities. However, they need to be viewed as an asset, instead of a drain, to their communities. Youth do have a lot to offer their communities, and, when given the opportunity, they have helped to produce many positive outcomes for the areas in which they live. Therefore, youth can be assets to the youth community as well as the broader community.

The following four cases focus on different examples of community asset assessments that integrated youth involvement into their communities and illustrate various ways that community asset assessment can be "youth friendly." Youth friendly places, for example, have been mapped as a way of encouraging positive youth development programming (Walker, 2006a).

The case examples will illustrate youth undertaking community asset studies that show the multifaceted aspects involved in planning and implementing these youth focused asset assessments. The cases derive from the United States and Canada: (1) Redwood City, California (John W. Gardner Center for Youth and Their Communities and Redwood City 2020); (2) San Francisco, California (Youth in Focus); (3) Vancouver, Canada (The Youth Friendly Health Services); and (4) Valley County, Nebraska (HomeTown Competitiveness).

1. Redwood City, California

Although youth involvement in community issues is still relatively scarce, it is not a new concept. In fact, a 1996 article in *The New York Times* tells of six urban middle school students who taught a class at Stanford University for a day (Stead, 1996). Despite their youth, the middle school students were the ideal instructors for the *Urban Youth and Their Institutions* lecture. The summer before, in conjunction with St. John's Educational Threshold, a local community center, they had conducted a neighborhood assessment of their local San Francisco neighborhood, and they based their teaching on this.

They collected data, made a comprehensive map of the area, and, from there, successfully lobbied to get a new park in their neighborhood (Stead, 1996). Although their story amazed many of the Stanford students, the youth center's director was not surprised in the least. In fact, he expressed the need for communities to start realizing the vast wisdom and potential that youth possess (Stead, 1996). Despite success stories in major news publications such as *The New York Times* that paint a very positive picture of involving youth in community initiatives, their involvement is rarely easy and is still full of complications and challenges.

These challenges can be seen in the initiative by Redwood City, California. Although school based family centers, as well as a myriad of other community and social services, had been added to the city, there was a definite lack of youth involvement in community decision making. To create more youth involvement, the John W. Gardner Center for Youth and Their Communities and the Redwood City 2020 agency joined forces to develop avenues for increased youth involvement and to gain knowledge about their perspectives on city issues (Fernandez, 2002). Redwood City 2020 represents a local collaborative effort to help children, youth, and families served by the Redwood City School District to succeed.

They began by involving 13 middle school students in an after school program that would identify services and various supports that would be needed at a new school based family center. The youth not only collected data, but they were fully involved in the process. They were to "develop, research, select the tools, analyze the data, generate findings, and develop concrete recommendation and actions" (Fernandez, 2002, p. 1). Although hopes were high for the project, planners admit that things did not go as they had planned. Policy makers in the community did invite the children to present their findings, but little policy change actually occurred as a result of the efforts.

Yet, despite the lack of concrete progress, positive effects were seen for both the youth and the community. First, the youth who participated agreed that they felt "lucky" to have been a part of a process. Also, they experienced some benefits of interacting and developing relationships with the adult facilitators. In fact, many of the students' teachers commented on noticeable, positive changes in the participating youth.

Also, the community saw an increase in mobilization of community resources. Furthermore, the work helped to alter how adults viewed youth and how youth viewed adults. People began to realize that youth are capable people, and youth, too, began to realize the complexities of processes that were involved in bringing about change.

Fernandes (2002) is very candid about the various challenges that the project encountered as well. First, a lot of attention needed to be paid to building upon the youths' strengths, while still providing them with adequate support and supervision, which the author acknowledges was a difficult balance to achieve. This was especially apparent with data analysis, particularly for youth who struggled with math. Many considered data collected through community action by youth to be a "messy" process. However, the project found that, although they were not held to a "purely scientific" standard, they still were able to identify some of the "most prevalent problems affecting youth, possible connections to the root causes, and ideas for change" (Fernandez, 2002, pp. 4–5).

City policy makers, however, did not always agree with the reliability and validity claimed. For example, even though the youth had an impressive 85% return rate on their surveys and a sample of 800 youth, policy makers wanted a larger sample size because there were approximately 3,000 middle school students.

Another major issue related to goals and reaching a common understanding between the adults and youth as to what the purpose of the research should be. In general, the youth were looking to have people listen to them and understand their points of view; the adults, rather, were striving to "fix" various problems that had been identified. To relieve this tension, those doing the research had to be very creative as to how they generated information.

One final concern was that of obtaining funding. The adults needed to be extremely cautious and remain vigilant about how the involvement of the youth was perceived by their funders. There was a debate as to whether funders would support this kind of organizing by youth rather than just have a large number of their opinions being surveyed (Fernandez, 2002). In essence, it was acceptable to tap their opinions but not to have them determine the actions taken as a result of the research.

2. San Francisco, California

An example of youth led research was found in the San Francisco Bay area through Youth in Focus, a nonprofit organization that is dedicated to empowerment through youth led research, evaluation, and planning. Its goal (London, Zimmerman, & Erbstein, 2003, p. 34) was to assist in developing and running projects that were "based on evaluative training methodology that offers youth meaningful leadership opportunities and addresses critical issues of power and social inequity." Also, they strived to combat the divide that existed between youth and adults in the community.

Youth tended to be excluded from community life and forced to grow up outside of it, but they still were expected to become active members when they got older. Youth in Focus tried to close this divide in expectations by getting both youth and adults to collaborate in the efforts. By doing this, they were hoping to help develop youths' sense of responsibility for their communities, increase their leadership skills and capacity, and develop further outlets for social action (London et al., 2003). Additionally, Youth in Focus identified a variety of benefits of youth led evaluation for youth participants.

First, they developed strong research, analytical, and writing skills, which would be useful to them in their academic lives and in the future (London et al., 2003). Also, they received invaluable job experience and job skills and increased their professional social network. Additionally, they enhanced their community organizing skills such as advocacy, public speaking, and other public communication skills, which could be valuable in future ventures.

The project allowed both youth and adults to engage in meaningful relationships that, otherwise, would not have existed. It was important to both the individual and the community because the project allowed youth who generally would have been completely excluded from the organization to become active and contributing members. This was essential because it enhanced youths' sense of pride and empowerment in feeling that their ideas mattered and actually could create some change.

The Youth in Focus model has been used at a variety of other community based organizations (CBO) in the area (London et al., 2003). First, Youth IMPACT, a program of the San Francisco Department of Children, Youth, and Their Families (DCYF), worked with Youth in Focus to develop a group of 10 high school students to become youth evaluators of 40 local community based organizations. The youth published their research, findings, and recommendations and distributed them to the various CBOs.

One interesting finding that was uniquely a youth developed idea was that of "trust." The youth evaluators selected trust as a main factor in determining whether a CBO was successful. This notion had never been considered before by DCYF when the evaluations were entirely run by adults. Also, the youth found that the influence CBOs had on clients was extremely limited; therefore, it pushed DCYF to support policy recommendations that increased community involvement with organizations that received assistance from DCYF. Finally, these youth continued their involvement in the city by helping to conduct asset and needs assessments and helping with the allocation process of youth funds.

3. Vancouver, Canada

One concrete and effective way of involving youth is to get them involved in community mapping. The Youth Friendly Health Services (YFHS) project, which was based in Vancouver, did just that. The aim of the project was to better understand what youth wanted from their community health center and what would make the Center more "youth friendly" (Amsden & VanWynsberghe, 2005). Community mapping was chosen as the preferred youth research tool because of its openness, its flexibility, and its ability to allow for story telling. Additionally, it allowed the youth to determine both the content and the structure of the end result.

First, it was necessary to create trust. As with the Youth IMPACT example, trust was potentially a major barrier for the participants. They needed to feel that their opinions would be taken seriously and that confidentiality would be respected. Additionally, taking their ideas seriously would contribute to their sense of empowerment, which was also vital to creating a successful mapping project (Amsden & VanWynsberghe, 2005).

From there, it was important to create an open space for participants to express their ideas. The youth researchers accomplished this by offering a variety of media for expression. Although participants could, and the majority did, use words to describe their thoughts, other materials such as paints and colored markers were available to those who wished to express their views through art. For example, one participant created an actual graffiti style train in which each compartment contained a different aspect of a community health center that he wished existed, such as a swimming pool and a dance hall. Finally, during the process, participants were encouraged to talk to one another. Researchers realized that surveys can be boring. Therefore, they wanted to create a "fun" atmosphere to keep the youth engaged. They also wanted to encourage the spreading of ideas between participants.

Once the data collection process was completed, youth researchers were fully involved in the coding and analysis. Admittedly, their involvement did make the process "messier," time consuming, and more complicated (Amsden & VanWynsberghe, 2005). However, because they were of the same age group as those who were surveyed, they were also able to clarify the meanings of things about which adult researchers were unclear. For example, youth had the insight to know that a "bouncy room" should be coded under "fun and recreation" whereas the adult researchers were perplexed as to how best to classify this response (Amsden & VanWynsberghe, 2005).

One unexpected issue that arose was the youths' own assumptions about themselves. Overall, youth did not feel as if they were conducting "real" research. This probably was due to the fact that the methodology of using personal voice and experience was foreign to the youth researchers. In the future, it was agreed that clearer explanations of the process would be helpful to further the youths' understanding the project as well as the youths' sense of empowerment. Delgado (2006), for example, stresses the importance of providing youth researchers with training on the research process and methods as a way of grounding them in this type of endeavor and showing them the various approaches toward answering the key questions they wish to address.

4. Valley County, Nebraska

Finally, an example from rural Nebraska shows that youth can also be integrated into ongoing community asset assessment efforts, instead of creating efforts that are purely youth led. Emery and Flora (2006) talk about an effort in a rural Nebraska community to create a spiral-up effect in which they were hoping to use one asset to increase other assets in the community. In this particular community, assets had been disappearing for a long time, and the community came together to try to revitalize itself. For example, one major concern they addressed was the flight of young people from their community to other communities that offered more opportunities (Emery & Flora, 2006). To combat this, the community decided to begin a leadership development program that included local high school students. It was an 8 month program with 16 participants, 4 of whom were current high school students. Their goals were to "increase [their] skills, to create awareness of leadership opportunities, and expand their understanding of the County" (Emery & Flora, 2006, p. 25).

As a result of the community's efforts, there was a noticeable change in how local leaders reacted to situations and approached the community's decline in assets. Also, more people were willing to become active participants and/or leaders in local government. Overall, this effort was somewhat unique because it focused on changing the entire community for the better, including making it better for the youth, which is not usually the case. Nevertheless, it highlights a variety of potential intervention goals that can result only from an asset foundation that can encompass the entire lifespan from young children to older adults.

CONCLUSIONS

Tensions between adults and youth can be found in almost all communities across the United States. The fact that they exist should not be considered "normal." Instead, one of the goals of asset assessments should be to address and minimize, if not totally eliminate, these tensions. Viewing youth as active and contributing partners in community efforts highlights that they, too, are assets or capital that cannot be ignored and that they have a vested interest in the well-being of their communities (Camino & Zelbin, 2002; Sherman, 2004). The quality of the relationships between youth and adults has important implications for youth having active and meaningful participation in programming, and for later interactions with adults as the youth, in turn, grow into adult status (Lekies, Baker, & Baldini, 2009; Serido, Borden, & Perkins, 2011).

Youth, however, should not be romanticized in any community asset assessment because they, like their adult counterparts, bring challenges to any effort to identify and mobilize a community's capital. Nevertheless, they should not be stigmatized, either. No segment of a community has a monopoly on a community's assets. Therefore, people should have their voices heard and influence felt in an inclusive community asset assessment regardless of their gender, ability, sexual orientation, documented status, race, age, or any other characteristics.

If community asset assessments are about investing in communities, then there is a definite "payback" when youth age in place and assume important leadership roles within these communities. Hopefully, they, in turn, will be more willing to share their knowledge and wisdom with future generations and act as role models and mentors to ensure that this happens.

10

Asset Assessments and
Latino Communities

" [T]he youthfulness and rapid growth of Latinos can be major assets
to the United States, fueling the growth of markets, staffing the
workforce, supporting financial systems such as Social Security, and
revitalizing communities. The positive dynamics stand in dramatic
contrast to the alarming demographic problems of other industrial
nations, such as Japan, Italy, France, and Germany."

(CISNEROS, *2008, p. 6*)

INTRODUCTION

The Latino community in the United States is a growing and very young segment
of the nation's population and is worthy of specific attention in this book. All
geographic regions of the country can count on having established or emerging
Latino communities. Asset assessment in these communities, as a result, represents important opportunities to both learn about these communities and help
guide community social work practice.

The demographic trends involving Latinos in the United States mean that this
community is no longer concentrated in select geographic regions of the country, and can be found in major urban areas, with small towns and rural areas
also experiencing rapid increases of Latinos (Delgado, 2011). Consequently, the
value of community asset assessments in this community of color has national,
rather than regional, implications. Naturally, adjustments will have to be made
to take into account local circumstances, for example, as in communities in
which Latinos who are undocumented represent a growing, if not significant,
segment of the community.

Asset assessments of urban communities of color bring with them a unique
set of rewards and challenges for community social workers and communities.
These communities, therefore, do require the introduction of innovative ways

of gathering and assessing information (Delgado, 2011). Three rewards have been selected for attention in this section: (1) richness of community assets; (2) collaboration as a central strategy; and (3) a young and growing community. these rewards benefit both the latino community and those undertaking a community asset assessment.

REWARDS

The undertaking of asset assessments in urban communities of color brings with it incredible rewards for both communities and participants in the assessment process. These rewards take on even greater significance when the community being assessed brings cultural traditions that are often misunderstood or totally overlooked by the dominant society.

1. Richness of Community Assets

Any community asset assessment of Latino communities will quickly uncover numerous assets that can be tapped in community capacity enhancement initiatives targeting this community (Delgado, 2007, 2011). The family is probably the most important protective factor in the life of Latino youth (Shetgiri, Kataoka, Ryan, Askew, Chung, & Schuster, 2009). In addition, Latino cultural traditions and familism are community assets (Bacallao & Smokowski, 2007). However, the presence of numerous cultural assets that are not typically encountered in scholarly articles and books will necessitate that any asset assessment be sufficiently sensitive to the role of culture in helping this community socially navigate its way through life in this society.

As noted in Chapter 2, cultural assets often represent an untapped resource in social interventions. Tapping these resources helps ensure that interventions are culturally grounded within a local context and increases the likelihood that interventions will succeed. Nevertheless, cultural assets are not fixed and certainly can change as a result of acculturation forces, for example.

Latino community assets have started to find their way into the professional literature, reflecting innovative thinking on the subject as a number of scholars across the nation have focused attention on them. For example, Smith-Morris (2007) did an asset study of a Mexican American community in Dallas, Texas, and describes three ways of operationalizing social capital: (1) use of memberships in local associations and networks; (2) degree of trust and adherence to norms; and (3) indicators of collective action. Innovative and multidimensional efforts to assess assets are very much in order and will undoubtedly emerge as community asset assessments continue to evolve in the future.

The importance of the arts and music within Latino culture should be taken into account in the development of an asset assessment. McDonald, Antunez, and Gottemoeller (2006–2007), for example, describe the use of arts as a way to assess the Latino community in New Orleans. The role of religion, too, must not be ignored, if we are to achieve a comprehensive understanding of Latino community assets. Latino Protestant churches, for example, are community assets that provide extensive instrumental, informational, and expressive services to the community and often do so in collaboration with other community institutions (Delgado, 2008; Sherman, 2003).

Latino small businesses have started to get attention, particularly as they are viewed for their role in creating a sense of community for residents and their economic power within these communities (Delgado, 2011). Sanchez-Jankowski's (2008) study of social change and resilience in low income multiracial urban neighborhoods found convincing evidence of the importance of small businesses in the social fabric of these communities. Small businesses have the potential to play influential roles in the social and economic life of low income/low wealth urban communities. These businesses, it must be emphasized, can be formal or informal. When informal, these are essentially unknown to the external community, making assessing them particularly difficult. An example of these informal businesses is baking or cooking for community or family functions, which has the potential to evolve into a bakery, restaurant, or catering business, given financial support and managerial consultation. Another example is repairing neighbors' cars in a driveway, which has the potential to evolve into a repair shop.

The role of Latino small businesses in creating and maintaining community social and economic fabric taps a variety of capital or assets such as social, economic, cultural, and human capital. The richness and diversity of formal and informal Latino small businesses must not be overlooked if practitioners are to obtain a comprehensive understanding of Latino community assets. Furthermore, these types of establishments also provide a wide range of social services such as referrals, translations, and credit (Delgado, 2009).

Cordasco and colleagues (2009) found that Latino youth, as compared to their parents, have a greater awareness and willingness to interact with adults outside of their immediate circle. As a result, they can help bridge cultural divides between adults and services and so are a social asset in Latino communities. Martyn and colleagues (2006) studied Latina adolescents and found that protective processes vary in type and strength over school and post-school periods, highlighting the dynamic power of assets over the lifespan, and the need to take age into account when assessing assets.

An ability to communicate in multiple languages is another community asset; for example, in the case of Latinos, use of Spanish connects the United States to Latin American countries and to Spain (Pomerentz, 2002). Also, if the community possesses language capabilities that are in short supply in the service provision or other sectors, members can be formally tapped to help organizations meet community needs. Latino youth serving as translators and interpreters increase family access to resources, knowledge, and information on a variety of domains such as education, employment, and social services. Thus, this role as "language broker" is a form of cultural and human capital and must be captured by any form of community asset assessment in communities in which English may not be the primary language used in daily transactions (Orellana, Dorner, & Pulido, 2003).

Bilingualism or multilingualism has the potential to be an asset to local social service, health care, education, and other helping agencies. For example, Reinschmidt, Hunter, Fernandez, Lacy-Martinez, Guernsey de Zapien, and Meister (2006) identified Latina natural healers (*promotoras*) as community capital who can be enlisted in their role as health educators and facilitators of routine and follow-up care. These individuals, however, are rarely known to those outside of their respective communities. Identification of this asset in an assessment, as a result, requires knowledgeable residents identifying them and brokering access to outsiders. These natural healers enjoy a long cultural tradition and are often turned to before, or even after, assistance is sought from health settings.

The topic of discrimination and prejudice toward Latinos is one that is inescapable in any effort to better understand the interplay between discrimination stress, coping strategies, self-esteem, and community assets. The ability to successfully navigate socially difficult situations, such as those posed by prejudice and discrimination, is an asset. Edwards and Romero (2008), for example, found that Mexican descent youth are resilient in coping with the experience of negative stereotypes and prejudice and that their self-esteem is able to withstand the impact of discrimination and prejudice. Gonzalez's (2009) study of Latino youth concludes that they experienced "a renewed commitment to their ethnic selves" when they were able to participate in activities and events that actively sought to undo negative stereotypes of themselves, and when their bilingualism was perceived to be an asset.

2. Collaboration as a Central Strategy

Collaboration is often an explicit or implicit goal of community asset assessments, and for very good reasons. The variety of Latino community assets cannot possibly be captured by one organization. Consequently, community asset assessments focused on this community must utilize collaborative partnerships, whenever possible, as a means of obtaining a comprehensive and in-depth picture of Latino community assets (Guerra & Valverde, 2007).

The theme should be particularly prominent in community asset assessments that involve dominant institutions and community residents. Collaboration between Latino families and dominant institutions, such as schools, is possible if staff respect and accept Latino cultural values and beliefs, and are willing and able to incorporate these cultural views into school–community collaborative initiatives (Olivos, 2009).

A collaborative approach can be labor intensive but can result in numerous benefits by increasing the likelihood of a comprehensive view of the community's assets. It also can result in the creation and strengthening of social capital between the various segments participating in these types of ventures. In addition, a collaborative approach during an asset assessment increases the likelihood of collaboration during the implementation of interventions based upon asset findings. Consequently, collaboration can best be viewed as an "investment" that will pay off in countless ways in future endeavors (Delgado, 2007).

3. A Young and Growing Community

The Latino community in the United States is here to stay (Pew Hispanic Center, 2011). It represents an increasingly growing segment of the United States population, too, and, as a result, will play an increasingly significant role in the future of this nation (Benitez, 2007; Hirschman & Massey, 2008; Rumbaut, 2006; Tienda & Mitchell, 2006). Consequently, any efforts to actively and meaningfully engage this population group will result in numerous benefits to these communities and the nation as a whole. Efforts to systematically identify, foster, and collaborate with indigenous assets represent the tapping of vast recourses.

It is important to take demographic profiles into account when conducting asset assessments of the Latino community. The youthfulness of the Latino population, for example, necessitates the development of asset assessments that can span a bilingual and bicultural perspective of what constitutes an asset. Latino older adults may speak only Spanish, while younger Latinos may be limited in their Spanish language competencies or may be bilingual. Models developed to reach and engage Latino youth will also offer potential for use, with necessary modifications, for other groups of color, and particularly those that are first generation in this country. In essence, the time, energy, and resources invested in these models will have considerable "payoffs" beyond Latino youth.

CHALLENGES

As has been discussed, there are a great number of Latino community assets or capital that are present in these communities and would benefit from a systematic assessment and incorporation into community interventions. However, as also discussed, Latino assets are certainly not easy to assess, for a variety of reasons. Four challenges stand out because of their importance: (1) heterogeneity of the latino community: (2) rapid demographic changes; (3) the role of acculturation; and (4) suspicion of outsiders.

1. Heterogeneity of the Latino Community

One of the major challenges Latino community asset assessments will face is the heterogeneity of this community (Motel, 2012; Patten, 2012). Although the label of "Latino" is often found in social work practice and literature, it may mistakenly convey a community with widely shared values, language dialects, history, and circumstances surrounding the lives of its members in the United States. It is true that there are common threads that bind this community together. However, the differences within and between Latino groups can be considerable, with far reaching implications for community social work practice and assessments, either need or asset focused.

In 2010, there was a total of approximately 51 million Latinos in the United States, with native born Latinos numbering approximately 32 million and foreign born Latinos accounting for approximately 19 million (Patten, 2012). Latino communities, as a result, will consist of both groupings, including what can be a sizable percentage of undocumented residents. Therefore, the differences in circumstances and outlooks related to documented status will mean that different assessment strategies and methods will be needed to take into account acculturation differences. This will increase the costs of community asset assessments.

English and Spanish language competencies will vary according to whether the residents are native or foreign born, their ages, and their acculturation levels. Youth are more likely to speak, write, and read English. Foreign born residents, in contrast, will be stronger with Spanish language skills. A percentage of Latino youth, however, may speak Spanglish (a combination of both Spanish and English). This, to which any researcher will testify, is a challenge in the wording of research questions and the research methods used to assess assets as well as needs.

Language competencies, of course, tie into acculturation levels of residents (Organista, 2007). Interviewing Latino families will often require different instruments that take into account different language abilities within a family and also contrasting values, from those that are considered "old world" Latino, such as interdependency and cooperation, to independence and competition. Reliance on folk healing practices and healers, too, may be considered "old world" (Berry-Caban & Crespo, 2008).

The role and cohesiveness of the family are still widely considered the cornerstone of a community asset (Saracho, 2007). Based upon their cornerstones research on Mexican families, Bacallao and Smokowski (2007) found that the acculturation gap between child and parent was an asset and not a deficit, resulting in Latino youth possessing language and social skills that help their parents socially navigate or broker their new cultural environment.

2. Rapid Demographic Changes

As noted earlier in this chapter, rapid Latino demographic changes can be found in both urban and rural communities across the United States (Delgado, 2011; Massey, 2008; National Research Council, 2006; Torres, 2006). Shifting demographic profiles, such as those caused by a rapid influx of Latinos who are undocumented, will pose particular challenges in conducting community asset assessments.

In some communities in which Latinos have recently arrived, there has been tension with other ethnic and racial groups (Chavez, 2008). Although there are possibilities of tension between different Latino groups, too, this has not materialized in a fashion that could severely hinder a community asset assessment. Torney-Purta, Barber, and Wilkenfeld's (2007, p. 111) study of 14 year old Latino students found, when compared to non-Latino students, that they "report more positive attitudes toward immigrants' rights but have lower civic knowledge and expected civic participation. These differences were apparent even when controlling for language, country of birth, and political discussions with parents." These findings, at least, may bode well for Latino communities that are experiencing rapid changes in composition as the result of Latino newcomer migration.

How community residents define themselves becomes an important local circumstance that must be taken into account in an asset assessment. For example, one recent trend shows that, in Latino communities, an increasingly sizable proportion of people identify themselves as "Indian" rather than "Latino." Decker (2011), based upon census figures, reports that there are 57,000 Native Americans in New York City who are of Latino origin from Latin America. These individuals have been called "Amerindians," with almost 50% of them originating in Mexico. Consequently, community asset assessments cannot lump all Latinos into a "Latino" category, and must, as a result, differentiate subgroups based on local circumstances.

3. The Role of Acculturation

The importance of acculturation in the development of a better understanding of the Latino community has gained significant recognition in the past decade (Delgado, 2008). An acculturation concept seeks to capture how Latinos have responded to environmental pressures related to English language acquisition and adoption of values commonly found among native residents of this country. Values such as competition, independence, and materialism, for example, strike at the core of what it means to be Latino in the twenty-first century.

Latino households can very easily consist of multiple generations, each of them with a particular level of acculturation related to their ability to speak, write, and converse in English, and to cultural values pertaining to family, religion, and strivings in this society. Interviews of household residents will uncover core assets, but also assets unique to individual members, depending upon their level of acculturation. In essence, there is no one prevailing perspective. Young generations, for example, may not share the same religious views as their parents or grandparents in the household. Religion, as a result, may be a powerful asset for grandparents, less so for parents, and may not even be an asset for youth.

4. Suspicion of Outsiders

There is little dispute that the Latino community in the United States is under siege from a variety of political circles, but particularly from those who subscribe to a harsh and punitive stance on undocumented immigration. The glare from this national spotlight has caused a tremendous amount of distrust in Latino communities that have a high concentration of undocumented residents (Chavez, 2008). This heightened level of distrust has spilled over into the arena of community practice regarding suspicion of outsiders, even including those who make serious efforts to better understand and reach this community. Also, this increased concern on the part of residents is at a level that is unprecedented in urban communities that historically already were leery of academics, government, and outsiders. Consequently, those making efforts to assess the assets or needs of this community must be prepared for increased scrutiny from residents and organizations that serve their needs.

This does not mean, however, that asset assessments in communities with high percentages of undocumented residents, for example, cannot be successful. It does mean that collaboration with trusted institutions that have institutional legitimacy within the community is essential. Also, very widespread publicity concerning the effort must be made, making such asset assessments that much more time consuming and expensive.

CASE ILLUSTRATIONS

1. Worcester, Massachusetts

Worcester is a city located approximately 40 miles west of Boston. Community asset assessments lend themselves to either a broad or a very specific focus. The case of Latino owned barbershops is an example of the latter. An asset assessment in the city of Worcester, Massachusetts, focused specifically on one type of small business within a highly circumscribed geographic area of the city (six blocks on Main Street South), where the majority of the Latino community resided (Delgado, 2008).

This asset assessment uncovered only two Latino owned barbershops in this area of the community. The low number was the result of increased competition from Latina owned beauty parlors serving both women and men, while barbershops served only males. (The beauty parlors were studied in a separate study, later.) The assessment provided rich information on the social services provided by these two barbershops, their histories within the community, and their willingness to collaborate with human service organizations in Latino focused interventions. The assessment, because of its highly focused nature, was relatively easy to plan and implement from a cost and administrative viewpoint.

2. Lawrence, Massachusetts

Lawrence, Massachusetts, is a city approximately 25 miles north of Boston. An asset assessment there involved a wider geographic area of the city than in

Worcester and focused on botanical shops (*botanicas*), which are Latino cultural variations of pharmacies (Delgado, 2008). This asset assessment built upon the findings of an earlier study of botanical shops in this area that focused on the experiences of developing a collaborative relationship between organizations providing HIV/AIDS services and botanical shops (Delgado & Santiago, 1998).

The depth of the second botanical shop study was much greater when compared to the Worcester study of barbershops above. Five botanical shops were identified and involved in the asset assessment. Each botanical shop provided data on types and number of social services provided, willingness to collaborate with human service organizations, the typical ailments customers presented, and the background and preparation of the owners. Interestingly, they provided an average of 3.4 separate types of social services and were willing to collaborate.

The ambitious goals of this study required interviewers to make multiple visits, have extensive training and support, and receive a very detailed debriefing after each botanical shop owner was interviewed. An additional challenge was that botanical shops can be quite controversial in Latino communities, as already noted, with residents either having very positive reactions to them or very negative reactions, depending upon their religious backgrounds and beliefs, with fundamentalist groups being more negative and Catholic groups being more accepting. The former often view these establishments as engaging evil forces. The latter do not share this perspective and can reconcile engaging in folk healing while still being devout Catholics. Consequently, botanical shops represent relatively more or less economic and cultural capital for different sectors of the Latino community.

3. Southern Florida

It is not unusual to have Latino owned small businesses named after a range of subjects related to the Latino background of the owner, such as the town or country of the owner, thereby distinguishing these businesses from conventional mainstream businesses in this country. In looking at the names, asset assessments can capture important information about a community in a highly innovative manner (Delgado, 2011). Consequently, gathering information on community assets such as Latino small businesses can necessitate including a variety of types of information. A number of scholars have sought to capture the meaning of this practice regarding naming a business (Delgado, 2011). Although both of the following studies focused on rural Latinos, their findings are equally applicable to urban Latino neighborhoods and, we believe, other groups of color in newcomer communities.

Bletzer (2003), for example, studied Latino owned small businesses in rural Southern Florida and found that the naming of grocery stores and restaurants reflected cultural expressions of both owner and customer Latino roots. Small business names reflected the "flavor and pride of Latino" identity and provided important information concerning Latino community composition and trends and the potential of these establishments for reaching specific sectors of the Latino community. Skelly and colleagues (2002) come to the same conclusion in their study of Latino stores (*tiendas*) in North Carolina. Bletzer (2003, p. 211) also notes that "The centrality and focal attraction of the neighborhood store within an urbanized area of immigrants... is replicated by a country store that creates a similar centrality in a rural area where few sources exist for the purchase of consumable necessities, such as food and household products."

Asset assessments of Latino small business naming practices must not restrict themselves to formal businesses. Every effort must also be made to accomplish the same goals involving informal businesses. Although the gathering of information on Latino small business naming practices represents a form of information that is usually not part of an asset assessment, this information is readily available and should be analyzed to achieve a more in-depth understanding of this form of Latino capital.

4. North Carolina

As addressed in Chapter 6, photovoice is a method that lends itself to use in community asset assessments. The following description of a North Carolina Latino photovoice project illustrates the potential use of this method for identifying Latino community assets (Streng, Rhodes, Ayala, Eng, Arceo, & Phipps, 2004, p. 403): "Over a one-year period, adolescents partnered with public health practitioners and researchers in: generating photo-assignments, taking photographs based on these assignments, using the photographs for photo-discussions, and defining themes based on these photo-discussions. A photograph exhibition and community forum raised awareness among local decision-makers and community members of the issues and assets of Latino adolescents and initiated a process toward change. From the participants' words and photographs emerged contextual descriptions of issues that both challenged and facilitated their adaptation and quality of life in their school and community."

The cultural content of photographs will differ based upon a variety of demographic characteristics. Latino youth often bring a blending of Latino and American cultural views based upon their lives in two different cultures, which will differ from that of Latino older adults. Photovoice facilitates the capturing and display of these cultural views that facilitate discussion and increase community awareness of their cultural assets, which, in turn, can be shared with those outside of their community.

CONCLUSIONS

Asset assessments take on greater significance when they target communities that do not have English as their primary language, are either new or have many members who have recently arrived, or have cultural values that put them at a distinct disadvantage in this society. All of these factors combine to make these communities, as in the case of Latinos, ones that can be discriminated against by the broader society. However, it would be incorrect to think of these communities, or any other oppressed community, as not having capital or assets.

This chapter has only touched upon the role of cultural capital in one community of color. Similar efforts in African American, Native American, and Asian American communities will uncover cultural capital that is often overlooked in community initiatives. O'Donnell and Karanja (2000, p. 75), for example, discuss transformative community practice as "the process by which people come to understand their own internal spirit and strength in order to develop alternative visions of themselves and their community." They discuss this model in regard to creating opportunities to build on the strengths and traditions of the largely African American Bronzeville community on the South Side of Chicago and identify a wide variety of assets in that community, both historically and later. Historical assets were jobs inside and outside the community, churches, clubs, cooperative businesses, African American/Black charities, music (jazz, blues, and gospel), and writers (Richard Wright and Gwendolyn Brooks). Later, even though its economy had declined, obvious and easily identifiable assets also included beautiful boulevards, lovely old homes, and physical proximity to a convention center, sports arenas, public transportation, and a central business district.

Carrying out capital assessments in Latino communities is not without its share of challenges, particularly in conceiving and inventorying what may be largely invisible capital to the outside world. However, the rewards of uncovering and utilizing these indigenous resources in community based initiatives have only recently been received. Similar challenges and rewards can be found in newly emerging communities of newcomers to the United States, particularly in geographic areas not already known for thriving communities of color.

11

Asset Assessments and Community Gardens

"In communities across the nation, advocates and organizations
are working hard to develop solutions to food system problems
and create innovative models that meet community needs...These
efforts are necessarily diverse; they represent local solutions to local manifestations of larger problems. However, they often share common goals,
such as making nutritious food more accessible, revitalizing
and empowering communities, and supporting local and sustainable
food production and distribution."

(POTHUKUCHI, JOSEPH, BURTON, & FISHER, *2002, p. 3*)

INTRODUCTION

The above quote by Pothukuchi and colleagues (2002) highlights both the importance of food security and nutrition as well as local solutions to achieve these. The
importance of food security is well understood by urban community residents
and those who work with them (Delgado, in press; Winne, 2008). In the case of
low income and low wealth urban communities, food security is compounded by
their limited access to fresh fruits and vegetables (Hess, 2009).

The emergence of what Lyson (2004) calls "civic agriculture" captures the
movement toward locally based agriculture and food production as a means of
helping to ensure food security, with important implications for urban communities. Community gardens represent one element of civic agriculture and
local efforts to meet nutrition needs, and one with a distinguished history in
the United States (Lawson, 2005). However, it is possible to engage in multiple
goals that provide food for a community but also educate and help to empower
the community in the process (De La Salle & Holland, 2010), bringing the food
justice movement within a community social work framework.

The professional literature reflects the popularity of community gardening for addressing a variety of community goals and needs. Wakefield and colleagues (2007) identify seven key benefits to community gardening: (1) improved access to food and fresh fruits and vegetables; (2) increased physical activity; (3) improved mental health; (4) improved security and safety; (5) increased community and human capital development; (6) increased social capital; and (7) improved local ecology and sustainability. Any combination, or all of these benefits, can be captured by a community asset assessment, with implications for the development of community initiatives focused on food and environmental justice themes (Delgado, in press). Pothukuchi (2004) provides a meta-analysis of several community food assessments, in part, to identify community assets that can be part of a comprehensive initiative to obtain a safe, culturally acceptable, nutritionally adequate diet.

Community gardens can be found throughout urban centers in the United States and the world, and in many different forms (Green, 2012; Lawson, 2005). Landauer and Brazil's (1990) book, *Tropical Home Gardens,* published over 20 years ago, represents what is arguably the first comprehensive study on the subject. It focuses on home gardens, or what we call community gardens, in the United States, Africa, Latin America, the Pacific Islands, and Southeast Asia. Hynes (1995), in one of the earliest books on the subject of urban gardens in the United States, specifically focused her research on inner cities and highlighted the importance of this form of capital in the life of low income families and their communities. Smith and Kurtz (2003), in one of the pioneer studies of community gardens involving the development of an inventory and classification, illustrate the diversity of types and locations in which community gardens can take hold.

Although urban communities, as already noted in Chapter 1, invariably consist of many different types of assets, the multifaceted benefits associated with community gardens make them an excellent example of a form of capital or asset that lends itself to asset assessments. Physically, they are not hidden and can be easily located, with the possible exception of home gardens that are not in easy public view. Rhoden (2002) highlights a variety of community gardens that can be found in urban communities: (1) individual and family plot gardens; (2) shared garden spaces for larger groups of residents; (3) school gardens; and (4) gardens serving nonprofit caregiving organizations, including houses of worship.

Community gardens can respond to a range of instrumental community needs such as food security, places for intergenerational and interethnic contact, and community beautification (Saldivar-Tanaka & Krasny, 2004). Expressive community needs, although much more difficult to measure but, nonetheless, equally important, can be met by having community gardens foster social capital bonding and bridging by providing a place and space for residents to gather and connect with each other. Additionally, expressive needs can be fostered that cross generations, cultures, and knowledge and abilities pertaining to growing food. Latino communities, for example, invariably include adult and older adult residents with agriculture backgrounds who understand the close association between food and land. Youth, however, may not share this agricultural history and knowledge about gardening, but can learn about them.

Fortunately, community gardens have been the subject of community asset assessments and lend themselves to participatory strategies. Ross and Simces (2008) note that a community food assessment is a participatory process that usually consists of four key "D" elements: (1) *Discovery* (identification of a community's resources and assets); (2) *Dreaming* (envisioning a future); (3) *Designing* (prioritizing and planning actions); and (4) *Delivering* (implementation and evaluation). These elements share many commonalities with community capacity enhancement paradigms, as covered in Chapter 5.

REWARDS

Community gardens represent capital that can be systematically assessed and mobilized in service to urban communities (Goddard, Doughill, & Benton, 2010; Twiss, Dickinson, Duma, Kleinman, Paulsen, & Rilveria, 2003). The importance of urban gardens and other green spaces in the life of communities has enjoyed a relatively long history from an asset or capital perspective (Hynes, 1995). Consequently, the professional literature has an abundance of case examples, research studies, and theoretical scholarship to help community practitioners integrate community gardens and other green space into asset assessments (Gearin & Kahle, 2006).

The rewards of assessing community gardens are numerous. However, only five will be discussed because of space limitations: (1) Community gardens are capital; (2) Community gardens lend themselves to green asset assessments; (3) Community gardens lend themselves to the use of a variety of research methods; (4) Community gardens increase the likelihood of healthy diets; and (5) Community gardens positively alter urban physical environments.

1. Community Gardens Are Capital

As noted earlier in this book and particularly in Chapter 2, community gardens are a form of capital (Oldham, 2011; Tavernise, 2011). Some scholars would go so far as to argue that community gardens can fall into various categories of capital. Hancock (2001, p. 278), for example, sees tremendous value in "green" community initiatives as vehicles for bringing together multiple forms of capital: "How then can community capital actually be created? What activities will simultaneously increase all four forms of capital at the community level? As a general rule, 'green' community economic development projects and strategies, which by definition are concerned with building ecological and economic capital, are also likely to increase human and social capital."

Elder (2005) argues that housing and green space represent two of the most important assets a city can possess. Krasney and Tidball (2009) found that community gardens were excellent contexts for the teaching of civic engagement and academic subject matter. Community gardens are capable of both individual and social transformation (Amin, 2008; Broad, 2009; Pudup, 2008). Brown (2011) illustrates the role of community gardens and farmers' markets to reach out to refugees in this country. There are over 24 farming projects throughout the country that focus on the nutritional needs of refugees from Africa, Southeast Asia, and other regions of the world. These gardens grow vegetables that were readily available in their home countries but are not so readily available in this country. Tortorello (2012) describes the potential of community gardens to provide a venue for cultural traditions to be continued through the planting of vegetables such as cowpeas, okra, and rice that have cultural significance to community residents.

Community gardens provide spaces and places in highly diverse communities for different racial and ethnic groups to come together and interact (Shinew, Glover, & Parry, 2004, p. 54): "Finding ways to alleviate racial tension is an important societal issue. A well-established strategy is to increase positive contact between members of different racial groups, which is hypothesized to lead to improved racial attitudes if the contact takes place under certain conditions. Bridging racial divides, however, has historically been a difficult process. Leisure settings can be ideal environments for interracial interaction to occur due to qualities of free choice and self-determination." Wills, Chinemana, and Rudolph (2011), for example, in a Johannesburg, South Africa, study of a community garden, found that it engendered trust between various groups. Consequently, community gardens can be used to promote racial harmony and reduce tensions within communities (Delgado, in press).

This same concept can apply to providing an opportunity for other groups to come together, such as people of different sexual orientations, gender identities, ages, or abilities. California is an example of a state that has a coordinated statewide effort to initiate, support, and increase school gardens. One of the benefits they note that enhances inclusiveness in a community is that they address multiple learning styles (California School Garden Network, 2010). Also, the American Horticultural Therapy Association (2011) notes that gardens can be beneficial for people with physical and mental disabilities and explains how they can be developed to be barrier free to promote access. One example of a model program of horticulture therapy is at the Perkins School for the Blind (2011) in Watertown, Massachusetts.

The Garden Mosaics Project brings youth and elders together in urban settings through community gardens (Cornell University Cooperative Extension New York City, 2012; Garden Mosaics, 2012). It was developed by Cornell University and has been implemented in many cities as well as internationally; it now is maintained and hosted by the American Community Gardening Association. Its mission is "connecting youth and elders to investigate the mosaic of plants, people, and cultures in gardens, to learn about science, and to act together to enhance their community" (Garden Mosaics, 2012). Among its suggested activities are the development of a "gardener's story" using oral history and photography to understand the relationship between a gardener's planting practices and advice and the gardener's culture; a community garden inventory; and a collage using maps and photographs of assets besides gardens in the community. The project reflects an asset based approach and underscores the positive benefits of community gardens. Those benefits also have more recently been recognized in the fact that the United States Department of Agriculture, in 2011, awarded Cornell University Extension in New York City and Washington State University Extension funding for a school pilot program, Healthy Gardens, Healthy Youth: A People's Garden. It is hoped that this pilot project will result in another nationwide model (Gold, 2011).

2. Community Gardens Lend Themselves to Green Asset Assessments

There are multiple examples that can be used to illustrate both the process and power of asset assessments involving the environment. Asset assessments can also be specifically focused on community food assessments. Green maps, not surprisingly, can cover a wide range of ecological factors, one of which is community gardening, which is experiencing a resurgence in popularity as this nation struggles with a prolonged recession. Common Ground (2004, p. 2.16) states that "Green maps, among their other virtues, offer the prospect of a 'common text' of ecological and cultural resources that can provide linkages between private visions and chronic public needs... the most successful projects in my view are those which combine youth projects with city-wide projects... Kids need skills and adults need to communicate their respect for youth initiatives without holding youth responsible for ecological problems which we adults have made ourselves."

The description of the goals provided by Pothukuchi and colleagues (2002, p. 6) of community food assessments parallels those of asset assessments covered in the previous sections of this book: "The Community Food Assessment approach reflects many fundamental aspects of the community food security movement, and contributes to it in important ways. It is integrative, and takes a systems approach. It involves collaboration between diverse stakeholders. It is solution-oriented, looking at assets and resources as well as problems. Community Food Assessments promote community food security by increasing knowledge about food-related needs and resources, by building collaboration and capacity, by promoting long-term planning, and by facilitating a variety of change actions including policy advocacy and program development."

3. Community Gardens Lend Themselves to the Use of a Variety of Research Methods

Community capital that can be assessed only by using one particular method effectively limits when and under what circumstances it can be a part of an assessment initiative. The relative ease and flexibility of research methods that can be used in assessing community gardens, though, are strengths of this type of asset because they allow local circumstances such as funding, time, and goals to dictate how the assessment will be conceptualized and implemented.

Pothukuchi (2004) undertook a meta-analysis of nine community food assessments (CFAs) involving community gardens and found a variety of research methods, including focus groups, key informants, and mapping, that were used to assess their effectiveness and why they can be considered assets. Community gardens also lend themselves to spatial mapping as a means of analyzing their influence within the community. In addition, observational and ethnographic methods bring an added dimension to community garden assessment, with the use of photography, too, allowing a visual representation to supplement other forms of qualitative and quantitative data (Blandrage, 2009).

4. Community Gardens Increase the Likelihood of Healthy Diets

The importance of proper nutrition in the lives of undervalued communities cannot be overly stressed. Lack of access to fresh fruits and vegetables and easy access to "junk foods" have often been identified as some of the major reasons for high rates of obesity and diabetes in population groups of color (Critser, 2003; Delgado, in press).

Alamo, Packett, Miles, and Kruger (2008) found that adults with a household member participating in a community garden consumed fruits and vegetables at a rate 1.4 times per day greater than those who did not participate. Participants were also 3.5 times more likely to eat fruits and vegetables five times per day. Ready access to fresh fruits and vegetables increases the likelihood of a more nutritious diet in low income and low wealth urban communities of color. Children are the focus of obesity prevention programs nationwide that sometimes include community gardening. In the case of children, the American Community Gardening Association (2010) suggests that community gardening with children may be done by organizations such as scout troops, day care centers, foster grandparent programs, and churches, which will help to bring together local organizations as well as individuals. In schools, they are used to increase nutrition awareness and healthy food choices of students, but they also contribute to understanding in other curricula areas such as science and social skills (Community Gardening Association, 2010). Finally, community gardens provide an opportunity for some form of physical exercise in the tending and harvesting of the gardens.

5. Community Gardens Positively Alter Urban Physical Environments

Altering the physical environment is one of the cornerstone goals of community capacity enhancement initiatives (Delgado, 2000). Community gardens not only alter physical environments but do so in a manner that results in multiple goals being achieved (Gearin & Kahle, 2006). Glover (2003, p. 190) also makes the observation: "Because initiatives undertaken to improve neighborhoods often focus on the physical environment, it is perhaps unsurprising that a community garden, initiated expressly to upgrade the streetscape within a neighborhood, is a grassroots endeavor that has been used with relative success." The Queen Anne Memorial Garden (located in a mid-sized city in the Midwestern United States), a community garden built to combat urban decline, offered residents a counter-narrative of themselves, by providing residents with an opportunity to alter their physical environment and, in the process, empower their community (Glover, 2003).

Community gardening is widely considered a path to urban revitalization. It attracts businesses and homebuyers, and enhances the quality of life in a community (Johnson, 2009). Furthermore, community gardens lend themselves to being planted in a wide variety of open spaces, enhancing the possibilities of this community asset appearing in the most unlikely of urban places (Moynihan, 2012). The potential benefits of community gardens make them an attractive form of capital that must be captured and mobilized, whenever possible, through community capacity enhancement projects resulting from asset assessments.

CHALLENGES

Although it is tempting to view community gardens as representing a win–win situation for urban marginalized communities, they certainly are not without challenges. Assessing community gardens as assets is very much dependent upon local circumstances. Three specific challenges have been identified for the purposes of discussion that address political, social, and methodological arenas: (1) community gardens as contested spaces; (2) community gardens as assets for a limited few; and (3) seasonal limitations and labor intensity.

1. Community Gardens as Contested Spaces

The presence of community gardens can be viewed as indicators of community assets. However, these same gardens can also be a focal point for tension. Urban land is expensive and, as a result, is often prized by developers and those elected officials who support them (Irazabal & Punja, 2009; Moynihan, 2012). Thus, community gardens can become spaces that are contested, as in the case of New York City when communities organized against Mayor Giuliani and city government bulldozing of gardens to make space for market rate apartments (Martinez, 2009; Schmetzkopf, 2002; Smith & Kurtz, 2003).

Although community social workers may find these contests relatively easy to analyze and take sides on, it becomes more complex when community gardens are replaced by low income and affordable housing. Land, in this instance, essentially affects two groups, both of which present "legitimate" needs. Specifically, there may be those who live in the community and welcome access to the benefits of gardens as well as those who wish to live in affordable housing and find that community gardens, although bringing great benefits, are not as important as housing itself.

2. Community Gardens as Assets for a Limited Few

The benefits of community gardens clearly go beyond those who own and cultivate plots (Glover, 2003, p. 190): "By converting decaying urban spaces into ornamental or vegetable gardens or both, residents transform neighborhood liabilities, namely abandoned, dilapidated lots into tangible (e.g., fresh produce, beautification, sitting gardens for recreation) and intangible neighborhood assets. In the context of urban revitalization, therefore, these 'assets' reflect a collective effort for positive neighborhood change."

Yet, the very nature of community gardens rests in limited plots of land that effectively limit the number of individuals who can successfully cultivate the land. Nevertheless, a broader perspective on who benefits from community gardens clearly will result in an increased number of residents beyond those who actually harvest the food. Beautification of a community benefits all residents, but particularly those who live in close proximity to the garden. Also, gardens are often created out of plots of land that generally were unattractive and, in many cases, magnets for criminal activity or the dumping of trash, abandoned cars, tires, etc. (Delgado, 2000). Therefore, taking geographic areas that have historically attracted criminal activities and transforming them into gardens also benefits the community because of a decrease in crime rates. Taking such a plot of land and transforming it into an oasis obviously benefits everyone in the community who lives near or walks by such an area.

3. Seasonal Limitations and Labor Intensity

Community gardens bring benefits during most seasons, depending upon their geographic location in the country. Winter months are usually time periods for planning, reflection, and evaluation by those who did gardening. Thus, gardens in sections of the country in which the winters are harsh present limited accessibility for community asset assessments since access to the gardens and assessment of their physical and nutritional benefits are seasonally limited. Therefore, capturing the richness of community gardens is best done during the seasons when they are operative.

Some data, however, can still be obtained during dormant periods, even though a picture of a community garden in the midst of winter in New England, for example, does not inspire any but the most dedicated gardener. However, important social capital goals can still be achieved and assessed during the off season because of bonds that were established while gardening.

On a final note, community gardens represent a form of capital that is both time and labor intensive. In other words, community gardens do not simply spring up overnight, and they require considerable thought, planning, and decision making by residents. Consequently, it is a form of capital that is dependent not only upon available land, unless they are rooftop based, but also upon many other factors.

CASE ILLUSTRATIONS

1. Toronto, Canada

Examination of which community asset assessments methods lend themselves to a particular capital is essential in maximizing efforts. As noted in Chapter 6, qualitative methods hold much promise in assessing community gardens, although quantitative methods can be used to measure factors such as increases in property values in housing located near community gardens, revenue generated through the selling of produce, food choices by residents, and the value of open space within a community's life. All these point to gardens fulfilling a variety of critical needs within a community, including generating various forms of capital.

A Toronto, Canada, study of community gardens illustrates the viability of using qualitative methods for assessment. Wakefield and colleagues (2007) utilized three primary methods for data gathering (participant observation, focus groups, and in-depth key informant interviews) as means of obtaining a comprehensive picture of the role and function of community gardens. The findings emphasize that community gardens were a vital part of a community's well-being (Wakefield et al., 2007, p. 100): "This study highlights the important role that community gardens play in the lives of gardeners, and how they enhance the health and well-being of gardeners and the broader community."

2. Upstate New York Inventory

Armstrong (2000) reports on one of the earliest efforts to carry out a community asset assessment and mapping of community gardens. This effort involved 20 community garden programs, representing 63 gardens, in upstate New York, and illustrated the multiple needs and reasons for the development of community gardens. This community asset assessment gathered data on the gardens for the purposes of informing community development and health promotion programs.

This assessment was selected because it had limited funding and illustrates the use of a methodology that, although with limitations, allowed for the gathering of data on a valuable community resource. Telephone interviews, a relatively inexpensive methodology, were used to assess the role and importance of community gardens. Counties with Cooperative Extension grants were targeted, and also officials, such as in offices of mayors and village clerks, for listings of garden program coordinators. Interviews lasted from 30 minutes to 3 hours, depending upon the complexity of the gardening program. It was found that, in addition to meeting a range of social, physical, and nutritional needs in the community, some of the gardens provided physical and psychological safe areas for residents to gather and plan social action and other community focused projects.

3. San Jose, California

Community gardens can either be initiated by community residents, or they can be part of an agency initiative. Asset assessments of the former will be more labor intensive than those focused on agency initiated gardens. Resident initiated gardens will require that researchers identify and locate individual gardeners to attempt to recreate the history of a garden, learn motivations for participation, and develop measures for assessing the effectiveness of these gardens. Data are arduous to obtain in resident initiated efforts and so do not facilitate the creation of in-depth case studies

In efforts initiated by agencies, however, it becomes easier to assess the capital of these gardens (Brown, 2011). These institutional efforts should have goals, objectives, and clear measures of process, output, and impact objectives. Process oriented data are more readily accessible and are particularly important in assessing the role of gardens for families and communities.

In a recent asset assessment of backyard community gardens in San Jose, California, a Latino community illustrates the many advantages that agency led projects have for facilitating community asset assessments (Brown, 2010). An agency project conducted by La Mesa Grande (The Green Table) sought to increase the availability of vegetables in this San Jose community. A total of 30 backyard gardens, each having two raised beds per house, were planted as part of this intervention. Raised beds served to reduce water consumption by 40% as well as the need for weeding, and allowed people who had to sit or who used wheelchairs to work them. One family, for example, reported saving an estimated $80 per week, having increased "healthier eating and physical activity" and having brought the family "closer together" because it involved the family rather than just one gardener (Brown, 2010, p. 16).

4. Dunedin, New Zealand

Community gardens can be found throughout the world. Furthermore, community gardens lend themselves to a variety of methods in community asset assessments, ranging from "low tech" to "high tech" methods. The reader may be amused by this case illustration of a high tech method. However, it highlights the challenges and possibilities of using highly scientific methods in service to communities, including the mapping of community gardens from a perspective that is very unique and full of potential.

Mathieu, Freeman, and Aryal (2007) report on a method for mapping community gardens that was not addressed in Chapter 6 and is clearly beyond the capabilities of those who are locally initiated, but it is worth mentioning as an illustration of a community asset assessment. They present data from an asset assessment undertaken in the city of Dunedin, New Zealand, that used satellite high-resolution multispectral Ikonos imagery to automatically map the extent, distribution, and density of private gardens in the city. This high technology assessment was able to identify 90.7% of the private gardens in the area and was also able to differentiate garden types.

The example of Dunedin, New Zealand, illustrates the potential advancements that can occur in community asset assessments as technology gets applied to community greenery and gardens. The reader, however, should not be intimidated into thinking that technological advances will make what community social work is familiar with obsolete. Technology will never replace the advantages of interacting with residents in face-to-face contact. However, technology can certainly supplement existing methods in a manner that can provide a more comprehensive picture of a community's gardening assets.

CONCLUSIONS

Ending this chapter with a case illustration involving a very high tech and specific method of assessment of community gardens shows how this field of community asset assessment is evolving in the twenty-first century, with promises of even more exciting developments to come. Community gardens have a long and distinguished history in urban America, and they, too, will undergo transformation as the civic agriculture movement evolves. Community gardens, in addition, fulfill a multitude of community focused goals that range from beautification to food security and fit well within a community assets paradigm. The importance of proper nutrition and physical activity in communities of color is well documented, and community gardens fulfill the need for nutritious foods and physical activity, in addition to converting what may be too many ugly urban spaces into beautiful community spaces.

The physical nature of this community asset lends itself quite well to be identified and studied. Those who garden these plots are accessible to be interviewed, and so are those who benefit indirectly because of proximity to their location. Community asset assessments focused on gardens are open to a variety of ways of assessing them. Community gardens, however, can also pose important challenges in the assessment process. Nevertheless, these challenges are far outweighed by the rewards that they bring to communities.

Future Rewards and Challenges

"Diversity is a social asset, part of the cultural commonwealth, requiring protection and nourishment."

(GOLDBARD, *2006, p. 48*)

12

Epilogue

"Finally, the study of community mapping is not the sole purview of 'scholars.' Community mapping practitioners are familiar with and working in local contexts. As practitioners, they accumulate, construct, and apply knowledge and techniques in real time, simultaneously producing new questions for research and enhanced practice."

(PARKER, *2006, p. 481*)

INTRODUCTION

This final chapter will focus on specific implications for social work education, training in the community, and the undertaking of research and evaluation pertaining to asset assessments in various types of urban communities across the country. The quote by Parker (2006) above about mapping is pertinent to all community asset assessments.

Community asset assessments come in many different shapes and sizes, and rarely does "one-size-fit-all" when discussing a community's assets and how best to identify, assess, and mobilize them. Asset assessments are first and foremost about practice, and in the case of this book, social work practice with, rather than for, communities. It should be noted, too, that, although this book has focused on urban areas of the country, rural assets do exist and are just as important in those communities as in urban communities, and a few examples have been cited throughout this book. However, the authors of this book have had urban practice experience and so drew from that context.

We have identified five key questions for community social work that we believe the profession must consider in embracing community asset assessment as a central part of our practice. Each of these implications addresses philosophical, ethical, and practical aspects of asset assessments.

1. How Do We Do No Harm?

Community social workers should not, under any circumstances, undermine a community's capital as a result of their intervention (Ellerman, 2007). Such action is not only detrimental to the community but also to the profession. Community capacity enhancement is about enhancing rather than detracting. Consequently, any form of community intervention, including an asset assessment, should not result in detrimental outcomes. Identifying various actors in an informal economy can, for example, result in authorities closing those businesses down because of various infractions or violations of the law, such as public health requirements for sale of food (Delgado, 2011). When an asset assessment results in such consequences, a community will have long memories of harm for very good reasons.

2. How Can We be Creative?

Social work must foster creativity and flexibility in practice in order to respond to rapidly changing community contexts (Walker, 2004). Some of these contexts may be so new that they have not yet appeared in social work academic classes, but practitioners and social work field placements may be far ahead of academics in thinking about ways of intervening in this new world, so to speak.

We need to be creative in how we think about assessments and all of the steps that follow once assessments are completed. Creativity fuels a capacity to venture into unknown territory and does so in a manner that can be highly contagious. However, creativity is not achieved without taking risks, which brings to the fore potential ethical and political concerns. A business as usual approach is unacceptable when addressing the assets and needs of urban based marginalized groups, and this is certainly the case when attempting to identify their assets and develop community capacity enhancing interventions.

Community asset assessment practice is still in its infancy compared to other social work practice, and that can be viewed as a drawback or an advantage. Clearly, asset assessments do not enjoy the long histories of their needs assessment counterparts. However, they are not burdened by this legacy, either. This frees us up to try new approaches and methods that are much more responsive to the communities to which we wish to reach out and that take into account the sociopolitical context of marginalized communities. In addition, creative approaches to increase community participation build upon a long tradition in social work from, for example, those settlement houses that were progressive and supported political action, that should be continued.

Creativity needs to be encouraged during all facets of social work education, and we as educators and practitioners must be prepared to model it for students. This does not mean, however, that we cannot be "scholarly" and "responsible" in the process of doing so. It does mean that we must be prepared to encourage new forms of practice in the field and even create or select field placements that are undertaking or willing to innovate in service to communities. As noted earlier, this takes on significance when identifying community assets in marginalized communities because of a history of neglecting these resources in the development of interventions.

3. Do We Have a Moral imperative?

There has been surprisingly little debate in the professional literature as to how almost a decade of conservative politics in the country has influenced the social work profession, with some notable exceptions. Discussion has taken place about how a human rights perspective, as noted earlier in this book, can serve as an organizing concept for community focused interventions. However, the authors of this book believe that the social work profession and, at the very least, those of us in community social work practice and scholarship, must play a more active and meaningful role in helping to redress the harm that has befallen urban marginalized communities, and the various subgroups in them that are marginalized by double or multiple oppressed statuses based on characteristics such as age, sexual orientation, or disability.

Social work historically has not been afraid of siding with unpopular causes and marginalized population groups. Some would argue that this has marginalized the profession; others, including us, however, would argue that this "moral" stance has enhanced and strengthened the profession. Apolitical stances are, in fact, political stances that effectively undermine whatever moral authority we can draw upon in giving voice to the voiceless in this society. We believe that bringing forth an asset perspective or paradigm helps ensure the likelihood that marginalized communities are not rendered invisible, and thereby voiceless, in determining what transpires within their environment, and in the external social policies that have an impact on their lives.

4. Is It a Panacea?

It would be tempting to think about asset assessments as representing a panacea for all the ills of marginalized urban communities in the United States and other countries. Unfortunately, even in our wildest dreams, this is certainly not the case. This is not to say that community asset assessments do not have tremendous potential for bringing together concepts that are positive or strengths based, and then applying them to subsequent interventions focused on undervalued groups and communities.

Our abilities as community social workers to be able to undertake needs as well as asset assessments do expand our capacities to be effective in urban communities. Many of the same "tools" are used in both types of assessments. However, the premises and set of values and principles forming the foundation for needs and assets certainly are different, and will never be mistaken for each other.

In addition, our quest as a profession to work cooperatively with other professions is increased when we embrace and contribute to community asset assessments because this is an emerging arena into which increasing numbers of helping professions are entering. Few, if any, professions are as capable as social work, however, to venture into all corners (formal and informal) of a community and engage in practice that is affirming, empowering, and participatory in character. That is one of the foremost strengths that we bring to this field, and it is one that we must continue to build upon through practice and scholarship.

5. Is Community Social Work in a Position to Lead This Movement?

We sincerely believe that no profession can or should own community asset assessments. Having said that, we also truly believe that social work is in an excellent position to help shape and make significant contributions to community asset assessments. Our knowledge of organizations, communities, urban social ecology, and marginalized groups puts community social work in an enviable position of transcending boundaries to include these systems and settings, leading to highly innovative approaches to assessments and interventions.

The profession's embrace of values stressing participatory democracy, empowerment, cultural diversity, and social justice sets the requisite foundation from which to launch community asset assessments that eventually can lead to interventions that successfully build upon a community's assets. Having social work play an influential practice and scholarly role in community asset assessments requires that the subject matter has a prominent place in social work education and practice. The field of community asset assessments will continue to progress as new technology is used to identify and assess assets, and new scholarship emerges to help us better understand how assets evolve and become incorporated into community capacity enhancement interventions.

CONCLUSIONS

The "art" and "science" of community asset assessments have been discussed. Clearly, these forms of assessments have multiple community uplifting agendas or goals, making them a legitimate form of community intervention. These agendas and goals, however, are not apolitical, once social justice considerations serve as their value base. Consequently, social justice principles can play a vital role in helping to shape the methods used and the questions that are asked.

Advances in the field in the past decade bode well for the future of community asset assessments and the role they can play in helping to empower communities, both urban and rural, and helping the organizations that serve these communities to do a better job. These goals take on even greater prominence when addressing marginalized urban communities across the United States. The "deficit" model is far too prevalent and will continue to attract more than its share of advocates. However, the "asset model," too, is here to stay and hopefully will continue to gain in popularity. We as community social workers should be positioned to take our place at the center of this movement!

REFERENCES

Abel, D. (2011, September 23). Crops, thefts rising at community gardens: Frustrated urban growers resort to defensive tactics. *The Boston Globe*, pp. A1, A6.

Access Project. (1999). *Getting the lay of the land on health: A guide for using interviews to gather information* (key informant interviews). Boston, MA: Author.

Adams, D., & Goldbard, A. (2005). *Creative community: The art of cultural development*. Self-published manuscript.

Adams, L. (2005). Social capital: The anatomy of a troubled concept. *Feminist Theory, 6*(2), 195–211.

Adamson, K., Baker, C., & Lewis, Y. (2007). Translating recommendations into reality: Community voices. *Preventing Chronic Disease, 4*(3), A45.

Adger, W. N., Hughes, T. P., Folke, C., Carpenter, S. R., & Rockstrom, J. (2005). Social-ecological resilience to coastal disasters. *Science, 309*(5737), 1036–1039.

Ahn-Redding, H. (2007). *The 'million dollar inmate': The financial and social burden of non-violent offenders*. Lanham, MD: Lexington Books.

Aja, G. N., Modeste, N. N., Lee, J. W., Montgomery, S., & Bellard, J. C. (2008–2009). Perceived importance of church-based assets to HIV/AIDS prevention and control in a Nigerian city. *International Quarterly of Community Health Education, 29*(2), 199–209.

Alamo, K., Packett, E., Miles, R., & Kruger, D. (2008). Fruit and vegetable intake among urban community gardeners. *Journal of Nutrition Education and Behavior, 40*(2), 94–101.

Alemeda County Public Health Department. (2007). *Setting the direction of the community assessment*. Oakland, CA: Author.

Alexander, T. E., & Cagle, V. M. (2009). *In their own words: LGBT youth writing the World Wide Web*. New York: GLAAD Center for the Study of Media & Society.

Alex-Assensoh, Y., & Assensoh, A. B. (2001). Inner-city contexts, church attendance, and African-American political participation. *The National Journal of Politics, 63*(3), 886–901.

Allen, J. O., Alaimo, K., Elam, D., & Perry, E. (2008). Growing vegetables and values: Benefits of neighborhood-based community gardens for youth development and nutrition. *Journal of Hunger & Environmental Nutrition, 3*(4), 418–439.

Allen-Meares, P., Gant, L., Shanks, T., & Hollingsworth, L. (2011). Embedded foundations: Advancing community change and empowerment. *The Foundation Review, 2*(3), 61–78.

Allison, K. R., Edmonds, T., Wilson, K., Pope, M., & Farrell, A. D. (2011). Community youth violence prevention: Positive youth development, and community mobilization. *American Journal of Community Psychology, 48*(1–2), 8–20.

Allison, K. R., & Rootman, I. (1996). Scientific rigor and community participation in health promotion research: Are they compatible? *Health Promotion International, 11*(4), 333–340.

Altschuld, J. W., & Kumar, D. D. (2009). *Needs assessment: An overview (Book 1).* Thousand Oaks, CA: Sage Publications.

Altschuler, A., Somkin, C. P., & Adler, N. E. (2004). Local services and amenities, neighborhood social capital, and health. *Social Science & Medicine, 59*(12), 1219–1229.

American Community Gardening Association. (2011). Starting a community garden. Retrieved July 20, 2011 from http://communitygarden.org/learn/starting-a-community-garden.php.

American Forests. (2012). Urban. Retrieved from http://americanforests.org/conservations/programs/urban/.

American Horticultural Therapy Association. (2011). About the American Horticultural Therapy Association. Retrieved from http://www.ahta.org/content.cfm?id-about.

Amin, A. (2008). Collective culture and urban public space. *City, 12*(1), 5–24.

Amsden, J., & VanWynsberghe, R. (2005). Community mapping as a research tool with youth. *Action Research, 3*(4), 357–381.

Anchan, J. P., & Katz, H. (2003). Capacity building and technology in the inner city. In D. Sutherland & L. Sokal (Eds.), *Resiliency and capacity building in inner-city learning communities* (pp.117–126). Winnipeg, Manitoba, Canada: Portage & Main Press.

Andersen, W. R. (2011). Using an asset-based community development initiative to attract and retain young people. *Journal of Extension, 42*(3), 1–5.

Anderson, L. (2009, Spring). Leadership, meaningful service, and engagement for all people. *The Voice:* Official Publication of the New York State Recreation and Park Society, Inc. New York: Saratoga Springs.

ArcNews Online. (2010, Spring). *GIS gives residents the tools to map their own parcels: The Beacon of Hope Resource Center Maps the "New" New Orleans.* Retrieved from http://www.esri.com/news/arcnews/spring10articles/the-beacon-of- hope.html.

Aref, F., Redzuan, M. B., & Emby, Z. (2009). Assessing sense of community capacity building in tourism development in Shiraz, Iran. *European Journal of Social Science, 7*(3), 126–132.

Arizmendi, L. G., & Ortiz, L. (2004). Neighborhood and community organizing in colonias: A case study in the development of promotoras. *Journal of Community Practice, 12*(1/2), 23–35.

Armstrong, D. (2000). A survey of community gardens in upstate New York: Implications for health promotion and community development. *Health & Place, 6*(4), 319–327.

Arneil, B. (2006). *Diverse communities: The problem with social capital.* New York: Cambridge University Press.

Aronson, R. E., Wallis, A. B., O'Campo, P. J., & Schafer, P. (2007a). Neighborhood mapping and evaluation: A methodology for participatory community health initiatives. *Maternal and Child Health Journal, 11*(4), 373–383.

Aronson, R. E., Wallis, A. B., O'Campo, P. J., & Schafer, P. (2007b). Ethnographically informed community evaluation: A framework and approach for evaluating community-based initiatives. *Maternal and Child Health Journal, 11*(4), 97–109.

Arrow, K. (1999). Observations on social capital. In P. Dasgupta & I. Serageldin (Eds.), Social capital (a multifaceted perspective, pp. 3–5). Washington, DC: World Bank.

Arundel, C., Clutterbuck, P., & Cleverly, S. (2005). *Putting theory into practice: Asset mapping in three Toronto neighborhoods.* Toronto, Canada: Caryl Arundel & Associates.

Asian Development Bank. (2001). *Social capital, local capacity building, and poverty reduction.* Woodland Hills, CA: Office of Environment and Social Development.

Aspy, C. B., et al. (2010). Youth assets and delayed coitarche across developmental age groups. *Journal of Early Adolescence, 30*(2), 277–304.

Aspy, C. B., Oman, R. E., Vesely, S. K., McLeroy, K., Rodine, S., & Marshall, L. (2004). Adolescent violence: The protective effects of youth assets. *Journal of Counseling & Development, 32*(3), 268–276.

Asset-Based Community Development Institute. (2001). *Asset mapping: A strengths-based approach.* Evanston, IL: Author.

Asset-Based Community Development Institute. (2009). Mercado Central.Retrieved from http://www.abcdinstitute.org/stories/mercado/.

Atkinson, R., & Willis, P. (2005). *Community capacity building—a practical guide.* University of Tasmania, Australia.

Bacallao, M. L., & Smokowski, P. R. (2007). The costs of getting ahead: Mexican family system changes after immigration. *Family Relations, 56*(1), 52–66.

Baines, S., & Hardill, I. (2008). 'At least I can do something': The work of volunteering in a community beset by worklessness. *Social Policy and Society, 7*(3), 307–317.

Baker, I. R., Dennison, B. A., Boyer, N. A., Seller, K. F., Russo, T. J., & Sherwood, N. A. (2007). An asset-based community initiative reduces television viewing in New York State. *Preventive Medicine, 44*(5), 437–441.

Balcazar, F. E., Keys, C. B., & Suarez-Balcazar, Y. (2001). Empowering Latinos with disabilities to address issues of independent living and disability rights: A capacity-building approach. In C. Keys & P. W. Dowrick (Eds.), *People with disabilities: Empowerment and community action* (pp. 53–70). New York: Haworth Press.

Bandura, A. (2006). Guide for creating self-efficacy scales. In F. Pajares & T. C. Urban (Eds.), *Self-efficacy beliefs of adolescents* (pp. 307–338). Charlotte, NC: Information Age Publishing.

Bankhead, T., & Erlich, J. L. (2004). Diverse populations and community practice. In M. Weil (Ed.), *Handbook of community practice* (pp. 59–83). Thousand Oaks, CA: Sage Publications.

Banks, S. (2008). Critical commentary: Social workers. *British Journal of Social Work, 38*(6), 1238–1149.

Barbour, R. S. (2005). Making sense of focus groups. *Medical Education, 39*(7), 742–750.

Barnidge, E., Baker, E. A., Motton, F., Rose, R., & Fitzgerald, T. (2010). A participatory method to identify root determinants of health: The heart of the matter. *Progress in Community Health Partnerships: Research, Education, and Action, 4*(1), 55–63.

Barron, S., Field, J., & Schuller, T. (Eds.). (2001). *Social capital: Critical perspectives.* New York: Oxford University Press.

Barrow, F. H. (2006). The International Classification of Functioning Disability, and Health (ICF). Retrieved from http://www.who.int/classifications/icf/en/.

Beacon of Hope Resource Center. (2011). *The iPhone app hits the streets of Gentilly.* Retrieved from http://www.beaconofhopenola.org/the-iphone-survey-app-hits-the -streets-of- gentilly.

Beaulieu, L. (2002). *Mapping the assets of your community: A key component for building local capacity.* Southern Rural Development Center, Mississippi State University.

Beckley, T. M., Martz, D., Nadeau, S., Wall, E., & Reimer, B. (2008). Multiple capacities, multiple outcomes: Delving deeper into the meaning of community capacity. *Journal of Rural and Community Development, 3*(1), 56–75.

Bedola, L. G. (2004). Race, connectedness and social capital in the United States. Paper presented at the Western Political Science Association Annual Meeting, Portland, OR, March 11–13, 2004.

Been, V., & Voicu, I. (2006). *The effect of community gardens on neighboring property values.* New York City: Furman Center for Real Estate and Urban Policy, New York University.

Benitez, C. (2007). *Latinization: How Latino culture is transforming the U.S.* Ithaca, NY: Paramount Books.

Berg, M., Coman, E., & Schensul, J. J. (2009). Youth action research for prevention: A multi-level intervention designed to increase efficacy and empowerment among urban youth. *American Journal of Community Psychology, 43*(3–4), 345–359.

Bergsgaard, M., & Sutherland, D. (2003). Hidden currency: Social and cultural capital in inner-city schools. In D. Sutherland & L. Sokal (Eds.), *Resiliency and capacity building in inner-city learning communities* (pp.189–206). Winnipeg, Manitoba, Canada: Portage & Main Press.

Berner, E., & Phillips, B. (2005). Left to their own devices? Community self-help between alternative development and neo-liberalism. *Community Development Journal, 40*(1), 17–29.

Berry-Caban, C. S., & Crespo, H. (2008). Cultural competency as a skill for health care providers. *Hispanic Health Care International, 6*(3), 115–121.

Best Practice Briefs. (1998–1999). The several forms of community mapping. Author, 4, 1–4.

Better Together. (2001). The arts and social capital. (http://www.bettertogether.org/ pdfs/Arts.pdf). Accessed November 20, 2009.

Bishop, B. J., Vicary, D. A., Browne, A. L., & Guard, N. (2009). Public policy, participation and the third position: The implication of engaging communities on their own terms. *American Journal of Community Psychology, 43*(1–2), 111–121.

Bisman, C. (2004). Social work values: The moral core of the profession. *British Journal of Social Work, 34*(1), 109–123.

Blanchet-Cohen, N., Ragan, D., & Amsden, J. (2003). Children becoming social actors: Using visual maps to understand children's view of environmental change. *Children, Youth & Environments, 13*(2), 1–10.

Blandrage, M. A. (2009). *Linking community revitalization, urban agriculture, and elementary education.* Rochester, NY: RIT Digital Media Library.

Bletzer, K. V. (2003). Latino naming practices of small-town businesses in rural Southern Florida. *Ethnology, 42*(3), 209–235.

Bloomberg, L., Ganey, A., Alba, V., Quintero, G., & Alcantara, L. A. (2003). Chicano-Latino Youth Leadership Institute: An asset-based program for youth. *American Journal of Health Behavior, 27*(Suppl. 1), S45–S54.

Blumenthal, D. S. (2006). A community coalition board creates a set of values for community-based research. *Preventing Chronic Disease: Public Health Research, Practice, and Policy, 3*(1), 1–7.

Bonham, V. L., Citrin, T., Modell, S. M., Franklin, T. H., Bleicher, E. W. B., & Fleck, L. M. (2009). Community-based dialogue: Engaging communities of color in the United States' Genetics Policy Convention. *Journal of Health Politics, Policy and Law, 39*(3), 325–359.

Bonmayor, R. (2008). Digital storytelling as a signature pedagogy for the new humanities. *Arts and Humanities in Higher Education, 7*(2), 188–204.

Bookman, A. (2004). *Starting in our own backyard: How working families can build community and survive the new economy.* New York: Routledge.

Born, P. (2008). *Community conversations: Mobilizing the ideas, skills, and passion of community organizations, governments, businesses, and people.* Toronto, Canada: BPS Books.

Borrup, T. (2003). Toward asset-based community cultural development: A journey through disparate worlds of community building. *Project for Public Spaces: Community Arts Network.*

Borrup, T. (2005). What's revolutionary about valuing assets as a strategy in cultural work? *Community Arts Network,* September, 1–9.

Bourdieu, P. (1986). The forms of capital. In J. Richardson (Ed.). *Handbook of theory and research for the sociology of education* (pp. 241-258). New York, NY: Greenwood Publishers.

Bowen, G. A. (2005). Local-level stakeholder collaboration: A substantive theory of community-driven development. *Community Development, 36*(2), 73–88.

Bradbart, M., & Braid, D. (2009). The devil is in the details: Defining civic engagement. *Journal of Higher Education Outreach & Engagement, 13*(2), 59–87.

Bradshaw, P. (1977). Conceptual tools: The concept of social need. In N. Gilbert & H. Specht (Eds.), *Planning for social welfare: Issues, models, and tasks* (pp. 290–298). Englewood Cliffs, NJ: Prentice Hall.

Brazg, T., Bekemeier, B., Spigner, C., & Huebner, C. E. (2010). Our community in focus: The use of photovoice for youth-driven substance abuse assessment and health promotion. *Health Promotion Practice, 12*(4), 502–511.

Breen, R. (2007). Art in the contested city. *Places, 19*(1), 98–99.

Brennan, M. A. (2007). Placing volunteers at the center of community development. *International Journal of Volunteer Administration, XXIV*(4), 5–13.

Brennan, M. A., Barnett, R. V., & Lesmeister, M. K. (2007). Enhancing local capacity and youth involvement in the community development process. *Community Development, 38*(4), 13–27.

Bridge, G. (2006). Perspectives on cultural capital and the neighborhood. *Urban Studies, 43*(4), 719–730.

Broad, G. M. (2009, November 11). *Gardens as sites for neighborhood communication: The case of Hollywood Community Gardens.* Los Angeles: Annenberg School for Communication University of Southern California, Urban Communication Foundation National Communication Association Pre-Conference Seminar.

Bronk, K. C. (2008). Early adolescent concepts of the good life and the good person. *Adolescence, 43*(6), 713–732.

Bronn, P. S. (2008). Intangible assets and communication. *Public Relations Research, Part III,* 281–291.

Brough, M. K., Bond, C., & Hunt, J. (2004) Strong in the City: Toward a strength based approach in indigenous health promotion. *Health Promotion Journal of Australia, 15*(3), 215–220.

Brown, L., LaFond, A., & Macintrye, K. (2001). *Measuring capacity building.* Chapel Hill, NC: University of North Carolina, Caroline Population Center.

Brown, M. B. (2006). Survey article: Citizen panels and the concept of representation. *The Journal of Political Philosophy, 14*(2), 203–225.

Brown, P. (1992). Popular epidemiology and toxic waste contamination: Lay and professional ways of knowing. *Journal of Health and Social Behavior, 33*(4), 267–281.

Brown, P. L. (2010, January 17). For Latino group, health and savings grow in backyard gardens. *The New York Times,* p. 16.

Brown, P. L. (2011, October 10). When the uprooted put down roots: For income and a taste of home, refugees turn to farming. *The New York Times,* p. A12.

Bryant, C. A., Forthofer, M. S., Brown, K. R. M., Landis, D. C., & McDermott, R. J. (2000). Community-based prevention marketing: The next steps in disseminating behavior change. *American Journal of Health Behavior, 24*(1), 61–68.

Bryce, H. J. (2006). Nonprofits as social capital and agents in the public policy process: Toward a new paradigm. *Nonprofit and Voluntary Sector Quarterly, 35*(2), 311–318.

Bryson, L., & Mowbray, M. (2005). More spray on solution: Community, social capital and evidence based policy. *Australian Journal of Social Issues, 40*(1), 91–106.

Buchanan, D. R., Miller, F. G., & Wallerstein, N. (2007). Ethical issues in community-based participatory research: Balancing rigorous research with community participation in community intervention studies. *Progress in Community Health Partnerships: Research, Education, and Action, 1*(2), 153–160.

Burrell, J. (2009). The field site as a network: A strategy for locating ethnographic research. *Field Method, 21*(2), 181–199.

Burris, S., Hancock, T., Lin, V., & Herzog, A. (2007). Emerging strategies for healthy urban governance. *Journal of Urban Health, 84*(Suppl. 1), 154–163.

Busch, R., & Mutch, M. (1998). Capacity building for harm reduction at the district level: Conceptual development and the dimension of practice. Paper presented at the Fourth Symposium on Community Action and Research and the Prevention of Alcohol and Other Drug Prevention. Kettil Brown Society Thematic Meeting, New Zealand.

Butterfoss, F. (2006). Process evaluation for community participation. *Annual Review of Public Health, 27,* 323–340.

Cahill, C., Sultana, F., & Pain, R. (2007). Participatory ethics: Politics, practices, institutions. *ACME: An International E-Journal for Critical Geographics, 6*(3), 304–318.

California School Garden Network. (2010). *Gardens for learning: Creating and sustaining your school garden.* Irvine, CA: California School Garden Network.

Calleson, D. C., Jordan, C., & Seifer, S. (2005). Community-engaged scholarship: Is faculty work in communities a true academic enterprise. *Academic Medicine, 80*(4), 317–321.

Cameron, J., & Gibson, K. (2005). Alternative pathways to community and economic development: The Latrobe Valley Community Partnering Project. *Geographical Research, 43*(3), 274–285.

Camino, L. (2005). Youth led community building: Promising practices from two communities using community-based service-learning. *Journal of Extension, 43*(1), 1–5.

Camino, L., & Zelbin, S. (2002). Making the transition to community youth development and emerging roles and competencies for youth-serving organizations and youth workers. *Community Youth Development Journal, Spring-Summer,* 70–78.

Cammarota, J. (2011). From hopelessness to hope: Social justice pedagogy in urban education and youth development. *Urban Education, 46*(4), 828–844.

Campanella, T. J. (2006). Urban resilience and the recovery of New Orleans. *Journal of the American Planning Association, 72*(2), 141–146.

Campbell, W. S. (2008). Lessons in resilience: Undocumented Mexican women in South Carolina. *Affilia, 23*(3), 231–241.

Canadian Association of Business Incubators. (Undated). Ontario, Canada: Author.

Cargo, M., & Mercer, S. L. (2008). The value and challenges of participatory research: Strengthening its practice. *Annual Review of Public Health, 29,* 325–350.

Carlson, E. D., Engebretson, J., & Chamberlain, R. M. (2006). Photovoice as a social process of critical consciousness. *Qualitative Research, 16*(6), 836–852.

Carson, A. J., Chappell, N. L., & Knight, C. J. (2007). Promoting health and innovative health promotion practice through a community arts centre. *Health Promotion Practice, 8*(4), 366–374.

Carr, J. H., & Servon, L. J. (2009). Vernacular culture and urban economic development: Thinking outside the (big) box. *Journal of the American Planning Association, 75*(1), 28–40.

Carroll, J. M., & Rosson, M. B. (2007). Participatory design in community infomatics. *Design Studies, 28*(3), 243–261.

Cashman, S. B., Adeky, S., Allen, A. J., Corburn, J., Israel, B. A., Montaño, J., Rafelito, A., Rhodes, S. D., Swanston, S., Wallerstein, N., & Eng, E. (2008). The power and the promise: Working with communities to analyze data, interpret findings, and get to outcomes. *American Journal of Public Health, 98*(8), 1407–1417.

Casswell, S. (2001). Community capacity building and social policy—what can be achieved? *Social Policy Journal of New Zealand, 17*(1), 22–35.

Castka, P., Bamber, C. J., & Sharp, J. M. (2004). Benchmarking intangible assets: Enhancing teamwork performance using self-assessment. *Benchmarking: An International Journal, 11*(6), 571–583.

Castledem, H., Gacuin, T., & First Nation, H. (2008). Modifying photovoice for community-based-participatory indigenous research. *Social Science & Medicine, 66*(6), 1393–1405.

Catalini, C., & Minkler, M. (2010). Photovoice: A review of the literature in health and public health. *Health Education & Behavior, 37*(3), 424–451.

Center for Universal Design. (1997). *The principles of universal design.* Raleigh, NC: North Carolina State University.

Chambers, R. (2006). Participatory mapping and geographic information systems: Whose map? Who is empowered and disempowered? Who gains and who loses. *Electronic Journal on Information Systems in Developing Countries, 25*(2), 1–11.

Charlier, N., Glover, M., & Robertson, J. (2009). Keeping kids smokefree: Lessons learned on community participation. *Health Education Research, 24*(6), 949–956.

Chaskin, R. J. (2001). Building community capacity. *Urban Affairs Review, 36*(3), 291–323.

Chaskin, R. J., Brown, P., Venkatesh, S., & Vidal, A. (2001). *Building community capacity*. New York: Aldine de Gruyter.

Chavez, L. R. (2008). *The Latino threat: Constructing immigrants, citizens, and the nation*. Palo Alto, CA: Stanford University Press.

Chavez, V., Israel, B., Allen, A. J., III, DeCarlo, M. F., Lichtenstein, R., Schutz, A., Bayer, I. S., & McGranaghan, R. (2004). A bridge between communities: Video-making using principles of community-based participatory research. *Health Promotion Practice, 5*(4), 395–403.

Checkoway, B. (1996). Adults as allies. Ann Arbor, MI: University of Michigan School of Social Work.

Checkoway, B. (2009). Community change for diverse democracy. *Community Development Journal, 44*(1), 5–21.

Checkoway, B., & Goodyear, L. (Eds.). (2002). *Youth participation in community evaluation research*. Ann Arbor: University of Michigan, Center for Community Change.

Checkoway, B., & Gutierrez, L. (Eds.). (2006). *Youth participation and community change*. New York: Haworth Press.

Chen, P., Weiss, F. L., & Nicholson, H. J. (2010). Girls Study Girls Inc.: Engaging girls in evaluation training through participatory action research. *American Journal of Community Psychology, 46*(1–2), 228–237.

Cheong, P. H., Edwards, R., Goulbourne, H., & Solomos, J. (2007). Immigration, social cohesion and social capital: A critical review. *Critical Social Policy, 27*(1), 24–49.

Chinman, M., Hannah, G., Wandersman, A., Ebener, P., Hunter, S. B., Imm, R., & Sheldon, J. (2005). Developing a community science agenda for building community capacity for effective preventive interventions. *American Journal of Community Psychology, 35*(3–4), 143–157.

Chino, M., & DeBruyn, L. (2006). Building true capacity: Indigenous models for indigenous communities. *American Journal of Public Health, 96*(4), 596–599.

Chow, J. C-C., & Crowe, K. (2005). Community-based research and methods in community practice. In M. Weil (Ed.), *The handbook of community practice* (pp. 604–619). Thousand Oaks, CA: Sage Publications.

Christie, L. (2006, June 15). Cities are hot again: After years of urban flight, Americans are finding the appeal of places like Philadelphia, Nashville and Seattle. Atlanta, GA: *CNNMoney*. Retrieved July 15, 2011 from http://money.cnn.com/2006/06/15/real_estate/return_to_cities/index.htm.

Christopher, S., Watts, V., McCormick, A. K., & Young, S. (2008). Building and maintaining trust in a community-based participatory research partnership. *American Journal of Public Health, 98*(8), 1398–1406.

Chu, W. C. K., Tsui, M-S., & Yan, M-C. (2009). Social work as a moral and political practice. *International Social Work, 52*(3), 287–298.

Chung, B., Corbett, C. E., Boulet, B. B., Cummings, J. R., Paxton, K., McDaniel, S., Mercier, S. O., Franklin, C., Mercier, E., Jones, L., Collins, B. E., Koegel, P., Duan, N., Wells, K. B., Glik, D., and Talking Wellness Group of Witnesses for Wellness. (2006). Talking wellness: A description of a community-academic partnered project to engage an African-American community around depression through the use of poetry, film, and photography. *Ethnicity & Disease, 16*(1), S-67–S-78.

Chutuape, K., Willard, N., Kapogiannis, B. G., & Ellen, J. M. (2009). Creative and tailored strategies needed to foster researcher-community partnerships. *American Journal of Public Health, 99*(3), 390–392.

Cisneros, H. G. (2008). An overview: Latinos and the nation's future. In H. G. Cisneros (Ed.), *Latinos and the nation's future* (pp. 3–13). Houston, TX: Arte Publico Press, University of Houston.

Clark, C. (2006). Moral character in social work. *British Journal of Social Work, 36*(1), 75–89.

Clark, J., & Clark, D. D. (1994). Creating tactile maps for the blind using a GIS. Bethesda, MD: American Congress on Surveying and Mapping/American Society for Photogrammetry and Remote Sensing International Proceedings, Retrieved July 19, 2011 from http://libraries.maine.edu/Spatial/gisweb/spatdb/acsm/ac94120.html.

Clark, M. J., Cary, S., Diemert, G., Caballos, R., Fuentes, M., Atteberry, I., Vue, F., & Trieu, S. (2003). Involving communities in community assessments. *Public Health Nursing, 20*(8), 456–463.

Clary, E. G., & Rhodes, J. E. (Eds.). (2006). *Mobilizing adults for positive youth development: Strategies for closing the gap between beliefs and behaviors (The Search Institute Series on Developmentally Attentive Community and Society).* Minneapolis, MN: Search Institute.

Cleaver, F. (2004). "The inequality of social capital and the reproduction of chronic poverty." *World Development, 33*(6), 893–906.

Cohen, D., & Prusak, L. (2001). *In good company: How social capital makes organizations work.* Boston, MA: Harvard Business School Press.

Cohen-Cruz, J. (2005). *Local acts: Community-based performance in the United States.* New Brunswick, NJ: Rutgers University Press.

Cohen-Cruz, J. (2007). *Between the edge and the root: Action Lab in Hunts Point.* (http://www.communityarts.net/readingroom/archivefiles/2006/07/between_theedg_1.php). Accessed May 26, 2009.

Cohousing Association of the United States. (2011). *What are the 6 defining characteristics of cohousing?* Bothell, WA: Cohousing Association of the United States. Retrieved July 15, 2011 from http://www.cohousing.org/six characteristics.

Coleman, J. S. (1998). Social capital in the creation of human capital. *American Journal of Sociology, 94*(S1), S121–S120.

Common Ground. (2004). *Approaches to community.* Victoria, B.C., Canada: Author.

Community Gardening Association. (2010). Research supporting the benefits of school gardens. Retrieved July 20, 2011 from http://www.kidsgardening.org/article/research-supporting-benefits-school-gardens.

Copeland-Carson, J. (2008). *Engaging community for sustainable revitalization: Key trends, strategies and recommendations.* San Francisco, CA: Copeland Carson & Associates.

Corburn, J. (2005). *Street science: Community knowledge and environmental health justice.* Cambridge, MA: MIT Press.

Corburn, J. (2009). *Toward the healthy city: People, places, and the politics of urban planning.* Cambridge, MA: MIT Press.

Cordasco, K. M., Asch, S. M., Bell, D. S., Guterman, J. J., Gross-Schulman, S., Ramer, L., Elkayam, U., Franco, I., Leatherwood, C. L., & Mangione, C. M. (2009). Risk and resilience in Latino community-based participatory research study. *Journal of Preventive Medicine, 37*(6), S217–S224.

Cornebise, J. (1998). Mapping community resources. *Community Technology Center Review,* January, 1–5.

Cornell University Cooperative Extension New York City. (2012). Garden mosaics. Retrieved from http://nyc.cce.cornell.edu/UrbanEnvironment/UrbanEcology/GardenMosaics/Pages/GardenMosaics.aspx.

Craig, W. J., & Elwood, S. A. (1998). *How and why community groups use maps and geographic information.* Minneapolis, MN: University of Minnesota Center for Urban and Regional Affairs.

Crampton, J. W. (2009). Cartography: Performative, participatory, political. *Progress in Human Geography, 33*(6), 840–848.

Crampton, J. W., & Krygier, J. (2006). An introduction to critical cartography. *ACME: An International E-Journal for Critical Geographies, 4*(1), 11–43.

Crane, K., & Mooney, M. (2005). *Essential tools: Community resource mapping.* Washington, DC: National Center on Secondary Education and Transition, U.S. Department of Education.

Crane, K., & Skinner, B. (2002). *Community resource mapping: A strategy for promoting successful transitions for youth with disabilities.* Rockville, MD: TransCen, Inc.

Critser, G. (2003). *Fat land: How Americans became the fattest people in the world.* Boston: Houghton Mifflin Co.

Cross, J. (2009). The old man and the storm [film]. Alexandria, VA: PBS Home Video.

Crowell, C. D. (2008). *Asset mapping as a tool in economic development and community revitalization:* A case study of Richmond, Ohio. Cincinnati, OH: University of Cincinnati, Design, Architecture and Planning.

Curley, A. M. (2010). Relocating the poor: Social capital and neighborhood resources. *Journal of Urban Affairs, 32*(1), 79–103.

Currid, E. (2007). How art and culture happen in New York. *Journal of the American Planning Association, 73*(4), 454–467.

Cuthill, M. (2002). Coolangatta: A portrait of community well-being. *Urban Policy & Research, 20*(2), 187–203.

D'Alonzo, K. T. (2010). Getting started in CDPR: Lessons in building community partnerships for new researchers. *Nursing Inquiry, 17*(4), 282–288.

Dabson, N. G., & Gilroy, A. R. (2009). From partnership to policy: The evolution of active living design in Portland, Oregon. *American Journal of Preventive Medicine, 37*(6, Suppl. 2), S436–S444.

Dahm, C. W. (2004). *Parish ministry in a Hispanic community.* Mahwah, NJ: Paulist Press.

Daly, M., & Silver, H. (2008). Social exclusion and social capital: A comparison and critique. *Theoretical Sociology, 37*(4), 537–566.

Davidson, A. (2012, July 15). The Bronx is yearning. *The New York Times Magazine,* p. 18.

Davidson, A., Schwartz, S. E. O., & Noam, G. G. (2008). Creating youth leaders: Community supports. *New Directions for Youth Development, 120*(Winter), 127–137.

Decker, G. (2011, July 4). More Hispanics are identifying themselves as Indians. *The New York Times,* p. A14.

Deeds, B. G., Strub, D. M., Willard, N., Castor, J., Ellen, J., Peralta, L., & Adolescent Trials Network for HIV/AIDS Interventions. (2006). Fertile ground: The role of a community asset assessment in 15 community-researcher partnerships promoting adolescent health. *Journal of Adolescent Health, 38*(2), 99–110.

DeFilippis, J., Fisher, R., & Shragge, E. (2006). Neither romance nor regulation: Re-evaluating community. *International Journal of Urban and Regional Research, 30*(3), 673–689.

DeFilippis, J., Fisher, R., & Shragge, E. (2009). What's left in the community? Oppositional politics in contemporary practice. *Community Development Journal, 44*(1), 38–52.

De La Salle, J., & Holland, M. (2010). *Agricultural urbanism: Handbook for building sustainable food and agriculture systems in 21st century cities.* Winnipeg, Canada: Green Frigate Books.

Delgado, L. H. (2012). Using data-driven tools to address foreclosures and distressed properties in Boston, Massachusetts. In *Proceedings from The Center for Community Progress Conference: Remaking America for the 21st Century--Reclaiming Vacant Properties.* New Orleans, LA: Center for Community Progress.

Delgado, M. (1995). Puerto Rican elders and natural support systems: Implications for human services. *Journal of Gerontological Social Work, 24*(3), 115–129.

Delgado, M. (1998a). *Social work practice in nontraditional urban settings.* New York: Oxford University Press.

Delgado, M. (1998b). Interpretation of Puerto Rican elder research findings: A community forum of research respondents. *Journal of Applied Gerontology, 16*(1), 317–332.

Delgado, M. (1999). *Community social work practice within an urban context: The potential of a community capacity-enhancement perspective.* New York: Oxford University Press.

Delgado, M. (2001a). *Where are all of the young men and women of color? Capacity enhancement practice and the criminal justice system.* New York: Columbia University Press.

Delgado, M. (2001b). *New arenas for community social work practice with urban youth: Use of the arts, humanities, and sports.* New York: Columbia University Press.

Delgado, M. (2002). *New frontiers for youth development in the twenty-first century: Revitalizing and broadening youth development.* New York: Columbia University Press.

Delgado, M. (2004). *Social youth entrepreneurship: The potential for youth and community transformation.* Westport, CT: Praeger Publishers.

Delgado, M. (2006). *Designs and methods for youth-led research.* Thousand Oaks, CA: Sage Publications.

Delgado, M. (2008). *Social work practice with Latinos: A cultural assets paradigm.* New York: Oxford University Press.

Delgado, M. (2009). *Older adult-led health promotion in urban communities: Theory and models.* Lanham, MD: Rowman & Littlefield.

Delgado, M. (2011). *Latino small businesses and the American dream: Community social work practice and economic and social development.* New York: Columbia University Press.

Delgado, M. (2012). *Prisoner re-entry at work: Adding business into the mix.* Boulder, CO: Lynne Rienner Publishers.

Delgado, M. (In Press). *Social justice and the urban obesity crisis: Implications for social work.* New York: Columbia University Press.

Delgado, M., & Barton, K. (1998). Murals in Latino communities: Social indicators of community strengths. *Social Work, 43*(4), 346–356.

Delgado, M., Jones, K., & Rohani, M. (2005). *Social work practice with refugees and immigrant youth in the United States*. Boston, MA: Allyn & Bacon.

Delgado, M., & Santiago, J. (1998). Botanical shops in a Puerto Rican/Dominican community in New England: Implications for health and human services. *Social Work, 43*(3), 183–176.

Delgado, M., & Staples, L. (2008). *Youth-led community organizing: Theory and action*. New York: Oxford University Press.

Delgado, M., & Zhou, H. (2008). *Youth-led health promotion in urban communities: A community capacity-enhancement perspective*. Lanham, MD: Rowman & Littlefield.

Denner, J., Kirby, D., Coyle, K., & Brindis, C. (2001). The protective role of social capital and cultural norms in Latino communities: A study of adolescent births. *Hispanic Journal of Behavioral Sciences, 23*(3), 3–21.

Dennis, S. F., Jr. (2006). Prospects for qualitative GIS at the intersection of youth development and participatory urban planning. *Environment and Planning, 38*(11), 2039–2054.

Dennis, S. F., Jr., Gaulocher, S., Carpiano, R. M., & Brown, D. (2008). Participatory photo mapping (PPM): Exploring an integrated method for health and place research with young people. *Health & Place, 15*(8), 466–473.

Denton, D., & Robertson, T. (2010). A kaleidoscope of innovation: Designing community impact in the Waterloo region. *The Philanthropist, 23*(3), 283–302.

DeRienzo, H. (2008). *The concept of community: Lessons from the Bronx*. Milan, Italy: IPOC de Pietro Condemi.

Diehl, A., Grabill, J. T., Hart-Davidson, W., & Iyer, V. (2008). Grassroots: Supporting the knowledge work of everyday life. *Technical Communication Quarterly, 17*(4), 413–434.

Diers, J. (2004). *Neighbor power: Building community the Seattle way*. Seattle: University of Washington Press.

Dika, S. L., & Singh, K. (2002). Applications of social capital in educational literature: A critical synthesis. *Review of Educational Research, 72*(1), 31–60.

Doel, M., Allmark, P., Conway, P., Cowburn, M., Flynn, M., Nelson, P., & Tod, A. (2010). Professional boundaries: Crossing a line or entering the shadows. *British Journal of Social Work, 40*(6), 1866–1889.

Domahidy, M. (2003). Using theory to frame community and practice. *Journal of the Community Development Society, 34*(1), 75–84.

Donaldson, L. P., & Daughtery, L. C. (2011). Introducing asset-based models of social justice into service learning: A social work approach. *Journal of Community Practice, 19*(1), 80–99.

Donoghue, E. M., & Sturtevant, V. E. (2007). Social science constructs in ecosystem assessments: Revisiting community capacity and community resiliency. *Society & Natural Resources, 20*(10), 899–912.

Downey, L. H., Ireson, C. L., & Scutcfield, F. D. (2009). The use of photovoice as a method of facilitating deliberation. *Health Promotion Practice, 10*(3), 419–427.

Duke, N. N., Borowsky, I. W., & Pettingell, S. L. (2011). Adult perceptions of neighborhood: Links to youth engagement. *Youth & Society, 44*(8), 408–430.

Dunn, C. E. (2007). Participatory GIS—a people's GIS? *Progress in Human Geography, 31*(5), 616–637.

Durlak, J. A., & DuPre, E. P. (2008). Implementation matters: A review of research on the influence of implementation on program outcomes and the factors affecting implementation. *American Journal of Community Psychology, 41*(4), 327–350.

Eaton, S. E. (2010). *Formal, non-formal and informal learning: The case of literacy, essential skills and language learning in Canada.* Calgary, AB: Eaton International Consulting Inc.

Ebrahim, S. (2004). Social capital: Everything or nothing? *International Journal of Epidemiology, 33*(4), 627.

Eck, J. E., Chainey, S., Cameron, J. G., Leitner, M., & Wilson, R. E. (2005). *Mapping crime: Understanding hot spots.* Washington, DC: Office of Justice Programs.

Edwards, L. M., & Romero, A. J. (2008). Coping with discrimination among Mexican descent adolescents. *Hispanic Journal of Behavioral Sciences, 30*(1), 24–39.

Eisinger, A., & Senturia, K. (2001). Doing community-driven research: A description of Seattle partners for healthy communities. *Journal of Urban Health, 78*(3), 519–534.

El Ansari, W. (2005). Collaborative research partnerships with disadvantaged communities: Challenges and potential solutions. *Public Health: The Journal of the Royal Institute of Public Health, 119*(8), 758–770.

El Ansari, W., Phillips, C. J., & Zwi, A. B. (2002). Narrowing the gap between academic professional wisdom and community lay knowledge: Perceptions from partnerships. *Public Health: The Journal of the Royal Institute of Public Health, 116*(1), 151–159.

Elder, R. F. (2005). Protecting New York City's community gardens. *New York University Environmental Law Journal,* 769–776.

Ellerman, D. (2007). Helping self-help: The fundamental conundrum of development assistance. *Journal of Socio-Economics, 36*(4), 561–577.

Elliot, C. (1999). *Locating the energy for change: An introduction to appreciative inquiry.* Winnipeg, Canada: International Institute for Sustainable Development.

Eloff, I., & De Wet, A. (2007). Opting for assets to enrich pre-school learning. *Early Child Development and Care, 177*(1), 1–13.

Eloff, I., & Ebersohn, L. (2001). The implications of an asset-based approach to early intervention. *Perspectives in Education, 19*(3), 147–157.

Elwood, S. (2006). Beyond cooptation or resistance: Urban spatial politics, community organizations, and GIS-based spatial narratives. *Annals of the Association of American Geographers, 96*(2), 323–341.

Emery, M., Fernandez, E., Gutierrez-Montes, I., & Flora, C. B. (2007). Leadership as community capacity building: A study on the impact of leadership development training on community. *Community Development, 38*(4), 60–70.

Emery, M., Fey, S., & Flora, C. (2006). Using community capitals to develop assets for positive community change. (www.ncrcrd.iastate.edu). Accessed December 13, 2009.

Emery, M., & Flora, C. (2006). "Spiraling-up": Mapping community transformation with community capitals framework. *Community Development, 37*(1), 19–35.

Emery, M., Wall, M., & Macker, D. (2004). From theory to action: Emerging entrepreneurship (E2), strategies to aid distressed communities grow their own. *Journal of the Community Development Society, 35*(1), 82–96.

Ennis, G., & West, D. (2010). Exploring the potential of social network analysis in asset-based community development practice and research. *Australian Social Work, 63*(4), 404–417.

Estabrook, M., Sakano, Y., Tubb, S. P., Varela, D., & Williams, R. (2005). *Grocery stores and social capital: A study of seven Cincinnati neighborhoods.* Cincinnati, OH: University of Cincinnati. (http:www.uc.edu/oldwebsite/summary-website/groceryrole-capital.pdf). Accessed October 30, 2009.

Evans, S. D. (2007). Youth sense of community: Voice and power in community contexts. *Journal of Community Psychology, 35*(6), 693–709.

Evans, W. D., Ulasevich, A., & Blahut, S. (2004). Adult and group influences on participation in youth empowerment programs. *Health Education & Behavior, 31*(5), 564–576.

Evenhouse, E. L. (2009). *The people know best: Developing civic participation in urban planning.* Berkeley, CA: University of California International and Area Studies.

Fahy, F., & O'Cinneide, M. (2009). Re-constructing the urban landscape through community mapping: An attractive prospect for sustainability? *Area (London, England: 1969), 41*(2), 167–175.

Fainstein, S. S. (2010). *The just city.* Ithaca, NY: Cornell University Press.

Falconi, J. L., & Mazzotti, J. A. (Eds.). (2007). *The other Latinos: Central and South Americans in the United States.* Cambridge, MA: Harvard University Press.

Farquhar, S. A., Michael, Y. L., & Wiggins, N. (2005). Building on leadership and social capital to create change in 2 urban communities. *American Journal of Public Health, 95*(4), 596–601.

Fenn, J. B., III, & Moore, S. (2010). *Rockwood cultural asset mapping: Building community and engaging residents.* Eugene: University of Oregon Press.

Ferguson, I., & Lavalette, M. (2006). Globalization and global justice. *International Social Work, 49*(3), 309–318.

Ferguson, R. F., & Dickens, W. T. (1999). Introduction. In R. F. Ferguson & W. T. Dickens (Eds.), *Urban problems and community development* (pp. 1–32). Washington, DC: Brookings Institution.

Ferlander, S. (2007). The importance of different forms of social capital for health. *Acta Sociologica, 50*(2), 115–128.

Fernandez, M. A. (2002). *Creating community change: Challenges and tensions in community youth research.* Stanford, CA: John W. Gardner Center for Youth and Their Communities.

Fernandez-Kelly, P. (2008). The back pocket map: Social class and cultural capital as transferable assets in the advancement of second-generation immigrants. *The Annals of the American Academy of Political and Social Science, 620,* 16–137.

Fetterman, D. M., & Wandersman, A. (Eds.). (2004). *Empowerment evaluation principles and practice.* New York: The Guilford Press.

Field, J. (2003). *Social capital (key issues).* New York: Routledge.

Field, J. (2008). *Social capital (key ideas).* New York: Routledge.

Field Museum. (2004). *Field Museum maps 'social assets' of Chicago's industrialized Lake Calumet region: Study identifies strengths of a community poised for change.* Chicago: Author.

Filbert, K. M., & Flynn, R. J. (2010). Developmental and cultural assets and resilient outcomes in First Nation young people in care: An initial test of an explanatory model. *Children and Youth Services Review, 32*(4), 560–564.

Fisher, P. A., & Ball, T. J. (2003). Tribal participatory research: Mechanisms of a collaborative model. *American Journal of Community Psychology, 32*(3–4), 207–216.

Fisher, R. (2004). History, context, and emerging issues for community practice. In M. Weil (Ed.), *Handbook of community practice* (pp. 34–58). Thousand Oaks, CA: Sage Publications.

Flaspohler, P., Duffy, J., Wandersman, A., Stillman, L., & Maras, M. A. (2008). Unpacking prevention capacity: An intersection of research-to-practice models and community-centered models. *American Journal of Community Psychology, 41*(3–4), 182–196.

Flint, R. W. (2010). Seeking resilience in the development of sustainable communities. *Research in Human Ecology, 17*(1), 44–57.

Flora, C. B., Flora, J. L., & Fey, S. (2004). *Rural communities: Legacy and change*, 2nd ed. Boulder, CO: Westview Press.

Flyvbjerg, B. (2006). Five misunderstandings about case-study research. *Qualitative Inquiry, 12*(2), 219–245.

Forman, J. (2004). Community policing and youth as assets. *Journal of Criminal Law and Criminology, 95*(1), 1–48.

Foster-Fishman, P., Nowell, B., Deacon, Z., Nievar, M. A., & McNann, P. (2005). Using methods that matter: The impact of reflection, dialogue, and voice. *American Journal of Community Psychology, 36*(4), 275–291.

Foth, M. (2004). *Encouraging residents to take ownership of an online community network through PAD: Participation, animation, design.* Brisbane, Australia: Creative Industries Research and Application Centre.

Foth, M. (2006). *Network action research.* Queensland, Australia: Queensland University of Technology.

Foth, M., & Adkins, B. (2005). A research design to build effective partnerships between city planners, developers, government and urban neighbourhood communities. *The Journal of Community Informatics, 2*(2), 116–133.4-H. (2012). Who we are. Retrieved from http://www.4-h.org/about/youth-development-organization/.

Fox, J., Suryanata, K., & Hershack, P. (Eds.). (2005) *Mapping communities: Ethics, values, practices.* Honolulu, HA: East-West Center.

Franklin, C., & Hopson, L. M. (2007). Facilitating the use of evidence-based practice in community organizations. *Journal of Social Work Education, 43*(3), 377–404.

Franklin, J., & Thomson, R. (2005). Special feature: (Re) claiming the social. *Feminist Theory, 6*(2), 161–172.

Fraser, H. (2005). Four different approaches to community participation. *Community Development Journal, 40*(3), 286–300.

Fraser, H. (2009). Trying to complete socially just, politically sensitive social work research. *Journal of Social Work, 9*(1), 87–98.

Freire, P. (1982). Creating alternative research methods. Learning to do it by doing it. In B. Hall, A. Gillette, & R. Tandon (Eds.), *Knowledge: A monopoly* (pp. 29–37). New Delhi, India: Society for Participatory Research in Asia.

Fremeaux, I. (2005). New Labour's appropriation of the concept of community: A critique. *Community Development Journal, 40*(3), 265–274.

Freudenberg, N. (2004). Community capacity for environment health promotion: Determinants and implications for practice. *Health Education & Behavior, 31*(4), 472–490.

Friedmann, J. (2007). *The wealth of cities: Towards an assets-based development of newly urbanized regions.* The Hague, Netherlands: UN-Habitat Award Lecture.

Fukuyama, F. (2002). Social capital and development: The coming agenda. *SAIS Review, XXII*(1), 23–37.

Gaarder, M. M., Munar, W., & Sollis, P. (2003). *Mapping community capacity among the Garifuna*. Washington, DC: Inter-American Development Bank, Economic and Sector Study Series.

Ganapalis, S. (2008). Critical appraisal of three ideas for community development in the United States. *Journal of Planning and Research, 27*(4), 382–399.

Gandelman, A. A., DeSantis, L. M., & Rietmeijer, C. A. (2006). Assessing community needs and agency capacity—An integral part of implementing effective evidence-based interventions. *AIDS Education and Prevention, 18*(Suppl. A), 32–43.

Garbarino, J., & Haslam, R. (2005). Lost boys: Why our sons turn violent and how we can save them. *Pediatrics & Child Health, 10*(8), 447–450.

Gardberg, N. A., & Fombrun, C. J. (2006). Corporate citizenship: Creating intangible assets across institutional environments. *Academy of Management Review, 31*(2), 329–346.

Gardner, J. F., & Mathias, E. A. (2009). Inclusion: Progress and promise: Beyond the disabling bubble. *The International Journal of Leadership in Public Service, 5*(2), 38–45.

Garden Mosaics. Retrieved August 22, 2012 from http://communitygardennews.org/gardenmosaics/index.htm.

Garrettson, M., Walline, V., Heisler, J., & Townsend, J. (2010). New medical school engages rural community to conduct regional health assessment. *Family Medicine, 42*(10), 693–701.

Gaynor, N. (2010). In-active citizenship and the depoliticization of community development in Ireland. *Community Development Journal, 46*(1), 27–41.

Gearin, E., & Kahle, C. (2006). Teen and adult perceptions of urban green space in Los Angeles. *Children, Youth and Environments, 16*(1), 25–48.

Gertler, B. (2003). Self-knowledge. In E. N. Zalta (Ed.), *Stanford encyclopedia of philosophy*. Retrieved June 15, 2004 (www.http://plato.stanford.edu/archives/spr2003/entries/selfknowledge).

Gertler, P., Levine, D. I., & Moretti, E. (2006). Is social capital the capital of the poor? The role of family and community in helping insure living standards against health shocks. *CEifo Economic Studies, 52*(3), 455–499.

Gesler, W., Hayes, H., Arcury, T., Skelly, A., Nash, S., & Soward, A. (2004). Use of mapping technology in health intervention research. *Nursing Outlook, 52*(3), 1142–146.

Ghirardelli, A., Quinn, V., & Foerster, S. B. (2010). Using geographic information systems and local food store data in California's low-income neighborhoods to inform community initiatives and resources. *American Journal of Public Health, 100*(11), 2156–2162.

Gibbon, M., Labonte, R., & Laverack, G. (2002). Evaluating community capacity. *Health and Social Care in the Community, 10*(5), 1–7.

Ginieniewicz, J. (2010). *The accumulation and transfer of civic and political assets by Argentinean migrants to Spain*. Manchester, UK: Global Urban Research Centre, University of Manchester.

Glantz, N., & McMahan, B. (2007). Introduction: The anthropology map merger. *Practicing Anthropology, 29*(4), 4–5.

Glöcker, H., Mkaga, M., & Ndezi, T. (2004). Local empowerment through community mapping for water and sanitation in Dar es Salaam. *Environment and Urbanization, 16*(1), 185–197.

Glover, T. D. (2003). The story of the Queen Anne Memorial Garden: Resisting a dominant cultural narrative. *Journal of Leisure Research, 35*(2), 190–212.

Goddard, M. A., Doughill, A. J., & Benton, T. G. (2010). Scaling up from gardens: Biodiversity conservation in urban environments. *Trends in Ecology and Evolution, 25*(2), 90–98.

Goebert, B., & Rosenthal, H. (2001). *Beyond listening: Learning the secret language of focus groups.* New York: John Wiley & Sons.

Gold, L. (2011, April 8). $1M will launch 70 school garden programs, 23 in N.Y. Cornell University Chronicle Online. Retrieved from http://www.news.cornell.edu/stories/April11/NYCgardens.html.

Goldbard, A. (2006). *New creative community: The art of cultural development.* Oakland, CA: New Village Press.

Goldman, J., Shilton, K., Burke, J., Estrin, D., Hansen, M., Ramanathan, N., Reddy, S., Samanta, V., & Srivastiva, M. (2008). *Participatory sensing: A citizen-powered approach to illuminating the patterns that shape our world.* Los Angeles, CA: Center for Embedded Networked Sensing, UCLA.

Goldman, K. D., & Schmalz, K. J. (2005). "Accentuate the positive!": Using an asset mapping as part of a community-health needs assessment. *Health Promotion Practice, 6*(2), 125–128.

Gonzalez, R. (2009). Beyond affirmation. *Hispanic Journal of Behavioral Sciences, 31*(1), 5–31.

Goodland, R., Burton, P., & Croft, J. (2005). *Effectiveness at what? The process and impact of community involvement in area-based initiatives.* Glasgow, Scotland: Scottish Centre for Research on Social Justice, University of Glasgow.

Goodman, R. M., Speers, M. A., McLeroy, K., Fawcett, S., Kegler, M., Parker, E., Smith, S. R., Sterling, T. D., & Wallerstein, N. (1998). Identifying and defining the dimensions of community capacity to provide a basis for measurement. *Health & Education Behavior, 25*(3), 258–278.

Goodyear, L., & Checkoway, B. (2003). Establishing the importance of youth participation in community evaluation and research. *Community Youth Development Journal, 4*(1), 54–55.

Gordon, H. R. (2010). *We fight to win: Inequality and the politics of youth activism.* New Brunswick, NJ: Rutgers University Press.

Grantmakers in Health. (2006). Assessing communities. *From the Ground Up,* February, 1–3.

Green, G. P. (2009). Community asset mapping and surveys. In R. Phillips & R. H Pittman (Eds.), *An introduction to community development* (pp. 155–165). New York: Routledge.

Green, G. P. (2010a). Natural amenities and asset-based development in rural communities. In G. P. Green & A. Goetting. (Eds.), *Mobilizing communities: Asset building as a community development strategy* (pp. 130–145). Philadelphia, PA: Temple University Press.

Green, G. P. (2010b). Community assets: Building the capacity for development. In G. P. Green & A. Goetting (Eds.), *Mobilizing communities: Asset building as a community development strategy* (pp. 1–13). Philadelphia, PA: Temple University Press.

Green, G.P. & Haines, A. (2008). *Asset building and community development, 2nd Ed.* Thousand Oaks, CA: Sage Publication.

Green, G. P., & Haines, A. (2012). *Asset building and community development,* 3rd ed. Thousand Oaks, CA: Sage Publications.

Green, J. J. (2008). Community development as social movement: A contribution to models of practice. *Community Development, 39*(1), 50–62.

Green, P. (2012, July 19). Tiny concrete jungles. *The New York Times,* pp.D1, D11.

Green, R., Gregory, R., & Mason, R. (2009). Preparing for social work practice in diverse context: Introducing an integrated model for class discussions. *Social Work Education, 28*(4), 413–422.

Grey, M. (2005). Dilemmas of international social work: Paradoxical processes in indigenisation, universalism and imperialism. *International Journal of Social Welfare, 14*(4), 231–238.

Griffin, D. G. (2010). School counselors and collaboration: Finding resources through community asset mapping. *Professional School Counseling, 13*(5), 248–256.

Grodach, C. (2010). Art spaces, public space, and link to community development. *Community Development Journal, 45*(4), 474–493.

Guerra, N. G., & Knox, L. (2008). How culture impacts the dissemination and implementation of innovation: A case study of the Families and Schools Together Program (FAST) for Preventing Violence with Immigrant Latino Youth. *American Journal of Community Psychology, 41*(3–4), 304–313.

Guerra, P. L., & Valverde, L. A. (2007). Latino communities and schools: Tapping assets for student success. *Principal Leadership, 8*(2), 40–44.

Gueye, M., Diouf, D., Chaana, T., & Tiomkin, D. (2005). *Community capacity enhanced strategy note: The answer lies within.* New York: HIV/AIDS Group Bureau for Development Policy, United Nations Development Programme.

Guion, L. A., Golden, J. H., & Diehli, D. C. (2010). *Maximizing the assets of a diverse community.* Gainesville: University of Florida, IFAS Extension.

Gutierrez, L., Lewis, E. A., Nagda, B. A., Wernick, L., & Stone, N. (2004). Multicultural community practice strategies and intergroup empowerment. In M. Weil (Ed.), *Handbook of community practice* (pp. 341–359). Thousand Oaks, CA: Sage Publications.

Haines, A. (2009). Asset-based community development. In R. Phillips & R. H. Pittman (Eds.), *An introduction to community development* (pp. 38–48). New York: Routledge.

Halifax, N. V. D., Meeks, J., & Khander, E. (2008). Photovoice in a Toronto community partnership: Exploring the social determinates of health with homeless people. *Progress in Community Health Partnerships: Research, Education, and Action, 2*(2), 129–136.

Hall, T., Lashua, B., & Coffey, A. (2008). Sound and everyday life in qualitative research. *Qualitative Inquiry, 14*(6), 1019–1040.

Han, H-R., Kang, J., Kin, K. B., Ryu, J. P., & Kim, M. T. (2007). Barriers to and strategies for recruiting Korean Americans for community-partnered health promotion research. *Journal of Immigrant Health, 9*(2), 127–146.

Hancock, T. (2001). People, partnerships and human progress: Building community capital. *Health Promotion International, 16*(3), 275–280.

Handwerker, W. P. (2006). The evolution of ethnographic research methods: Curiosities and contradictions in the qualitative research literature. *Reviews in Anthropology, 35*(1), 105–118.

Hardcastle, D. A., Powers, P. R., & Wenocur, B. (1997). *Community practice: Theories and skills for social workers.* New York: Oxford University Press.

Hardcastle, D. A., Powers, P. R., & Wenocur, B. (2011). *Community practice: Theories and skills for social workers,* 3rd ed. New York: Oxford University Press.

Hardi, P., & Pinter, L. (2007). City of Winnipeg quality-of-life indicators. In M. S. Sirgy, D. Rahtz, & D. Swain (Eds.), *Community quality-of-life indicators* (pp. 127–176). Amsterdam: Springer Publishers.

Hardina, D. (2004). Guidelines for ethical practice in community organizing. *Social Work, 49*(3), 595–604.

Harlem Children's Zone. (2012). Changing the odds. Retrieved from http://www.hcz.org/?gclid=CIqXnPuQ27ECFaZlOgodpXkAXA, August 8, 2012.

Harley, J. B. (1988). Maps, knowledge, and power. In D. E. Cosgrove & S. Daniels (Eds.), *The iconography of landscape* (pp. 277–312). Chicago: University of Chicago Press.

Harley, J. B. (1989). Deconstructing the map. *Cartographics, 26*(2), 1–20.

Harper, G. W., & Carver, L. J. (1999). "Out-of-the-mainstream" youth as partners in collaborative research: Exploring the benefits and challenges. *Health Education & Behavior, 26*(2), 250–265.

Harpham, T. (2007). The measurement of community social capital through surveys. In I. Kawachi, S. V. Subramanian, & D. Kim (Eds.), *Social capital and health* (pp. 51–62). New York: Springer Publishers.

Harrison, L., & Falk, I. (1997). Good thinking good practice: Research perspectives on learning and work. 5th Annual International Conference on Post-compulsory Education and Training, Gold Coast, Queensland, 26–28 November 1997, *4*(1), 41–58.

Hart, D., Donnelly, T. M., Youniss, J., & Atkins, R. (2007). High school community service as a predictor of adult voting and volunteering. *American Education Research Journal, 44*(1), 197–219.

Haugh, H. (2005). The role of social entrepreneurship in regional development. *International Journal of Entrepreneurship and Small Business, 2*(4), 346–357.

Haugh, H. (2007). Community-led venture creation. *Entrepreneurship Theory and Practice, 31*(2), 161–182.

Haynes, K. S. (1998). The one hundred-year debate: Social reform versus individual treatment. *Social Work, 43*(10), 501–509.

Hays, R. A., & Kogl, A. M. (2007). Neighborhood attachment, social capital building, and political participation: A case study of low-income and moderate-income residents of Waterloo, Iowa. *Journal of Urban Affairs, 29*(2), 181–205.

Healy, L. M. (2007). Universalism and cultural relativism in social work ethics. *International Social Work, 50*(1), 11–28.

Healy, L. M. (2008). Exploring the history of social work as a human rights profession. *International Social Work, 51*(6), 735–748.

Heath, S., Brooks, R., Cleaver, E., & Ireland, E. (2009). *Researching young people's lives.* Thousand Oaks, CA: Sage Publications.

Heinze, H. J., Jozefowicz, D. M. H, & Toro, P. A. (2010). Taking the youth perspective: Assessment of program characteristics that promote positive development in homeless and at-risk youth. *Children and Youth Services Review, 32*(10), 1365–1372.

Hergenrather, K. C., Rhodes, S. D., Cowan, C. A., Bardhoshi, G., & Pula, S. (2009). Photovoice as community-based participatory research: A qualitative review. *American Journal of Health Behavior, 33*(6), 686–698.

Heritage, Z., & Dooris, M. (2009). Community participation and empowerment in healthy cities. *Health Promotion International, 24*(Suppl. 1), i45–i55.

Herlihy, P. H., & Knapp, G. (2003). Maps of, by and for the peoples of Latin America. *Human Organization, 62*(4), 303–314.

Hernandez-Cordero, L. J., Ortiz, A., Trinidad, T. S., & Link, B. (2011). Fresh Start: A multilevel community mobilization plan to promote youth development and prevent violence. *American Journal of Community Psychology, 48*(1–2), 43–55.

Hero, R. E. (2007). *Racial diversity and social capital: Equality and communities in America.* Terre Haute, IN: University of Notre Dame Press.

Hess, D. J. (2009). *Localist movement in a global economy: Sustainability, justice, and urban development in the United States.* Cambridge, MA: MIT Press.

Hillier, A. E. (2007). Why social work needs mapping. *Journal of Social Work Education, 43*(2), 205–221.

Hirschman, C., & Massey, D. S. (2008). Places and peoples: The new American mosaic. In D. S. Massey (Ed.), *New faces in new places: The changing geography of American immigration* (pp. 1–21). New York: Russell Sage Foundation.

Hodge, D. R. (2005). Developing a spiritual assessment toolbox: A discussion of the strengths and limitations of five different assessment methods. *Health & Social Work, 30*(4), 314–323.

Hodge, D. R., & Limb, G. E. (2010). A Native American perspective on spiritual assessment: The strengths and limitations of a complementary set of assessment tools. *Health & Social Work, 35*(2), 121–131.

Hodgson, D.C., & Schroeder, R.A. (2002). Critical dilemmas of counter-mapping community resources in Tanzania. *Development and Change, 33*(1), 79–100.

Hodgson, D. L., & Schroeder, R. A. (2003). Dilemmas of counter-mapping community resources in Tanzania. *Development and Change, 33*(1), 79–100.

Hoefer, R. (2012). *Advocacy practice for social justice.* Chicago, IL: Lyceum Books, Inc.

Hoey, B. A. (2008). *What is ethnography?* http://www.brianhoey.com/General%20Site/general_defn- ethnography.htm. Accessed December 9, 2011.

Hoff, R., Mahfood, J., & McGuiness, A. (2010). *Sustainable benefits of urban farming as a potential brownfields remedy.* Bridgeville, PA: The Mahfood Group.

Hohenemser, L. K., & Marshall, B. D. (2002). Utilizing a youth development framework to establish and maintain a youth advisory committee. *Health Promotion Practice, 3*(2), 155–165.

Holland, J. (2009). Young people and social capital. *Young, 17*(4), 331–350.

Hollingshead, L. D., Allen-Meares, P., Shanks, T. R., & Grant, L. M. (2009). Using the miracle question in community and planning. *Families in Society, 90*(3), 332–335.

Horowitz, C. R., Robinson, M., & Seifer, S. (2009). Key issues in outcome research: Community-based participatory research from the margin to the mainstream. *Circulation, 119,* 2633–2642.

Hu, W. H. (2002). *Youth community asset mapping initiative report: Environmental Youth Alliance.* Vancouver, Canada: Environmental Youth Alliance.

Hudson, L. E., Jr., & Santora, E. D. (2003). Oral history: An inclusive highway to the past. *The History Teacher, 36*(2), 206–220.

Humm-Delgado, D. (1980). Planning issues in local interagency collaboration. In J. O. Elder & P. R. Magrab (Eds.), *Coordinating services to handicapped children: A handbook for interagency collaboration* (pp. 163–178). Baltimore, MD: Paul H. Brooks Publisher.

Hung, Y. (2004). East New York farms: Youth participation in community development and urban agriculture. *Children, Youth and Environments, 14*(1), 20–31.

Hustedde, R. J. (2009). Seven theories for seven community developers. In R. Phillips & R. H. Pittman (Eds.), *An introduction to community development* (pp. 20–37). New York: Routledge.

Hyland, S. E., & Owens, M. (2005). Revitalizing urban communities through a new approach to computer mapping. In S. E. Hyland (Ed.), *Community building in the twenty-first century* (pp. 101–132). Santa Fe, NM: The School of American Research Press.

Hynes, H. P. (1995). *A park of Eden: America's inner-city gardeners.* White River Junction, VT: Chelsea Green.

Imm, P. S., Kehres, K., Wandersman, A., & Chinman, M. (2006). Mobilizing communities for positive youth development: Lessons learned from neighborhood groups and communities. In E. G. Clary & J. E. Rhodes (Eds.), *Mobilizing adults for positive youth development* (pp. 137–157). New York: Springer Publishers.

Innes, J. E. (2004). Consensus building: Clarification for the critics. *Planning Theory, 3*(1), 5–20.

Innes, J. E., & Booher, D. E. (2004) Reframing public participation: Strategies for the 21st century. *Planning Theory & Practice, 5*(4), 419–436.

Irazabal, C., & Punja, A. (2009). Cultivating just planning and legal institutions: A critical assessment of the South Central Farm struggle in Los Angeles. *Journal of Urban Affairs, 31*(1), 1–23.

Israel, B. A., Schulz, A. J., Estrada-Martinez, L., Zenk, S. N., Viruell-Fuentes, E., Villarruel, M., & Stokes, C. (2006). Engaging urban residents in assessing neighborhood environments and their implications for health. *Journal of Urban Health, 83*(3), 523–539.

Iwasaki, Y., Bartlett, J., MacKay, K., Mactavish, J., & Ristock, J. (2006). Mapping nondominant voices into understanding stress-coping mechanisms. *Journal of Community Psychology, 36*(6), 702–722.

Jaccard, J., & Jacoby, J. (2010). *Theory construction and model-building: A practical guide for social scientists.* New York: Guilford Press.

Jackson, S. E., Cleverly, S., Poland, B., Burman, D., Edwards, R., & Robertson, A. (2003). Working with Toronto neighborhoods toward developing indicators of community capacity. *Health Promotion International, 18*(4), 339–350.

Jaeger, P. T., & Xie, B. (2009). Developing online community accessibility guidelines for persons with disabilities and older adults. *Journal of Disability Policy Studies, 20*(1), 55–63.

James, D. (2004). Those slippery intangibles: How a business performs is not dependent on black and white issues. *Future Shock.* (http://www.amerin.com.au/Those_ slipperyintangibles.pdf). Accessed December 13, 2009.

Janesick, V. J. (2007). Oral history as a social justice project: Issues for the qualitative researcher. *The Qualitative Report, 12*(1), 111–121.

Jarrett, R. L., Sullivan, P. J, & Watkins, N. D. (2004). Developing social capital through participation in organized youth programs: Qualitative insights from three programs. *Journal of Community Psychology, 33*(1), 41–55.

Jeffrey, B., & Troman, G. (2003). Time for ethnography. *British Educational Research Journal, 30*(4), 535–548.

Johnson, J. C., et al. (2009). Building community participatory research coalitions from the ground up: The Philadelphia Area Research Community Coalition. *Progress in Community Health Partnerships: Research, Education, and Action, 3*(1), 61–72.

Johnson, J. H. (2002). A conceptual model for enhancing community competitiveness in the new economy. *Urban Affairs Review, 37*(6), 763–779.

Johnson, T. A. (2009, May 24). Roots in South L.A.; I love my community—that's why I'm working to bring it the beauty and benefits of trees. *Los Angles Times*, p. 40.

Jones, K. R. (2009). Influences of youth leadership within a community-based context. *Journal of Leadership in Education, 7*(3), 246–264.

Jones, L., Meade, B., Forge, N., Mini, M., Jones, F., Terry, C., & Norris, K. (2009). Chapter 2. Begin your partnership: The process of engagement. *Ethnicity & Disease, 19*(Special Supplement), S6–8–S6–16.

Jurokowski, J. M., & Paul-Ward, A. (2007). Photovoice with vulnerable populations: Addressing disparities in health promotion among people with intellectual disabilities. *Health Promotion Practice, 8*(4), 358–365.

Jurokowski, J. M., Rivera, Y., & Hammel, J. (2009). Health perceptions of Latinos with intellectual disabilities: The results of a qualitative pilot study. *Health Promotion Practice, 10*(1), 144–155.

Kanuha, V. K. (2000). "Being" native versus "going native": Conducting social work research as an insider. *Social Work, 45*(5), 439–447.

Karuppannan, J. (2005). Mapping and corrections: Management of offenders with Geographic Information Systems. *Corrections Compendium, 30*(1), 1–10.

Kasmel, A., & Andersen, P. T. (2011). Measurement of community empowerment in three communities in Rapla (Estonia). *International Journal of Environmental Public Health, 8*(3), 799–817.

Kasumagic, L. (2008). Engaging youth in community development: Post-war healing and recovery in Bosnia and Herzegovina. *International Review of Education, 54*(4), 375–392.

Katz, D. L. (2004). Representing your community in community-based participatory research: Differences made and measured. *Preventing Chronic Disease: Public Health, Research, and Policy, 1*(1), A12.

Kay, A. (2006). Social capital, the social economy and community development. *Community Development Journal, 41*(2), 160–173.

Kearney, S. C. (2009). *The community garden as a tool for community empowerment: A study of community gardens in Hampden County*. Amherst, MA: Graduate School of the University of Massachusetts, Master of Landscape Architecture Thesis.

Kegler, M. C., Rigler, J., & Honeycutt, S. (2010). How does community context influence coalition in the formation stage? A multiple case study based on the Community Coalition Action Theory. *BMC Public Health, 10*(1), 90–100.

Kegler, M. C., Rigler, J., & Honeycutt, S. (2011). The role of community context in planning and implementing community-based health promotion projects. *Evaluation & Program Planning, 34*(3), 246–253.

Kelly, C. M., Hoehner, C. M., Baker, E. A., Ramierez, L. K. B., & Brownson, R. C. (2006). Promoting physical activity in communities: Approaches for successful evaluation of programs and policies. *Evaluation and Program Planning, 29*(3), 280–292.

Kelly, D. C. (2009). In preparation for adulthood: Exploring civic participation and social trust among young minorities. *Youth & Society, 40*(4), 526–540.

Kerka, S. (2003). Community asset mapping: Trends and issues alert. ERIC ED 481324.

Khanlou, N., & Peter, E. (2009). Participatory action research: Considerations for ethical review. *Social Sciences & Medicine, 60*(10), 2333–2340.

Khwaja, A. I. (2004). Is increasing community participation always a good thing? *Journal of the European Economic Association, 2*(2–3), 427–436.

Kim, J., & Kaplan, R. (2004). Physical and psychological factors in sense of community: New urbanist Kentlands and nearby Orchard Village. *Environment and Behavior, 36*(3), 313–340.

Kim, Y. C., & Bell-Rokeach, S. J. (2006). Civic engagement from a communication infrastructure perspective. *Communications Theory, 16*(2), 173–197.

Kim-Ju, G., Mark, G. V., Cohen, R., & Garcia-Santiago, O. (2008). Community mobilization and its application to youth violence prevention. *American Journal of Preventive Medicine, 34*(3S), S5–S12.

King, C., & Cruickshank, M. (2011). Building capacity to engage: Community engagement of government engagement? *Community Development Journal, 46,*(1), 5–28.

King, N. K. (2004). Social capital and nonprofit leaders. *Nonprofit Management & Leadership, 14*(4), 471–448

Kinloch, V. (2007). Youth representations of community, art, and struggle in Harlem. *New Directions for Adult and Continuing Education, 116*(1), 37–49.

Kissane, R. J., & Gingerich, J. (2004). Do you see what I see? Nonprofit and resident perceptions of urban neighborhood problems. *Nonprofit and Voluntary Sector Quarterly, 33*(2), 311–333.

Knominga, P., & van Staveren, I. (2007). Beyond social capital: A critical approach. *Review of Social Economy, 65*(1), 1–9.

Knox, K. (2009). *Asset based community development in practice: Current models, costs, benefits and outcomes.* York, England: Joseph Rowntree Foundation.

Kolzow, D. E., & Pittman, R. H. (2009). The global economy and community development. In R. Phillips & R. H. Pittman (Eds.), *An introduction to community development* (pp. 324–338). New York: Routledge.

Korsching, P. F., & Allen, J. C. (2004). Locality based entrepreneurship: A strategy for community economic vitality. *Community Development Journal, 39*(4), 385–400.

Kothari, A., Driedger, S. M., Bickford, J., Morrison, J., Sawada, M., Graham, I. D., & Crighton, E. (2008). Mapping as a knowledge translation too for Ontario Early Years Centres: Views from data analysts and managers. *Implementation Science, 3*(4), 1–7.

Krasney, M. E., & Tidball, K. G. (2009). Community gardens as contexts for science, stewardship, and civic action learning. *Cities and the Environment, 2*(1), 1–18.

Kretzmann, J. P., & McKnight, J. (1993). *Building communities from the inside out: A path toward finding and mobilizing a community's assets.* Evanston, IL: Center for Urban Affairs and Policy Research, Northwestern University.

Krieger, J., Rabkin, J., Sharify, D., & Song, L. (2009). High post walking for health: Creating built and social environments that support walking in a public housing community. *American Journal of Public Health, 99*(S3), S593–S599.

Kristjanson, P., Radeny, M., Battenweek, I., Ogutu, J., & Natenbaert, A. (2005). Livelihood mapping and poverty correlates at a meso-level in Kenya. *Food Policy, 30*(5–6), 568–583.

Krueger, R. A., & Casey, M. A. (2009). *Focus groups: A practical guide for applied research,* 4th ed. Thousand Oaks, CA: Sage Publications.

Kusenbach, M. (2003). Street phenomenology. *Ethnography, 4*(3), 455–485.

Kwon, M. (2002). *One place after another: Site-specific art and locational identity.* Cambridge, MA: MIT Press.

Labonte, R. (2004). Social inclusion/exclusion: Dancing the dialectic. *Health Promotion International, 19*(1), 113–121.

Labonte, R., & Laverack, G. (2001). Capacity building and health promotion, part 1:For whom and for what purpose? *Critical Public Health, 11*(a), 111–127.

Lachapelle, P., Emery, M., & Hays, R. L. (2010). The pedagogy and the practice of community visioning: Evaluating effective community strategic planning in rural Montana. *Community Development, 41*(2), 176–191.

Landau, J. (2007). Enhancing resilience: Families and communities as agents for change. *Family Process, 49*(3), 351–365.

Landauer, K., & Brazil, M. (Eds.). (1990). *Tropical home gardens.* Tokyo, Japan: United Nation's Press.

Lange, E. A., & Fenwick, T. J. (2008). Moral commitments to community: Mapping social responsibility and its ambiguities among small business owners. *Social Responsibility Journal, 4*(1/2), 41–55.

Langer, J. (2005). *The mirrored window: Focus groups from a moderator's point of view.* Ithaca, NY: Paramount Market Publishing, Inc.

Larson, C., Schlundt, D., Patel, K., Goldzweig, I., & Hargreaves, M. (2009). Community participation in health initiatives for marginalized populations. *The Journal of Ambulatory Care Management, 32*(4), 264–270.

Larson, R., Walker, K., & Pearce, N. (2005). A comparison of youth-driven and adult-driven youth programs: Balancing inputs from youth and adults. *Journal of Community Psychology, 33*(1), 57–74.

Lasker, R. D., & Lasker, E. S. (2006). Broadening participation in community problem solving: A multidisciplinary model to support collaborative practice and research. *Journal of Urban Health, 80*(1), 14–47.

Lather, P. (2006). Paradigm proliferation as a good thing to think with: Teaching research in education as a wild profusion. *International Journal of Qualitative Studies in Education, 19*(1), 35–57.

Laughlin, D. L. (2008). *Defining and exploring public space: Young people's perspective from Regent Park, Toronto.* Waterloo, Canada: University of Waterloo.

Laverack, G. (2006a). Evaluating community capacity: Visual representation and inter-pretation. *Community Development Journal, 41*(3), 266–276.

Laverack, G. (2006b). Using a "domains" approach to build community empowerment. *Community Development Journal, 41*(1), 4–12.

Lawson, J. L. (2005). *City bountiful: A century of community gardening in America.* Berkeley: University of California Press.

Lee, J. A. B. (2001). *The empowerment approach to social work practice: Building the beloved community,* 2nd ed. New York: Columbia University Press.

Lekies, K. S., Baker, B., & Baldini, J. (2009). Assessing participation in youth community action projects: Opportunities and barriers. *Community Development, 40*(4), 346–358.

Lempa, M., Goodman, R. M., Rice, J., & Becker, A. B. (2008). Development of scales measuring the capacity of community-based initiatives. *Health Education Behavior, 35*(3), 298–315.

Lennie, J. (2005). An evaluation capacity-building process for sustainable community IT initiatives. *Evaluation, 11*(4), 390–414.

Leposky, J., Kick, E. L., & Williams, J. P. (2003). The construction of the local and the limits of contemporary community building in the United States. *Urban Affairs Review, 38*(3), 417–445.

Lerner, R. M., & Benson, P. L. (Eds.). (2002). *Developmental assets and asset-building communities: Implications for research, policy, and practice.* (The Search Institute Series on Developmentally Attentive Community and Society.) Minneapolis, MN: Search Institute.

Levi, M. (1996). Social and unsocial capital: A review essay of Robert Putnam's "Making Democracy Work." *Politics and Society, 24*(1), 45–55.

Levy, S. R., Anderson, E. E., Issel, L. M., Willis, M. A., Dancy, B. L., Jacobson, K. M., Fleming, S. G., Copper, E. S., Berrios, N. M., Sciammarella, E., Ochoa, M., & Hebert-Beirne, J. (2004). Using multilevel, multisource needs assessment data for planning community interventions. *Health Promotion Practice, 5*(1), 59–68.

Levy, S. R., Baldyga, W., & Jurkowski, J. M. (2003). Developing community health promotion interventions: Selecting partners and fostering collaboration. *Health Promotion Practice, 4*(3), 314–322.

Li, H., Meng, L., & Wang, Q. (2008). Political connections, financing and firm performance: Evidence from Chinese private firms. *Journal of Development Economics, 87*(2), 283–299.

Li, Y., & Marsh, D. (2008). New forms of political participation: Searching for expert citizens. *British Journal of Political Science, 38*(2), 247–272.

Liamputtong, P. (2011). *Focus group methods: Principle and practice.* Thousand Oaks, CA: Sage Publications.

Lieberman, A., & Harris, D. (2007). Acknowledging adult bias: A focus-group approach to utilizing beauty salons as health-education portals for inner-city adolescents. *Health Promotion Practice, 8*(3), 205–213.

Lietz, C. A., Langer, C. L., & Furman, R. (2006). Establishing trustworthiness in qualitative research in social work. *Qualitative Social Work, 5*(4), 441–458.

Lin, N. (1999). Building a network theory of social capital. *Connections, 22*(1), 28–51.

Lindau, S. T., et al. (2011). Building community-engaged health research and discovery infrastructure on the South Side of Chicago: Science in service to community priorities. *Preventive Medicine, 52*(3–4), 200–207.

Linnan, L., Ferguson, Y., Wailewski, Y., Lee, A. M., Yang, J., Solomon, F., et al. (2005). Using community-based participatory research methods to reach women with health messages: Research from the North Carolina BEAUTY and Health Pilot Project. *Health Promotion Practice, 6*(2), 164–173.

Liou, J. (2004). Community capacity building to strengthen socio-economic development with spatial asset mapping. Paper presented at the Third Annual FIG Regional Conference, Jakarta, Indonesia.

London, J. K., Zimmerman, K., & Erbstein, N. (2003). Youth-led research and evaluation: Tools for youth, organizational, and community development. *New Directions for Evaluation, 98*(1), 33–46.

London, R. A., Pastor, M., Jr., Servon, L. J., Rosner, R., & Wallace, A. (2009). The role of community technology centers in promoting youth development. *Youth & Society, 42*(2), 199–228.

Long, D. A., & Perkins, D. D. (2007). Community social and place predictors of sense of community: A multilevel and longitudinal analysis. *Journal of Community Psychology, 35*(5), 563–581.

Lopez, J. (2009, August 29). Eastside dreams; young Latinos want to create an arts district of their very own in Boyle Heights. *Los Angeles Times*, p. D1.

Loukaiton-Sideris, A. (2000). Revisiting inner-city strips: A framework for community and economic development. *Economic Development Quarterly, 14*(2), 165–181.

Lowrie, K. W., Solitace, L., & Himmelfarb, K. (2011). Building capacity for community-based brownfields remediation and redevelopment: An innovative technical assistance model. *Remediation: The Journal of Environmental Cleanup Costs, Technologies, and Techniques, 21*(2), 101–115.

Lu, J., & Halseth, G. (2009). The practice of principles: An examination of CED groups in Vancouver, B.C. *Community Development Journal, 44*(1), 80–110.

Luke, D. A. (2005). Getting the big picture in community science: Methods that capture context. *American Journal of Community Psychology, 35*(3/4), 185–200.

Lum, D. (2003). *Culturally competent practice: A framework for understanding diverse groups and justice issues, 2nd edition.* Pacific Grove, CA: Brooks/Cole.

Lydon, M. (2003). Community mapping: The recovery (and discovery) of our common ground. *Geomatica, 57*(2), 131–143.

Lynn, M. (2006). Discourses of community: Challenges for social work. *International Journal of Social Welfare, 15*(2), 110–120.

Lyon, L. (1999). *The community in urban society.* Prospect Heights, IL: Waveland Press, Inc.

Lyons, T., & Reimer, B. (2006). A literature review of capacity frameworks: Six features of comparison. Paper presented at the NRRN Conference, Twillingate, NFLD, Canada.

Lyson, T. A. (2004). *Civic agriculture: Reconnecting farm, food, and community.* Medford, MA: Tufts University Press.

Maclellan-Wright, M. F., Anderson, D., Barber, S., Smith, N., Cantin, B., Felix, R., & Raine, K. (2007). The development of measures of community capacity for community-based funding programs in Canada. *Health Promotion International, 22*(3), 299–306.

Maginn, P. J. (2007). Towards more effective community participation in urban regeneration: The potential of collaborative planning and applied ethnography. *Qualitative Research, 7*(1), 25–43.

Magis, K. (2010). Community resilience: An indicator of social sustainability. *Society & Natural Resources, 23*(5), 401–416.

Maines, S. (2006, December 24). "To develop maps for the blind that are created by the blind": Graduate student draws on personal experience, faculty support in comprehensive project to create tactile diagrams of campus. LJWorld.com. Retrieved July 19, 2011 from http://www2.ljworld.com/news/2006/dec/24/develop_maps_blind_are_crea ted_blind/.

Mallach, A. (2006). *Bringing buildings back: From abandoned properties to community assets.* Montclair, NJ: National Housing Institute.

Mallach, A. (2010). *Bringing buildings back: From abandoned properties to community assets,* 2nd ed. Montclair, NJ: National Housing Institute.

Maman, M., Lane, T., Ntogwisangu, J., Modiba, P., Vanrooyen, H., Timbe, R., Visrutaratna, S., & Fritz, K. (2009). Using participatory mapping to inform a community-randomized trial of HIV counseling and testing. *Field Methods, 21*(4), 368–387.

Manzo, L. C., & Perkins, D. D. (2006). Finding common ground: The importance of place attachment to community participation and planning. *Journal of Planning Literature, 20*(4), 335–350.

Marinetto, M. (2003). Who wants to be an active citizen? *Sociology, 37*(1), 103–120.

Marre, A. W., & Weber, B. A. (2010). Assessing community capacity and social capital in rural America: Lessons from two rural observatories. *Community Development, 41*(1), 92–107.

Marshall, C., & Rossman, G. B. (2011). *Designing qualitative research,* 5th ed. Thousand Oaks, CA: Sage Publications.

Marshall, P. A., & Rotimi, C. (2001). Ethical challenges in community-based research. *The American Journal of the Medical Sciences, 322*(5), 241–245.

Martin, B., & Varney, W. (2000). Nonviolent action and people with disabilities. *Civilian-Based Defense, 15*(1), 4–16.

Martinez, I. L., Cater-Pokras, O., & Brown, P. B. (2009). Addressing the challenges of Latino health research: Participatory approaches in an emergent urban community. *Journal of the National Medical Association, 101*(9), 908–914.

Martinez, M. (2009). Attack of the butterfly spirits: The impact of movement framing by community garden preservation activists. *Social Movement Studies, 8*(4), 323–339.

Martyn, K. K., Reifsnider, E., Barry, M. G., Trevino, M. B., & Murray, A. (2006). Protective processes of Latina adolescents. *Hispanic Health Care International, 4*(2), 111–124.

Massey, D. S. (Ed.). (2008). *New faces in new places: The changing geography of American immigration.* New York: Russell Sage Foundation.

Matarasso, F. (2007). Common ground: Cultural action as a route to community development. *Community Development Journal, 42*(4), 449–458.

Mathie, A., & Cunningham, G. (2003a). From clients to citizens: Asset-based community development as a strategy for community-driven development. *Development in Practice, 13*(5), 474–486.

Mathie, A., & Cunningham, G. (2003b). *Who is driving development? Reflections on the transformative potential of asset-based community development.* Antigonish, NS, Canada: Coady International Institute.

Mathieu, R., Claire Freeman, C., & Aryal, J. (2007). Mapping private gardens in urban areas using object-oriented techniques and very high-resolution satellite imagery. *Landscape and Urban Planning, 81*(3), 179–192.

Mattessich, P. W. (2009). Social capital and community building. In R. Phillips & R. H. Pittman (Eds.), *An introduction to community development* (pp. 49–57). New York: Routledge.

Mattessich, P. W., & Monsey, B. (1997). *Community building: What makes it work.* St. Paul, MN: Wilder Research Center.

Mayer, M. (2003). The onward sweep of social capital: Causes and consequences for understanding cities, communities, and urban movements. *International Journal of Urban and Regional Research, 27*(1), 110–123.

Mayer, S. E. (1994). *Building community capacity: The potential of community foundations*. Minneapolis, MN: Rainbow Research, Inc.

Mazereeuw, B. (2005). *Urban agriculture report*. Waterloo, Canada: Region of Waterloo Growth Management Strategy.

McClusky, K., & McClusky, A. (2003). From at risk to enriched in the inner city: The role of grandparents and parents. In D. Sutherland & L. Sokal (Eds.), *Resiliency and capacity building in inner-city learning communities* (pp. 63–81). Winnipeg, Manitoba, Canada: Portage & Main Press.

McDonald, M., Antunez, G., & Gottemoeller, M. (2006–2007). Using the arts and literature in health education. *International Quarterly of Community Health Education, 27*(3), 264–278.

McElroy, T. A., Davis, A., Hunt, C., Dadul, J., Stanba, T., & Larson, C. (2011). Navigating a way forward: Using focused ethnography and community readiness to study disability issues in Ladakh, India. *Disability & Rehabilitation, 33*(1), 17–27.

McFarland, D. A., & Thomas, R. J. (2006). Bowling young: How youth voluntary association influence adult political participation. *American Sociological Review, 71*(3), 401–425.

McIntyre, A. (2003). Through the eyes of women, photovoice and participatory research as tools for re-imagining gender, place and culture. *Gender, Place & Culture, 10*(1), 47–66.

Mckernan, S. M., & Sherraden, M. (Eds.). (2008). *Asset building and low-income families*. Washington, DC: The Urban Institute.

McKnight, J. L., & Kretzmann, J. P. (1996). *Mapping community capacity*. Evanston, IL: Institute for Policy Research Northwestern University.

McLaren, P. (1998). *Life in schools: An introduction to critical pedagogy in the foundations of education*, 3rd ed. New York: Longman Publishers.

Meridian Consulting. (2006). *A community needs/asset assessment of services for victims of domestic and sexual violence in New Hampshire*. Amherst, MA: Author.

Mertens, D. M., & Ginsburg, P. K. (2008). Deep in ethical waters: Transformative perspectives for qualitative social work research. *Qualitative Social Work, 7*(4), 484–503.

Mertzel, C., Moon-Howard, J., Dickerson, D., Ramjohn, D., & VanDevanter, N. (2008). Making connections: Community capacity for tobacco control in an urban African American community. *American Journal of Community Psychology, 41*(1–2), 74–88.

Miah, M. R. (2003). Empowerment zones, microenterprises, and asset building. In R. A. English (Editor-in-Chief), *Encyclopedia of Social Work,* 19th ed. (2003 Suppl., pp. 38–47). Washington, DC: NASW.

Michigan State University. (2000). The several forms of community mapping. *Best Practice Briefs, 4*, 1–4.

Michiotis, S., Cronin, B., & Devletoglou, H. (2010). Revealing hidden issues and assessing intangible assets in organisations and communities. *International Journal of Decision Sciences, Risk and Management, 2*(3–4), 308–326.

Miller, E. K., & Scofield, J. L. (2009). Slavic Village: Increasing active living into community development through partnerships. *American Journal of Preventive Medicine, 37*(Suppl. 2, 6), S377–S385.

Miller, G. (2008). Collaborative action research: A catalyst for enhancing the practice of community youth mapping. Doctoral Dissertation, University of Victoria, Victoria, BC, Canada.

Minkler, M. (Ed.). (1999). *Community organizing and community building for health.* New Brunswick, NJ: Rutgers University Press.

Minkler, M. (2004). Ethical challenges for the "outside" researcher in community-base d-participatory-research. *Health Education & Behavior, 31*(6), 684–697.

Minkler, M. (2005). Community-based research partnerships: Challenges and opportunities. *Journal of Urban Health, 82*(Suppl. 2), H3–H-12.

Mitchell, C., DeLange, N., Moletsane, R., Stuart, J., & Buthelezi, T. (2005). Giving a face to HIV and AIDS: On the uses of photo-voice by teachers and community health care workers working with youth in rural South Africa. *Qualitative Research in Psychology, 2*(3), 257–270.

Mittelmark, M. B., Wise, M., Nam, E. W., Santos-Burgoa, C., Fosse, E., Saan, H., Hagard, S., & Tang, K. C. (2006). Mapping national capacity to engage in health promotion: Overview of issues and approaches. *Health Promotion International, 21*(2), 91–98.

Molloy, J. K. (2007). Photovoice as a tool for social justice workers. *Journal of Progressive Human Services, 18*(1), 39–55.

Molnar, D., & Kammerud, M. (1977). The problem analysis: The Delphi Technique. In N. Gilbert and H. Specht (Eds.), *Planning for social welfare* (pp. 153–163). Englewood Cliffs, NJ: Prentice Hall, Inc.

Moloney, M. (2005, September 1). 'Those who suffer write the songs': Remembering Frank Harte 1933–2005. *The Journal of Music.* Retrieved from http://journalofmusic.com/focus/those-who-suffer-write-songs.

Molyneux, C., Wassenaar, D., Peshu, N., & Marsh, K. (2005). "Even if they ask you to stand by a tree all day, you will have to do it (laughter)…!: Community voices on the notion and practice of informed consent for biomedical research in developing countries." *Social Sciences & Medicine, 61*(2), 443–454.

Montgomery, J. (2005). *Community strengthening through urban sociability.* Victoria, BC, Canada: Urban Cultures Ltd.

Montoya, M. J., & Kent, E. E. (2011). Dialogical action: Moving from community-based to community-driven participatory research. *Qualitative Health Research, 21*(7), 1000–1011.

Moore, K. A., & Lippman, L. H. (Eds.). (2005). *What do children need to flourish?: Conceptualizing and measuring indicators of positive development.* (The Search Institute Series on Developmentally Attentive Community and Society.) Minneapolis, MN: Search Institute.

Moore, L. V., & Roux, A. V. D. (2005). Associations of neighborhood characteristics with the location and type of food stores. *American Journal of Public Health, 96*(2), 325–331.

Moreno, M-J. (2004). Art museums and socioeconomic forces: The case of a community museum. *Review of Radical Political Economics, 36*(4), 506–527.

Morgan, A., & Ziglio, E. (2007). Revitalising the evidence base for public health: An assets model. *IUHPE-Promotion & Education, 14*(Suppl. 2), 17–22.

Morse, S. (2011). Communities revisited: The best ideas of the last hundred years. *National Civic Review, 100*(1), 8–13.

Morsillo, J., & Prilleltensky, I. (2007). Social action with youth: Interventions, evaluation, and psychopolitical validity. *Journal of Community Psychology, 25*(6), 1–16.

Moser, C. (2008). Assets and livelihood: A framework for asset-based social policy. In C. Moser & A. A. Dani (Eds.), *Assets, livelihoods, and social policy* (pp. 43–83). Washington, DC: The International Bank for Reconstruction and Development, The World Bank.

Motel, S. (2012). *Statistical portrait of Hispanics in the United States, 2010.* Washington, DC: Pew Hispanic Center.

Mowbray, C. T., Woolley, M. E., Grogan-Kaylor, A., Grant, L. M., Gilster, M. F., & Shanks, T. R. W. (2007). Neighborhood research from a spatially oriented strengths perspective. *Journal of Community Psychology, 35*(5), 667–680.

Mowbray, M. (2005). Community capacity building or state opportunism? *Community Development Journal, 40*(3), 255–264.

Moynihan, C. (2012, August 22). Trespassing to plant flowers, and a flag: Effort to save a lot from development. *The New York Times*, p. A21.

Murphy, P. W., & Cunningham, J. V. (2003). *Organizing for community controlled development: Renewing civil society.* Thousand Oaks, CA: Sage Publications.

Nakkula, M. J., Foster, K. C., Mannes, M., & Bolstrom, S. (2010). Community sustainability: Orlando's healthy community initiative. *Building Healthy Communities for Positive Youth Development, 7*(1), 89–100.

Nakkula, M. J., Foster, K. C., Mannes, M., & Lewis, S. (Eds.). (2010). *Building healthy communities for positive youth development.* (The Search Institute Series on Developmentally Attentive Community and Society.) Minneapolis, MN: Search Institute.

Nam, E. W., & Engelhardt, K. (2007). Health promotion community mapping: The Korean situation. *Health Promotion International, 22*(2), 155–162.

National Association of Social Workers. (2008). *Code of Ethics.* Washington, DC: Author.

National Association of Social Workers. (2011a). *Position statement diversity & cultural competence.* Washington, DC: Author.

National Association of Social Workers. (2011b). *Position statement on social justice.* Washington, DC: Author.

National Research Council. (2006). *Multiple origins, uncertain destines: Hispanics and the American future.* Washington, DC: Author.

Navarro, V. (2002). A critique of social capital. *International Journal of Health Services, 32*(3), 423–432.

Necheles, J. W., Hawes-Dawson, J., Ryan, G. W., Williams, L. B., Holmes, H. N., Wells, K. B., Valana, M. E., & Schuster, M. A. (2007). The teen photovoice project: A pilot study to promote health through advocacy. *Progress in Community Health Partnerships: Research, Education, and Action, 1*(3), 2219–2229.

Netting, F. E., Kettner, P. M., & McMurty, S. L. (2004). *Social work macro practice*, 3rd ed. Boston, MA: Pearson.

Newman, S. D., et al. (2011). Community advisory boards in community-based participatory research: A synthesis of best practices. *Preventing Chronic Disease Dialogue, 8*(3), 1–10.

Nicholas, L. (2004). Participatory program planning: Including program participants and evaluators. *Evaluation and Program Planning, 25*(1), 1–14.

Nicotera, N. (2007). Measuring neighborhood: A conundrum for human service researchers and practitioners. *American Journal of Community Psychology, 40*(1/2), 26–51.

Norris, F. H., Stevens, S. P., Pfefferbaum, B., Wyche, K. F., & Pfefferbaum, R. L. (2008). Community resilience as a metaphor, theory, set of capacities, and strategy for disaster readiness. *American Journal of Community Psychology, 41*(2), 127–150.

Norton, B. L., McLeroy, K. R., Burdine, J. N., Felix, M. R. J., & Dorsey, A. M. (2002). Community capacity: Concept, theory, and methods. In R. J. DiClemente, R. A. Crosby, & M. C. Kegler (Eds.), *Emerging theories in health promotion practice and research: Strategies for improving public health* (pp. 194–227). San Francisco, CA: Jossey-Bass.

Nowak, D. J., et al. (2010). *Sustaining America's urban trees and forests*. Washington, DC: Department of Agriculture.

Noy, D. (2008). Power mapping: Enhancing sociological knowledge by developing generalizable analytical public tools. *The American Sociologist, 39*(1), 3–18.

NYS Community Improvement Through Youth (CITY) Project. (2012). The City Project: Community Improvement Through Youth. Retrieved from http://128.253.16.77/city/.

O'Donnell, S. M., & Karanja, S. T. (2000). Transformative community practice: Building a model for developing extremely low income African-American communities. *Journal of Community Practice, 7*(3), 67–84.

O'Looney, J. (1998). Mapping communities: Place-based stories and participatory planning. *Journal of the Community Development Society, 29*(2), 201–237.

O'Meara, P., Chesters, J., & Han, G-S. (2004). Outside-looking in: Evaluating a community capacity building project. *Rural Sociology, 14*(2), 126–141.

ONCE (La Organización Nacional de Ciegos Españoles). (2012). *Museo Tiflológico*. Madrid, Spain. Retrieved from http://museo.once.es/.

O'Toole, T. P., Kathuria, N., Mishra, M., & Schukart, D. (2005). Teaching professionalism within a community context: Perspectives from national demonstration project. *Academic Medicine, 80*(4), 339–343.

Ohmer, M. L., & Korr, W. S. (2006). The effectiveness of community practice interventions: A review of the literature. *Research on Social Work Practice, 16*(2), 132–145.

Oldham, J. (2011, August 22). Demand for locally grown produce spurs rise of urban farms. *The Boston Globe*, p. A4.

Oliver, M. (2001). Forward. In T. M. Shapiro & E. N. Wolff (Eds.), *Asset for the poor: The benefits of spreading asset ownership* (pp. xi–xiii). New York: Russell Sage Foundation.

Oliver-Smith, A. (2005). Communities after catastrophe: Reconstructing the material, reconstructing the social. In S. E. Hyland (Ed.), *Community building in the twenty-first century* (pp. 45–70). Santa Fe, NM: School of American Research Press.

Olivos, E. M. (2009). Collaboration with Latino families. *Intervention in School and Clinic, 45*(2), 109–115.

Oman, R., Vesely, S., Mcleroy, K., Harris-Wyatt, V., Aspy, C., Rodine, S., & Marshall, L. (2002). Reliability and validity of the youth asset survey (YAS). *Journal of Adolescent Health, 31*(3), 247–255.

Onwuegbuzie, A. J., & Leech, W. L. (2006). Linking research questions to mixed methods data analyses procedures. *The Qualitative Report, 11*(3), 474–498.

Orellana, M. F., Dorner, L., & Pulido, L. (2003). Accessing assets: Immigrant youth's work as family translators or "para-phrasers." *Social Problems, 50*(4), 505–524.

Organista, K. C. (2007). *Solving Latino psychosocial and health problems: Theory, practice, and populations.* New York: John Wiley & Sons.

Overcamp-Martini, M. (2007). Theory for the public good? Social capital theory in social work education. *Advances in Social Work, 8*(1), 196–207.

Ozanne, J. L., & Anderson, L. (2010). Community action research. *Journal of Public Policy & Marketing, 29*(1), 123–137.

Pacheco, J. S., & Plutzer, E. (2008). Political participation and cumulative disadvantage: The impact of economic and social hardships on young citizens. *Journal of Social Issues, 64*(3), 571–593.

Pain, R. (2004). Social geography: Participatory research. *Progress in Human Geography, 28*(5), 652–663.

Pan, R. J., Littlefield, D., Valladolid, S. G., Tapping, P. J., & West, D. C. (2005). Building healthier communities for children and families: Applying asset-based community development to community pediatrics. *Pediatrics, 115*(Suppl.), 1185–1187.

Paranagamage, P., Austin, S., Price, A., & Khandokar, F. (2010). Social capital in action in urban environments: An intersection of theory, research, and practice literature. *Journal of Urbanism: International Research on Placemaking and Urban Sustainability, 3*(3), 231–252.

Parker, B. (2006). Constructing community through maps? Power and praxis in community mapping. *The Professional Geographer, 58*(4), 470–484.

Parker, E. A., Meiklejohn, B. M., Patterson, C. M., Edwards, K. D., Preece, C., Shuter, P. E., & Gould, T. (2006). Our games our health: A cultural assets for promoting health in indigenous communities. *Health Promotion Journal of Australia, 17*(2), 103–108.

Parker, R. N., Alcaraz, R., & Payne, P. R. (2011). Community readiness for change and youth violence prevention: A tale of two cities. *American Journal of Community Psychology, 48*(1–2), 97–105.

Pastor, M., Morello-Frosch, R., & Sadd, J. L. (2005). The air is always cleaner on the other side: Race, space, and ambient air toxics exposures in California. *Journal of Urban Affairs, 27*(2), 127–148.

Patten, E. (2012). *Statistical portrait of the foreign-born in the United States, 2010.* Washington, DC: Pew Hispanic Center.

Pennell, J., Noponen, H., & Weil, M. (2005). Empowerment research. In M. Weil (Ed.), *The handbook of community practice* (pp. 620–635). Thousand Oaks, CA: Sage Publications.

Peredo, A. M., & Chrisman, J. J. (2004). Toward a theory of community-based enterprises. *Academy of Management Review, 31*(2), 309–328.

Perkins, C. (2007). Community mapping. *The Cartographic Journal, 44*(2), 127–137.

Perkins School for the Blind. (2011). *History of horticulture at Perkins.* Watertown, MA: Perkins School for the Blind. Retrieved July 20, 2011 from http://www.perkins.org/inside-perkins/pappas-horticultural- center/history.htmlm.

Pew Hispanic Center. (2009). *Between two worlds: How Latino youths come of age in America.* Washington, DC: Author.

Pew Hispanic Center. (2010). *Statistical portrait of Hispanics in the United States, 2008.* Washington, DC: Author.

Pew Hispanic Center. (2011). *2010 Census.* Washington, DC: Pew Research Center.

Phillips, R. (2004). Artful business: Using the arts for community economic development. *Community Development Journal, 39*(2), 112–122.

Phillips, R., & Pittman, R. H. (2009). A framework for community and economic development. In R. Phillips & R. H. Pittman (Eds.), *An introduction to community development* (pp. 3–19). New York: Routledge.

Pineda, C. (2006). *Mapping your community's faith-based assets.* Cambridge, MA: Harvard University Kennedy School of Government.

Pinkett, R. (2003). Community technology and community building: Early results from the Creating Community Connections Project. *The Information Society, 19*(4), 365–379.

Pitre, P. E. (2009). Parents involved in community schools v. Seattle School District 1. *Education & Urban Society, 41*(5), 544–561.

Pomerantz, A. (2002). Language ideologies and the production of identities: Spanish as a resource for participation in a multilingual marketplace. *Journal of Cross-Cultural and Interlanguage Communication, 21*(2–3), 275–302.

Poole, D. L. (1998). Building community capacity to promote social and public health. *Health & Social Work, 22*(3), 163–170.

Popple, K., & Stepney, P. (2008). *Social work and the community: A critical framework for practice.* New York: Palgrave Macmillan.

Portes, A. (1998). Social capital: Its origins and applications in modern sociology. *American Review of Sociology, 24*(1), 1–24.

Portes, A., & Landbolt, P. (1996). Unsolved mysteries: The Tocqueville Files II: The downside of social capital. *The American Prospect, 7*(26). Retrieved from http://prospect.org/article/unsolved-mysteries-tocqueville-files-ii-1.

Pothukuchi, K. (2004). Community food assessment. *Journal of Planning and Research, 23*(4), 356–377.

Pothukuchi, K., Joseph, H., Burton, H., & Fisher, A. (2002). *What's cooking in your food system? A guide to community food assessment.* Venice, CA: Community Food Security Coalition.

Public Laboratory for Open Technology and Science. (2012). *Balloon Mapping kit.* Retrieved from http://publiclaboratory.org/home.

Pudup, M. B. (2008). It takes a garden: Cultivating citizen-subjects in organized garden projects. *Geoforum, 39*(3), 1228–1240.

Putnam, R. D. (2000). *Bowling alone: The collapse and revival of American community.* New York: Simon & Schuster.

Pyles, L. (2006). Toward a post-Katrina framework: Social work as human rights and capabilities. *Journal of Comparative Social Welfare, 22*, 79–88.

Quave, J. M., & Rankin, B. (2006). Does it pay to participate? Neighborhood-based organizations and the social development of urban adolescents. *Children and Youth Services Review, 28*(11), 1229–1250.

Quinn, B. (2005). Arts festivals and the city. *Urban Studies, 42*(5/6), 927–943.

Raeburn, J., Akerman, M., Chuengsatiansup, K., Mejia, F., & Oladepo, O. (2007). Community capacity building and health promotion in a globalized world. *Health Promotion International, 21*(Suppl. 1), 84–90.

Rappaport, N., Alegria, M., Mulvaney-Day, N., & Boyle, B. (2008). Staying at the table: Building sustainable community-research partnerships. *Journal of Community Psychology, 36*(6), 693–701.

Rattray, N. (2006). *A user-centered model for community-based web-GIS.* Park Ridge, IL: Urban and Rural Information Systems Association.

Raymond, C., Bryan, B., Macdonald, D., Cast, A., Strathern, S., Grandgirard, A., & Kalivas, T. (2009). Mapping community values for natural capital and ecosystem services. *Ecological Economics, 68*(5), 1301–1315.

Reason, P. (2006). Choice and quality in action research practice. *Journal of Management Inquiry, 15*(2), 187–203.

Reed, B. G. (2004). Theorizing in community practice: Essential tools for building community, promoting social justice, and implementing social change. In M. Weil (Ed.), *Handbook of community practice* (pp. 84–102). Thousand Oaks, CA: Sage Publications.

Reimer, B. (2006). The rural context of community development in Canada. *Journal of Rural and Community Development, 1*(3), 155–175.

Rein, M. (1977). Planning by what authority? Social planning: The search for legitimacy. In N. Gilbert & H. Specht (Eds.), *Planning for social welfare: Issues, models, and tasks* (pp. 50–69). Englewood Cliffs, NJ: Prentice Hall.

Reinschmidt, K. M., Hunter, J. B., Fernandez, M. L., Lacy-Martinez, C., Guernsey de Zapien, J., & Meister, J. (2006). Understanding the success of Promotoras in increasing chronic diseases screening. *Journal of Health Care for the Poor and Underserved, 17*(2), 256–264.

Reisch, M. (2012). Interventions with communities. In C. A. Glisson, C. N. Dulmus, & K. M. Sowers (Eds.), *Social work practice with groups, communities, and organizations* (pp. 81–130). New York: John Wiley & Sons.

Rhoden, J. (2002). Growing healthy communities through urban gardening. *New Life Journal, 3*(5), 1–3.

Richard, A. (2003). *Cultural assets for Latino community building in East Palo Alto.* San Francisco, CA: Wildflowers Institute.

Riley, K. A. (2009). Reconfiguring urban leadership: Taking a perspective on community. *School Leadership and Management, 29*(1), 51–63.

Ritchie, D., Parry, O., Gnich, W., & Platt, S. (2004). Issues of participation, ownership and empowerment in a community development programme: Tackling smoking in a low-income area in Scotland. *Health Promotion International, 19*(1), 51–59.

Robinson, J., & Perkins, D. D. (2009). Social development needs assessment in China: Lessons from an international collaborative field school in Guangxi Zhuang Autonomous Region. *China Journal of Social Work, 2*(1), 34–51.

Robinson, J. W., & Meikle-Yaw, P. A. (2007). Capital and community capacity with signature projects: A case study of two diverse Delta Communities. *Journal of Extension, 45*(2). (http://www.joe.org/joe/200april/a4.php). Accessed June 12, 2009.

Rodine, S., Oman, R. F., Vesely, S. K., Aspy, C. B., Tolma, E., Marshall, L., & Flur, J. (2006). Potential protective effect of the community involvement asset on adolescent risk behaviors. *Journal of Youth Development: Bridging Research and Practice, 1*(1), 1–17.

Rodriguez, M. C., & Morrobel, D. (2004). A review of Latino youth development research and a call for an asset orientation. *Hispanic Journal of Behavioral Sciences, 26*(2), 107–127.

Rogler, L. H., Barreras, O., & Cooney, R. S. (1981). Coping with distrust in a study of intergenerational Puerto Rican families in New York City. *Hispanic Journal of Behavioral Sciences, 3*(1), 1–17.

Ronning, L. (2009). Social capital: An asset or a liability to entrepreneurial activity. *International Journal of Entrepreneurship and Small Business, 7*(2), 232–252.

Ross, L. (2011). Sustaining youth participation in a long-term tobacco control initiative: Considerations of a social justice perspective. *Youth & Society, 43*(2), 681–704.

Ross, M. G. (1967). *Community organization: Theory, principles, and practice.* New York: HarperCollins College Division.

Ross, N. J., Renold, E., Holland, S., & Hillman, A. (2009). Moving stories: Using mobile methods to explore the everyday lives of young people in public care. *Qualitative Research, 9*(5), 605–623.

Ross, S., & Simces, Z. (2008). *Community food assessment guide.* Vancouver, B.C., Canada: Provincial Health Services Authority.

Rossing, B. (2000). Identifying, mapping and mobilizing our assets. Unpublished manuscript.

Rotary International. (2008). *Community Assessment Tools: A companion piece to communities in action.* Evanston, IL: Author.

Rotegard, A. K., Moore, S. M., Fagermoen, M. S., & Rutland, C. M. (2010). Health assets: A concept analysis. *Nursing Studies, 47*(4), 513–525.

Rothman, J., Teresa, J., & Erlich, J. L. (1994). Appendix A: Fostering participation and promoting innovation—Handbook for human service professionals. In E. J. Thomas & J. Rothman (Eds.), *Intervention research: Design and development for human service* (pp. 377–426). New York: Haworth Press.

Royse, D., Staton-Tindall, M., Badger, K., & Webster, J. M. (2009). *Needs assessment.* New York: Oxford University Press.

Rumbaut, R. G. (2006). The making of a people. In M. Tienda & F. Mitchell (Eds.), *Hispanics and the future of America* (pp. 16–65). Washington, DC: The National Academic Press.

Rusch, L. (2010). Rethinking bridging: Risk and trust in multiracial community organizing. *Urban Affairs Review, 45*(4), 483–506.

Saegert, S. (2006). Building civic capacity in urban neighborhoods: An empirically grounded anatomy. *Journal of Urban Affairs, 28*(5), 275–294.

Sail, R. M., & Abu-Samah, A. (2010). Community development through community capacity building: A social science perspective. *Journal of American Science, 6*(2), 68–76.

Saldivar-Tanaka, L., & Krasny, M. E. (2004). Culturing community development, neighborhood open space, and civic agriculture: The case of Latino community gardens in New York City. *Agriculture and Human Values, 21*(4), 399–412.

Saleeby, P. W. (2011). Using the International Classification of Functioning, Disability, and Health in social work settings. *Health & Social Work, 36*(4), 303–305.

Salem, E., Hooberman, J., & Ramirez, D. (2005). MAPP Chicago: A model for public health systems development and community building. *Journal of Public Health Management & Practice, 11*(5), 393–400.

Sanchez-Jankowski, M. (2008). *Cracks in the pavement: Social change and resilience in poor neighborhoods.* Berkeley, CA: University of California Press.

Santo, C. A., Ferguson, N., & Trippel, A. (2010). Engaging urban youth through technology: The Youth Neighborhood Mapping Initiative. *Journal of Planning Education and Research, 30*(1), 52–65.

Saracho, O. (2007). Hispanic families as facilitators of their children's literacy development. *Hispanic Journal of Behavioral Sciences, 6*(2), 103–117.

Sarkissian, W., Bunjamin-Mau, W., Umemoto, K., & Cook, A. (2009). *Speakout: A step-by-step to speakouts and community workshops.* Oxford, England: Earthscan.

Saunders, P. (2008). Measuring wellbeing using non-monetary indicators: Deprivation and social exclusion. *Family Matters, 76*(1), 8–17.

Save the Children. (2000). *Children and participation: Research, monitoring and evaluation with children and young people.* London: Author.

Scarinci, I., Johnson, R. E., Hardy, C., Marrion, J., & Partridge, E. E. (2009). Planning and implementation of a participatory evaluation strategy: A viable approach in the evaluation of community-based participatory programs addressing cancer disparities. *Evaluation and Program Planning, 32*(3), 221–228.

Schafer-McDaniel, N. J. (2004). Conceptualizing social capital among young people: Towards a new theory. *Children, Youth and Environment, 14*(1), 140–150.

Schensul, J. J. (2005). Strengthening communities through research partnerships for social change: Perspectives from the Institute for Community Research. In S. E. Hyland (Ed.), *Community building in the twenty-first century* (pp. 191–218). Santa Fe, NM: The School of American Research Press.

Schensul, J. J. (2009). Community, culture and sustainability in multilevel dynamic systems intervention science. *American Journal of Community Psychology, 43*(4), 241–256.

Schlossberg, M. (Undated). *Asset mapping and community development planning with GIS: A look at the heart of West Michigan United Way's innovative approach.* Ann Arbor, MI: University of Michigan, Urban, Technology and Environmental Planning.

Schmetzkopf, K. (2002). Incommensurability, land use, and the right to space: Community gardens in New York City. *Urban Geography, 23*(4), 323–343.

Schreiner, M., & Sherraden, M. (2007). *Can the poor save? Savings and asset building in individual development accounts.* New Brunswick, NJ: Transaction.

Schuler, D. (2004). *Community networks and the evolution of civic intelligence.* Olympia, WA: The Public Sphere Project, The Evergreen State College.

Schuller, T. (2002). The complementary roles of human and social capital. (http://www.oecd.org/dataoecd/5/48/182524.pdf). Accessed November 20, 2009.

Schwartz, L., Sable, M. R., Dannerbeck, A., & Campbell, J. D. (2007). Using photovoice to improve family planning services for immigrant Hispanics. *Journal of Health Care for the Poor and Underserved, 18*(4), 757–766.

Scott, S. M. (2007). Walking the walk: An assets-based approach to transforming neighborhood dynamics and reclaiming forgotten virtues in urban Atlanta. Paper presented at the Annual Meeting of the American Public Health Association, Washington, DC.

Seider, S. C., Gillmor, S., & Rabinowicz, S. (2011). The impact of community service learning upon the expected political voice of participating college students. *Journal of Adolescent Research, 27*(1), 44–77.

Seippel, O. (2006). Sport and social capital. *Acta Sociologica, 49*(2), 169–183.

Semenza, J. C., & Krishnasamy, P. V. (2007). Design of a health-promoting neighborhood intervention. *Health Promotion Practice, 8,* 243–256.

Semenza, J. C., March, T. L., & Bontenpo, B. D. (2006). Community-initiated urban development. *Journal of Urban Health, 84*(1), 8–20.

Serido, J., Borden, L. M., & Perkins, D. F. (2011). Moving beyond youth voice. *Youth & Society, 42*(1), 44–63.

Severson, K. (2011, August 15). At vacant homes, foraging for fruit: Roaming harvesters work to feed others and themselves. *The New York Times,* p. A11.

Seyfang, G. (2004). Working outside the box: Community currencies, time banks and social inclusion. *Journal of Social Policy, 33*(1), 49–71.

Seymour, W. (2007). Exhuming the body: Revisiting the role of the visible body in ethnographic research. *Qualitative Health Research, 17*(9), 1188–1197.

Shah, S. (2011). *Building transformative youth leadership: Data on the impacts of youth organizing.* New York: Funders' Collaborative on Youth Organizing.

Sharpe, P. A., Greaney, M. L., Lee, P. R., & Royce, S. W. (2000). Assets-oriented community assessments. *Public Health Reports, 115*(2–3), 205–211.

Shaw, I. (2005). Practitioner research: Evidence or critique? *British Journal of Social Work, 35*(8), 1231–1248.

Shaw, M. C. (2008). Community development and the politics of community. *Community Development Journal, 43*(1), 24–36.

Shaw, S., Bagwell, S., & Karmowska, J. (2004). Ethnoscapes as spectacle: Reimagining multicultural districts as new destinations for leisure and tourism consumption. *Urban Studies, 41*(10), 1983–2000.

Sherman, A. L. (2003). *The community service activities of Hispanic Protestant congregations.* Terre Haute, IN: The Center for the Study of Latino Religion, Notre Dame University.

Sherman, R. F. (2004). The promise of youth is in the present. *National Civic Review, 93*(1), 50–55.

Sherwood, K. E., & Dressner, J. (2004). *Youth organizing: A new generation of social activism.* Philadelphia, PA: Public/Private Ventures.

Shetgiri, R., Kataoka, S., Ryan, G., Askew, L., Chung, P., & Schuster, M. (2009). Risk and resilience in Latinos: A community-based participatory research study. *American Journal of Preventive Medicine, 37*(6), S217–S224.

Shinew, K. J., Glover, T. D., & Parry, D. C. (2004). Leisure spaces as potential sites for interracial interaction: Community gardens in urban areas. *Journal of Leisure Research, 36*(3), 336–355.

Shirlow, P., & Murtagh, B. (2004). Capacity-building, representation and intracommunity conflict. *Urban Studies, 41*(1), 57–70.

Short, A., Guthman, J., & Raskin, S. (2007). Food deserts, oases, or mirages? Small markets for food security in the San Francisco Bay Area. *Journal of Planning Education and Research, 26*(3), 352–364.

Sieber, R. (2006). Public participation geographic information systems: A literature review and framework. *Annals of the American Geographers, 96*(3), 491–507.

Siegel, P. B. (2005). Using an asset-based approach to identify drivers of sustainable growth and poverty reduction in Central America: A conceptual framework. Washington, DC: World Bank Policy Research Paper No. 3475.

Silver, D., Weitzman, B., & Bretcher, C. (2002). Setting an agenda for local action: The limits of expert opinion and community voice. *Policy Studies Journal, 30*(3), 362–378.

Simpson, L., Wood, L., & Daws, L. (2003). Community capacity building: Starting with people not projects. *Community Development Journal, 38*(4), 277–286.

Singer, A., Hardwick, S. W., & Brettell, C. B. (Eds.). (2008). *Twenty-first century gateways: Immigrant incorporation in suburban America.* Washington, DC: Brookings Institution Press.

Siranni, C. (2007). Neighborhood planning as collaborative democratic design. *Journal of the American Planning Association, 75*(4), 373–387.

Sites, W., Chaskin, R. J., & Parks, V. (2007). Reframing community for the 21st century: Multiple traditions, multiple challenges. *Journal of Urban Affairs, 29*(5), 519–541.

Skelly, A. H., Arcury, T. A., Gesler, W. M., Cravey, A. J., Dougherty, M. C., Washburn, S. A., & Nash, S. (2002). Sociospatial knowledge networks: Appraising community as place. *Research in Nursing and Health, 25*(2), 159–170.

Skerratt, S., & Hall, C. (2011). Community ownership of physical assets: Challenges, complexities and implications. *Local Economy, 26*(3), 170–181.

Smit, J., & Bailkey, M. (2006). *Building community capital and social inclusion through urban agriculture.* Ottawa, Canada: International Development Research Centre.

Smith, C. R., & Kurtz, H. E. (2003). Community gardens and politics of scale in New York City. *The Geographical Review, 93*(2), 193–212.

Smith, L. T. (2005). On tricky ground: Researching the Native in the age of uncertainty. In N. K. Denzin & Y. S. Lincoln (Eds.), *Handbook of qualitative research* (pp. 85–107). Thousand Oaks, CA: Sage Publications.

Smith, M. R. (2009). *'Social capital,' the encyclopedia of informal education.* (http:www/infed.org/biblio/social_capital.htm). Accessed September 19, 2009.

Smith, N., Littlejohns, L. B., Hawe, P., & Sutherland, L. (2008). Great expectations and hard times: Developing community indicators in a health communities initiative in Canada. *Health Promotion International, 23*(2), 119–126.

Smith, N., Littlejohns, L. B., & Roy, D. (2003). *Measuring community capacity: State of the field review and recommendations for future research.* Ottawa, ON, Canada: Health Policy Research Program, Canada.

Smith, N., Littlejohns, L. B., & Thompson, D. (2001). Shaking out the cobwebs: Insights into community capacity and its relation to health outcomes. *Community Development Journal, 36*(1), 30–41.

Smith-Morris, C. (2007). Social capital in a Mexican-American community in Dallas, Texas. *Urban Anthropology and Studies of Cultural Systems and World Economic Development, 36*(4), 425–456.

Smits, P. A., & Champagne, F. (2008). An assessment of the theoretical underpinnings of practical participatory evaluation. *American Journal of Evaluation, 29*(4), 427–442.

Snow, L. (2008). Strategies for sustainable small town and rural development. (http://www.consumerenergy.com/appslpdf/Snow.pdf). Accessed June 11, 2009.

Sobel, J. (2002). "Can we trust social capital?" *Journal of Economic Literature, 40*(1), 139–154.

Soja, E. W. (2010). *Seeking spatial justice.* Minneapolis: University of Minnesota Press.

Solomon, F., Linnan, L., Wasilewski, Y., Less, A. M., & Young, J. (2004). Observational study in ten beauty parlors: Results informing development of the North Carolina BEAUTY and Health Project. *Health Education & Behavior, 31*(6), 790–806.

Specht, H., & Courtney, M. E. (1995). *Unfaithful angels: How social work has abandoned its mission.* New York: The Free Press.

Squazzoni, F. (2007). Local community development initiatives from the bottom-up: The role of community development corporations. *Community Development Journal, 44*(4), 500–514.

Staeheli, L. A. (2008). Citizenship and the problem of community. *Political Geography, 27*(1), 5–21.

Staples, L. (Ed.). (2004). *Roots to power: A manual for grassroots organizing.* Westport, CT: Praeger Publisher.

Stead, D. (1996, January 7). BLACKBOARD; Stanford Gets Street Smart. *The New York Times,* pp. 4A, A8.

Stehlik, D., & Buckley, A. (2008). Participative inquiry using community-as-researche rs-approach: The Balingup Model. *Sustaining Gundwana, 9*(1), 1–18.

Stein, B. J. (2012, July 12). From the editor: What's wrong with the Bronx.*Mott Haven Herald.* http://motthavenhearld.com/2012/07/12/from-the-editor-whats-wrong-wit h-the-bronx/#comments. Retrieved July 30, 2012.

Stern, J. A. (2006). Guest editorial: The roots of human rights advocacy and a call to action. *Social Work, 51*(2), 101–105.

Stern, M. J., & Seifert, S. C. (2007). *Culture and urban revitalization: A harvest document.* Philadelphia: University of Pennsylvania, School of Social Policy & Practice.

Stewart, D. W., Shamdason, P. M., & Rook, D. (2006). *Focus groups: Theory and practice.* Thousand Oaks, CA: Sage Publications.

Stewart, W. P., Liebert, D., & Larkin, K. W. (2004). Community identities as visions for landscape change. *Landscape and Urban Planning, 69*(2–3), 315–334.

Stokols, D., Grzywacz, J. G., McMahan, S., & Phillips, K. (2003). Increasing the health promotive capacity of human environments. *American Journal of Health Promotion, 18*(1), 4–13.

Strack, R. W., Magill, C., & McDonagh, K. (2004). Engaging youth through photovoice. *Health Promotion Practice, 5*(1), 49–58.

Streng, J. M., Rhodes, S., Ayala, G., Eng, E., Arceo, R., & Phipps, S. (2004). Realidad Latina: Latino adolescents, their school, and a university use photovoice to examine and address the influence of immigration. *Journal of Interpersonal Care, 18*(4), 403–415.

Sturtevant, V. (2006). Reciprocity of social capital and collective action. *Community Development, 37*(1), 52–64.

Suarez-Balcazar, Y., Hellwig, M., Koubam J., Redmond, L., Martinez, L., Block, D., Kohrman, C., & Peterman, W. (2006). The making of an interdisciplinary partnership: The case of the Chicago Food System Collaborative. *American Journal of Community Psychology, 38*(1–2), 113–123.

Suarez-Balcazar, Y., & Kinney, L. (2006). Realities and myths of safety issues for community researchers working in a marginalized African American community. *American Journal of Community Psychology, 37*(3), 303–309.

Sutton, S. E., & Kemp, S. P. (2006). Integrating social science and design inquiry through interdisciplinary design charrettes: An approach to participatory community problem solving. *American Journal of Community Psychology, 28*(2), 125–129.

Svendsen, G. L. H., & Sorensen, J. F. L. (2007). There's more to the picture than meets the eye: Measuring tangible and intangible capital in two marginal communities in rural Denmark. *Journal of Rural Studies, 4*(8), 453–471.

Swaans, K., Broerse, J., Meincke, M., Mudhara, M., & Bunders, J. (2009). Promoting food security and well-being among poor and HIV/AIDS affected households: Lessons from an interactive and integrated approach. *Evaluation and Program Planning, 32*(1), 31–42.

Talen, E. (2000). Bottom-up GIS: New tool for individual and group expression in participatory planning. *Journal of the American Planning Association, 66*(3), 279–294.

Talen, E., & Shah, S. (2009). Neighborhood evaluation using GIS: An exploratory study. *Environment and Behavior, 39*(5), 583–615.

Tavernise, S. (2011, September 9). Vegetable gardens are booming in a fallow economy. *The New York Times,* pp. A13–14.

Taylor, A. W., Williams, C., Dal Grande, E., & Herriot, M. (2006). Measuring social capital in a known disadvantaged urban community—health policy implications. *Australian & New Zealand Health Policy, 3*(2), 1–8.

Taylor, M. (2007). Community participation in the real world: Opportunities and pitfalls in new governance spaces. *Urban Studies, 44*(2), 297–317.

Tebes, K. (2005). Community science, philosophy of science, and the practice of research. *American Journal of Community Psychology, 35*(3/4), 213–230.

Teitelman, A., et al. (2010). Youth's strategies for staying safe and coping. *Journal of Community Psychology, 38*(7), 874–885.

Teufel-Shone, N. I., Siyuja, T., Watahomigie, H. J., & Irwin, S. (2006). Community-based participatory research. Conducting a formative assessment of factors that influence youth wellness in the Hualapai community. *American Journal of Public Health, 96*(9), 1623–1628.

Theokas, C., & Lerner, R. N. (2006). Observed-ecological assets in families, schools, and neighborhoods: Conceptualization, measurement, and relations with positive and negative developmental outcomes. *Applied Developmental Science, 10*(2), 61–74.

Thomas, H. (2007). From radicalism to reformism. *Planning Theory, 6*(3), 332–335.

Thomas, L. R., Donovan, D. M., & Sigo, R. L. W. (2010). Identifying community needs and resources in a Native community: A research partnership in the Pacific Northwest. *International Journal of Mental Health Addiction, 8*(2), 362–373.

Thompson, T. E. (2009). *Youth leading with their heads.* Victoria, B.C., Canada: University of Victoria.

Throsby, D. (1999). Cultural capital. *Journal of Cultural Economics, 23*(1), 3–12.

Throsby, D. (2006). On the sustainability of cultural capital. Research paper. Sydney, Australia: Macquarie University.

Tice, K. (2009). Needs and asset assessments. *Michigan Nonprofit Association, 10*(1), 1–2.

Tienda, M., & Mitchell, F. (2006). *Multiple origins, uncertain destines: Hispanics and the American future.* Washington, DC: National Research Council.

Titterton, M., & Smart, H. (2008). Can participatory research be a route to empowerment? A case study of a disadvantaged Scottish community. *Community Development Journal, 43*(1), 52–64.

Torney-Purta, J., Barber, C. H., & Wilkenfeld, B. (2007). Latino adolescents' civic development in the United States: Research results from the IEA Civic Education Study. *Journal of Youth & Adolescence, 36*(2), 111–125.

Torre, M. E., & Fine, M. (2007). Theorizing audience, products and provocation. In P. Reason & H. Bradbury (Eds.), *Handbook of action research* (pp. 407–419). Thousand Oaks, CA: Sage Publications.

Torres, A. (Ed.). (2006). *Latinos in New England.* Philadelphia, PA: Temple University Press.

Torres, M. I., Marquez, D. X., Carbone, E. T., Stacciarini, J-M. R., & Foster, T. W. (2008). Culturally responsive health promotion in Puerto Rican communities: A structuralist approach. *Health Promotion Practice, 9*(2), 149–158.

Tortorello, M. (2011, August 4). What's left behind. *The New York Times,* pp. D1, D5.

Tortorello, M. (2012, June 14). The seeds of survival. *The New York Times,* pp. D1, D4.

Trader-Leigh, K. (2008). *Understanding the role of African American church and clergy on community crisis response.* Washington, DC: Joint Center for Political and Economic Studies Health Policy Institute.

Trevillion, S. (2008). Research, theory, and practice: Eternal triangle or uneasy bedfellows? *Social Work Education, 28*(4), 440–450.

Tulloch, D. (2007). Many, many maps: Empowerment and online participatory mapping. *First Monday, 12*(2), 1–18.

Turner, N. E., & Pinkett, R. D. (2000). *An asset-based approach to community building and community technology.* Cambridge, MA: MIT Media.

Twiss, J., Dickinson, J., Duma, S., Kleinman, T., Paulsen, H., & Rilveria, L. (2003). Community gardens: Lessons from California healthy cities and communities. *American Journal of Public Health, 93*(8), 1435–1438.

Ungar, M., Manuel, S., Mealey, S., Thomas, G., & Campbell, C. (2004). A study of community guidelines: Lessons for professionals practicing with and in communities. *Social Work, 49*(4), 550–561.

United Nations. (1948). *The Universal Declaration of Human Rights.* New York: Author.

United Nations. (2010). *Human Development Report 2010, 20th Anniversary Edition (The real wealth of nations: Pathways to human development).* New York: United Nations Development Programme.

United States Census Bureau. (2010). *20th Anniversary of Americans with Disabilities Act: July 26.* Washington, DC: United States Census Bureau. Retrieved July 14, 2011 from http://www.census.gov/newsroom/releases/archives/facts_ or_features special editions/cb10-ff13.html.

United States Geological Survey. (2007). *GIS.* (http://egsc.usgs.gov/isb/pubs/gis_ poster/). Accessed December 9, 2011.

Valaitis, R. (2005). Computers and the Internet: Tools for youth empowerment. *Journal of Medical Internet Research, 7*(5), 1–20.

Valaitis, R., & O'Mara, L. (2005). Enabling youth participation in school-based computer-supported community development in Canada. *Health Promotion International, 20*(3), 260–268.

Van Staveren, I. (2003). "Beyond social capital in poverty research." *Journal of Economic Issues, 37*(2), 415–423.

Van Willigen, J. (2005). Community assets and the community-building process: Historical perspectives. In S. E. Hyland (Ed.), *Community building in the twenty-first century* (pp. 25–44). Santa Fe, NM: The School of American Research Press.

VanderVen, K. (Ed.). (2008). *Promoting positive development in early childhood: Building blocks for a successful start (The Search Institute Series on Developmentally Attentive Community and Society).* Minneapolis, MN: Search Institute.

Vaugh, L. M., Rojas-Guyler, L., & Howell, B. (2008). "Picturing" health: A photovoice pilot of Latina girls' perceptions of health. *Community Health: The Journal of Health Promotion and Maintenance, 31*(4), 305–316.

Vega, M. Y. (2009). The change approach to capacity-building assistance. *AIDS Education and Prevention, 21*(Suppl. B), 137–151.

Veiller, L. (1900–1901). "The Tenement-House Exhibition of 1899." *Charities Review, 10,* 19–25.

Veenstra, G., Luginash, I., Wakefield, S., Birch, S., Eyles, J., & Elliott, S. (2005). Who you know, where you live: Social capital, neighborhood and health. *Social Science & Medicine, 60*(12), 2799–2818.

Verity, F. (2007). Community capacity building—A review of the literature. *Australia: Finders University of South Australia, School of Social Administration and Social Work.*

Verter, B. (2003). Spiritual capital: Theorizing religion with Bourdieu against Bourdieu. *Sociological Theory, 21*(2), 150–174.

Wade, M. (2007). *Community mapping: A how-to handbook for grassroots women's organizations.* New York: Huairou Commission.

Wakefield, S., Yeudall, F., Taron, C., Reynolds, J., & Skinner, A. (2007). Growing urban health: Community gardening in South-East Toronto. *Health Promotion International, 22*(2), 92–111.

Wakefield, S. E., & Poland, B. (2005). Family, friend or foe? Critical reflections on the relevance and role of social capital in health promotion and community development. *Social Science & Medicine, 60*(12), 2819–2832.

Waldern, B. (2006). Community research mythology. *The Qualitative Report, 11*(1), 55–79.

Walker, J. A. (2006a). Intentional youth programs: Taking theory to practice. *New Directions for Youth Development, 112,* 75–92.

Walker, J. E. (2006b). Building from strength: Asset-based community development. *Communities & Banking,* Winter, 25–27. (http:www.bos.frb.org/commdev/c&b/2006/winter/building.pdf). Accessed February 3, 2010.

Walker, S. (2004). Community work and psychosocial practice—Chalk and cheese or birds of a feather? *Journal of Social Work Practice, 18*(2), 161–175.

Walters, K. L., Stately, A., Evans-Campbell, T., Simoni, J. M., Duran, B., Schultz, K., Stanley, E. C., Charles, C., & Guerrero, D. (2009). "Indigenist" collaborative research efforts in Native American communities. In A. R. Stiffman (Ed.), *The field researcher survival guide* (pp. 146–173). New York: Oxford University Press.

Wang, C. C. (2006). Youth participation in photovoice as a strategy for community change. In B. Checkoway & L. M. Gutierrez (Eds.), *Youth participation and community change* (pp. 147–162). New York: Haworth Press.

Wang, C. C., Cash, J. L., & Powers, L. S. (2000). Who knows the streets well as the homeless? Promoting personal and community action through photovoice. *Health Promotion Practice, 1*(1), 81–89.

Wang, C. C., & Pies, C. A. (2004). Family, maternal, and child health through photovoice. *Maternal and Child Health, 8*(2), 95–102.

Wang, C. C., & Redwood-Jones, Y. A. (2001). Photovoice ethics: Perspectives from Flint Photovoice. *Health & Education Behavior, 28*(5), 560–572.

Warren, J. (2010). *What is grassroots mapping?* The Public Laboratory for Open Technology and Science: Grassroots Mapping. Retrieved from http://grassroots-mapping.org/about/.Warren, J. (2012). *Grassroots mapping with balloons and kites.* Cambridge, MA: MIT Media Lab. Retrieved from http://www.media.mit.edu/research/groups/1950/grassroots-mapping-balloons-and-kites.

Watson, V, (2006). Deep difference: Diversity, planning and ethics. *Planning Theory, 5*(1), 31–50.

Weil, M. (Ed.). (2004a). *Handbook of community practice.* Thousand Oaks, CA: Sage Publications.

Weil, M. (2004b). Introduction: Contexts and challenges for 21st-century communities. In M. Weil (Ed.), *Handbook of community practice* (pp. 3–33). Thousand Oaks, CA: Sage Publications.

Weiss, M. (2003). *Youth rising.* Oakland, CA: Applied Research Center.

Weissbourd, R. (2010). Lessons from the field: How 21st century community development can inform federal policy. *Journal of Comprehensive Community Development, 1*(1), 1–10.

Weller, S., & Bruegel, I. (2009). Children's 'place' in the development of neighborhood social capital. *Urban Studies, 46*(3), 629–643.

Wertheimer, M. R., Beck, E. L., Brooks, F., & Wolk, J. L. (2004). Community partnerships: An innovative model of social work education and practice. *Journal of Community Practice, 12*(3), 123–140.

Wheeler, W., & Roach, C. (2005). *Community-based youth leadership: A pathway to civic engagement.* Takoma Park, MD: Innovation Center for Community & Youth Development.

Wiles, R., Charles, V., Crow, G., & Heath, S. (2008). Researching researchers: Lessons for research ethics. *Qualitative Research, 6*(3), 283–299.

Williams, C. C., & Windebank, J. (2000). Self-help and mutual aid in deprived neighborhoods: Some lessons from Southampton. *Urban Studies, 37*(1), 127–147.

Williams, K. J., Bray, P. G., Shapiro-Mendoza, C. K., Reiez, I., & Peranteau, J. (2009). Modeling the principles of community-based participatory research in a community health assessment conducted by a health foundation. *Health Promotion Practice, 10*(1), 67–75.

Williment, K. (2009). It takes a community to create a library. *Partnership: The Canadian Journal of Library and Information Practice and Research, 4*(1), 1–7.

Wills, J., Chinemana, F., & Rudolph, M. (2010). Growing or connecting? An urban food garden in Johannesburg. *Health Promotion International, 25*(1), 33–41.

Wilson, N., Dasho, S., Martin, A. C., Wallerstein, N., Wang, C. C., & Minkler, M. (2007). Engaging young adolescents in social action through photovoice. *The Journal of Early Adolescence, 27*(2), 241–261.

Wilson, N., Minkler, M., Dasho, S., Carrillo, R., Wallerstein, N., & Garcia, D. (2006). Training students as facilitators in the Youth Empowerment Strategies (YES!) Project. *Journal of Community Practice, 14*(1), 201–217.

Winnie, M. (2008). *Closing the food gap: Resetting the table in the land of plenty.* Boston, MA: Beacon Press.

Wiseman, J. (2006). Local heroes? Learning from recent community strengthening initiatives in Victoria. *Australian Journal of Public Administration, 65*(2), 95–107.

Witkin, B. R., & Altschuld, J. W. (1995). *Planning and conducting needs assessments: A practical guide.* Thousand Oaks, CA: Sage Publications.

Witten, K., Exeter, D., & Field, A. (2003). The quality of urban environments: Mapping variation in access to community resources. *Urban Studies, 40*(1), 161–177.

Wong, I. (2009). *Knowledge synthesis: Creating inventory of community assets.* The Monieson Centre's Knowledge Impact in Society. (www.easternontarioknowledge. ca). Accessed November 11, 2009.

Wong, N. T., Zimmerman, M. A., & Parker, E. A. (2010). A typology of youth participation and empowerment for children and adolescent health promotion. *American Journal of Community Psychology, 46*(1–2), 100–114.

World Health Organization. (2002). *Towards a common language for functioning disability and health: ICF, The international, disability, and health.* Geneva, Switzerland: United Nations.

Wronka, J. (2008), *Human rights and social justice: Social action and service for the helping and health professions.* Thousand Oaks, CA: Sage Publications.

Xenos, M., & Moy, P. (2007). Direct and differential effects of the Internet on political and civic engagement. *Journal of Communication, 57*(4), 704–718.

Yohalem, N., & Wilson-Ahlstrom, A. (2010). Inside the black box: Assessing and improving quality in youth programs. *American Journal of Community Psychology, 45*(3–4), 350–357.

Yonas, M. A., Burke, J. G., Rak, K., Bennett, A., Kelly, V., & Gielen, A. C. (2009). A picture is worth a thousand words: Engaging youth in CBPR using creative arts. *Progress in Community Health Partnerships: Research, Education, and Action, 3*(4), 349–358.

Yoo, S., Butler, J., Elias, T. I., & Goodman, R. M. (2009). The 6-step model for community empowerment: Revisited in public housing communities for low-income senior citizens. *Health Promotion Practice, 10*(2), 262–275.

Yoon, I. (2009). A mixed-method study of Princeville's rebuilding from the flood of 1999: Lessons on the importance of invisible community assets. *Social Work, 54*(1), 19–28.

Yosso, T. J. (2005). Whose culture has capita? A critical race theory discussion of community cultural wealth. *Race Ethnicity and Education, 8*(1), 69–91.

Yosso, T. J., & Garcia, D. G. (2007). "This is no slum": A critical race theory analysis of community cultural wealth in culture clash's Chavez Ravine. *Aztlan: A Journal of Chicano Studies, 32*(1), 145–179.

Youth in Focus. (2002). *Youth rep step by step: An introduction to youth-led research and evaluation.* Oakland, CA: Author.

Zautra, A., Hall, J., & Murray, K. (2008). Community development and community resilience: An integrated approach. *Community Development, 39*(3), 130–147.

Zeldin, S. (2004). Youth as agents of adult and community development: Mapping the processes and outcomes of youth engaged in organizational governance. *Applied Developmental Sciences, 8*(2), 75–90.

Zhou, M., & Kim, S. S. (2006). Community forces, social capital, and educational achievement: The case of supplementary education in the Chinese and Korean immigrant communities. *Harvard Educational Review, 76*(1), 1–29.

Zust, B. L., & Moline, K. (2003). Identifying underserved ethnic populations within a community: The first step in eliminating health care disparities among racial and ethnic minorities. *Journal of Transcultural Nursing, 14*(1), 66–74.